The Conservative Aesthetic

The Conservative Aesthetic

Theodore Roosevelt, Popular Darwinism, and the American Literary West

Stephen J. Mexal

LEXINGTON BOOKS
Lanham • Boulder • New York • London

Published by Lexington Books
An imprint of The Rowman & Littlefield Publishing Group, Inc.
4501 Forbes Boulevard, Suite 200, Lanham, Maryland 20706
www.rowman.com

6 Tinworth Street, London SE11 5AL, United Kingdom

Copyright © 2021 The Rowman & Littlefield Publishing Group, Inc.

All rights reserved. No part of this book may be reproduced in any form or by any electronic or mechanical means, including information storage and retrieval systems, without written permission from the publisher, except by a reviewer who may quote passages in a review.

British Library Cataloguing in Publication Information Available

Library of Congress Cataloging-in-Publication Data

Names: Mexal, Stephen J., author.
Title: The conservative aesthetic : Theodore Roosevelt, popular Darwinism, and the American literary West / Stephen J. Mexal.
Description: Lanham : Lexington Books, [2021] | Includes bibliographical references and index. | Summary: "The Conservative Aesthetic explores a circle of western writers and artists that rose up around Theodore Roosevelt in the late nineteenth century. It makes the case that their unique alloy of popular Darwinism and western mythmaking represent an aesthetic component of American conservatism that has long been overlooked"—Provided by publisher.
Identifiers: LCCN 2021004071 (print) | LCCN 2021004072 (ebook) | ISBN 9781793632616 (cloth) | ISBN 9781793632630 (paper) | ISBN 9781793632623 (epub)
Subjects: LCSH: Conservatism and literature—United States—History—19th century. | American literature—West (U.S.)—History and criticism. | American literature—19th century—History and criticism. | Conservatism—United States—History—19th century. | Authors, American—Political and social views. | West (U.S.)—Intellectual life—19th century.
Classification: LCC PS169.C67 M49 2021 (print) | LCC PS169.C67 (ebook) | DDC 809/.933581—dc23
LC record available at https://lccn.loc.gov/2021004071
LC ebook record available at https://lccn.loc.gov/2021004072

Contents

Preface		vii
Acknowledgments		ix
Introduction: The Old Iron Days		1
PART I: GENTLEMEN OF THE WEST (1880–1884)		**17**
1	Roosevelt in the Badlands	19
2	Wister Goes West	31
3	Frederic Remington's Vanishing West	41
4	A Self-Made Man	53
5	Remington and the Art of Scientific Representation	65
6	Wister's Legal Education	71
7	"Buffalo Bill" Cody and the Selling of the West	79
PART II: THE EARLY HISTORY OF CONSERVATISM (1689–1880)		**93**
8	The Nature of Freedom	95
9	Emerson's Great Man Theory of History	105
10	Darwin Comes to America	117
11	The Redeemers, the Socialists, and Conservatism After the Civil War	127

PART III: SELLING A DARWINIAN WEST (1884–1890) — 137

12 Equal to All Occasions — 139
13 Cody and the Queen — 153
14 The Cowboy of Dakota — 159
15 Remington's Great White West — 167
16 Natural Inequality and the Course of Progress — 173
17 The Ghost Dance — 181

PART IV: IN SEARCH OF A PRACTICAL HISTORY (1890–1895) — 187

18 The Johnson County War — 189
19 The World's Columbian Exposition — 195
20 The Boone and Crockett Club — 201
21 Environmental Conservation and Political Conservatism — 209
22 The Science of Western History — 219
23 A Practical Conservatism — 227
24 The Evolution of a Cowboy — 233
25 The Bronco Busters — 243
26 Progress, Populism, and the Lure of War — 249

PART V: CUBA AND THE NEW WEST (1896–1902) — 255

27 The Rush of War — 257
28 The Cowboy Regiment Abroad — 267
29 Rewriting a Legacy — 281
30 *The Virginian* and the White House — 293

Epilogue: The Cowboy President — 305
Works Cited — 313
Index — 335
About the Author — 353

Preface

A few years into George W. Bush's presidency, I became slightly obsessed with a series of press photographs of Bush taken at his ranch near Crawford, Texas. In the photos, Bush was wearing blue jeans, aviator sunglasses, boots, and a cowboy hat. It looked like he was dressed for clearing chaparral—which, it turned out, was exactly what he was doing. It seemed obvious the photos were intended as some kind of political performance. They recalled similar photos of then president Ronald Reagan taken at his own ranch in California, nearly twenty years earlier. Reagan, too, had worn blue jeans, aviator sunglasses, boots, and a cowboy hat.

It occurred to me that their western garb was speaking in a kind of language I hadn't really thought about before. The cowboy hats seemed to signal something about Bush and Reagan's shared political conservatism and its connection to a long-standing set of myths about the American west. They seemed designed to pluck conservatism free of its modern entanglements with racism, classism, and authoritarianism and present it instead as something romantic and accessible. I wanted to learn more about how the symbols of the west had shaped the underpinnings of modern conservatism.

I soon realized that most books on American political conservatism began with the emergence of the modern conservative political movement in the decades after World War II. Many of those books were about campaigns, donors, and political maneuverings. Relatively few covered the mythic or imaginative underpinnings of conservatism. Relatively few covered conservatism before the New Deal. And there was very little research connecting the prewar American west to the aesthetics and the habits of mind that would later be recognized as the core of American conservatism. I was looking for an accessible introduction to the western aesthetics of American conservatism, one that explored the people and ideas at the heart of the mythmaking.

To put it differently, my question about why Bush and Reagan wore those cowboy hats was not really answered by any existing book on American conservatism.

In a way, I wrote this book to try to answer it.

Acknowledgments

Portions of this book appeared in a significantly different form in an article published in *Western American Literature*. My thanks to the University of Nebraska Press for their permission to reprint "'My dear Judge': Owen Wister's *Virginian*, Oliver Wendell Holmes, Jr., and Natural Law Conservatism" from *Western American Literature* 51.3 (2016): 279–311.

For ideas, suggestions, and encouragement, thanks are due to Erica L. Ball, Marlin Blaine, Christine Bold, Robert L. Gunn, Cathryn Halverson, William R. Handley, David Kelman, Michael Lemon, Brian Michael Norton, Irena Praitis, Robert Yusef Rabiee, Justin Race, and Nicolas S. Witschi. I'm especially grateful to an anonymous reviewer, Lana L. Dalley, and Richard Hutson, all of whom took the time to read the manuscript in a spirit of generosity and respond with thoughtful suggestions for revision.

At California State University, Fullerton, the Department of English, Comparative Literature, and Linguistics has been a warm intellectual home, filled with smart and accomplished colleagues who are also genuinely fun people. I am ever grateful for their collegiality. Special thanks are due to Carlen Pope, who helps the whole operation run smoothly. Material support for this book was provided by a university-funded sabbatical as well as by a summer research fellowship from the College of Humanities and Social Sciences.

I'm thankful for the research assistance provided by Thomas J. McCutchon at the Rare Book and Manuscript Library at Columbia University, Pamela Pierce at the Theodore Roosevelt Center at Dickinson State University, as well as librarians at the Theodore Roosevelt Papers at the Library of Congress and the Theodore Roosevelt Collection at the Houghton and Widener libraries at Harvard University.

At Lexington Books, I'm grateful to Jessica Thwaite and Holly Buchanan for their interest and support.

Thanks also go to my wife Sharon and son Warren. Yet perhaps my greatest acknowledgment should go to my daughter Parker. Unlike her brother, she was not thanked in the last book, as she was not yet born. In order to maintain my unblemished record of equal sibling treatment, I had to spend nearly a decade writing this book so that she could be thanked in one, too.

Introduction
The Old Iron Days

In the summer of 1901, three years after leading what the press called a "cowboy regiment" to military victory in Cuba, Vice President Theodore Roosevelt traveled to Colorado Springs for a speech and a reunion of the Rough Riders.[1]

For Roosevelt, the Cuban campaign had been an opportunity to test his theory that the values of the so-called primitive American west—values from a supposedly less-developed past—had practical utility in the present. They could be used to win the battles of merit that characterized contemporary life, whether on the battlefield, in the boardroom, or on the campaign trail.

The Rough Riders had made Roosevelt nationally famous. Some had denounced the way in which the public's eagerness for military romance turned the deaths of real men into little more than "a side show to the great Roosevelt circus," as one writer objected at the time.[2] For others, the widespread embrace of Roosevelt's hero-westerner image—a persona characterized by editor Poultney Bigelow as "Cowboy Napoleon"—was little more than a reckless national delusion.[3]

Yet few could deny that Roosevelt's decades-long project of trying to figure out the historical and philosophical significance of the American west had paid off in spectacular fashion. Since 1880, he and his friends had discussed how the region had provided a kind of game field on which the bloody history of American conquest had been played; how it had helped birth what he called a unique group of "frontier folk"; how it had existed in a permanent temporal gulf, like a pocket watch lagging well behind the well-regulated clockwork of eastern modernity; how its ruthless equality made unsparingly clear what, in his view, were the Darwinian divisions between strong and weak.[4]

These ideas had been tested in the crucible of Cuba. And they had turned Roosevelt into something of an intellectual man of action, one of the most famous writers and statesmen in America. Just a few months after returning home from Cuba, he was elected governor of New York. Two years after that, he was vice president of the United States. Though he couldn't know it yet, six weeks after his speech in Colorado, the assassination of McKinley would make him president.

Officially, he was in Colorado Springs to give a speech celebrating the state's "quarto-centennial," its twenty-fifth anniversary of statehood. The third annual Rough Riders' reunion had been scheduled for the following day.

His midmorning speech at Acacia Park was before a cheering crowd that reporters estimated to be as large as 10,000. The speech was largely about America's century-long western expansion, a story in which a legacy of violence was turned into something grand and romantic. The conquest of the west, he said, was the story of men who claimed "victory after victory in the ceaseless strife waged against wild men and wild nature." It was, he declared dramatically, "the great epic feat in the history of our race."[5]

Yet Roosevelt was more interested in what that history could do today, in the present. The process of western expansion, he said, had permanently altered the character of all Americans. He claimed the men who had immigrated to western territories like Colorado possessed the sort of "daring and hardihood and iron endurance" that was necessary then, but was still necessary now.[6]

He said it was crucial to conserve the skills and values that had been cultivated by the frontier west. Later, he would be even more explicit about the usefulness of America's western history, arguing that as time went on, America would "need a greater and not a less development of the fundamental frontier virtues."[7] He was making an argument for a kind of practical conservatism: a sensibility that conserved qualities associated with America's history in large part because those qualities were useful in the modern age. The future, he said, depended on the "peculiarly American characteristics" that had been cultivated by the America's history of western expansion.[8] The past should be fuel for the present.

What were those characteristics? He implied that a kind of evolution had selected brave, self-reliant, tenacious individuals for success in the American west. There had been "scant room for the coward and the weakling in the ranks of the adventurous frontiersmen," he pointed out. However, he continued, the life-or-death hazards that characterized the Darwinian past had faded in recent decades. "The old iron days have gone, the days when the weakling died as the penalty of inability to hold his own," he said. Yet it was imperative that Americans continue to "preserve the iron quality which made our forefathers and predecessors fit."[9] Even if natural law no longer demanded such mortal stakes, he suggested, Darwinian fitness was still the commanding principle of the west, one Americans neglected at their peril.

To this way of thinking, modern society had made Americans in danger of becoming soft, prone to shirking the kind of work necessary for national greatness. But all that could yet be fixed, Roosevelt suggested, by making use of the aggressive self-reliance that had conquered the American west. What America needed now, he proclaimed, were "the iron qualities that must go with true manhood."[10] Those qualities had once been necessary for mere survival. But today, they were needed to guard against national decline. After all, America was now a global actor: a nation with a "part which hereafter, whether we will or not, we must play in the world at large," as he put it.[11] It was as if he was presenting himself—Theodore Roosevelt, American Warrior-Cowboy—as proof of a new axiom: the tools of the frontiersman were now the tools of empire. To wield those tools was to become an engineer of progress.

The crowd cheered its approval. Throughout, Roosevelt was utterly confident in his basic conservative vision of America: his faith that the "old iron days"—the skills and mental habits cultivated by the Darwinian scrabblings of the frontier west—could be put to use in forging the country's future.

Roosevelt had long harbored conservative tendencies, even aristocratic and occasionally authoritarian ones. He valued social equality significantly less than he valued the sort of structures that allowed for the emergence of what he saw as naturally superior individuals. As he had put it a few years earlier, he had little patience for those who "cant about 'liberty' and the 'consent of the governed,' in order to excuse themselves for their unwillingness to play the part of men."[12]

But now here he was, exhorting Americans to once again act as in the iron days of old. In a way, the Colorado speech was a distillation of a set of ideas that he and his friends had been discussing for decades: a vision of a conservatism that could fulfill the old Jeffersonian dream of an America led by a naturally selected aristocracy.

This book is about an idea. It's about the emergence, in the late nineteenth century, of a uniquely American conservatism, one that was shaped both by romantic myths about frontier self-reliance as well as by the popular Darwinism of the day. But even though this book is about ideas, it foregrounds some of the individuals who actually developed and promoted them.

In the final decades of the nineteenth century, a circle of writers, thinkers, and artists who were acquiring tremendous cultural influence—a kind of informal westerners' club—rose up around Theodore Roosevelt. They had much in common. All were white, male, and enjoyed some degree of economic privilege; most were college educated; and many traveled west for the first time as young men after experiencing a personal tragedy in the east. For many in the circle, the west seemed to represent not just an intriguing exercise for their intellects, but an opportunity for personal regeneration: a chance to disappear into the past and start again.

That circle included Owen Wister, the nervous young Harvard graduate who longed to be a musician, resigned to being a lawyer, and ended up a writer. On the advice of his doctor, he first traveled west in an attempt to cure his neurasthenia. The most reactionary of all the figures in Roosevelt's circle, Wister was obsessed with western lynching. With jurist Oliver Wendell Holmes Jr. as a mentor and friend, he acquired literary prominence by telling stories about men he called the "true aristocracy": those he thought were fit to stand outside the law and above their fellow citizens.[13]

It also included Frederic Remington, the artist, journalist, novelist, illustrator, and sculptor who, despite his prodigious talents, was never fully welcomed into the Porcellian Club bonhomie of Wister and Roosevelt. Remington was an established illustrator by the time Wister and Roosevelt began work on their western-inspired books and stories, and his dynamic illustrations of white rangy cowboys and sterile western landscapes thrilled their imaginations. His work would forever be wed to Roosevelt's theory of practical conservatism when his sculpture "The Bronco Buster" was used to commemorate Roosevelt and the Rough Riders at the end of the Cuban invasion.

Also in Roosevelt's orbit was the young historian Frederick Jackson Turner. During his doctoral studies at Johns Hopkins, Turner had been trained to think of history as a science governed by natural laws that could be discerned and analyzed. Inspired by Roosevelt's book *The Winning of the West*, Turner developed arguably the first conservative theory of American history. He argued that retrogressions into the "past" of the American frontier west helped propel ongoing development in the east.

On the outskirts of the circle was William "Buffalo Bill" Cody, whose traveling western spectaculars made him one of the nineteenth century's preeminent showmen. Perhaps earlier than anyone, Cody intuited how the American west made it easy for legends to become true and for truths to become legend. After killing a Cheyenne warrior and then incorporating that killing back into his theater show, Cody acquired a worldwide reputation as an emissary of America's frontier past. His wild west shows told a romantic, nostalgia-soaked story about America's western frontiers, painting them as places where fitness was established through ruthless battles for soil and honor and survival.

And of course the group included Roosevelt himself. Today many remember Roosevelt as America's barrel-chested twenty-sixth president with a reputation as a progressive reformer. But in the mid-1880s, he wasn't any of those things.[14] He was a wiry young man, just barely out of college, who in a few short years had endured the devastating deaths of his father, mother, and new wife. As if still acting on a childhood promise to "make my body"—a sort of Lamarckian self-reinvention—Roosevelt sought solace in Dakota Territory, where he developed an informal theory of individualism, historical development, and the far west.[15] He thought that the American west cultivated a rugged self-reliance that, if properly harnessed, could confer crucial advantages in the ongoing Darwinian competitions that drove historical progress.

Of course, these figures hardly represented the last word in western writing, popular Darwinism, or conservatism. Other authors, such as Frank Norris, a critic of laissez-faire capitalism, or Jack London, a professed socialist, were similarly interested in the intersection of masculinity, Darwinism, and the American west.[16] And of course there were a number of figures in the late nineteenth century who espoused ideas which can reasonably be called conservative. What made Roosevelt and his circle distinctive was not just their influence in the intertwining worlds of politics and popular culture, but the unique way in which popular Darwinism and the romance of the west elevated their conservative sensibilities into something approaching an aesthetic.

These men are hardly unknown figures. They have been the objects of both serious study and popular fascination for over a century. In recent years, scholars have begun to look more closely at the racial ideologies that underpinned their frontier mythmaking, or to the ways in which Roosevelt, Remington, Wister and others were enmeshed in a web of conservative economic interests that linked western development with the New York banking and cultural elite.[17] This book builds on a number of those studies.[18]

Similarly, the conservative political beliefs held by of many of these men have been well documented.[19] Yet their efforts to forge a set of narratives from an alloy of popular Darwinism and western mythmaking—that is, the aesthetic component of their conservatism—have been often overlooked.

To be clear, though, this book does not unearth some previously undiscovered archival bombshell. Its contributions are chiefly interpretive: telling old stories in new ways. This book brings together a number of different figures' biographies in order to make interpretive claims about their letters, journals, and published writing, and weaves those claims into a single accessible narrative.

To varying degrees, they all considered themselves writers. In 1888, Roosevelt said, "I'm a 'literary feller,' not a politician, nowadays."[20] In that spirit, this book is interested in how their writing revealed their romantic beliefs about the history of the American west far more than it is in the accuracy of those beliefs. As James Fenimore Cooper put it, "history, like love, is so apt to surround her heroes with an atmosphere of imaginary brightness."[21]

Yet while this book is a story of writers and cultural figures, it's also a story of ideas. These men have never been considered intellectuals, and rightly so. But even if they didn't fully realize it, they were creating a new way to think about American freedom, one that arguably made perfect sense to white, privileged young men like themselves. Fusing Emersonian self-reliance with Darwinian philosophy, they yoked both to new myths about conservativism and progress in the American west.

Today, of course, American conservatism means something quite different than what it used to. Readers accustomed to the ideological contours of contemporary politics might feel the form of conservatism presented here seems distant, like an ancient language whose surviving morphemes are just barely discernable in our own. That distance, though, is part of the point. There are ample divergences between nineteenth- and twenty-first-century conservative ideas, but there are meaningful continuities, too. This book suggests an early example of a uniquely American conservatism. But the myth of the American west that emerges in their writing—with its uncritical embrace of individualism, its latent antidemocratic convictions, its certainty that the land was the rightful inheritance of white men—is also connected to conservatism today, in ways innumerable to count.

In case it isn't obvious, this is a book about men without women. And it's a book about white men specifically. But it's not coincidental that a book about American conservatism is also a book about white men. Roosevelt and his circle seem to have been inspired almost exclusively by writers and adventurers who were white and male, even though the actual American west was considerably more diverse. Women, of course, were everywhere in the nineteenth-century American west, yet were often overlooked in popular representations of the region.[22] Roosevelt and Wister might easily have been inspired by any number of western women authors, including by Caroline Kirkland, the early frontier writer; by Emma Ghent Curtis, the Colorado writer and suffragist whose 1889 cowboy novel *The Administratrix* preceded Wister's rise by a number of years; or, later, by Montana women like Frances McElrath, whose 1902 novel *The Rustlers*, published one month before Wister's *The Virginian*, was similarly inspired by the violent class conflict of the Johnson County War.[23]

Yet Roosevelt, Wister, and the rest didn't merely overlook the experiences of western women. They used the west to actively promote a particular model of masculinity. For them, masculinity became something of a romantic spectacle, brimming with ambition and nostalgia for the American past. Telling stories about the American west, and overcoming the challenges it presented, underwrote one particular type of masculinity, making it seem as if male authority had been selected by nature itself.[24]

For Roosevelt and his circle, their own whiteness and masculinity were often invisible. As we might say today, they often universalized their own privilege, assuming that what was true for them was true of everyone. This universalism made it easy for them to overlook the experiences of nonwhites and women—to assume a kind of elegant, yet fundamentally dishonest, detachment. In writing his pseudo-Darwinian genealogy of the cowboy, for example, Wister blithely ignored Remington's advice to emphasize the historical significance of Mexican cowboys. Later, Roosevelt would downplay the contributions of the Black cavalry units that saved his life in Cuba. And all of them were at least indifferent to, if not outright pleased by, the violent depopulation of America's indigenous peoples. In a million tiny ways, Roosevelt and his circle often acted as if the privileges of educated, wealthy white males were not privileges at all, but instead simply the way things were.[25]

The conservatism of Roosevelt, Wister, and the rest was rough-hewn. They were writers, artists, and historians in possession of what philosopher Michael Oakeshott would later call a "conservative disposition," but they were not intellectuals or activists.[26] For that matter, the word "conservatism" barely even existed in America when Roosevelt was born. For them, conservatism was new and unbroken ground. They were tilling it as they went along.

In that spirit, this book doesn't chart specific policy developments or political machinations, but rather the emergence of a general conservative aesthetic: the core ideas that have, for a century or more now, rooted conservatism in the American soil. These include a belief in the absolute power of the individual; an orientation toward maintaining the historical status quo; a sense that society should be ordered by the laws of nature; a feeling that certain rules apply to some groups more than others; an innate suspicion of collectivism; a faith that inequality is not just acceptable but natural; and a belief in a hierarchical society. Those ideas came to life with vivid clarity when these men told stories about the hazards of the American west.

This book does not pretend to be the definitive story of conservatism in America. Even so, some might object that it dulls too many of the reactionary edges from conservatism. While this book does grapple with some of Roosevelt, Wister, and Remington's thinking about race and immigration, it does not make the case that their particular strain of American conservatism had its roots solely or entirely in a culture of white supremacy. That does not mean they were somehow free of America's larger history of systemic racism. They were obviously the beneficiaries of a nation structured to reward whiteness, and they often conflated American civilization with white identity. Yet their conservative ideas were often framed as appeals to natural law or democratic feeling.

Such impartial-sounding appeals may strike observers of contemporary conservatism as mere rhetorical posturing. Since World War II, American conservative politics have been so tightly intertwined with white identity that nearly any conservative idea could reasonably be interpreted as an appeal to white racism. But it is worth trying to understand older ideas on their own terms, apart from their subsequent applications. Although the word "meritocracy" didn't exist at the time, and today we are rightly suspicious of the way the concept effaces any number of unearned racial and economic advantages, Roosevelt and his circle were often using the American west to imagine a nation that in their minds would be governed by its best citizens.

Roosevelt and his circle too often overlooked the ways in which existing hierarchies of economics, race, gender, education, and family status conferred meaningful social benefits. As a result, what they emphasized in place of those hierarchies—so-called rugged individualism, Darwinian fitness, and the romance of the American west—yoked their conservatism to western individualism, not to eastern social registers or southern racial feudalism. This focus offered them a kind of plausible deniability of their own racial and class privilege. It gave them the ability to champion supposedly objective, universal qualities like "merit" or "fitness" while still envisioning a hierarchical society. In their minds, the west simply offered the best place to cultivate the sort of individualism that would ensure national greatness.

The conservatism of Roosevelt and his circle is best understood as a set of aesthetic tendencies: as beliefs about human progress, the good life, self-determination, and moral and civic order. This book tries to understand those tendencies as undergirding the conservatism that was emerging in embryonic form at the end of the nineteenth century.

What are some key characteristics of that conservatism? One is a general orientation toward the past, or what might be called a conservative temporality. These men were all interested in imagining the American past, and were shadowed by a vague sense that in the onrush of modernity, something—some ineffable quality of the republic, of its citizens—had been diminished along the way.

Another core characteristic is the belief that a hierarchical, undemocratic society is a more natural, and therefore better, society. These men were not seeking to create a hereditary aristocracy, but they did tend to hold the belief that society flourishes if led by its best and brightest: its "natural aristocracy," as Thomas Jefferson put it.[27]

That said, their conservativism didn't demand a restoration. This is perhaps the most paradoxical and poorly understood component of American conservatism as it was developed by Roosevelt and others: that it actually looks forward, not backward. Theirs was a practical conservatism, seeking not to return to the past but rather to use it to shape the future. Their conservatism was predicated in part on the belief that the freedoms of the American past held practical utility for the American present. In their search for what Van Wyck Brooks would later call a "usable past," they homed in on the history proffered by America's western frontiers.[28]

The belief that America's past contained a wellspring of freedom was not an entirely new one, of course. A number of Enlightenment-era philosophers, including John Locke and Jean-Jacques Rousseau, subscribed to the belief that individual liberty had its conceptual origins in a long-ago mythical state of nature.[29] Yet for those Enlightenment thinkers, the state of nature had generally been an origin point, not a return destination. For Locke and Rousseau, it was not possible or even desirable to return to the state of nature.[30] For them, progress was a straight line from state-of-nature primitivism to modern civilization: once humans had developed beyond the state of nature, they could never again return. Roosevelt and his circle, in contrast, seemed to be developing a new way of thinking about the concept. For them, the American west was not just a source of freedom but also a site of its regeneration: a state of nature to which they could still return, strip away the artifice of civilization, and demonstrate their natural fitness.

In general, they thought that America's history of frontier conquest represented two things at once. First, it offered a kind of toolkit for solving contemporary problems. The qualities they romantically associated with life on the range—self-reliance, hard work, tenacity, honor, a certain quickness of wit and of gun—were also qualities that they felt equipped someone to be a great man of history. And second, they thought that western living was, in a general sense, a good way to measure the mettle of a man. For a white easterner to thrive in the far reaches of the west was to receive a kind of certificate of ontological superiority. In their imaginations, the west was an arduous land where eastern men tested themselves by walking the knife-edge of existence. And to walk that blade without tumbling into the abyss meant that they could return to the east as new and better men, hardened and equipped for leadership by the compressive forces of the west.

Or that was the idea, anyway. But it was an idea they held close to their hearts, one they developed over countless books and articles and performances and paintings. They seemed to genuinely believe that the west offered a proof of manly superiority. But then again, they also wanted to believe it. After all, it was not just a bygone generation of adventurers who had ventured to the undeveloped corners of the continent. They had gone there, too.

For them, the far west was not just a point in space, but a point in time. Traveling there meant going back to an earlier, less-developed America. It created an opportunity for a deliberate retrogression: an opportunity to return on a temporary basis to an earlier and, in their minds, a less-developed age, in order to recover the sort of self-reliant hardihood that might be put to use solving the problems of modernity.

This emphasis on self-reliance is worth underscoring. By the end of the nineteenth century, a political belief system that emphasized the absolute freedoms of the individual, largely free of obligations to kin and class and community—what was most often simply called *individualism*—had begun its long, slow migration from being associated largely with the political left to being associated largely with the political right.

In general, they held the belief that American identity was built by adhering not to traditional ties of ethnicity or blood, but instead to a set of ideas. By the late nineteenth century, an upstart collection of American political philosophers was beginning to give one particular idea—socialism—new credibility. Socialism was an idea that needed to be contested by other ideas. And so the effort that Roosevelt, Wister, Cody, and others devoted to cultivating a new belief in American individualism became a political act. Their writings suggested that America's future lay not in some unknown, left-leaning universe of cooperative socialism and trades unionism. For them, America's future instead lay in its past: in its well-explored and time-tested emphasis on self-reliant individualism.

The influence of Darwin was integral as well. Since the Enlightenment, political philosophers have used nature to provide a transcendent justification for individual freedom. For Roosevelt and his circle, Darwin allowed their individualism to assume the air of modern science. Darwin and his many popularizers held that competitive struggle drove species development. The Lamarck-influenced "American school" of evolutionary theory held that individuals could create their own adaptive advantages. Individuals, according to this Lamarckian reasoning, could through sheer force of will choose to succeed in the great competitions that were the chief engines of progress. For Roosevelt and his circle, Darwinism offered a scientific warrant for American faith in the individual, making self-reliance a natural law in more ways than one.[31]

Many studies of American conservativism suggest it emerged in its clearest form shortly after World War II.[32] In the ten years after the war, Barry Goldwater first ran for elective office, Whittaker Chambers published his anticommunist memoir *Witness*, and William F. Buckley founded the Intercollegiate Society of Individualists and the *National Review*. These figures are all central to the creation story of the modern conservative movement.

It was also in this period that historian Russell Kirk published *The Conservative Mind*, one of the earliest intellectual histories of conservatism. Three years before, literary critic Lionel Trilling had dismissed conservatism as a series of "irritable mental gestures which seek to resemble ideas."[33] Kirk wanted to prove such assumptions wrong. *The Conservative Mind* sought to demonstrate a broad continuity in conservative thinking, inspired by a set of writers and thinkers stretching from Edmund Burke's critique of the French Revolution up until mid-century America. Yet in choosing to emphasize centuries of transatlantic conservatism, Kirk was also choosing to downplay any qualities unique to American conservatism in specific. After all, Burke's conservative defense of centuries of monarchical stability would seem to apply rather poorly to America, a nation which lacked a tradition of monarchical stability altogether, let alone one worth conserving.

One of Kirk's early insights was that one of Trilling's points about liberalism—that it was "a large tendency rather than a concise body of doctrine"—was true of conservatism, too.[34] So Kirk was wide-reaching when searching for examples of conservative thought, looking to literary figures as much as to political philosophers and statesmen. As several contemporary scholars have suggested, political worldviews are often better understood in the realm of aesthetics—through stories and symbols and values—than purely in the realm of facts.[35]

Since Kirk, a number of historians of politics, economics, culture, and literature have turned their attention to the story of conservatism in America.[36] Although many of those studies quite reasonably continue to focus on the rise of the conservative movement after World War II—a rise which includes Kirk himself—there have been a number of efforts to trace the origins of American conservatism to the 1930s and even earlier.[37]

However, most studies on American conservatism have been, quite understandably, studies of conservative politics. To this way of thinking, the story of conservatism in America is a story of elections, laws, corporate interests, and advocacy groups. As a result, the notion of conservatism as a kind of imaginative aesthetic—shaped equally by stories and paintings and science and myths—has not been studied as fully as it might be.

In short, the story of a western-influenced American conservatism, emerging decades before the birth of the modern conservative movement, has not yet been fully told. This was a conservatism born not of economic ideology nor of campaign maneuverings, but of art, literature, and ideas. And it is a story best told from the perspective not of professional politicians, but of young men grappling with books and stories and their own dreams of America.

The book begins in the early 1880s, when many of these men first went west, and concludes at the turn of the twentieth century, after Roosevelt and the Rough Riders had tested his theory of practical conservatism in Cuba.

Part I, Gentlemen of the West (1880–1884), details Roosevelt, Wister, Remington, and Cody's early years in the west. They all seemed to feel that the land was somehow precarious: the last breath of a fading era as well as the birthplace of something new. For them, telling stories about the west meant also telling stories about a land unsullied by human hands. It also meant trying to bring the rest of America more fully in line with the laws of nature as they saw them.

Part I introduces these men through a few moments of critical importance. It charts their early years, their first significant exposures to the west, and the way in which they seized on the region as an object of interpretation. It also pays careful attention to the emergence of their ideas about time, history, nature, and individualism. They were each cultivating a new kind of conservatism, honed on the whetstone of their ideas about the west. They were building, as one of Remington's friends later put it, a "cowboy philosophy."[38]

In Part II, The Early History of Conservatism (1689–1880), the book's timeline moves backward to explain the emergence of American conservatism as a relatively coherent set of ideas. One premise of this section is the notion that individual freedom has always depended on our understanding of the laws of nature. Beginning with John Locke's theory of the state of nature and tracing it forward through Thomas Jefferson, it also investigates what has long been viewed as the intellectual origin point of conservatism: Burke's reflections on the French Revolution. Burke, too, wanted to make sure that human ideas about freedom followed certain principles of nature.

This section also explores Ralph Waldo Emerson's nineteenth-century writings on history, conservatism, and individualism. Today, most scholars accentuate Emerson's affinity for democratic individualism and minimize the significance of his ideas to American conservatism. Yet as one contemporary of Emerson's observed, in the aftermath of his theory of self-reliance, a split opened up between individualists and socialists, and Emersonian individualism began to be associated with the political right.

While all this was happening, the very definition of conservativism was just beginning to settle into its modern usage. The word "conservatism," which barely existed at all in the decades before the Civil War, was well on its way to being established in the decades after.

Part II also notes the substance and influence of Darwin's development hypothesis, first published on the eve of the Civil War. After the war, American thinkers like William Graham Sumner reshaped Darwinian natural selection so it interlocked perfectly with American individualism. There were other significant ideas fomenting, of course. The white southern redeemers sought to reconstruct the antebellum racial feudal system. On the left a new generation of economists were building the philosophical architecture for American socialism. All of this created an opening for a new type of conservatism.

Part III, Selling a Darwinian West (1884–1890), tells how Roosevelt began to see the west as a kind of experiment station for his theory of American history. That theory held that individual merit, as determined through competition or battle, determined an individual's place in the natural order, and it was a succession of those merit-testing competitions that propelled the wheel of American history. A few years after buying his ranch, Roosevelt tried to join a group seeking to find and execute alleged cattle rustlers. The attraction to extrajudicialism—the idea that elite individuals in the west knew better than courts of law—would go on to be a defining characteristic of Roosevelt and Wister's thinking about the west.

Part III also investigates Cody's wild west show at the peak of its popularity, as well as Remington's rise as a kind of illustrator-adventurer. *Harper's* magazine sent Remington to South Dakota to cover the simmering tensions between U.S. Army and the Lakota. Cody had been dispatched as well. Both saw the conflict, which soon erupted at Wounded Knee, as characteristic of the west: an opportunity to make society more natural by realigning it with the law of survival.

In Part IV, In Search of a Practical History (1890–1895), the book explores Wister's first significant taste of writerly acclaim, which he found by telling stories about western vigilantism. Like Roosevelt, Wister felt that law simply worked differently in the far west. In so-called primitive conditions, the right type of man could be judge, jury, and executioner. The majority of this section occurs in and around the 1893 World's Fair in Chicago. Wister, Remington, Cody, and Roosevelt all attended. Cody performed, Wister worked on a story, Remington exhibited paintings, Frederick Jackson Turner unveiled his new theory of American history, and Roosevelt's Boone and Crockett Club exhibited a rustic cabin to promote the club's unique blend of wildlife conservation and political conservatism.

In Part V, Cuba and the New West (1896–1902), the book charts two intertwining yearnings: Remington's simmering desire to see a war and Roosevelt's desire to fight in one. To them, war seemed like a generational inheritance denied, and both believed their experiences in the west made them uniquely equipped for Cuba. Many writers and politicians were describing Cuba as a new "state of nature," using the same language that had once been used to describe America's western frontiers.[39]

Cuba was also a place to test their theory of practical conservatism: the belief that retrogressions into a so-called primitive frontier could select America's best and bravest men. Roosevelt assembled a cavalry regiment that the press christened the Rough Riders, named after Cody's latest wild west extravaganza. It was perhaps the most visible example of his desire for a usable past. In Roosevelt's mind, the Rough Riders' connection to America's western past made the whole enterprise more likely to advance the values of civilization. This section also tells the story of the Rough Riders' charge up Kettle Hill, aided by the African American Ninth and Tenth Calvary Regiments. Over time, Roosevelt downplayed the contributions of the Black soldiers, implying that the Darwinian struggle represented by Cuba applied to certain types of westerners, but not to others.

For his part, Remington spun his own misrepresentations of the war. In an illustration for *Scribner's* magazine to accompany one of Roosevelt's articles, he painted the Rough Riders charging San Juan Hill, an event he had never witnessed, and a hill they had never charged. But the truth, he seemed to concede, mattered less than the legend. A few months after his inauguration as governor of New York, Roosevelt attended Cody's show, which had incorporated a fictionalized recreation of the Rough Riders battle in Cuba based in part on Remington's painting. Roosevelt had the disconcerting experience of watching his real experiences twisted into a theater spectacle. Afterward, though, he pronounced the show accurate. The romance had become reality.

For Roosevelt, Wister, Remington and the rest, the American west wasn't delimited by the borders of Wyoming or Dakota Territory or even the California coast. More than anything else, for them the west was an idea. They were obsessed with its aesthetics, with the role its shifting borders had played in the development of the nation, with the many ways its signs and symbols could be rendered useful.

But at the core of their interest was a new kind of conservatism, one that was unique to America. That conservatism held that the sparsely populated land west of the Mississippi River was a kind of laboratory for American progress, one where the nation's fittest individuals—its smartest, its bravest, its most self-reliant—could still be selected. The west still held the promise of a secular and even scientific American Eden. In their minds, it could be the primitive fields from which the nation's future might yet flourish: an untapped bounty of the country's last, best men.

NOTES

1. "Cowboy Regiments," 1.
2. Sullivan, 2.
3. Bigelow, 283.
4. Roosevelt *Winning Volume I*, 101.
5. Kegel, 6.
6. Kegel, 6.
7. Roosevelt "Pioneer," 56.

8. Kegel, 6.
9. Kegel, 6.
10. Kegel, 9.
11. Kegel, 9.
12. Roosevelt "Strenuous," 18. See also Watts, 63–66.
13. Wister *Virginian*, 95.
14. Hofstadter argues Roosevelt's reputation as a reformer is surprising, given his long-standing lack of "interest in the human goals of reform" (*American* 290).
15. Robinson *Brother*, 50. For more on the significance of the American west to the American cult of individualism, see Barlow, 111–142; Nelson, 81–104; and Richardson *How*, 111–123.
16. Kaplan, 261–266.
17. See Bederman, 170–215; Bold *Frontier*, 65–79; Cox *How*, 75–96; Kuenz, 98–128; and Slotkin, 156–193 on the many links between western cattle ranching, New York finance, conservative politics, and western cultural myths.
18. This book would not have been possible without the foundational work of certain scholars that, while cited elsewhere, are worth singling out here. White's early study of Remington, Wister, and Roosevelt, *The Eastern Establishment and the Western Experience*, provided important groundwork. In addition, Payne's biography of Wister; Scharnhorst's biographical study of Wister's western fiction; Samuels and Samuels's biography of Frederic Remington; Bogue's biography of Turner; Russell's biography of Cody; and Reddin's study of wild west shows have collectively provided the biographical groundwork for this book. Finally, Splete and Splete's collection of Remington's letters, *Frederic Remington—Selected Letters*; Kemble Wister's collection of Wister's letters, *Owen Wister Out West*; Jacobs's study and collection of Turner's letters, *The Historical World of Frederick Jackson Turner*; and Morison's multivolume *Letters of Theodore Roosevelt* have all served as vital collections of primary source documents. Unless otherwise noted, all cited correspondence is drawn from these published collections of letters.
19. See Kammen, 267; Hawley, 107; Kuenz, 104; and Rydell and Kroes, 97.
20. TR letter to Brander Matthews, October 5, 1888, in Brander Matthews letters.
21. Cooper, 225. Wrobel reminds that romantic, mythic depictions of particular regions were a writerly choice. Travel writers offered detailed, if subjective, accounts (21–32).
22. See Jenson and Miller, 18–20; Woodworth-Ney, 33–64; and Halverson, 1–35.
23. Lamont, 1–9, 31–52. See also Baym, 1–11.
24. See Rico, 1–11. See also Bederman, 170–215.
25. For more on Roosevelt, whiteness, and the American west, see Pierce, x–xvii and Richardson *How*, 115–128. For more on the role of the American west in Wister and Roosevelt's conception of masculinity, see Worden, 35–80.
26. Oakeshott, 153.
27. Cappon, 388.
28. Brooks, 40.
29. See Ellingson, 81–84; Mexal, 8–10.

30. Cooper *Rousseau*, 18.

31. In addition to Hofstadter's *Social Darwinism*, see Bannister for a more recent evaluation of Darwin's social influence. For a study of the many late-century competing theories of evolution, see Bowler.

32. Allitt, 159.

33. Trilling, xv.

34. Trilling, xvi–xvii.

35. See Ankersmit, 47; Lakoff, 69; and Smith *Stories*, 15. For more on literary aesthetics and conservatism specifically, see Zunac.

36. The recent literature on postwar American conservatism is vast. For an overview of book-length studies drawn largely from the past thirty years, see Brennan's *Turning Right in the Sixties*, Burns's *Goddess of the Market*, Farber's *The Rise and Fall of Modern American Conservatism*, Himmelstein's *To the Right*, Lichtman's *White Protestant Nation*, Lowndes's *From the New Deal to the New Right*, McGirr's *Suburban Warriors*, Nash's *The Conservative Intellectual Movement in America*, Perlstein's *Before the Storm*, Richardson's *To Make Men Free*, Robin's *The Reactionary Mind*, Schoenwald's *A Time for Choosing*, Schneider's *The Conservative Century*, and Tanenhaus's *The Death of Conservativism*. Nearly all of these studies are histories of political and economic change, though, and tend to elide the aesthetic, narrative dimension of American conservatism.

37. For literature on conservatism before World War II, see the first half of Allitt's *The Conservatives*, Kolko's *The Triumph of Conservatism*, McCloskey's *American Conservatism in the Age of Enterprise*, Olmsted's *Right out of California*, Postell and O'Neill's collection *Toward an American Conservatism*, and Richardson's *How the South Won the Civil War*.

38. Thomas "Recollections," 354.

39. Clark *Cuba*, 275.

Part I

GENTLEMEN OF THE WEST (1880–1884)

Chapter 1

Roosevelt in the Badlands

Two weeks after graduating from Harvard in 1880, twenty-one-year-old Theodore Roosevelt boarded a train in New York with his younger brother Elliott, thrilled at the journey that lay in front of him. Roosevelt had become engaged to a tall young woman named Alice Lee earlier that year. He wanted to mark the culmination of his college career and bachelorhood with an epic hunting trip to a part of the country he had never visited before: the American west.

Roosevelt had been looking forward to the trip for a long time. He was still recovering from the devastating death of his father two years earlier. At the age of nineteen, he had suddenly been left without a man to show him how to move through the world. "I expect to enjoy the western trip greatly, as I think it will build me up," he had told his mother before he left.[1] Before he had even seen the west, he seemed to believe it was not only a place. It was a force of nature, something that would actively build him.

By August 22, the Roosevelt brothers had settled at Wilcox's farm in Illinois and gotten in three days' worth of shooting.[2] "I feel twice the man for it already," Roosevelt exulted in a letter to his sister Anna.[3] The west, he had already decided, was a place that built his manhood.

Roosevelt had been born to a family that had known power and influence for over a hundred years. His father was a fourth-generation New Yorker, a plate-glass magnate and an influential Manhattan philanthropist who ten years earlier had helped found the Metropolitan Museum of Art and the Museum of Natural History. His mother was a socialite and the daughter of a powerful Georgia slaveholder and plantation owner. Roosevelt had been raised in a luxurious three-story brownstone on East 20th Street in Manhattan. He had never wanted for any material thing.

But in the west, it was easy to forget he was born to the American gentry. Hundreds of miles west of New York, a kind of superficial equality reigned. Roosevelt boasted in a letter to his sister that he and his brother went about "dressed about as badly as mortals could be," unshaven, wearing dirty boots. He found the local farmers "pretty rough" yet still deserving of his respect. They had an easy self-reliance that Roosevelt found immensely attractive. "I like them very much; like all rural Americans they are intensely independent," he wrote. He prided himself that he and his brother were able to shoot as well as they could, and work just as hard without succumbing to exhaustion. "I do'n't wonder," Roosevelt mused, "at their thinkking us their equals [sic]."[4]

He did not say that they were equal, merely that the men would have been justified in thinking them so. But he liked that the west allowed for the fiction of equality. In the west, Roosevelt found a laboratory for his earliest political beliefs, principles that stressed self-reliance and shunned government control.

In the place of traditional social divisions of the east, Roosevelt found that the west cultivated a sort of physical democracy in which differences could be explained by deficits in self-reliance. The ultimate marker of a man was the degree to which he did not need others. If Roosevelt was as physically capable as the locals, then social differences no longer much mattered. Under the wide-open skies of the west, he seemed ready to believe, relationships between citizens were simply different.

Roosevelt and Elliott made it back to New York by the end of September. Even though the hunting had not been what he was expecting, Roosevelt thought the trip had been high adventure. He had broken both his guns and been thrown headfirst from a wagon and bitten by a snake.[5] What could be better?

The following year, Roosevelt first got into politics by running for a seat in the New York State Legislature. Over the course of his long political career, he would drift far from his youthful beliefs in the absolute powers of individualism and would acquire a reputation as a reformer and a progressive. He would never fully abandon conservatism, though. One contemporary observer later noted the way Roosevelt represented "the union of radical and conservative ideas and of conservative and radical action."[6] Yet in his later years, Roosevelt's conservatism would hardly be absolute. After completing his second term as president, Roosevelt urged his party to "champion a system of increased Governmental control, paying no heed to the cries of worthy people who denounce this as Socialistic."[7] His early endorsement of a laissez-faire society driven by "intensely independent" individuals would, in time, fade.

But it would be a long time before Roosevelt would come to this point. Early in his political and literary career, he embraced wholeheartedly a rough-and-tumble individualism that he saw as the natural order of the universe. The notion that individuals and societies were both governed by Darwinian natural law was by then a common one, promoted by thinkers such as Herbert Spencer and others, but Roosevelt sharpened his personal theories about the natural state of the individual on the whetstone of the American west.

For Roosevelt, westerners exemplified the truest and best type of Americans. Much later, he would muse that "I owe more than I can ever express to the West." His west, though, was less about a region than it was about a certain type of person. As he explained it, working and living with westerners allowed him to "get into the mind and soul of the average American of the right type."[8] This ideal American was friendly, hardworking, and unrelentingly self-reliant. For a young Theodore Roosevelt, this wasn't just the way of the west. It was a law of nature.

By the time he crossed the Ohio River for the first time, Roosevelt had been courting Alice Hathaway Lee for nearly two years. They had first met when Roosevelt had gone to visit the family of his Harvard classmate Richard Saltonstall. Roosevelt was already enmeshed in a dense network of family friends and future business acquaintances: The Saltonstalls lived in Chestnut Hill, seven miles away from where Roosevelt was going to school in Cambridge, and right next to Richard's uncle, George Cabot Lee of the Boston banking firm Lee, Higginson and Company.[9] Lee's father had cofounded the firm in 1848.[10] The same firm would later hire Owen Wister in late 1883.

Lee's daughter Alice was just seventeen, nearly three years younger than Roosevelt, but Roosevelt noticed her immediately. Shortly after they met, Roosevelt vowed to "win her [. . .] if it were possible."[11] He first proposed to her in June 1879. She didn't say no, but she didn't say yes, either. But in January of the following year, Alice agreed. They formally announced their engagement on Valentine's Day of that year.

On October 27, 1880, a month after he and Elliott returned from their hunting trip out west, Roosevelt and Alice married in Brookline, Massachusetts. It was Roosevelt's twenty-second birthday. After the death of his father, things were back on track. He had graduated magna cum laude from Harvard earlier that year, had just begun studying law at Columbia, and now was getting married. After a short honeymoon, he and Alice moved into 6 West 57th Street, New York.[12] Roosevelt was intoxicated with love, writing in his diary that he and Alice were "one in *everything*."[13] They stayed up late, slept in, ate at home. In the evenings, they would sit together while Roosevelt read aloud from Walter Scott's *Quentin Durward* or Keats's poems.[14]

He began to think of himself as a writer. The following spring, he started work in earnest on the manuscript which would become his first book, *The Naval War of 1812*.

He also began to think he might like to run for office. Roosevelt's nascent political ambitions were viewed as odd by many in his social circle. Politics was not seen as an intellectual pursuit suitable for educated men of means like Roosevelt. It was a disreputable sea of vote-grubbing and patronage. But Roosevelt wanted to invent a more intellectual politics. He complained about the overeducated men of "little practical experience" whose "training in the theory of politics has been gained solely by the study of foreign books."[15] What was needed, he thought, was someone to fuse the practical with the intellectual. Roosevelt wondered if he could create a uniquely American fusion of theory, politics, and writing.

He was surprised to find that even the local Republican bosses laughed at the prospect of him getting involved in politics. Men who had been raised by families like the Roosevelts simply didn't do things like that. Party bosses told him that "politics were 'low'; that the organizations were not controlled by 'gentlemen'; that I would find them run by saloon-keepers, horse-car conductors, and the like, and not by men with any of whom I would come in contact outside."[16] One cousin warned that "his own father would not have liked it," adding that the "Roosevelt circle as a whole had a profound distrust of public life."[17]

Roosevelt tried to pass off these concerns, quipping that they only meant that "the people I knew did not belong to the governing class," and he, for one, "intended to be one of the governing class."[18] But his family had a point. Roosevelt was deeply interested in intellectual and scientific discovery, and he didn't want to join politics for the wrong reasons. As he continued to work on *The Naval War*, he began to think more about how politics was the bolt that joined abstract ideas with practical action. Politics were a way to do important work in the world, but it had to mean something. To be something other than the purview of saloonkeepers and horsecar drivers, politics had to be directed from an intellectual edifice. He just first had to build that edifice.

In November 1881, he was elected to the New York State Assembly from the Twenty-First District. He would go on to serve three consecutive one-year terms, and in 1883 he was elected Minority Leader. Yet he kept hearing the siren call of the west.

In the summer of 1883, Roosevelt met a forty-one-year-old former naval officer named Henry Honychurch Gorringe. Gorringe had garnered some minor notoriety a few years earlier for the role he played in relocating the obelisk popularly called "Cleopatra's Needle" from Alexandria, Egypt, to Central Park, New York. They chatted about *The Naval War of 1812*, which had been published the previous year, but the conversation eventually turned to hunting. After Roosevelt mentioned that he wanted to hunt some of the remaining wild bison in America, Gorringe suggested a trip to the Little Missouri River in Dakota Territory. Gorringe planned to accompany him, but then cancelled at the last minute. So Roosevelt packed his bags and his guns, kissed his pregnant wife goodbye, and left by himself on September 3, 1883.[19]

Five days later, he arrived by train in the town of Little Missouri, on the bank of the river just opposite the new settlement of Medora. He arrived on the same day that the two lines of the Northern Pacific were finally connected with a ceremonial golden spike near Gold Creek, Montana, marking the nation's latest transcontinental railroad line.

What once had been a prairie was poised to become a modern trade center of iron and industry. Roosevelt had come to Dakota looking for something that would not, he suspected, be there for long: an austere west of horses, campfires, and guns. Reading the press coverage of the golden spike connecting the two lines in a large ceremony attended by Ulysses S. Grant, Roosevelt must have thought that the west was rapidly disappearing. Henry Villard, the president of the Northern Pacific, had his men attach the final rail to a live telegraph wire, so that when he hammered in the ceremonial golden spike, it signaled the branch office in New York that the line was complete.[20] In one dramatic collision of gold and steel, the west spoke to the east at the speed of electricity. The country was shrinking.

But for the time being, the west felt as big as it ever had. A French nobleman named the Marquis de Morès had come to the Little Missouri river valley a few months before Roosevelt. He had opened a meat-packing business, made a small fortune, and even founded his own town, which he named after his wife Medora. His was perhaps a common dream of western individualism, where space still seemed boundless. Here, it was not just that every man could be his own boss. Every man could be his own mayor.

Little Missouri was then a desolate place, more train stop than town. On the journey there, Roosevelt could see a stark prairie stretching nearly as far as he could see. It was a part of the country that everyone called the Badlands.

Originally named by French Canadian trappers and fur traders who called them *mauvaises terres*, literally "bad lands," the Badlands were formed by millennia of mineral deposits followed by dramatic wind and water erosion, resulting in a series of steep and sweeping rock formations. One author of a U.S. Geologic Survey report commented in 1870 that the region "resembles a gigantic city abandoned and fallen to decay."[21]

Peering out the window, Roosevelt might have seen stacks of buffalo hides and bones, bleaching in the September sun and waiting to be hauled off back east. The bones would be ground up and used as a filter in eastern sugar refineries.[22] However, indirectly, men hunting bison in the Badlands were connected by the railroad to genteel Boston women in bustle gowns, stirring sugar into their tea. The skulls and skins made the metaphor clear: bloodshed in the west sustained civilization in the east.

In Little Missouri, the twenty-four-year-old Roosevelt disembarked and stood on the train platform. Other than the train depot and the Pyramid Park Hotel, the town seemed entirely uninhabited. That suited him fine. He grabbed his duffle bag and headed for the hotel.[23]

The next day, Roosevelt went to an abandoned army post to meet the ranch hand who had reluctantly agreed to serve as his hunting guide. The hardened Joe Ferris thought that Roosevelt was just another New York "dude." His studious-looking eyeglasses were, Ferris thought, a sure sign that Roosevelt wouldn't be much use on the hunting trail.[24] Nonetheless, he took Roosevelt to the Chimney Butte ranch, where he lived with his brother Sylvane and their partner William J. Merrifield.[25]

The ranch was a simple one-room log cabin with a dirt roof, abutted by a horse corral and a chicken coop. To another person of Roosevelt's comfortable upbringing, it might have seemed sparse, even squalid.

Roosevelt loved it.

The west allowed for a romantic sort of individual freedom, one in which governmental regulation hid snugly in an overcoat of mythic history. On the one hand, the Badland ranches seemed entirely beyond the reach of the long arm of the federal government. After all, there was virtually nothing else there. It made it easy to believe that one was living in the "wild woods and uncultivated waste of America," as philosopher John Locke had put it centuries earlier.[26] On the other hand, though, the land was in nearly every possible dimension intertwined with the government. Claimed by the government, protected by the government, with ownership laws and grazing laws created by the government, the Badlands perfectly symbolized the modern west. The land offered a fantasy of existence outside of governmental authority, but only as long as you didn't think too hard about it.

Roosevelt could already sense that the region was passing quickly into the romantic glow of history. "It was right and necessary that this [western] life should pass," as he later put it. "The great unfenced ranches, in the days of 'free grass,' necessarily represented a temporary stage in our history."[27] The implied tension between individual freedoms, tending outward and away from government regulation, and social planning, tending toward governmental authority, was not a new one. But to Roosevelt, it certainly seemed new. He seemed to be imagining himself standing on a kind of temporal precipice, watching the final days of the American frontier as it wheeled off the edge and spun wildly toward the canyon floor below.

By the early 1880s, Roosevelt had been thinking about staking a claim in the west for some time. Even before coming to the Badlands, he invested in a cattle business started by two of his college classmates, Hubert E. Teschemacher and Frederic O. de Billier. In 1879, the year after they graduated Harvard, they had moved to Wyoming Territory and made $34,031 in less than a year. Roosevelt joined another Harvard friend, Richard Trimble, along with the journalist John Bigelow in investing in their company. On October 30, 1882, Roosevelt invested $10,000 and Teschemacher and de Billier soon reincorporated to account for their three new investors.[28]

Over the next ten years, Teschemacher's and de Billier's company would steadily grow in size and power. Wealthy stockgrowers, many of them transplanted eastern elites, banded together to stifle competition and protect their own class interests. They began to act like a sort of landed gentry, manipulating laws and professional practices to protect themselves. Workers began to resent them for it. These class tensions would eventually come to a head when Teschemacher, de Billier, and nineteen other cattle ranchers hired a posse of gunmen to find and execute as many as seventy ranch-hands and cowboys who they alleged were cattle rustlers.[29] This attempted mass lynching inspired Owen Wister to begin working on a series of stories that would eventually coalesce into his novel *The Virginian*.

Of course, Roosevelt could not foresee the rise of this new sort of western aristocracy. After making his first investment in a western cattle company and seeing the Badlands for the first time a year later, he simply wanted a more authentic attachment to the west. Almost from the first moment he disembarked the train, he was awestruck by the landscape. Decades later, he would still be able to close his eyes and see clearly the "vast silent spaces," the "lonely rivers," the endless "plains where the wild game stared at the passing horseman."[30] For Roosevelt, the hardships of the unsparing land—in stark contrast to the comforts of his New York home—were what made the west worthwhile.

In later years, Roosevelt recalled the Badlands as a glorious space of work and redemption. During those first hunting trips, even when near-freezing rain was pouring down in sheets, he still hauled Joe Ferris out of the cabin to hunt bison. He grew increasingly certain that some part of him belonged in the west. For Ferris's part, his initial concern about the fitness of the "four-eyed tenderfoot" slowly dissipated. It didn't take long before Roosevelt impressed him with his gritty ability to "stand an awful lot of hard knocks."[31]

Roosevelt had just become the youngest minority leader in the history of the New York Assembly. Ferris remembered Roosevelt saying that the west offered him a chance to "get away from politics."[32] But Roosevelt's west wasn't apolitical in an absolute sense, just in a technical one. There may have been no glad-handing or canvassing for votes, but as he rode in the pouring September rain, Roosevelt was soaking up a different sort of political philosophy. He was refining what it meant—to his mind, anyway—to be an individual in America.

To be in the west, Roosevelt felt, was to walk the knife-edge of human existence. "We knew toil and hardship and hunger and thirst," he explained, "and we saw men die violent deaths as they worked among the horses and cattle, or fought in evil feuds with one another; but we felt the beat of hardy life in our veins, and ours was the glory of work and the joy of living."[33] To live and work in the west was to feel the thrum of life where others could not; it was to claim the honor of work when others would not. Being a westerner meant thinking of yourself as assiduously self-reliant. And being assiduously self-reliant, for Roosevelt, meant being alive.

By the end of the hunting trip, Roosevelt had decided it was not enough to be invested in someone else's ranch. He wanted his own. Sylvane Ferris and William Merrifield agreed to work for him, and one evening, sitting on a log near Cannonball Creek, Roosevelt took out his checkbook and wrote Merrifield and Ferris a check for 14,000 dollars, instructing them to buy several hundred head of cattle for the Chimney Butte Ranch.[34] It was done. He was a westerner.

By the time he got back to New York, Roosevelt was already finding a way to work his new western identity into conversations and letters, telling a fellow assemblyman that he "was forced to take up some out-of-doors occupation for the summer, and now have a cattle ranch in Dakotah."[35]

Roosevelt was also thrilled to be back with Alice, whose belly grew steadily bigger in the first months of 1884. He peppered his letters to his "Darling Wifie" with professions of his love, writing that he hated to "leave my bright sunny little love."[36]

On February 12, 1884, their daughter Alice Lee Roosevelt was born. Afterward, the new mother did not look well. The next day, Roosevelt nervously telegraphed his old nursemaid that his wife was "only fairly well."[37]

Two days later, Roosevelt marked his diary with an enormous black *X* that took up almost a tenth of the page. "The light has gone out of my life," he wrote.[38] His mother, Martha Bulloch Roosevelt, had succumbed suddenly to typhoid fever and died that day. A few hours later—four years to the day after she and Roosevelt had gotten engaged—Alice Hathaway Lee Roosevelt died of kidney failure.

Shaken with grief, Roosevelt sought to escape New York as soon as possible. By the end of April, he felt increasingly ambivalent about his political career, no longer willing to "stay in public life unless I can do so on my own terms."[39] He wanted to return to the west.

For the next several years, Roosevelt spent as much time as possible in Dakota Territory. He quietly bought and built a second, larger ranch that he named Elkhorn, thirty-five miles north of Medora.[40] "The country is growing on me," he wrote his sister in June, adding with apparent relief that he was sleeping well, but leaving the obvious unstated: before coming west, he had not been sleeping very well at all.[41]

He appreciated the solitude. "Nowhere," he wrote the following year, "not even at sea, does a man feel more lonely than when riding over the far-reaching, seemingly never-ending plains; and, after a man has lived a little while on or near them, their very vastness and loneliness and their melancholy monotony have a strong fascination for him."[42] This was not an unwanted loneliness, though. It was an important theme in the story Roosevelt was beginning to tell himself about the west. The story was a simple one: the west is where a man goes to be alone. And it is only the man who is alone, the man who is totally self-reliant, who is truly a man.

In expanding his ranch, Roosevelt was arguably driven more by matters literary than economic. In April, as if grateful for the distraction, he noted all the work he needed to do. But the work he was anticipating wasn't ranching; it was writing. For "the next few months I shall probably be in Dakota," he announced seven weeks after their deaths, sounding relieved that there "will be plenty of work to do writing."[43]

Yet he was no mere eastern poseur. "I didn't play; I *worked*, while on my ranch," he once said irritably, as if accustomed to being defensive on the matter.[44] He worked with the rest of the hands when they branded the calves and gathered the cattle for market. He felt his body changing from all the time spent with horse and rope and gun. He was becoming "well hardened," he wrote his sister in June, gloriously exhausted at having just spent "*thirteen hours in the saddle.*"[45]

While the actual pleasure he derived from spending thirteen hours on a horse was debatable, he certainly enjoyed the idea of it. He was drawn to the romance of western life as much as the reality. More than anything, Roosevelt wanted to figure out what the American west, as an idea, really meant. By 1884, *The Naval War of 1812* had already gone through three editions, establishing him as a successful historian. But Roosevelt was beginning to realize that mountains, hunting, and cowboys fired his literary imagination in a way that naval history never could.

In less than a decade, he would publish a number of books about the American west. The region would continue to spur his literary output for years to come. His first western book, *Hunting Trips of a Ranchman* (1885), was followed by his biography of Thomas Hart Benton, the Missouri senator and staunch advocate of western expansion (1887), which was followed immediately by *Ranch Life and the Hunting Trail* (1888) and the first two volumes of his four-volume history *The Winning of the West* (1889). Several years later, he returned to his experiences in the Badlands in *The Wilderness Hunter* (1893).

Roosevelt never claimed he was an intellectual, or even a particularly original thinker. He once told the founding president of Cornell University that he had "come to the conclusion that I have mighty little originality of my own. What I do is to try to get ideas from men whom I regard as experts along certain lines, and then try to work out those ideas."[46] Yet his prolificity on the western frontier amounted to an attempt to discover a political theory of the American west. For Roosevelt, who had a great love of science, the west was a type of laboratory in which various theories of individualism could be synthesized and tested. It wasn't that the west simply allowed for more freedom, in the way that unfenced land allowed for longer rides. It was that the west—or, more precisely, the way Americans thought about the west—actually created a new type of individual freedom. This type of freedom simultaneously involved a theory of individuals, nature, civil society, and land use. Seeking to escape his grief into the stark loneliness of the Badlands, Roosevelt began assembling this theory in the summer and fall of 1884, when he first began writing the essays and books in which he sought to explain the west—*his* west—to America.

NOTES

1. Qtd. in Putnam, 199.
2. Robinson *Brother*, 113.
3. TR letter to Anna Roosevelt, 22 August 1880. Unless otherwise noted, all correspondence from Roosevelt is from Elting E. Morison's multivolume *Letters of Theodore Roosevelt*.
4. TR letter to Anna Roosevelt 22, August 1880.
5. TR letter to Corinne Roosevelt, 12 September 1880.
6. Qtd. in Abbott, 260.
7. Roosevelt "Trusts," 654.
8. Roosevelt *Autobiography*, 119–120.
9. Di Silvestro, 15.
10. Boston, 34.
11. Roosevelt "Personal Diary," 25 January 1880. Roosevelt made this vow "a year ago last Thanksgiving," or on November, 28, 1878.
12. Di Silvestro, 20.
13. Roosevelt "Personal Diary," 12 December 1880.
14. TR letter to Martha Bulloch Roosevelt, 31 October 1880.
15. Roosevelt "Colonial," 230.
16. Roosevelt *Autobiography*, 56.
17. Qtd. in Pringle, 57.

18. Roosevelt *Autobiography*, 56.
19. TR letter to Anna Roosevelt, 3 September 1883. See also Putnam, 308–309.
20. Leeson, 422.
21. Qtd. in "Bad," 389.
22. Vollweiler, 36.
23. Roosevelt *Autobiography*, 94, Vollweiler, 37.
24. Hagedorn, 11.
25. Roosevelt *Autobiography*, 94.
26. Locke *Second Treatise*, 33.
27. Roosevelt *Autobiography*, 94.
28. Gressley, 125–127. Although historians have spelled his name in different ways, the 1880 *Harvard Register* lists it as "de Billier" ("Subscribers" 249).
29. Smith *War*, 194.
30. Roosevelt *Autobiography*, 93.
31. Qtd. in Hagedorn, 38.
32. Qtd. in Hagedorn, 38.
33. Roosevelt *An Autobiography*, 93–94.
34. Hagedorn *Roosevelt*, 43.
35. TR letter to Jonas S. Van Duzer, 20 November 1883. For a contemporary analysis of the romantic allure of ranching, see Cook "Romance," 223–243.
36. TR letter to Alice Lee Roosevelt, 6 February 1884.
37. TR telegram to Dora Watkins, 13 February 1884.
38. Roosevelt "Personal Diary," 14 February 1884.
39. TR letter to Simon Newton Dexter North, 30 April 1884.
40. Brinkley 168–171.
41. TR letter to Anna Roosevelt, 17 June 1884.
42. Roosevelt *Hunting* 197.
43. TR letter to Simon Newton Dexter North, 30 April 1884.
44. TR letter to James Brander Matthews, 7 December 1894.
45. TR letter to Anna Roosevelt, 17 June 1884.
46. TR letter to Andrew Dickson White, 26 December 1899.

Chapter 2

Wister Goes West

The first time Owen Wister ever saw Theodore Roosevelt, Roosevelt had blood pouring down his face.

It was in the old Harvard gymnasium, when eighteen-year-old Wister was a freshman and Roosevelt a junior. The scrawny Roosevelt, sporting a thick pair of sideburns, was fighting in an intramural boxing championship in the lightweight class. After the referee called time on a round, Roosevelt put his gloves down. His opponent promptly popped him in the nose. The spectators began to boo and hiss. Roosevelt held up his glove for silence. "It's all right," he announced in his clear, earnest voice. He walked over and shook his opponent's hand to show there were no hard feelings. "He didn't hear him."[1]

Wister had been deeply impressed, and thought he glimpsed a "prophetic flash" of the person Roosevelt was to become. That, he seemed to think, was how to be a man.[2]

Wister was tall and pale, with keen, dark eyes, hair that he parted carefully down the center, and a mustache that he kept neatly waxed and curled at the ends. Like Roosevelt, he was born into a family that had long known power and prestige. (Decades later, while spending the night at Roosevelt's White House, it would occur to him that he was the fourth generation of his family to have stayed there.[3]) His family was composed of two intertwining strains that did not blend easily: a slaveholding, conservative aristocratic class, and an artistic, creative liberal class.

His maternal grandmother, Fanny Kemble, was an English writer and actress famous throughout Europe and America for her poetry, memoirs, and talent at bringing Shakespeare to life onstage. She married Pierce Mease Butler, a southern slaveholder who was the grandson of a South Carolina delegate to the Constitutional Convention.

Their marriage was tumultuous from the start. Due to her acting career, Kemble was frequently away from their Philadelphia home when her children were young. In 1848, after years of resisting her husband's entreaties to become a "traditional" wife and mother, Kemble found herself served with divorce papers. It was only after months of legal wrangling that Kemble won custody of her children, including the woman who would become Owen Wister's mother.

Wister's mother had inherited her own mother's intellectual and artistic sensibilities. Wister's father, who had been taught by reformist educator Bronson Alcott, became a prominent Philadelphia physician. Wister grew up in a household that guaranteed his membership among the American elite. But thanks to his grandmother, he also grew up in a household where writers like Henry James and William Dean Howells were considered family friends.

Shortly before Wister's first birthday, his family's two sides were pulled apart by the Civil War. His mother had inherited her own mother's antislavery, Union sympathies. Other family members mirrored Wister's grandfather's Confederate allegiances. When Wister was one year old, his grandfather Pierce was arrested on charges of high treason for allegedly trying to send weapons to Confederate forces in Georgia. (He was eventually released only after pledging not to undermine the North any further.)[4]

Wister was born into a family that wove together two opposing strains of American thought: southern pro-slavery conservatism and northern individualism. He would be the last owner of the land enriched by generations of the people enslaved by his family.[5]

Wister's father always assumed his son would take his place among the gentry of the Atlantic coast. But Wister had been a slightly odd child. He was often sick and, like his grandmother, was drawn to the symphony and opera.

Once Wister arrived at Harvard in the fall of 1878, in addition to paying social calls to some of Boston's notable families, including the Cabots, the Lodges, and the Holmeses, he also began attending the opera as often as he could—once attending five different operas in a week. His father did not approve. He worried the opera was distracting Wister from his studies, but he also implied it was faintly unmanly. "Five nights to the opera is rather too much for a mature man," he said. For a "boy who has work to do the next day" and "requires a good deal of sleep," he told his eighteen-year-old son, such musical indulgence "is utterly bad."[6]

But Wister persisted. He got a piano for his room and decided to major in music. In the spring of his sophomore year, Wister was elected to Harvard's top final club, the Porcellian. There he furthered his relationship with Roosevelt, who was also a member. The club also brought him closer to jurist Oliver Wendell Holmes Jr., who had been a member when he attended Harvard nearly twenty years before.[7]

In the spring of 1880, Holmes—a thirty-nine-year-old Civil War veteran, an established lawyer, and legal scholar who had already done a stint as a professor at Harvard Law—was considerably older than Wister. Like Wister, Holmes was born to the Atlantic gentry. His own father, Holmes Sr., was an eminent physician, professor, and poet who was friends with Ralph Waldo Emerson and the other members of the Boston literary elite.

Even though Wister and Holmes were separated by a twenty-one-year age gap, they enjoyed each other's company. Holmes was tall and lanky with seemingly boundless energy, and took a liking to Wister. Holmes, who never had children, occasionally invited Wister over to his house for drinks and dinner. Wister, the youngest at these parties, rarely said much, as he felt he was there mostly "to be seen and not heard," yet he still fondly recalled the sound of ice clinking in the pitcher as the brilliant Holmes mixed drinks while holding forth on some subject or another.[8]

Though perhaps neither of them knew it, Holmes was already training Wister to think like a lawyer. At the time, Wister had no intentions of joining the bar. Despite his father's disapproval, Wister was quite talented at music, and intended to pursue it as a career. After graduating *summa cum laude* with a degree in music, Wister went to Europe and auditioned on the piano for Franz Liszt at Richard Wagner's house in Germany. After his audition, Liszt wrote to his old friend Fanny Kemble that her grandson had a pronounced talent for music, and Wister stayed for a winter's study at the prestigious Conservatoire de Paris.[9]

He returned home to start what his father hoped would be an illustrious career in investment banking with Lee, Higginson and Company. It should have been a good fit for the twenty-three-year-old Wister, almost like working for family. One of the partners, George C. Lee, was Roosevelt's father-in-law. And despite his father's insinuations that Wister's love of music was somehow unmanly, it was not out of place there. Henry Lee Higginson, another partner, had founded the Boston Symphony Orchestra.

But the work was terrifically boring. Despite the promise of a job, business had slumped, and so Wister was housed instead in the Union Safe Deposit Vaults. There he sat on a high, hard stool and calculated interest at 2.5 percent for prolonged stretches. He wasn't sure how long he could keep it up.[10] He continued his friendship with Holmes, and was thrilled when, at one Porcellian Club party, Holmes picked up his plate and glass and moved across the room to sit next to Wister.[11]

The two men talked about books, history, and ideas, not just law. They had conversations about the historian and novelist Henry Adams (Adams's novel *Democracy* had been published anonymously in 1880, and Wister claimed to have deduced Adams's authorship long before it was publicly confirmed), the prolific realist Henry James, the French literary naturalist Emile Zola, and others.[12] Wister always liked talking about books, and began to think he might want to be a writer.

He started working on a manuscript. Like many beginning writers, he eagerly showed his drafts to a friend. Unlike many beginning writers, though, for Wister that family friend was William Dean Howells, the so-called dean of American letters who had just spent nearly ten years as editor of the prestigious *Atlantic Monthly*. Howells politely suggested that the book "be never shown to a publisher."[13]

Wister knew Howells was right. And whether it was the bad news from Howells, the tedium of work, or something else altogether, Wister's health, which had never been robust, began to degenerate. One side of his face was semiparalyzed for more than a month in what was likely an attack of Bell's palsy. His reflexes slowed, and even blinking seemed laborious. "I wish I were a stronger person," Wister lamented to his father. "It will prevent my ever doing much."[14] He didn't want to believe that he was constitutionally, intractably weak—*unfit*—yet all available evidence seemed to be indicating as much.

He needed a change. To start, he and his father agreed that he could not remain a clerk forever. His efforts at writing had panned out, and he reluctantly agreed to give up the dream of being a composer. It felt as if there were only one choice left: law school.

He did admire Holmes. Holmes was a lawyer, yet also lived a full, intellectual life. In the fall of 1884, Wister told his father that the romance of music and the tedium of clerking would both be put away. "I would go to the Harvard Law School," he recalled saying, "since American respectability accepted lawyers, no matter how bad, which I was likely to be, and rejected composers, even if they were good, which I might possibly be."[15]

Neurasthenia was the name that late-nineteenth-century medical doctors gave to a mysterious combination of stress-related ailments that seemed mostly to afflict bourgeois professionals.[16] The disease was first identified by Dr. George M. Beard, a New York neurologist who in 1869 had invented the term to describe the "nervous exhaustion" that seemed to afflict a growing number of Americans.[17] Beard thought the disease was caused by the cool climate of the northeastern United States and the relentless striving that characterized modern urban capitalism. Neurasthenics' symptoms seemed endless. They included headaches, dilated pupils, irritability, insomnia, drowsiness, feelings of fear or anxiety, muscle spasms, exhaustion, dyspepsia, or any number of other ailments.[18] It was an umbrella of maladies, an ineffable disease of upper-class modernity brought on by the droning stresses of the Gilded Age economy.

By the mid-1880s, Dr. Silas Weir Mitchell—Wister's first cousin, once removed—had established himself as one of the preeminent authorities on neurasthenia.[19] He was the inventor of the "rest cure," which was frequently used to treat female neurasthenics. The cure was not particularly complicated. It mostly involved doing as little as possible, often for weeks at a time. As Mitchell explained it in an 1875 lecture, the physician should simply say to the patient, "You are ill. Remain in bed for a month."[20] Mitchell's rest cure was eventually used to treat to a number of prominent women, including social worker and activist Jane Addams, William Dean Howells's daughter Winifred Howells, writer Charlotte Perkins Gilman (who turned her experience of the cure into the short story "The Yellow Wall-paper"), and Virginia Woolf.[21]

For male neurasthenics, though, Mitchell tended not to prescribe the "rest cure" but the "west cure." As he explained in his book *Wear and Tear: Or, Hints for the Overworked*, he was concerned about the upper classes along the Atlantic coast. He thought that traveling, "especially in the West," could alleviate the countless stressors that came from living in America's "teeming city hives."[22]

> The man who lives an out-door life—who sleeps with the stars visible above him—who wins his bodily subsistence at first hand from the earth and waters—is a being who defies rain and sun, has a strange sense of elastic strength, may drink if he likes, and may smoke all day long, and feel none the worse for it. Some such return to the earth for the means of life is what gives vigor and developing power to the colonist of an older race cast on a land like ours. A few generations of men living in such a fashion store up a capital of vitality which accounts largely for the prodigal activity displayed by their descendants, and made possible only by the study contest with Nature which their ancestors have waged. That such a life is still led by multitudes of our countrymen serves to keep up our pristine force and energy. The country is continually contributing vitality to the towns.[23]

Mitchell was convinced that men had drifted too far from such an "out-door life." This was a conservative argument about neurology and America alike. It suggested that the original fount of American vitality lay in the past, and to recreate those bygone conditions would allow the well to be replenished. Spending too much time in the modern city had exhausted the vitality of men like Wister. The only cure was to "return to the earth." To return to the west.

He advised as much to Wister. "You don't feel kindly to your race, you know," he pointed out. He was trying to say that Wister was an unabashed elitist, and some experience with the great democratic masses might be good for him. "There are lots of humble folks in the fields you'd be the better for knowing."[24] Wister thought that maybe he was right. If nothing else, it would give him something to do before he started law school in the fall.

On June 30, 1885, he boarded the Limited Express at the Philadelphia train station.[25] He planned to follow his doctor's orders and shore up his vitality through a journey into America's frontier past.

The nominal reason for Wister's trip was illness. "I went West that July day to cure a headache I had waked and slept with since February," he later explained.[26] But the cure took effect almost instantly. And to his surprise, traveling west changed the way he thought about politics and the sweep of American history.

Wister arrived in Wyoming on July 3 and stayed on a ranch belonging to Frank Wolcott. The New York-born Wolcott was a fierce ex-lawman and powerful ranchman. He had risen to the rank of major in the Union army, traveled west to Wyoming, and served as a U.S. marshal before getting into ranching in the mid-1870s.[27]

Wister knew he was following in the footsteps of several of his Harvard classmates. Teschemacher and de Billier, both class of 1878, were already junior cattle barons, and of course Roosevelt had purchased his ranch in Dakota Territory two years earlier.[28]

Along with Frank Wolcott and every other powerful rancher in the territory, Teschemacher and de Billier were members of the Wyoming Stock Growers Association. By the time Wister arrived, cattle were big business, and enterprising easterners had been trying to recreate genteel club life in the frontier west. The leading ranchers and investors of the region gathered at the informal headquarters of the region's cattle business: the Cheyenne Club. Built in 1881 "for the comfort of men of wealth," as one early account put it, the Cheyenne Club was a grand brick edifice that had cost an incredible $40,000.[29] It housed gentlemen of means as well as the local board of trade, and was set up to receive the current trading prices for stock in the Chicago and eastern markets. Wealthy landowners and speculators would gather to gossip, play cards, drink wine, and, of course, cut deals involving thousands of head of cattle and acres of range land. One reporter, visiting the Cheyenne Club three years before Wister, wrote that it was like "a young Wall Street. Millions of dollars are talked of as lightly as nickels and all kinds of people are dabbling in steers."[30]

The club was nice enough, but the twenty-four-year-old Wister was mostly awestruck at the pellucid mass of western space. "The sky—there is none," he wrote in his journal. "It looks really like what it scientifically is—space. The air is delicious."[31] This western land, he decided, represented an opportunity to start it all again.

Looking west to the Laramie Mountains and east to the Great Plains, Wister thought that the sheer scale signified something about the role the west would play in America's future. The west was "a very much bigger place than the East," he wrote. The "future America is just bubbling and seething in bare legs and pinafores here." The west, he began to believe, was the inevitable site of the American future. That future, though, wouldn't be a continuation of the past. Instead, the west would be "like Genesis," a divine-gifted opportunity to begin the world anew.[32]

A few days after drawing this comparison, Wister witnessed a disagreement at a ranch and doubled his commitment to the analogy: "In the Old Testament Lot and Isaac and Uncle Leban and the rest had times not unlike this—only guns weren't invented."[33] He was just beginning to play with a new idea: the notion that going west represented not just a spatial shift, but a temporal shift. It was like going back in time, to the days of the Old Testament. This lent a geographic dimension to his nascent conservatism. To return to or conserve a particular historical moment would no longer require a grand restoration or redemption. It would simply require a train ride. Temporality had been replaced by geography.

But Wister also knew the west wasn't frozen in history. Even if going there in 1885 was like witnessing Genesis, such a comparison would not be apt for very long. The American west would be slowly crowded by urban modernity, Wister wrote, trying to capture the grand, sweeping sense of history he felt. The west would make room "for Cheyennes, Chicagos, and ultimately inland New Yorks—everything reduced to the same flat prairies-like level of utilitarian civilization." Out of the primeval genesis of cattle ranching and flintlock, a social and economic elite would naturally emerge. And over time, the west would inevitably be dominated by a traditional social and economic order: "Branans and Beeches will give way to Tweeds and Gay Goulds—and the ticker will replace the rifle."[34]

Wister's visit to Wyoming was short. But it was enough to change his life for good. In time, he would become the greatest living bard of the American west. His stories about cowboys and ranchers would eventually be read by people from all over the nation and praised by the president.

On his way back to the Atlantic coast to start law school, the twenty-five-year-old Wister thought more about the theory of civilizational advancement—the move from Genesis to modernity—and the role he thought the west should play in the grand sweep of history. He was clearly thinking about the pace of social change. "Puritanism," he mused, "is the protest of one stage of civilization against a later stage at which itself in its turn is bound to arrive." In other words, conservative impulses were not directed toward the past, but toward the future. "Whatever dissensions arise are only the result of some portion of this great progressive organism getting ahead of the rest, or pulling contrary to the general direction of development."[35] The west, he seemed to think, could reshape the flow of history. It was the inevitable "general direction of development"—it was pulling America into the future—yet it was also like Genesis: a perfectly preserved reminder of civilization's earliest beginnings. It was with this mindset—equating the west with the inevitable future, and that inevitable future as one that ran contrary to any progressive ideas that might "get ahead of the rest"—that Wister returned to Boston in August 1885, ready to study American law in earnest.

NOTES

1. Wister *Roosevelt*, 5.
2. Wister *Roosevelt*, 5.
3. Wister *Roosevelt*, 106.
4. Payne, 6–9.
5. Bell Jr., 495.
6. Qtd. in Payne, 32.
7. Payne, 32–36.
8. Wister *Roosevelt*, 129.
9. Wister *Roosevelt*, 22.
10. Wister *Roosevelt*, 22.
11. Payne *Owen*, 64.
12. Wister *Roosevelt*, 130, 147–151.
13. Wister *Roosevelt*, 23.
14. Payne, 72.
15. Wister *Roosevelt*, 27.
16. Gosling, xii. See also Lears, 47–58.
17. Gosling, 9.
18. Beard, 39–117.
19. Mitchell was married to Wister's mother's cousin. Wister referred to Mitchell's son, Langdon Mitchell, colloquially as his "cousin"; Langdon was in fact his second cousin (Wister *Roosevelt*, 23). See Bell Jr., 487.
20. Mitchell "Rest," 84.
21. Poirier "Weir," 15.
22. Mitchell *Wear*, 74, 9.
23. Mitchell *Wear*, 7–8.
24. Qtd. in Payne, 76.
25. Payne *Owen*, 77.
26. Qtd. in Scharnhorst *Owen*, 8.
27. Bold *Frontier*, 74.
28. Payne, 80.
29. Bancroft *History*, 797.
30. Qtd. in Sobel, 156.

31. OW journal 3 July 1885 in Wister *Owen*, 30. Unless otherwise noted, all journal entries from Wister are from Fanny Kemble Wister's *Owen Wister Out West*.
32. OW journal 2, 6 July 1885.
33. OW journal, 16 July 1885.
34. OW journal, 16 July 1885.
35. OW journal, 2 August 1885.

Chapter 3

Frederic Remington's Vanishing West

During his first trip west to Montana in 1881, long before he had established himself as an influential illustrator, painter, sculptor, and writer, a stocky nineteen-year-old named Frederic Remington found himself harking back to the western-themed books and paintings he had pored over as a young boy.

Like many of his childhood friends in upstate New York, as a boy Remington had been obsessed with Washington Irving's 1830s-era western books such as *A Tour of the Prairies* and *The Adventures of Captain Bonneville*, along with any books detailing the exploits of Meriwether Lewis and William Clark.

But the young Remington was especially taken with the work of Pennsylvania artist George Catlin, who had first traveled west in 1830 to begin the massive undertaking he thought of as his life's work: painting portraits of as many Plains Indians as possible. The "history and customs of such a people, preserved by pictorial illustrations, are themes worthy the life-time of one man," Catlin had proclaimed grandly.[1] By 1836, Catlin had assembled a traveling "Indian Gallery" of his paintings, essentially inventing the nation's first traveling western show. As a boy Remington loved looking at those paintings, which had been reproduced, republished, and exhibited countless times by the year he was born.

During that first trip to Montana, Remington thought back to men like Catlin, dead for almost a decade, or Irving, who had been dead for almost two, and felt as if was "sweating along their tracks."[2] He was walking in the footprints of an earlier generation of western mythmakers, and knew he was seeing the west in the way those writers and artists wanted him to see it.

One cold night, Remington came upon the campfire of a wagon freight worker. The man was old and grizzled, wearing a cotton shirt open at the neck. He offered Remington bacon and hot coffee.

The two talked late into the night. Like Remington, the man was from New York and had gone west at a young age. Back then, the west had been Iowa, but he had "followed the receding frontiers," as Remington put it, "always further and further west."

"And now," the old man declared, "there is no more West. In a few years the railroad will come along the Yellowstone and a poor man can not make a living at all."[3]

It was at that moment, Remington later recalled, that his attitude toward the west changed. At once, he knew the "wild riders and the vacant land were about to vanish forever, and the more I considered the subject the bigger the Forever loomed."[4] The west, as men like Catlin and Irving and even this old-timer had known it, was not long for late-century America.

So Remington set himself on the task of trying to capture the west for posterity, just as Catlin had done a half-century earlier. "Without knowing exactly how to do it," he recalled, "I began to try to record some facts around me." He knew, though, that this sort of record-keeping wasn't purely about documenting the present. "If the recording of a day which is past infringes on the increasing interest of the present," he thought, "be assured there are those who will set this down in turn and everything will be all right in the end." In other words, documenting what he called the "living, breathing end of three American centuries of smoke and dust and sweat" was akin to a type of time travel. It meant working in the present, yet capturing the past, all for the benefit of the future.[5]

He did not have a sketchbook or even any real paper with him, but he sketched out a scene on some spare wrapping paper, put it into a small envelope, and sent it off to *Harper's* magazine in New York. He had never done anything for publication beyond his college newspaper and knew he was taking a chance. But when Charles Parsons, the art director at *Harper's*, opened the odd proposal, he saw something unusual in its unrefined simplicity. He decided to take a chance, too. Parsons was intrigued by the scene Remington had drawn, along with its unconventional paper and its distant-seeming Wyoming postmark. Parsons passed it off to William A. Rogers, an experienced illustrator.[6]

Rogers smoothed out the crumpled little sketch, admired it, and then redrew it on wood for publication. (Later, Remington finally got a chance to meet Rogers, who had all but forgotten about the little cowboy sketch on wrapping paper. It "was you who introduced me to the public," Rogers recalled Remington telling him. "That was my first appearance and I was mighty glad I fell into the hands of an artist who knew a cowboy saddle and a Western horse."[7])

Remington's original submission did not survive, but the published version of his sketch depicted a party of five cowboys in a meadow, startled out of their slumber by a lone army scout on horseback. Scrambling for their spurs and gun-belts, the cowboys eye the scout anxiously. The scout, resting his rifle across his saddle, is scowling and pointing gesturing to the left—the west—of the illustration, as if telling them they are not allowed there any longer and need to move along.

Though Remington always professed his documentary aspirations—wanting to record for posterity the "wild riders and the vacant land" that "were about to vanish forever"—the drawing didn't actually document any particular part of the west. Remington had done the work in Montana but mailed it from Wyoming, as if it might have been drawn in either place. And when it finally appeared in print in the February 25, 1882, issue of *Harper's Weekly*, the caption claimed it depicted an Arizona scene. "Cow-boys of Arizona: Roused by a Scout" ran as a full-page illustration credited to "W.A. Rogers from a Sketch by Frederic Remington."[8] His west was more a placeholder than an actual place.

Even at a young age, Remington was tugged between the two artistic poles of documentation and representation. He wanted his art to be documentary, like a visual historian recording something specific in the west. But his work was more often representative, depicting the general idea of the west. It didn't matter if the sketch contained Montana cowboys or Wyoming cowboys or real cowboys at all. It was just as easily put to use representing a scene from Arizona. All the same, when Remington drew an imagined scene and then claimed he had "record[ed] some facts," he wasn't being entirely deceptive. As he began to realize, the past was brought into existence by the pencil. His art became a kind of beautiful lie that seemed to reveal something true about the American past, a truth his audience would in time be eager to believe.

Remington was born in Canton, New York, in 1861 to Seth Remington and Clarissa Sackrider. Some of his earliest memories of his father involved writing, politics, and war. Seth Remington had been part owner of a newspaper, the St. Lawrence *Plaindealer*. But just eight weeks after his son's birth, he traveled to New York City to enroll in the first U.S. Volunteer Calvary in what some northerners were already beginning to call the War for the Suppression of the Rebellion.[9]

After the war, Seth Remington was known as "Colonel Remington" for the remainder of his life. He returned to publishing and in 1873 bought an interest in the Ogdensburg *Journal*.[10] He was a kind of warrior-writer, a regional player whose very name carried a history of wartime valor. In the way of most young boys, his son wanted to be just like him.

At age thirteen, Remington enrolled in military school in Vermont before transferring the following year to another military academy in Massachusetts. He didn't exactly look like conventional military material. He was growing into a rather large young man. Describing himself to a friend at the time, he said he could "spoil an immense of amount of good grub at any time of the day," adding that "I go a good man on muscle."[11] His hair was short and bristly, and though he was about five feet eight inches, he weighed 180 pounds, big for his height. He was supposed to be training to be a disciplined American warrior, and for a while, tried to think of himself as such. "There is nothing poetical about me," he wrote with terse pride. He seemed to think that the way to be a man was to be like his father: brave and commanding, all iron and muscle.

But he was also nurturing an interest in art, and shared a love of military-themed art with his friend. ("Your favorite subject is soldiers," Remington told him. "So is mine."[12]) Remington mailed his shaky, still unformed sketches to his friend, and in return, requested pictures of a specific type of American in a specific type of scene. "Don't send me any more women or any more dudes," he begged. "Send me Indians, cowboys, villains, or toughs. These are what I want."[13]

By his third year in the academy, it would have been clear to almost anyone, Remington included, that he did not belong in the military. Growing up in the shadow of his father—war hero, newspaperman, local Republican party leader—Remington must have been stumbling about for his own path to greatness, slowly realizing that his talents, whatever they were, were not the same as his father's. He was ill-suited to the military, with no special aptitude for writing or politics.

But he had always liked sketching. So in the fall of 1878, he enrolled in the Yale School of Fine Arts in New Haven. Though they would not meet for another several years, just then Owen Wister was starting at Harvard, 200 miles up the coast, and making his father leery with talk of majoring in music. Remington's family likewise seemed nervous about his interest in art. In their view, art wasn't really a profession—at best it was unseemly for an upward-bound family like the Remingtons—and it certainly wasn't a very manly thing to do.[14]

Yale College was still the exclusive purview of men (the undergraduate college would not, in fact, enroll women for nearly another century), except for the School of Fine Arts. The year Remington enrolled, there were a total of thirty art students at Yale. Including Remington, only seven of them were men. The only first-year male art student was Remington.[15] As a student in the School of Fine Arts rather than Yale College proper, Remington was not exactly a Yale man, although he tried to play the part on his trips home. For someone aspiring to the manly world of his father, spending time in the feminine world of art school must have been at times dispiriting.

But he did make at least one older friend, a twenty-three-year-old named Poultney Bigelow, whose father was a New York diplomat, writer, onetime newspaper publisher, and politician. Bigelow edited the student newspaper, and on November 2, 1878, published Remington's first illustration. It was part of the series "College Riff-Raff," a full-page cartoon depicting an injured football player with his arm in a sling, his foot bandaged, and head wrapped in dressings.

Remington's interest in drawings of football injuries echoed his earlier interest in drawings of "Indians, cowboys, villains, or toughs." Despite rejecting a future with the military, he was still attracted to the romantic courage evoked by pictures of cowboys and injured football heroes. He was more interested in the image of battle than in actual battle.

There was nothing unusual about this. A drawing allowed for a kind of shortcut around direct experience. A person does not have to actually suffer a broken arm to appreciate the bravery and pathos conjured by a picture of an injured football player.

The most basic job of an artist, Remington was learning, was to create the illusion that people were familiar with experiences they had not actually experienced. He was beginning to exercise his skill at representation, which meant depicting the world's underlying types—the general idea of a soldier, a cowboy, a football player—rather than the specifics of its visible exterior.[16]

But it would not take long before a shattering event caused Remington to flee the stuffy Yale art classroom and the entire Atlantic coast. In the summer after his first year at Yale, Remington returned home to Canton where he began to court a college student two years older named Eva Caten. They kept in touch when Remington returned to New Haven in the fall. His second year was going better than his first. He made the football team, which offered kind of a refuge of masculinity. (Decades later, during one of the country's first of many debates about the safety of football, Remington would insist that any attempts to make football safer threatened to "emasculate" the game, such that it would be "robbed of its heroic qualities."[17]) Several weeks after 6,000 spectators gathered to watch Yale and Princeton battle to a scoreless draw, Remington went home to Ogdensburg for Christmas break.

As soon as he arrived, he realized something was deeply wrong. His father was stricken with tuberculosis and had degenerated rapidly. On February 18, 1880, he died at the age of forty-six. Remington was just eighteen years old. He never returned to Yale.[18]

Grief-stricken and adrift, Remington tried his hand at a few different jobs, but wasn't driven toward anything in particular. Six months after his father's death, he wrote to Eva's father and asked for his daughter's hand in marriage. Lawton Caten flatly turned him down. Much like Theodore Roosevelt would later go west to escape his own grief over the loss of his wife and mother, Remington seemingly felt like something wild inside him was tugging him westward.

A few months later, he was making plans for a trip to Montana.

When he left New York on August 10, 1881, the local newspaper reported that the nineteen-year-old Remington "intends to make a trial of life on a ranche" in Montana.[19] After a connection in Chicago, he took the railroad west from St. Paul into western Dakota Territory, where he boarded a stagecoach for Miles City, Montana.

Remington quickly realized his romantic dreams of ranch life were unlikely to come true. The type of western life he wanted was not, it turned out, easy to come by. After all, he did not want to be a mere ranch hand; he wanted to be a ranch owner. But the funds required to get started in the cattle ranching business were far beyond the means of a Yale Art School dropout, even if that dropout was the son of a New York businessman.

He learned about Teschemacher and de Billier, who were on track to make $34,031 profit that fall. (The following year, Roosevelt would join with Poultney Bigelow's father to invest in their cattle company.) Remington knew there was wealth and adventure to be had in ranching, and he knew Teschemacher and de Billier were already enormously successful. Unfortunately, they had started with an initial investment of $158,600 in cash and cattle. Even with the small estate he stood to inherit from his father, he simply didn't have access to that kind of capital.[20]

Yet the west, he seemed to believe, still offered opportunities. A man just had to know where to look. Even in the dark, listening to old men recalling older times and telling him "there is no more West," he knew there was still *something* there.

He would later write that once the sun set in Montana, it created a "wild charge in the dark." The darkness of the west was overpowering. At night, a person "cannot see; you whirl through a canon cut in the mud; you plough through the sage-brush and over the rocks clatter and bang."[21] Remington, too, was stumbling in the dark, trying to find the type of man he could be. And on one such night, after his chance encounter with the grizzled old New Yorker, Remington tried to "record some facts" through his art. He mailed off his little wrapping paper sketch. By late October, he would be back in New York.

Thrilled that a New York publisher had actually wanted something he had drawn, he went to Manhattan to meet with George William Curtis of *Harper's Weekly* to discuss the possibility of additional work. Although it would be another three years before he would get anything else published in *Harper's*, that one sale was enough to fire Remington's belief in himself and in his art.

When he turned twenty-one on October 4, Remington inherited around $10,000 from his father's estate.[22] Much as his future friends Roosevelt and Wister would fund their own western adventures with family money, Remington felt the money would allow him finally to live a life of rugged western individualism. (Also like his future friends, he seemed not to fully grasp the irony of needing a healthy inheritance to fund a life of manly self-reliance.) Five months after coming into his inheritance, Remington had boarded a train for Kansas, where he planned to follow a former Yale classmate into the sheep ranching business.[23]

But it didn't take long for the grim reality of sheep ranching to settle in. It didn't have any of the romance of the wide-open cattle ranges of Wyoming and Montana, for one thing. He still wanted to document the west, but there was little that seemed worth documenting. Kansas in mid-March was a brown flatness, all half-frozen mud and scrawny trees. It was a west that had been stripped of all its poetry and color and romance, if it ever had any to begin with.

When he wrote home, he tried to make the nearby town of Peabody seem more exciting than it was. "Man just shot down street—must go," he wrote tersely in one letter.[24] It wasn't true—no shooting had taken place—but he was having fun experimenting with the ways that the west could come alive not through documentation, but through representation. He wanted to get at an *idea* of the west, whether or not he had actually witnessed the thing. A kind of lie that told the truth.

By 1884, he had sunk all of his inheritance into the ranch and had nothing to show for it. He returned to the east and finally married Eva Caten. Then he went to Kansas again to give it one more try.

In later years, he never spoke about his failed sheep ranching enterprise. It did not exactly match the masculine image he wanted to portray. He instead explained those years by claiming, falsely, that he had gone to Montana to work as a cowboy.[25] But in trying to make sense of that turbulent time, he wasn't just inventing a cowboy heritage. He was also turning his profligacy into virtue. It had been his inheritance that allowed him to go west and try his hand at self-reliant ranching. But now that the money was gone, he was forced to actually shift for himself. "Now that I was poor I could gratify my inclination for an artist's career," he explained.[26]

With few options remaining, Remington announced that he planned to go west and find his fortune. He was not, however, planning to go anywhere physically. He instead retreated to a makeshift studio and began to paint western scenes from his imagination. He put these paintings for sale on consignment at W. W. Findlay in Kansas City. They sold quickly. He did a few more.[27]

Emboldened, he submitted another sketch to *Harper's Weekly*, "Ejecting an 'Oklahoma Boomer,'" depicting a small, multiracial group of cavalry escorting a forlorn party of squatters from Indian Territory. Like his last sketch, this one was also redrawn, this time by Thure de Thulstrup. Remington also submitted an article to go with the drawing, and *Harper's* bought that, too. The art ran on the cover of *Harper's Weekly* on March 28, 1885.

Even though he had only lived in the west for a short period of time, in later years, he would return for a number of visits to the fount of his original inspiration. Yet many of his friends seemed to think him a natural son of the west, much like the similarly eastern Roosevelt and Wister. One of those friends, playwright Augustus Thomas, later spun romantic—and exaggerated—stories of how Remington's "young manhood was spent in the far West, at work with the cow-boys and near the soldiers and Indians whose picture historian he was destined to become."[28]

But Remington was also, perhaps even without realizing it, cultivating a set of beliefs about the west and its role in American history. As Thomas explained it, Remington's western "education reinforced the independence of his nature." The west amplified his natural individualism. Remington first "adopted the cow-boy habit and point of view," Thomas elaborated, "and finally assimilated the cow-boy philosophy."[29] Remington was coming around to the belief that drawings of cowboys, like other signifiers of the west, were not just romantic images. They carried their own histories and ideas, their own philosophy.

Over the next several decades, this "cow-boy philosophy" would emerge piecemeal, as Remington pursued illustration, painting, sculpture, journalism, and eventually fiction with increasing success. Back in New York in the fall of 1885, he had the chance to try to convince the East Coast publishing establishment, face-to-face, of the virtues of this philosophy.

He scheduled a meeting with J. Henry Harper, the head of the Harper publishing house. Remington had decided to take a chance and not wear conventional business dress to the meeting. Instead, he strode into the Harper offices on Franklin Square, tall and bristle-haired and weighing nearly two hundred pounds, dressed so that he "looked like a cowboy just off the ranch," as Harper later recalled. Remington had brought samples of his art, which Harper deemed "very crude" yet with "all the ring of new and live material."[30] But he also wanted to test his storytelling skills: his ability to represent the west without strictly documenting it.

He began to spin a fantastic tale of shrewd bravery and iron nerves. Until just a few days ago, he told Harper, he had been stranded in a small western town with no more than a quarter to his name. He had gone to a saloon, where he saw two professional gamblers "plucking a man who looked like an Eastern drummer." Remington watched the card game for a few minutes and then told the salesman that it was probably time to go to bed. When the two gamblers shot Remington a look of pure fury, Harper recalled him saying, Remington "whipped out his gun, told the card-sharpers to hold up their hands, and covered his retreat until he and his befriended companion were safe in the man's bedroom and had locked and barricaded the door."[31] Remington told Harper that he had then stayed up all night guarding against their return, gun at the ready.

In the morning, Remington concluded triumphantly, the salesman was so thankful that he offered to pay Remington's way to New York City, which it so happened was his destination as well. As soon as he arrived, Remington said, he had come immediately to see J. Henry Harper.[32]

The story was pure fiction, of course, but it didn't matter. Harper believed it completely.[33] As well he should have. Its message was custom-crafted for Harper himself. It suggested Remington was a tough and self-reliant gentleman westerner, the type of man who could shepherd tenderfoot easterners through the darkness of America's western wild.

Remington's meeting with Harper worked better than he could have hoped. Harper bought two of Remington's sketches on the spot and agreed to send him to Arizona to report on Geronimo's lengthy evasion of the American military forces. The Chiricahua Apache leader had been leading a tenaciously fierce resistance against the U.S. efforts to expand into Apache territory. The desert southwest, Geronimo later explained, was a gift from God to the Apaches. The United States was trying to take away "the liberty to return to that land which is ours by divine right."[34] Even from Geronimo's perspective, American nature meant a divine right to American freedom. The federal government might have agreed in principle. It just seemed to think that American nature meant freedom for some Americans, not for all.

By June 8, 1886, Remington was making his way into Arizona Territory. In March, Geronimo had agreed to surrender, but at the last minute, slipped away with a party of around fifty Apache. No one had been able to find him since. For many white Americans, Geronimo's continued freedom was widely seen as an affront not just to the American military, but to the nation as a whole. As one frustrated former army officer put it, "what can the United States soldier, mounted on his heavy American horse, with the necessary forage, rations, and camp equipage, do against this supple untiring foe? Nothing, absolutely nothing."[35] The continued existence of Geronimo's band was sorely testing the belief that the American west had somehow produced a better, fitter nation. One week of the type of work that it would take to catch Geronimo, the officer complained, "will kill the average soldier and his horse; [yet] the Apache thrives on it. The frontiersman, as he now exists, is simply a fraud as an Indian-fighter."[36]

After the meeting in which Remington had impressed Henry Harper with his cowboy clothes and western exploits, *Harper's* had sent Remington to illustrate the efforts made by General Nelson Miles to find Geronimo. He kept a journal where he tried to make pretentious, scientific-sounding classifications of the various western types he observed. The west was a place where any evolutionary differences between people and nations, he thought, was readily apparent.

The native New Mexicans of Spanish or Indian descent, he wrote, were "a very degraded set."[37] Mexicans, similarly, were "not a virtuous people," in part because "selfishness and various other low traits predominate." In his mind, he was able to track their place on the great imagined line of evolutionary progress in part because of the clarity of the west, which magnified all differences. "The people in this country have studied economy until they can live on a melon and stick of sugar cane and don't have to work more than one day a week," he scoffed. "They study economy of living and working, the general effect of which is a natural decay. Poverty and the Cross rule the race, indolence and averice [sic] are hand maidens, and ignorance and decay are the results."[38]

Remington saw himself as a kind of anthropologist-adventurer, making Darwinian judgments about the degeneracy of the different races he observed. In contrast, the industrious "frontiersmen"—the white settlers—"all exhibit rough bearded and tanned faces with a very marked stamp of physical courage plainly stamped on their physiogony [sic]."[39]

He also got to meet General Nelson A. Miles, who commanded 5,000 U.S. soldiers along with some Apache scouts and civilian militias. Miles was effusively warm to Remington in the apparent hopes of keeping the fruitless hunt for Geronimo out of the newspapers for a while. Both men seemed to make a mental note to keep in touch. (Years later, Miles would hire Remington to do the illustrations for his memoir.) But the trip wasn't shaping up to be what Remington had hoped. Geronimo had a well-deserved reputation as a skilled guerilla warrior responsible for the deaths of hundreds of American soldiers. After some agents in Deming told him it was simply too dangerous to chase after him, Remington decided to abandon the Geronimo angle.

But the trip gave him further opportunity to hone his cowboy philosophy. He noted that "the cow-boys of whome I meet many are quiet, determined and very courteous."[40] Following their example, he acquired an elegant sombrero and a pair of Colt revolvers. And he was eager to assign some kind of grand significance to the interplay between eastern civilization and western violence. While in Tucson, Remington paid the Indian warden of a local church to show him around the chapel. The next morning, he was shocked to learn that the warden had gotten drunk that night and murdered another man's wife. Remington realized that "the dollar I gave him yesterday to show me through the church was the bottom of whiskey and murder."[41]

Remington thought the episode was significant. It did seem similar to the situation with Geronimo, in that both involved white easterners trying to exert their influence on the indigenous tribesmen of the west. Even with the best of intentions, violence erupted in their wake.

But that wasn't the similarity that Remington saw. Tracing cause-and-effect in the deserts of the American southwest, where the arid wind forbade any durable footprints and history was always renewing itself, was tricky business. "I am in no wise to blame" for the bloodshed, he told himself, "as I could not controll [sic] the destiny of the dollar."[42]

It was true that he didn't directly kill the woman, of course. But the lesson he extracted was telling. Even though he admitted his dollar was at "the bottom" of the murder, Remington still saw himself as blameless. To Remington, the west seemed like a land without a past, where a man's actions never followed him into the future unless he wanted them to.

NOTES

1. Catlin, 2.
2. Remington "A Few," 16.
3. Remington "A Few," 16.
4. Remington "A Few," 16.
5. Remington "Few," 16.
6. Samuels *Frederic*, 35.
7. Rogers, 245.
8. Samuels *Frederic*, 36.
9. Samuels *Frederic*, 7–8, Crafts, 181.
10. Samuels *Frederic*, 9–14.
11. FR letter to Scott Turner [1877]. Unless otherwise noted, all letters from Remington are from Allen P. Splete and Marilyn D. Splete's *Frederic Remington: Selected Letters*.
12. FR letter to Scott Turner, 3 March 1877.
13. FR letter to Scott Turner [1877].
14. Samuels *Frederic*, 23.
15. Samuels *Frederic*, 23.
16. As Tatum argues, Remington seemed to understand that "the mind's eye strategically alters the truth(s) of the past even as it represents it" (152).
17. Qtd. in Samuels *Frederic*, 27.
18. Samuels *Frederic*, 28.
19. Qtd. in Samuels *Frederic*, 33.
20. Gressley, 125–127.
21. Remington "Chasing," 55.
22. Vorpahl *Frederic*, 28.
23. Samuels *Frederic*, 38.

24. Samuels *Frederic*, 42.
25. Thomas "Recollections," 354.
26. Qtd. in Editorial Staff n.p.
27. Samuels *Frederic*, 54–55.
28. Thomas "Recollections," 354.
29. Thomas "Recollections," 354.
30. Harper, 604.
31. Harper, 604.
32. Harper, 604.
33. Samuels *Frederic*, 62.
34. Geronimo, 214.
35. Qtd. in Bourke, 467–468.
36. Qtd. in Bourke, 468.
37. Qtd. in Samuels *Frederic*, 69.
38. Qtd. in Samuels *Frederic*, 76.
39. Qtd. in Samuels *Frederic*, 69.
40. Qtd. in Samuels *Frederic*, 69.
41. Qtd. in Samuels *Frederic*, 72.
42. Qtd. in Samuels *Frederic*, 72.

Chapter 4

A Self-Made Man

When he wasn't riding or hunting, Roosevelt spent much of his time in the Badlands mentally tinkering with a set of ideas about American freedom and the way it shaped what he called, in *The Winning of the West*, the "American character."[1] Of all the men Roosevelt met in the Badlands, none shared his elite upbringing or East Coast background. Many were not even born in America.

But one of the things that Roosevelt began to believe about the west was that it was a terrific homogenizing force. It took men of different backgrounds, often from different nations or races, and made them into westerners. Shortly after founding Elkhorn Ranch, he observed that the many foreign-born cowboys, men who started off as "wild spirits from every land," quickly became "undistinguishable from their American companions."[2] Simply living in the west made onetime strangers into a cohesive band of Americans.

In Roosevelt's view, the west was a beneficent agent of assimilation. It tamed "wild spirits" from foreign lands, making them Americans in temperament if not in citizenship. This type of assimilation required a unified and cohesive national identity, something for people to assimilate *to*. The west boiled America down to a single homogenous draft. It distilled a national character.

This belief in a single American character made some of Roosevelt's ideas about the west seem incongruous. For example, two words he repeatedly used to refer the west were "vigor" and "freedom." In 1885, he said he loved the "freedom" of ranch life, the "vigorous, open-air existence it forces a man to lead."[3] Three years later, he repeated the sentiment, praising the "abounding vigor" and the "bold restless freedom" of ranching on the plains.[4]

He seemed to conclude that the west's assimilating power was a consequence of the vigorous existence it demanded. Because the west lacked many of the comforts of the east, survival required unusual vigor. Many could not stand it. For those who could, such collective exertion carved away unnecessary flab. What remained was a hard, lean citizenry.

But the notion that vigor led to assimilation was at odds with his other significant belief, that the west was a land of unusual freedom. A territory full of absolutely free individuals isn't likely to also be a territory in which there is a high degree of similarity across individuals. To put it another way, the sort of civil order that produces national homogeneity is hardly the sort of thing that is easily created by an excess of individual freedom.

Yet this paradox was explained by another theory he was testing. Another way of thinking about the homogeneity produced by the west was through the lens of Darwin's development hypothesis. Homogeneity, seen one way, is a product of evolution. The only reason "squirrel" denotes a recognizable category of rodent is because millennia of natural selection gradually created the family *Sciuridae*. Similarly, Roosevelt thought, the west selected the American character by demonstrating to people their place in the so-called natural order. Individual freedom was merely a component of this process.

In the west, Roosevelt thought, everyone was not equally free all the time. Shaped on the one hand by his understanding of naturalists like Darwin and, on the other, by his reading of early western novelists like James Fenimore Cooper and Mayne Reid, Roosevelt began to develop a set of beliefs about individual freedom and civil society, and to test those theories against the events and experiences he observed in the west.

He was coming to see the west as a Darwinian proving ground. Men mustered as many liberties as they were able in an attempt to establish their place in the social order. Ranching, he wrote in one revealing moment, "is very exciting, and is done in company, under the stress of an intense rivalry between all the men," making it so "the unfit are weeded out by a very rapid process of natural selection."[5]

This was a crucial breakthrough in his thinking. In Roosevelt's west, *free* was just another word for *more fit*.

Roosevelt had been a sickly child, thin and asthmatic. Family members described him as having a "gallant spirit" housed in a "puny and fragile body."[6] His illness was an inheritance, something he was born with. His siblings were not much healthier. Anna had a spinal defect, Elliott got a number of upper respiratory infections, and Corinne eventually acquired asthma as well.[7] From an early age, he had a clear sense that he was not, in a Darwinian sense, fit.

Roosevelt grew up in a world in which Darwin's theories had essentially always existed. Darwin had published *On the Origin of Species* when Roosevelt was just eleven months old. As Roosevelt became a boy and later a young man, Darwin's development hypothesis was always there, an omnipresent part of post-Civil War intellectual life.

Over a half-century before Roosevelt was born, Erasmus Darwin—Charles's grandfather—had published his massive two-volume study titled *Zoonomia*. It made the case that volition—an organism's individual will—produces permanent biological changes. It was a principle that Erasmus was convinced could be seen in the tadpole, "which acquires legs and lungs, when he wants them." It was also a principle he thought extended to humans. He believed any changes produced by such "habits of life" could become permanent.[8] Individual will could literally remake an individual.

Erasmus Darwin's theories of such "transmutations" were refined fifteen years later by French naturalist Jean Baptiste Lamarck. Lamarck claimed that individuals could create new genetic inheritances not just for themselves but for their descendants, all through sheer force of will. One of Lamarck's favorite examples of this principle involved the giraffe. By reaching for leaves, Lamarck thought, giraffes stretched their necks and legs and then passed on those traits to their progeny.[9] In his mind, that was why giraffes were tall—because they tried to be. Lamarck thought that a combination of environment and volition produced an organism's biological inheritance. The principle of transmutation meant that individual effort determined biology.

But shortly after Roosevelt's birth, *On the Origin of Species* began to overturn that principle. Under Darwin's development hypothesis, acquired characteristics were not necessarily transmitted to subsequent generations, meaning that individual will might be biologically irrelevant.

So Roosevelt, after suffering another bad asthma attack when he was around eleven years old, might have been surprised when his father somberly told him that his body was not his master. Physiology, he said, was subordinate to the will.

"Theodore," his father said, "you have the mind but you have not the body, and without the help of the body the mind cannot go as far as it should. You must *make* your body. It is hard drudgery to make one's body, but I know you will do it."[10]

Your body, his father was telling him, is not your inheritance. Your body is your own, and it can be remade with tireless effort and an unshakable will. Roosevelt looked up in determination. *"I'll make my body,"* he announced.[11]

The previous year, Charles Darwin had borrowed the phrase "survival of the fittest" from Herbert Spencer and incorporated it for the first time into the fifth edition of *On the Origin of Species*. Darwin, as Roosevelt would later say, "succeeded in effecting a complete revolution in the thought of the age, a revolution as great as that caused by the discovery of the truth about the solar system."[12] Throughout his boyhood, Darwin's ideas had been a key part of Roosevelt's education. Roosevelt's pledge to make his body was a promise to become fitter in a musculoskeletal sense, but also to become fitter in a Darwinian sense.

His father's emphasis on volition was more Lamarckian than it was Darwinian. Theodore Roosevelt Sr. was advising something fairly straightforward: building muscle and cardiopulmonary health through exercise. Nonetheless, his counsel would have resonated with Roosevelt, who was already a fervent student of natural history. And it was Lamarck, rather than Darwin, who advocated the significance of such changes in physiology as a result of will or environment in determining the place of an individual in the natural order. Such fusions of Darwinism and Lamarckianism were still common and gained credence with the work of the American school of evolutionary theorists.

About four years later, Roosevelt made a funny series of drawings for his mother and sister that he called "Illustrations on the Darwinian Theory." In one of these, Roosevelt depicted himself evolving from a crane, in the other, from a giraffe. He signed the drawings "Cranibus Giraffinus."[13] Roosevelt did not literally believe he evolved from a giraffe, of course. He was just having fun, making a joke about natural selection. Yet his choice of a giraffe as his evolutionary forbear, as opposed to a bear or moose or wolf, was not arbitrary. He *was* thin and angular, rather like a giraffe. More importantly, his cartoon suggested two interrelated beliefs, even at such a young age. First, it implied a belief that physiology was determined in a Darwinian sense. Roosevelt knew he did not choose to inherit his frail body, in the same way that in the cartoon he did not choose his giraffish forebears. In the drawing as well as his studies, his body was something inherited, not something self-made.

However, this view was complicated by the second belief suggested by the drawing, which was that biology was *not* determined—that a person could, indeed, make his body. The Latin suffix *–inus*, as in Roosevelt's pseudonym "Giraffinus," usually indicates a relationship of possession or origin. The joke was that Roosevelt's life would be ultimately determined by his giraffe ancestors. For Lamarck, though, the giraffe was an example of an animal which was *not* governed by its inherited nature.[14] It needed a longer neck, so it developed one. The giraffe, in other words, is simultaneously a symbol of Darwin's inherited, immutable characteristics and of Lamarck's environmentalist, mutable physiology. For Roosevelt, it meant bodies that had been inherited, but also bodies that had been made.

That same year Roosevelt met Ralph Waldo Emerson, the bard of American self-invention, while on a family trip to Egypt. By then the sixty-nine-year-old had begun to grow frail—the smile of the "mystic, dreamy" intellectual now seemed, as Roosevelt's sister Corinne recalled, "somewhat vacant"—but he received his fellow Americans graciously.[15] Roosevelt's father clearly thought the moment would make an impression on his children, and perhaps especially on his eldest son. Roosevelt had spent the day touring the tombs of Beni Hasan, where the Egyptian elite were buried during the Bronze Age and the bones of Egypt's half-forgotten great men had long since turned to dust. Then, in the evening, he met Emerson, who wrote that "Nature suffers nothing to remain in her kingdoms which cannot help itself."[16]

After pledging to make his body, Roosevelt would spend hours exercising in a converted room that the family called the "piazza," hefting his body weight and eventually learning to box. In later years, one of his sister's most vivid memories was "seeing him between horizontal bars, widening his chest by regular, monotonous motion," a dedication "which eventuated in his being not only the apostle but the exponent of the strenuous life."[17] As he grew older, and especially after he graduated college, Roosevelt began to look for new places in which his body could be reconstructed. He sought new challenges that would allow him to leverage Lamarckian transmutation against Darwinian survival. He wanted to make his body into one of society's fittest.

He eventually found those challenges in the vast prairies of the Dakota Badlands.

Out on his ranch, Roosevelt felt like he was finally experiencing a world he had only seen in books. He had lined his shelves at Elkhorn with the sort of books "no ranchman who loves sport can afford to be without," as he put it.[18] Just as his beliefs about the power of the individual had been shaped by Emerson and Darwin, his beliefs about the west had been shaped by other writers. Even the way he dressed while on his ranch—in what he thought of as a traditional frontiersman's outfit of leather tunic and breeches—was shaped by the writers he loved as a boy.

As a child, one of his favorite storytellers had been the Irish writer Mayne Reid. Reid's novel *The Scalp-Hunters* told a story that resonated deeply with Roosevelt: a tenderfoot adventure seeker feels his body transform into something harder and stronger as he presses ever deeper into the arid core of the American southwest.

Reid had come to the United States at the age of twenty-one, joined a New York volunteer regiment, and went west in 1846. After returning home to Ireland, Reid refashioned himself as an adventure novelist, eventually publishing over forty novels and adventure stories for boys. *The Scalp-Hunters*, the 1851 novel for which he was best known in Roosevelt's time, evokes a rugged, romantic west, a land "unfurrowed by human hands."[19] It tells the story of Henry Haller, a young adventure seeker from the south who falls in with a group of Santa Fe traders. Haller promptly transforms himself into a western mountain man, getting "armed to the teeth" and donning a deerskin hunting shirt.[20] He then indulges what was already a common American fantasy: he goes west and reinvents himself. As Haller and the party go deeper into the territories, Haller feels his body transform: his "strength increased" and he experiences "a buoyancy of spirits and a vigour of body, I had never known before."[21]

The Scalp-Hunters was a powerful fantasy. It invited readers to imagine a land of startling beauty and looming danger. But for Roosevelt the fantasy was especially personal. His near-crippling asthma often required him to be taken away from the stifling humidity of New York, "away on trips to find a place where I could breathe," as he later recalled.[22] The arid west was just the type of place where he could easily imagine his lungs filling with cool, clean air. For the novel's protagonist, the west was also a place to remake himself, to feel a "vigour of body" he had never known. *The Scalp-Hunters* told a very simple and very seductive tale: that the American west was a place that took soft, eastern city boys and turned them into lean men of tempered iron.

Roosevelt was enthralled by the spirit of manly exploration that emanated from Reid's novels. Even decades later, when writing his autobiography, Roosevelt still thought fondly of Reid's books and other boys' adventure stories, and vividly recalled trying to translate Reid's romantic tales into the real world, to bring his "adventures in realistic fashion before me."[23]

About ten years after first reading Reid and promising to make his body, Roosevelt finally went west, telling his mother that he thought the trip would "build me up."[24] Simply being in the west, he was saying, would be a physical and evolutionary challenge that would enable his self-creation. In New York and Cambridge, he had to seek out physical training to supplement his regular life. But in the west, regular life *was* training.

For the rest of Roosevelt's life, the role that the American west played in the story of his self-fashioning would be the stuff of national legend. One reporter saw Roosevelt traveling west in April 1885 and thought he seemed weak and out of place. The reporter described the twenty-six-year-old Roosevelt as a "pale, slim young man with a thin piping voice and general look of dyspepsia," a "boyish looking" young man with a "slight lisp, a short red mustache and eye glasses": in brief, a "typical New York dude."[25]

But not too many years later, Roosevelt had transformed into a barrel-chested man approaching 200 pounds. In the minds of many Americans—including Roosevelt himself—it was the west that had propelled this transformation. One Kansas City writer summarized this belief by noting the exercise regimen Roosevelt had needed to attain a weight of even 135 pounds, until at last he "went West and lived in the open until he was normal for his height and had muscles which even a prize fighter could respect."[26]

Roosevelt was able to accomplish this transformation in part because when he went west, he was traveling to an idea as much as to a place. And that idea was one that had been created in large part by stories: by the romantic adventures of Mayne Reid but also, and perhaps more durably, by the exploits of Nathaniel "Natty" Bumppo, the frontiersman hero of five novels written by James Fenimore Cooper. It was the fictional Bumppo—who famously dressed in buckskin leather—that Roosevelt was most clearly emulating when he donned his fringed shirt and trousers and went riding through the Badlands.

Roosevelt was exposed to the works of Cooper at an early age. In 1871, his family had taken a vacation to the Adirondack Mountains. In the late evenings, once it got too dark to play, Roosevelt's father would gather the children around the campfire and read aloud from Cooper's novel *The Last of the Mohicans*. Roosevelt had fought sleep and tried to pay attention.[27]

He did eventually get around to reading Cooper on his own. Twice in his massive history *The Winning of the West*, Roosevelt referred to Cooper's fiction to illustrate a historical point about America.[28] Once he had finished his ranch house at Elkhorn in 1885, he loved sitting around the hearth on winter nights listening to the pine logs crackle, pleased that he had stocked the place with ample books—especially those by Cooper, an author he supposed "no man, east or west, would willingly be long without."[29]

Cooper was born in 1789 to a prominent family in upstate New York. Although he published in a wide range of genres, by the time Roosevelt was a boy, Cooper's most enduring works were a series of five novels published between 1823 and 1841 known as the "Leatherstocking Tales." All featured a canny rural hero named Natty Bumppo.

Published during a time of territorial expansion, the Leatherstocking Tales created a new hero for a young nation that had its gaze fixed steadily on the western frontier. Western expansion was hardly a peaceful process, of course. Two years after the 1826 publication of *Last of the Mohicans*, the second book in the series, Andrew Jackson was elected president. Jackson styled himself as the first democratic president: a rugged product of the frontier who was proud to be a veteran of the Indian wars. After taking office, Jackson redoubled his Indian fighter persona, strengthening and accelerating policies of what was called "Indian removal."

Removal involved the forced relocation of a number of Native American tribes. In later years, it would be most clearly exemplified by the Trail of Tears, in which a number of different tribes were violently relocated to the western territories between 1831 and 1838. For some tribes, this process involved a forced march from their historical homelands in the south to Indian Territory west of the Mississippi River. Thousands of Indians died in the process, including as much as a third of the entire Cherokee nation.[30]

For Cooper's readers, the conflicts facing Bumppo would have resonated with the actual process of western expansion in the age of Jackson. The fictional Bumppo fought to expand British settlements westward during the

French and Indian War, making it easy, if anachronistic, for readers to see him as a defender of the nation that would eventually become America. This seemingly straightforward arithmetic—for whites, western settlement meant conquering and displacing Indians—would be returned to by Mayne Reid and countless other writers over the course of the nineteenth and early twentieth centuries.

Part of what made Bumppo a compelling hero was his proud resistance to modernity. He had little patience for anything unrelated to the time-tested practicalities of woodcraft and battle. As Cooper put it in the novel, Bumppo acquired knowledge in primitive fashion, "from the lights of nature."[31] He was an appealing paradox: a harbinger of progress through retrogression.

Another reason Bumppo remained an iconic character for several generations of Americans was not just what he did, but also how he looked. In a few short years, his leather clothes became an icon of western expansion. (It was probably not coincidental that Mayne Reid, in *The Scalp-Hunters*, outfitted his protagonist almost exactly like Bumppo.[32]) For Roosevelt, as for many nineteenth-century readers who saw Bumppo as a quintessential American hero, Bumppo *was* that buckskin clothing.

Of course, Cooper had not conjured Bumppo entirely out of thin air. He based Bumppo's character and clothing in large part on Daniel Boone, the Pennsylvania frontiersman who cut a wider path through the Cumberland Gap in 1775, making it possible for loggers and settlers to move westward into Kentucky and Tennessee.[33] The fictional Bumppo, like his real-life predecessor Boone, was viewed by many as a character who had made America possible. Boone fought against Loyalist troops in the Revolutionary War and enabled western expansion into Kentucky. For many, his struggles for political independence and his struggles for western expansion became fused. His transformation from man to myth occurred in part because of a simple, irresistible belief: *To fight for western territory is to fight for American freedom.*

So Roosevelt must have thought it seemed appropriate to don the same clothes as Mayne Reid's hero Haller, who was dressed like Bumppo, who in turn was dressed like Boone. When he went to Dakota Territory after the death of his wife, Roosevelt made a conscious choice to dress in a way that fit with his mythic conception of the west. He was going to a real, physical place, but he outfitted himself like a character in a book. Donning the persona of a rough-and-tumble 1884 rancher, Roosevelt decided to dress like a 1757 fictional woodsman.

Out on the range, Roosevelt did occasionally dress like his cowboys, in a flannel shirt and tall alligator-skin boots. But he loved to dress like Bumppo and Boone, and devoted several pages of his 1885 book *Hunting Trips of a Ranchman* to extolling the virtues of the frontiersman's outfit.[34] The book's frontispiece featured an engraving of Roosevelt in just such an outfit, taken from a studio photograph by Julius Ludovici. In it, the twenty-six-year-old Roosevelt is wearing his fringed leather tunic and matching breeches. His hunting knife, which he had purchased at the jeweler Tiffany & Co. before leaving New York, is tucked into his cartridge belt, and he holds his .45-75 Winchester rifle diagonally across his body.[35] The look is completed by his dark fur hunting hat and neckerchief, and his serious, if slightly uneven, gaze. (Perhaps feeling they would spoil the effect, Roosevelt had elected not to wear his eyeglasses when posing for the photograph.)

Roosevelt tried to defend the outfit on the grounds of practicality, claiming it was suited to occasions "where there will be much rough work."[36] At the same time, the outfit was hardly embraced by other ranch workers. The other cowboys—men who were presumably doing some rough work of their own—didn't wear anything like it.

In other words, Roosevelt was dressing in costume and he knew it. In the mid-1880s, he was obsessed with western clothes and what they meant, noting the precise details of shirts, boots, and hats in his diary and exploring the clothes of cowboys and trappers in detail in several of his published works.[37] All the same, he was not a poseur. He was an enthusiastic hunter and horseman, with a high tolerance for the many discomforts of western rural life. And he wasn't entirely dissembling when he emphasized his outfit's suitability for hunting.

But if the fringed buckskin wasn't useless, its symbolic value far exceeded its practicality. Despite his claims to simple, unadorned utility, Roosevelt simply loved dressing like his boyhood heroes, Haller and Bumppo and Boone and all the rest. In more ways than one, he wanted to walk in their moccasins.

A few years later, in *Ranch Life and the Hunting Trail*, he tried to claim that the fringed outfit was more common than it actually was—that it was, in fact, a sort of national costume that had gone unchanged for centuries. "It was the dress in which Daniel Boone was clad when he first passed through the trackless forests of the Alleghanies [*sic*] and penetrated into the heart of Kentucky," he wrote. It was also "the dress worn by grim old Davy Crockett when he fell at the Alamo" in 1836.[38]

Affecting a grand, mythic tone, Roosevelt deliberately blurred time and space to explain the significance of the outfit. The clothing was also worn, he continued, by the "the wild soldiery of the backwoods" when they "marched to victory over Ferguson and Pakenham, at King's Mountain and New Orleans; when they conquered the French towns of the Illinois; and when they won at the cost of Red Eagle's warriors the bloody triumph of the Horseshoe Bend."[39]

These were all completely different battles, in completely different times, fought by completely different individuals. Yet Roosevelt saw a meaningful continuity among them. In his view, they were all fought by a single, cohesive "wild soldiery of the backwoods": a militia of gritty gentlemen clad in buckskin hunting tunics. In donning that same costume, Roosevelt was participating in the same process of western expansion. He was merely the latest in a hardscrabble individualist lineage stretching back to Daniel Boone. To this way of thinking, the west explained conquest and conquest explained the west.

During his time in the Badlands, Roosevelt was constantly honing a theory of the American west, which was simultaneously a theory of American freedom and American history. It was a theory rich enough to fill several books and propel his future political career. But much of it can be condensed into a simple story about America, one Roosevelt told in multiple forms for virtually his entire life. That story went something like this:

The American west was a prize that was won through violent struggle. It was a proving ground, a battlefield of natural selection, in which only the most fit men prevailed through strenuous effort. The environment selected those men, creating a new race of Americans. And those Americans, born of the blood and sage grass of the west, were proven natural rulers of men who would rightly win other lands much as they had won the west. Superiority in the American west meant a natural superiority in the world.

Like most of his educated peers who had grown up in the age of Darwin, Roosevelt believed that environment determines populations. But unlike scientists who believed that such natural selection occurs over thousands of generations, Roosevelt seemed to think that the American west had begun to produce a new race—a buckskin-clad "backwoods stock," as he put it—relatively quickly.[40]

He speculated that such a change had begun on one of America's first frontiers, in the foothills of the Alleghany Mountains west of the British colonies in the late eighteenth century. It was there, he thought, that the "frontier folk" began to emerge.[41] These early westerners were "Americans by birth and parentage, and of mixed race; but the dominant strain in their blood was that of the Presbyterian Irish—the Scotch-Irish as they were often called."[42] This population was not racially homogenous in a strict sense—it "mingled with the descendants of many other races"—but its experiences in the west produced a "stock" of homogenous westerners. As evidence, Roosevelt counted Andrew Jackson, Samuel Houston, David Crockett, Daniel Boone, Meriwether Lewis, and William Clark, the "most prominent backwoods pioneers of the west and southwest, the men who were the leaders in exploring and settling the lands, and in fighting the Indians, British, and Mexicans."[43]

By the mid-1880s, Roosevelt seemed to believe that this "American stock" had created a new and superior race of individuals. It was a group that had bred a sort of natural aristocracy in the ever-receding borders of the American west. And he intended to be one of them.

NOTES

1. Roosevelt *Winning I*, 265.
2. Roosevelt *Hunting*, 6.
3. Roosevelt *Hunting*, 14.
4. Roosevelt *Ranch*, 24.
5. Roosevelt *Hunting*, 16–17.
6. Robinson *Brother*, 19.
7. Morris, 40.
8. Darwin *Zoonomia*, 394, 395.
9. Lamarck, 122.
10. Robinson *Brother*, 50.
11. Robinson *Brother*, 50.
12. Roosevelt "History," 11.
13. Robinson *Brother*, 83–87.
14. Hawley, 36–39.
15. Robinson *Brother*, 65.
16. Emerson "Self-Reliance," 162.
17. Robinson *Brother*, 50.
18. Roosevelt *Hunting*, 12.
19. Reid *Scalp*, 1.
20. Reid *Scalp*, 29.
21. Reid *Scalp*, 34.
22. Roosevelt *Autobiography*, 13.
23. Roosevelt *Autobiography*, 14.
24. Qtd. in Putnam, 199.
25. Qtd. in White *Eastern*, 83.
26. Cushing, 395.
27. Roosevelt *Diary*, 8 August 1871.
28. Roosevelt *Winning I*, 326; Roosevelt *Winning II* 137. For an analysis of Cooper's representation of the west and the broader scientific effort to do the same, see Gunn, 17–51.
29. Roosevelt *Hunting*, 12.
30. The historical consensus is that there were 4,000 Cherokee deaths during removal out of a population of roughly 20,000. However, Thornton argues that a mortality figure of 8,000, of a total population of 22,000, is more accurate (84, 92–93).
31. Cooper, 156.
32. Reid *Scalp*, 27.
33. Faragher *Daniel*, 20–21.
34. Roosevelt *Hunting*, 34.
35. McCullough, 478.

36. Roosevelt *Hunting*, 34.
37. Roosevelt "Personal Diary," 16 August 1884.
38. Roosevelt *Ranch*, 81.
39. Roosevelt *Ranch*, 81.
40. Roosevelt *Winning I*, 101.
41. Roosevelt *Winning Volume I*, 101.
42. Roosevelt *Winning Volume I*, 102.
43. Roosevelt *Winning I*, 103.

Chapter 5

Remington and the Art of Scientific Representation

After his trip to the southwest for *Harper's*, in the fall of 1886, Remington traveled back to New York to look up his old Yale friend Poultney Bigelow, who had risen to become the editor of *Outing* magazine. He made an appointment at the magazine's Nassau Street offices and went to show Bigelow what he'd been up to, leaving behind the cowboy getup he'd used to make an impression over at *Harper's*.

Bigelow was impressed with how far the twenty-four-year old Remington had come from the seventeen-year-old he'd first met back in New Haven. "Here was the real thing," Bigelow thought, examining Remington's sketches of cowboys and ranchers and Indians. These "were the men of the real rodeo, parched in alkali dust, blinking out from barely opened eyelids under the furious rays of an Arizona sun." He looked at Remington's signature in amazement. The sketches were almost like the work of a completely different man. Even without the costume he had donned for *Harper's*, it was clear Remington "had turned himself into a cowboy," Bigelow marveled.[1] He bought every drawing Remington was offering. Over the next year, seventy-one of Remington's illustrations would appear in the pages of *Outing* alone.[2]

As his illustrations appeared in a number of national magazines, Remington started to become an established, name-brand artist. He was also becoming wealthy. In 1887, he and Eva moved to a luxurious new home at 360 West 58th Street in Manhattan.[3]

On the advice of his editors at *Harper's*—who wanted him to be a documentarian, not merely an artist—Remington traveled with a camera, a piece of gear that was then still somewhat unusual for an artist. He developed a working method he liked. He would make a quick sketch with pencil or watercolor, note the colors to make sure his final draft was accurate, and finally take photographs.[4] Although a few illustrators criticized Remington for using photographs, Remington's work had long been shaped by the tools of scientific and technological realism.

Until the late nineteenth century, artists tended to paint galloping horses with their front legs splayed out to the front and their hind legs splayed to the back, somewhat like a rocking horse. No one knew for certain how horses looked mid-gallop; they moved too fast for the human eye to process accurately. Whether during the gallop all four legs left the ground, one leg remained touching at any given moment, or something else entirely, was all ultimately subject to guesswork.

In 1872, one wealthy horseracing enthusiast had decided he wanted a firm answer to the question. Leland Stanford was a railroad tycoon, former California governor, and a founding member of the California Republican Party who would go on to establish Stanford University. He had enough money to find out the answer. He contacted a photographer named Eadweard James Muybridge to see if he could help.

Born in England, Muybridge had come to San Francisco in 1855. After the war, he became known for his stunning landscape photographs of the American west, particularly his 1867 photos of the Yosemite Valley. Muybridge tried out a new high-speed photography method on Occident, Stanford's prize Standardbred whose very name—coming from the Latin word for the setting sun—perfectly symbolized the west. It was a blurry photograph, but Muybridge was able to capture Occident at full gallop, legs completely off the ground, frozen in midair.

Stanford wanted to continue the horse studies, but Muybridge, who had suffered a serious head injury in stagecoach accident, began to exhibit increasingly erratic behavior. He learned that he was not the biological father of his six-month-old son. He traveled north from San Francisco to Calistoga, in the Napa Valley, to find the man he suspected of paternity: a local drama critic who had exchanged letters with Muybridge's wife. When Muybridge found him, he shot him at point-blank range.

The man died and Muybridge was arrested. But Stanford was so eager to resume their photographic studies that he paid for Muybridge's defense lawyer. He argued that his client had been so dramatically changed by the stagecoach accident that it had crippled his self-control, leading to a state of temporary insanity. In February 1875, the jury acquitted Muybridge and found the murder had been a justifiable homicide.

In June 1878, the summer before Remington's first semester at Yale, Muybridge was ready to try it again. He set up a series of twenty-four cameras in sequence at the edge of Stanford's racetrack, with each camera rigged to take a shot by a thread stretched across the track. The result, a collection of six photographs he titled *The Horse in Motion*, was turned into series of silhouettes printed on a glass disc, which could be projected by a device Muybridge invented called a "Zoöpraxiscope." The rapid-fire viewing of the frame sequence produced an effect akin to motion picture, similar to a zoetrope.[5]

Humans had never seen fluid, real-time motion that had been frozen and dissected in such a way. Unlike many paintings or illustrations of a galloping horse, which often depicted the horse's legs extended outward, here the horses legs were tucked *inward*, nearly under its belly, as if it were lying down to sleep. In reviewing Muybridge's study for *Century* magazine, George E. Waring Jr. (whose son was a close friend of Owen Wister's at Harvard), admitted to having a common reaction: "the first impression of absurdity is inevitable."[6] The animal was caught in a pose no one had ever witnessed. Even though the gait was perfectly natural, on first glance it looked deeply *un*natural.

The photographs went against every conventional depiction of a galloping animal. They could "never by any ordinary process be reconciled with the conventional horse of the artist, ancient or modern," Waring thought.[7] Yes, it was a horse, and yes, it was galloping, but it didn't look like a picture anyone had ever seen before.

Waring took this one step further, wondering if artists could ever truly represent a galloping horse. It was "not so much a question whether the artist shall reproduce the positions of Muybridge's photographs," he speculated, "as whether he shall attempt to paint a galloping horse at all, since he cannot indicate the *action*, which is the essence of the gallop."[8] Waring was getting at a very basic question of art, one that had been given new urgency in the age of photography: could artists document the real world at all?

And there was another problem. Thanks to generations of painters, people knew, or at least thought they knew, how a horse galloped. But when "an attempt is made to represent them in another way," Waring suggested, "our conventional natures revolt at the innovation."[9] In other words, artists had already taught generations to see a horse's gallop in a particular way. Even if that way was incorrect, it could not easily be unlearned. As a result, "whether or not artists should abandon their old method of representing the galloping horse" had become an urgent question.[10]

It was a question that Frederic Remington thought he knew the answer to.

In the mid-1880s Remington's career was still gathering steam, but in ten short years, he would be widely acknowledged to be one of the best illustrators alive, a reputation that he enjoyed in large part because of the new way he developed of drawing horses. As one journalist proclaimed, Remington "has mastered the art of representing by a stroke the action of a fiery pony, as in the sudden leap of a *broncho* into the air," or "how a horse ought to hold his foot when standing, walking and running." The acclaim he won for his western realism—his perceived accuracy in documenting ranchers and Indians and soldiers—was to a certain degree a residue of his equine realism. "One reason why many of his Indian and soldier pictures are good," the writer concluded, "is that the horses in them are so excellent."[11] His horses offered an interpretive shortcut for discerning the realism of his cowboys and ranchers. After all, many easterners were ill-equipped to determine whether a particular cowboy seemed realistic or not, but most could judge the realism of a moving horse.

Remington acquired this reputation for documentary realism in part because he was one of the first artists to consistently incorporate the results of Muybridge's study into his work. As early as 1886, he began working depictions of the kinetically correct gallop into his work.[12] In 1887, when Remington began working on Roosevelt's *Ranch Life and the Hunting Trail*, he would still occasionally draw horses in the traditional splayed gallop.[13] But he soon embraced the new, and more scientifically accurate, way of documenting the west.

As George Waring Jr. predicted in 1882, popular artists did not merely document the world; they shaped how people saw it. He got the details wrong, though. Waring thought humans had seen horses galloping incorrectly for so long that it was too late to change their perceptions.

He was mistaken. By the end of the century, one writer could wonder at how "stiffly unnatural the rocking-horse courser of art of yesterday appears bedsides the fiery instantaneity of Mr. Frederic Remington's mustangs!" He marveled at how "grotesquely unreal, impossible, these instantaneous attitudes seemed when Mr. Muybridge first photographed them some ten or fifteen years ago!"[14] Horse paintings from a century ago now looked simply wrong. It was as if the world had changed. But of course it had not changed in the slightest. Horses galloped the same way they always had. But humans' perception of their gallop had been changed completely.

This, Remington was beginning to realize, was the power of the artist in the age of mass media. Artists, photographers, and even writers could completely change the way Americans saw animals, nature, or their country. And in doing that, they could change the country itself. Representation could actually *become* documentation. Our subjective perceptions of the world might, under certain circumstances, be inseparable from the world itself.

Intellectuals like Emerson had long wondered whether humans could have accurate knowledge of anything beyond their own perceptions. Remington's success with the new, Muybridge-influenced gallop seemed to suggest that it didn't really matter. Even if the world did exist outside of humans' perceptions, no one would—or could—know if it did without those same tools of human perception. Artists, Remington realized, had taught generations how to "see" a horse's gallop. After Muybridge, they had to teach them all over again. That horses, existing outside of human perception, galloped the same way they always had was irrelevant. Humans now *perceived* horses as galloping differently. The artists' subjective representations had functioned as a documentation of reality itself.

For all intents and purposes, Remington was realizing, it was men like him and others he had yet to meet—aspiring gentlemen adventurers like Theodore Roosevelt and Owen Wister, armed with pen and brush and camera—who could become the unacknowledged legislators of the world people thought they knew.

NOTES

1. Bigelow, 304.
2. Vorpahl *My*, 22.
3. Samuels *Frederic*, 90.
4. Samuels *Frederic*, 73–74.
5. Palmquist and Kailbourn, 412–413.
6. Waring Jr., 384.
7. Waring Jr., 385.
8. Waring Jr., 387.
9. Waring Jr., 387.
10. Waring Jr., 386.
11. Jones, 186, 189, 190.
12. For a conclusive analysis of Muybridge's influence on Remington, see Samuels *Frederic*, 83–85.
13. Samuels *Frederic*, 252–253.
14. Fletcher, 388.

Chapter 6

Wister's Legal Education

When Owen Wister returned to Massachusetts to start law school in August 1885, he was still thinking about Wyoming. It was a kind of an American Eden, representing at once America's future and its inevitable fall from that perfect state of possibility. There, he thought, was where the country was going: out among the undulating prairies and the stoic men on tired horses and the still-unfenced land. Wister wanted to be at the knife-edge of an ever-unsheathing history. But he also seemed to realize that law—the rules of men and civil society—helped propel the blade.

Once he started attending classes at Harvard Law, Wister resumed his friendship with Oliver Wendell Holmes Jr. and regularly met Holmes and his wife for dinner at their Boston house on Saturday and Sunday evenings. In between his law classes, he and Holmes began regularly spending time together: going to concerts, to Saturday Club gatherings, or to dinners with William Dean Howells and William James.[1]

Harvard Law was then at the forefront of a revolution in legal education. Christopher Columbus Langdell had been appointed dean of the law faculty in 1870 and was transitioning the school away from a lecture method of instruction toward a brand-new "case method" of teaching law.[2] Rather than having a professor explain a legal principle that emerged as a result of particular decisions, which was the way it used to work, the new case method had students directly read the relevant cases and then figure out the relevant legal principle and how it was applied. This meant that when Owen Wister arrived at Harvard Law in 1885, his education was dramatically different than it would have been had he attended fifteen or twenty years earlier, when Holmes had attended. The new case method also would have suggested to Wister that legal principles didn't exist apart from the decisions that composed them, and that those decisions existed in narrative form. Wister's legal education, to put it more strongly, would have been built around the idea that legal principles comprise certain types of stories, and that law, by that same logic, is a type of narrative.[3]

But the time he spent with chatting with Holmes may have provided Wister with a better education than the time he actually spent in the law classroom. Wister was not particularly interested in law school, but he was interested in law. He began thinking seriously about the nature and authority of law and was particularly struck by what he saw as Holmes's neutral observation of the law.

Law, Wister believed, existed outside of human preferences and politics. Holmes's "mission is the Law and to declare what it is; never to assert or to further any humanitarian or political bent," he later mused. "The law is a rule for him to observe, not a tool to carry out his preferences."[4] Wister was becoming something of a legal foundationalist: that is, he was coming to hold the belief that the law was a neutral "rule to observe," one that seemingly existed outside of human wishes and preferences. He arrived at this belief in part through his conversations with Holmes, but also through his reading of Holmes's groundbreaking 1881 book *The Common Law*.

Holmes had been appointed to the Supreme Judicial Court of Massachusetts in 1883, two years before Wister started law school. Before that, he had been a professor at Harvard Law in the early 1870s as well as in the 1882–1883 academic years. In 1876, he had begun working on the series of essays and lectures that would ultimately become *The Common Law*.

Common law is distinct from civil law, which has been passed by legislatures and literally written into existence. In contrast, common law is shaped solely by precedent. It is frequently referred to as "judge-made law," in the sense that a legislative or governing body has not articulated a particular code. Common law emerges accretively, through a slow series of judgments that build on one another. Over many years, judges come to a slow consensus—each reading and respecting the decisions of a prior case—and thus a "common law" allowing or forbidding a particular thing emerges.

For Holmes, precedent did not create the law; it merely indicated it. It indicated an invisible, unarticulated, and unlegislated law, but a law nonetheless. As Holmes wrote, through "a series of successive approximations—by a continual reconciliation of cases," such laws would steadily become more visible and articulated.[5] His theory of common law held that basic, foundational laws existed outside of conscious human preferences, and that those laws were steadily brought into focus by the additive nature of common law decisions.

What was useful about the common law, Holmes explained, was that "it decides the case first and determines the principle afterwards." Lawyers and judges, "like other men, frequently see well enough how they ought to decide on a given state of facts without being very clear as to the *ratio decidendi* [the rationale]," and it is only later that it is possible to "state the principle which has until then been obscurely felt."[6] The legal principle, in other words, had been there all along—humans simply hadn't discovered it yet.

One stylistic trick Holmes developed was to speak the law as if it were alive. "The life of the law has not been logic: it has been experience," he wrote. Law even had a body: evolving independent of human reason, it "embodies the story of a nation's development."[7] Law, for Holmes, had a "life," one that was not shaped deliberately by human reason, but rather inadvertently, by human instincts. The conclusion seemed inevitable: if law was alive, then it was subject to the laws of evolution.

Holmes, like most intellectuals of his day, was greatly influenced by the work of Darwin. He held the common belief that all living things were on a linear evolutionary track from simplicity to complexity, and were constantly battling for resources.[8] But Holmes was one of the first to advance the idea that law was the product of its own kind of evolution. He did not think that law depended on the human past; he suggested instead that law somehow had its own past. For Holmes, law was a thing in itself. It existed in a symbiotic relationship with human civilization, yet possessed its own unique life and evolutionary trajectory, one that judicial decisions were constantly uncovering.[9]

Holmes thought this was related to a natural conservatism inherent to both humans and the law. In the margins of his own copy of *The Common Law*, next to the published line "the degree to which [law] is able to work out desired results depend[s] very much upon its past," he wrote, "Imagination of men limited—can only think in terms of the language they have been taught. Conservative instinct."[10] Humans had certain conservative instincts, he thought, but the common law did, too. It only changed slowly, and was relentlessly backward-looking.

There were many ways in which the law marched in retrograde. "Every important principle," he wrote, was at bottom the "result of instinctive preferences and inarticulate convictions." Through adjudication, "ancient rules maintain themselves," and "new reasons more fitted to the time have been found for them."[11] Legal concerns were resolved by those "instinctive preferences," which in turn revealed contemporary applications of the "ancient rules" of law. All this, to put it simply, amounted to a stirring defense of a conservative legal philosophy: the solution to the dilemmas of the present lay in uncovering the rules of the past.

In trying to formulate his theory of the common law, Holmes eventually hit upon the idea that all law is based on a single principle of liability. All "tests of liability are external," as he put it, meaning that an individual was liable for harms if an "ideal average prudent man" would be liable in an equivalent situation.[12] The standard for legal liability lay in an imagined person, a sort of fiction that Holmes acknowledged was an ideal being: an "average man, the man of ordinary intelligence and reasonable prudence. Liability is said to arise out of such conduct as would be blameworthy in him."[13]

In sum, Holmes was trying to discover the ways in which law existed separately from actual humans. Law had its own life, its own evolutionary trajectory, and, in adjudicating, humans should test the law against a fictional human of reasonable prudence. Like his young friend Wister, who was just beginning to wonder if he might be a writer, Holmes depended on his imagination to illuminate the dark spots on his cognitive map of the world. He imagined the law as a sort of slow-moving creature, half-buried in historical muck, that humans were steadily uncovering and learning more about. Central to his theory of jurisprudence was someone who did not exist at all: a fictional person who was at once perfectly average and flawlessly ideal. In his mind, flesh-and-blood defendants were in some sense competing with this fleshless "average man."

The principle of competition united much of Holmes's ideas about metaphysics and the law. Later in life, Holmes admitted that he came "devilish near to believing that might makes right."[14] This belief in the moral value of competition was a direct consequence of his understanding of Darwin. According to Darwin's theory of evolutionary competition, the victor of a particular conflict illuminates the principle underlying the conflict. Holmes seemed to believe that certain unchanging principles exist outside of the rules and whims of men and that social conflicts revealed those principles.

The Common Law was a significant work of legal scholarship, one that arguably eventually propelled Holmes to the bench of the Supreme Court. But part of what endeared him to Wister was that it was also an essentially conservative explanation of the law. Holmes believed that judges were beholden less to the conflicts of their age and more to an unchanging common law. In his view, law sought to uncover foundational, timeless principles by adhering to the past. For Holmes, this required imagining a normative "ideal being" and then certifying the results of a natural process of competition.

It was his work on the common law that had helped elevate Holmes from the faculty of Harvard Law to the Massachusetts Supreme Judicial Court in 1883. And once Wister returned from Wyoming to begin law school in 1885 and began dining regularly with Holmes, it was this same theory of law that the two men would have discussed at length: on their long walks, over dinner, over drinks.

In later years, Wister conflated Holmes's aristocratic demeanor with his conservative legal ideas. Once, Wister and Holmes were walking past the Parker House hotel on School Street in Boston. It was a fine, genteel establishment for the city's intellectual class, where the Saturday Club—a literary society that once counted Louis Agassiz, Ralph Waldo Emerson, Asa Gray, and Henry Wadsworth Longfellow as members—regularly met. Wister suggested they go and have a drink together.

Holmes paused, as if uncomfortable, even though the Parker House was hardly a ramshackle tavern. As Wister recalled it, Holmes insisted they to go his house instead. "I don't somehow cotton to the notion of our Judges hobnobbing in hotel bars and saloons," Holmes said. "The Bench should stand aloof from indiscriminate familiarities." Wister interpreted this episode as agreeable evidence that Holmes was an "aristocrat in morals as in mind," observing no real difference between Holmes's legal philosophy as a judge and his general bearing as an aristocrat.[15]

Many years later, when Holmes was on the Supreme Court of the United States, Wister drew a distinction between Holmes and fellow justice Louis Brandeis that similarly suggested he conflated Holmes's ideas about law with Holmes's status as a member of an Anglo-American aristocracy. "I doubt if any gulf exists more impassable than the one which divides the processes of a Holmes from those of a Brandeis," Wister wrote of the equally formidable Brandeis, who was Jewish. "Holmes descends from the English Common Law, evolved by the genius of a people who have built themselves the greatest nation in a thousand years; Brandeis, from a noble and ancient race which has radiated sublimity in several forms across the centuries, but has failed in all centuries to make a stable nation of itself."[16] For Wister, legal principles were akin to a racial inheritance: something to be transmitted through particular individuals. This was similar to Holmes's own view that the common law was a living entity discoverable only by select cases and individuals over time.

But Wister was jarringly literal about this. For Wister, legal principles were actually carried in the blood of particular individuals. It wasn't just that Holmes was educated in the tradition of English Common Law; for Wister, Holmes genetically "descends from the English Common Law." This is in part why Wister repeatedly lionized Holmes as an "aristocrat." For Wister, Holmes's legal authority was just as biologically determined as Brandeis's Jewishness. "*Liberty defined and assured by Law*," Wister wrote, "is a principle as alien to the psychology of that race [Jews] as it is native with Holmes and his ancestors."[17] A law devoted to fairness and freedom, in other words, is "native" to particular ethnic groups. The racist implication was unavoidable: society should follow the legal and governmental direction of certain groups, and not others, if it wished to be free.

Perhaps without realizing it, Wister was revealing something not just about Holmes, but about himself. Both seemed to believe that law was located in the past (in precedent, for Holmes; in ancestry, for Wister), and that a just and good civil society would ensue if members of a select group of society's "fittest" (judges, for Holmes; whites, for Wister) molded society in accordance with that past.

In other words, they shared what might reasonably be called a conservative worldview. Wister would not have called it a conservative worldview, of course. He thought it was just the way things were. In his view, Holmes's principles were barely even principles; they were instead an apolitical mechanism for allowing competing interests to battle. Survival would anoint the winner. Holmes's "mission is the Law and to declare what it is; never to assert or to further any humanitarian or political bent," Wister explained. "The law is a rule for him to observe, not a tool to carry out his preferences; and those who try to label him *radical* miss him as wholly as if they tried to label him *conservative*."[18] For Wister and Holmes alike, the Darwinian principle of competition was neither liberal nor conservative; it was simply the order of the universe.

But applying Darwinian principles to social principles—as in Holmes's self-professed belief that "might makes right"—was hardly a neutral act. It was instead thoroughly conservative, in the sense that it would often certify preexisting inequities as merely "natural." It made social power part of the natural order of the universe.

And of course, there is nothing more political than the pretense of not being political. One thing Holmes taught Wister was that humans needed not just to observe the laws of nature, but to help them along if necessary. The desire to bring society in harmony with Darwinian law was part and parcel of his conservatism. This was an aristocratic view of law and nature alike, one that later led Holmes's biographer to note that Holmes at times "seemed to espouse a kind of fascist ideology."[19]

Holmes's approval of eugenics, for example, which Wister seems to have shared, offers an illustration of the way in which they saw *natural* as synonymous with *apolitical*. Eugenics was a belief system that often united otherwise-incompatible political worldviews. It was embraced by some progressives who wanted to marshal science in the service of an ever-more-perfect society, but also by certain conservatives like Holmes, who believed that society flouted the laws of nature at its peril. When Holmes later sat on the Supreme Court, the court would uphold a Virginia law instituting forced sterilization of the mentally unfit. Holmes's majority decision wasn't rooted in abstract notions of the public good or civic duty but in the brutal laws of nature. "It is better," he wrote, if "society can prevent those who are manifestly unfit from continuing their kind." His conclusion was ruthless: "Three generations of imbeciles are enough."[20]

The law, he was saying, was not really a human thing at all. It was instead subject to the principles of natural selection. Because, in his mind, the unfit—"imbeciles," in this case—had already lost the grand battle for survival, society would be justified in enacting the inevitable natural consequences by sterilizing them. For him, the logic was simple, bracing in its clarity: Human society reflects a nonhuman natural order, and the success or failure of society depends on the degree to which it accedes to the laws of that order.

Holmes's view of eugenics was, in this sense, closely related to his view of the law. For Holmes, the common law was different from the human-created rules governing civil society. Through successive decisions, certain members of the elite would uncover more of that external law. Eugenics, too, involved a law external to humans—natural selection—that nonetheless governed society which certain members of the elite could enforce. Both common law and eugenics presume a hierarchical society in which certain members of the elite interpret and apply principles derived from an external, transcendental order. This view was apparently shared by Wister, who admired Holmes as an "aristocrat in thought and conduct" and thought the eugenics decision was one of several especially good "illustrations of Holmes's mind."[21]

Wister, in short, came to share Holmes's conservative intellectual framework, particularly as it applied to law and social order. Wister looked up to Holmes his entire life, and was mentored by the older Holmes at a formative time. In the mid-1880s, Wister was establishing his adult identity, studying the law, and making regular trips to the American west to muse on "the virtues and the vices of [that] extraordinary phase of American social progress."[22] It was around this time, too, that he began working on the series of western stories and sketches that would eventually coalesce into his life's greatest work.

After his second or third journey to the west, Wister began urging Holmes to make a trip to the western states and territories. In 1888, Wister happily reported to his mother that Holmes had decided to take "a great big jaunt all over the West in a director's car," even if it meant they would miss their regular weekend dinners for a time.[23]

Wister, too, was soon off on another journey to the Wyoming ranchlands. He would soon begin applying his legal thinking to his beliefs about the west. If it was true that the west represented the next phase of "American social progress," then it was particularly important that America understand the west correctly.

NOTES

1. Wister *Roosevelt*, 130; Payne, 94–95.
2. Stevens, 35–72.
3. For more on Langdell's influence, see Coquillette and Kimball, 304–343.
4. Wister *Roosevelt*, 135.

5. Holmes Jr. "Codes," 213. See also Stoner Jr., 1–9.
6. Holmes Jr. "Codes," 212–213.
7. Holmes Jr. *Common*, 115.
8. Novick *Collected*, 9, 29–30.
9. Novick *Collected*, 45–46.
10. White *Common*, 4.
11. Holmes Jr. *Common*, 133.
12. Holmes Jr. *Common*, 140, 171.
13. Holmes Jr. *Common*, 141.
14. Qtd. in Alschuler, 10.
15. Wister *Roosevelt*, 130.
16. Wister *Roosevelt*, 134–135.
17. Wister *Roosevelt*, 135, italics in original.
18. Wister *Roosevelt*, 135, italics in original.
19. Novick *Honorable*, xvii.
20. Holmes Jr. "Buck," 104.
21. Wister *Roosevelt*, 145, 142.
22. OW journal, 20 June 1891.
23. Qtd. in Payne, 104.

Chapter 7

"Buffalo Bill" Cody and the Selling of the West

A few years earlier—two weeks before Henry Honychurch Gorringe first encouraged Roosevelt to travel to Dakota Territory—a small show called "The Wild West, Rocky Mountain, and Prairie Exhibition" had opened at the Omaha fairgrounds in Nebraska Territory. Wild West shows had been around at least since George Catlin had first exhibited his paintings of Plains Indians in the 1830s, launching a traveling western show which later enchanted a young Frederic Remington.

But this particular Wild West show caught the imagination of Americans like none before. One enthusiastic audience member reported that the show's charismatic ringmaster had "out-Barnumed" circus magnate P. T. Barnum.[1] That ringmaster was a thirty-seven-year old westerner named William Frederick Cody. But he liked everyone to call him "Buffalo Bill."

That first show contained a number of elements that were popular enough to ensure a place in Cody's future shows for decades to come. There was a sharpshooting act, Indian bareback riding and other ersatz-anthropological displays of Indian life, and a cowboy musical act. There was a dramatic reenactment of an Indian attack on the Deadwood mail coach, a Pony Express presentation, and an act featuring bull-riding and roping that anticipated the emergence of the modern rodeo.[2]

But in large part, the legitimacy of the show depended on Cody's real-life experiences as a scout. The program featured an exciting story of Cody's killing of a Cheyenne warrior, accompanied by a full-page drawing of Cody scalping him.[3]

The show was not an immediate success, and Cody groused that he had not made that much money. The next season he partnered with a man much like himself: a charismatic westerner who had parlayed his military experience into a series of successful turns on the stage. Nathan Salsbury had turned to acting after a stint in the Union army. It was Salsbury who would guide Cody to places of which he could scarcely dream. From their first partnership in the fall of 1883 until Salsbury's death in 1902, Cody's professional fate would be intertwined with Salsbury's, the manager and principal owner of Buffalo Bill's Wild West show.

It certainly was not a foregone conclusion that the show would be a success. One early show program included a solemn article that called for a dramatic reconsideration of the cowboy.[4] In just a few short years, there would be a near-complete turnaround in the public estimation of the cowboy. Men like Cody, Remington, Roosevelt, Wister, and others would succeed in completely changing the public perception of the cowboy, even though none of them, including Cody, ever actually worked as a cowboy.[5] By the turn of the twentieth century, they had recast the cowboy into a romantic, self-reliant natural aristocrat.[6] But when Cody and Salsbury were getting ready for the show's second season, that conception of the cowboy simply didn't exist.

On the contrary, cowboys were widely seen as filthy, uneducated, itinerant laborers. Hardly modern knights; for many, they were a subclass of criminals. Two years before Cody launched his show, President Chester A. Arthur had used part of his Annual Message to Congress to denounce the "armed desperadoes known as 'Cowboys,'" identifying their "acts of lawlessness and brutality" as threats to Arizona Territory.[7]

But from its inception, the Wild West show worked to transform these stereotypes. The show's program stressed cowboys' "reputable trade," emphasizing their economic and agricultural function. And Cody went even further. The cowboy was not just useful, the show insisted. He had been "falsely imagined" and "little understood." Indeed, the cowboy was actually something of a natural aristocrat, possessing many of the "qualities that form the romantic hero of the poet, novelist and historian."[8]

Developing a line of thought that Owen Wister would pick up in subsequent years, the program suggested that far from being a lower-class reprobate, the cowboy was better understood as a member of the Anglo-American upper classes. "Composed of many 'to the manner born,'" it gently argued, using Shakespeare's famous description of the aristocracy, cowboys were "recruited largely from Eastern young men." The cowboy was a future titan of military and business, one who "often develops into the most celebrated ranchman, guide, cattle king, Indian fighter and dashing ranger."[9] Just two short years after the president had identified cowboys as a chief threat to national security, Cody and his Wild West show were asking America to think of cowboys not as criminals at all, but instead as a kind of perfect paradox: simultaneously romantic vestiges of American individualism and peers in America's natural aristocracy.

Cody's family had immigrated to Kansas Territory in 1854, when he was eight years old. In Iowa, his father Isaac had long nurtured western dreams, and missed a chance to go to California with the Gold Rush. When one of his children had a fatal horse accident the year before, the devastating loss provided just the impetus he needed to finally go west.[10]

Earlier that year, President Franklin Pierce had signed the Kansas-Nebraska Act, first proposed by Illinois senator Stephen A. Douglas, in an effort to balance the slave and free states in the western states and territories. This was yet another expression of the ongoing hope that a racist and an antiracist America could peacefully coexist. Decades earlier, the Missouri Compromise of 1820 had prohibited slavery in the northern parts of the former Louisiana Territory. After the Treaty of Guadalupe Hidalgo ended the Mexican-American War in 1848 and dramatically expanded the western territories of the United States, an 1850 set of laws tried again to define what it meant to be free in the American west.

Among other things, the bills admitted California as a free state, passed a new Fugitive Slave Act, and organized the territory of New Mexico under the principle of what was called "popular sovereignty." The principle at the core of the Kansas-Nebraska Act, popular sovereignty was promoted by northern Democrats like Douglas as a democratic compromise over the question of western slavery, in that it would defer the issue to the individual voting settlers of a territory, who would simply vote on whether or not to allow it. The perverse genius of popular sovereignty was that it said that individual freedom didn't come from God or nature, but from other individuals with the right to vote. Popular sovereignty subjected individual liberty to the democratic whims of whites.

Like many adherents to the loose philosophy of Manifest Destiny, Douglas had believed that America's "promised land is westward."[11] Voicing what most people had long concluded—that the future of the union lay in how the issue of freedom in the American west got resolved—Douglas argued that there was a "power in this nation greater than either the North or the South," namely "the great West," where could be found "the hope of this nation—the resting place of the power that is not only to control, but to save, the Union."[12] For Douglas, popular sovereignty was a good middle ground between abolition and slavery.

It also allowed him to avoid taking a clear stand one way or the other. Douglas established a hierarchy of two competing approaches to liberty. He took one type of freedom—individual liberty—and subordinated it to another: democratic rule. "We ought to be content with whatever way they [the people] decide the question" of slavery, Douglas wrote.[13] But because there were few limitations on who "they" were, the creation of Kansas Territory instantly caused a rush of pro- and anti-slavery settlers ready to battle for their cause. All knew that this would be a sort of tournament of democracy. Each faction was competing for a type of liberty that was incompatible with the type of liberty valued by their opponents.

The inrush of pro-slavery settlers from Missouri and "free staters" from Illinois and elsewhere created a powder keg that erupted into what became known as "Bleeding Kansas." New York clergyman Henry Ward Beecher took up donations to buy rifles for the free staters fighting the pro-slavery "border ruffians," as New York *Tribune* publisher Horace Greeley called them. In 1856, the radical abolitionist John Brown, who had come to Kansas the previous year, led a party of free staters to a settlement on Pottawatomie Creek, where they executed five border ruffians with broadswords.

But Isaac and eight-year-old William were there at the beginning. For the rest of his life, Cody would be able to clearly recall arriving in Kansas and thrilling to the sights: the sea of white-covered wagons groaning over the hills on their way to Utah and California, the horsemen with huge pistols and knives tucked into their belts, the armed cavalry, the Indians.[14] It was romantic, but it was a romance that had been created by a larger political dynamic.

Of course, Isaac hadn't come to Kansas for political reasons. Like many other settlers, Isaac just wanted to get rich. Still, he recognized that his presence in Kansas could not be separated from larger political issues. Being in the west, the future Buffalo Bill learned, was not without symbolic value. It *meant* something.

Isaac was a farmer and a pioneer with an ineradicable sense of wanderlust, but his son also remembered him as something of a natural politician.[15] At one point in the arid Kansas summer of 1854, Cody watched as his father was coaxed into giving an impromptu speech at Rively's store, a popular gathering place for pro-slavery immigrants from Missouri. Because Isaac's brother Elijah hailed from Missouri, the Missourians must have concluded that Isaac was like them, a border ruffian.

Cody remembered that Isaac tried to politely demur, but the small crowd didn't let it go. After much prodding, Cody watched his father reluctantly climb up on a box that served as a small stage and began to speak. As Cody later recounted in his memoir, the audience listened intently to what Isaac had to say. "The question before us to-day is, shall the territory of Kansas be a free or a slave state," he began slowly. "I was one of the pioneers of the State of Iowa, and aided in its settlement when it was a territory, and helped to organize it as a state." He continued by adding that he "voted that it should be a *white* state," and concluded, "I believe in letting slavery remain as it now exists, and I shall always oppose its further extension."[16]

The border ruffians realized he was only trying to placate them. The pro-slavery crowd began to shout him down. "Get down from that box!" one called out. "You black abolitionist, shut up!" shouted another.[17] Cody watched in horror as one of the Missourians leaped up onto the box next to his father, pulled out a huge bowie knife, and stabbed him. The shopkeeper quickly grabbed Isaac and hurried him home. He eventually had to retreat to his brother's house in Missouri to recuperate before he felt well enough to return to Kansas.

For Cody, his father's failed performance on that makeshift western stage contained a number of lessons. One was the function of western conservatism in America's national conversation over freedom. Isaac had, after all, simply advocated "letting slavery remain as it now exists," and even voiced support for statewide segregation. But for trying to conserve the status quo—for not wanting to expand slavery, merely to maintain it—he was deemed an "abolitionist" by the hostile crowd. As Cody later interpreted the episode, Isaac's laissez-faire conservatism inadvertently turned him into something of a freedom fighter. Someone who merely wanted to continue the established order suddenly became, as Cody dramatically put it, a man who "shed the first blood in the cause of the freedom of Kansas."[18]

But if one lesson Cody learned was political, another was theatrical. After Isaac had recovered and returned from Missouri, it was made clear to him that he would be hanged if he dared to remain in the territory. As Cody told the story, a posse of horsemen had come and surrounded the Cody house one night. Thinking quickly, Isaac donned his wife Mary's bonnet and shawl and hurried out of the house to hide in the cornfield. The disguise had worked, Cody realized. The men "neither halted him nor followed him."[19] A costume saved his life.

In short, some of Cody's earliest lessons of the frontier west involved a firsthand view of the politics of settlement and popular sovereignty. From his father he realized how easily political conservatism in the west could sound like a full-throated love of universal liberty. And he saw how the west was a land where everyone was potentially an actor. It was a place where he would soon make a career by distilling these qualities into one of the most popular American entertainment spectacles of the late nineteenth century.

It wasn't long after arriving in Kansas that Cody met what he called a "genuine Western man." He was a tall, rangy fellow wearing a broad-brimmed "California hat" and a full buckskin suit, just like Natty Bumppo or Daniel Boone. Cody was taken with the westerner's buckskin suit, his beautiful bridle and lariat, his skill with horses. He wanted nothing more than to "become as skillful a horseman as he was," as he later recalled.[20] From that moment, he never got free of the magnetic pull of the west. As he got older, he came to crave the romantic sensation of feeling "as only a man can feel who is roaming over the prairies of the far West, well armed, and mounted on a fleet and gallant steed." This feeling, he thought, was a "perfect freedom."[21]

Cody grew into a charismatic westerner in a wide-brimmed hat, much like the man who had captured his imagination as a boy. By the time he turned twenty-one, he had grown to six feet in height, with a warrior's body—which he clad in buckskin, naturally—and a full mustache and goatee, topped with long, wavy hair flowing out from under his hat.[22] He had also gotten married to Louisa Frederici, and had the first of four children. Friends remembered him as "tall, stalwart and of magnificent physique," yet also a "daring rider, and a most expert rifleman."[23] In the late 1860s, he contracted with the Kansas Pacific railroad to hunt bison to feed the 1,200 laborers who were building the railroad. He only worked for Kansas Pacific for 18 months, but in that short time he reportedly killed 4,280 bison, earning him a hefty salary and the nickname "Buffalo Bill" from the roadhands.[24]

In 1869, the twenty-three-year-old Cody met a dime novelist and playwright named Edward Z. C. Judson, better known by his pen name, Ned Buntline. The tall, dashing man who people called "Buffalo Bill" caught Buntline's imagination, and by the end of the year he had published *Buffalo Bill, King of the Border Men*, the first of many books and stories about Cody. In time, the character of Buffalo Bill became a dime novel staple, a kind of mythic hero of American individualism. By some estimates, over 550 dime novels featuring Cody's exploits—most heavily embellished, if not wholly invented—were eventually published.[25]

In 1872, Buntline convinced Cody to play himself in a stage play he had written titled *The Scouts of the Plains*. When Buntline gave him a copy of the piece of dialogue he had to learn, Cody stared at his lines in horror, realizing he would have to memorize them. He thought it would take him about six months. Buntline had given him less than a day. At showtime, Cody donned his usual buckskin suit—the "costume" Buntline had instructed him to wear—and peeked out at the packed house.[26]

Once he stepped onstage, it didn't take long for Buntline and Cody both to realize that Cody was a terrible actor. When the time came for Cody's lines, he froze. But he had natural charisma and a terrific gift for showmanship. Thinking fast, Buntline improvised, inviting Cody to "tell us all about the hunt."

Cody did, and rapidly warmed to the occasion. By the end of the play, Cody recalled, "I took up fifteen minutes, without once speaking a word of my part; nor did I speak a word of it during the whole evening."[27] Buntline and Cody both seemed to realize that Cody should not be trying to act out a scripted character. Cody should simply be character he was already becoming.

For the next several years, Cody took steps to blur the lines between William F. Cody, the man, and Buffalo Bill, the character. These efforts culminated in 1876, when Cody shed real blood in his theatrical costume, dramatically taking the "first scalp for Custer."

On June 25, 1876, while leading the Seventh Cavalry Regiment in a battle against the Arapaho, Lakota, and northern Cheyenne tribes, Lieutenant Colonel George Custer, along with nearly a third of his regiment, was killed in a brief and bloody battle. Most white Americans were shocked. The Indian Wars were, after all, premised on a certain assumption of inequality. Spreading white civilization throughout the continent was seen by many whites as a sort of divine mission, made morally justifiable because whites were presumed to be simply *better* than nonwhites. Custer's death raised uncomfortable questions about how superior white American civilization really was.

The death became a national symbol of outrage. A long investigative article in a Chicago newspaper surveyed some of the shock and fury felt by the western states and territories. In Salt Lake, the reporter noted, citizens claimed they could raise a regiment of frontiersmen in ten days for a military response to Custer's death. Detroit grieved at having to "add Custer and his men to the list of martyrs" of the Indian Wars. And in Aurora, Illinois, there was the racist hope that the army would simply "annihilate the redskins."[28] Nor was the shock limited to the west. Two weeks after the battle, the *New York Times* published Brigadier General Alfred H. Terry's report of the "great disaster," along with his (incorrect) assumptions that the Indians must have lost an equivalent proportion of warriors, and that there had to have been "a number of white men fighting with the Indians."[29]

Cody knew Custer personally; they had met almost nine years earlier in Kansas. In the spring of 1867, Cody had been ordered to help Custer and ten others travel the 65-mile journey from Fort Hays to Fort Larned as quickly as possible. Cody remembered the trip as sealing the relationship between the two men and recalled Custer saying he would have liked to have Cody as a scout in his regiment. If Cody ever needed work, Custer added, he should come see him.

Of course, neither man could foresee the cruel irony by which Custer's name would inadvertently help give Cody all the work he could ever want.

By 1876, Cody and Buntline had settled into a regular theater season. Between tours, Cody would pick up more scouting or guide work. At the close of the season that year, he was eager to return to Dakota Territory to fight in the Great Sioux War, as it would come to be called, in part because the violence would provide new material for the stage shows. His role in the show was basically as a raconteur, and he always needed violent new material for his yarns.

Cody met up with the Fifth Cavalry and traveled to the Red Cloud Agency, the federal outpost charged with disbursing funds to, and encouraging the "civilizing" of, Indian tribes in the area. Cody and the Fifth had been ordered to scout the land between the Black Hills and the Red Cloud Agency. They were just returning to Fort Laramie when a messenger arrived with news of Custer's death, along with orders for the Fifth Calvary to move to the Big Horn region.[30]

As Cody later told it, the men rushed to reach War Bonnet Creek to head off the Cheyenne. On July 17, Cody spied a large party of Cheyenne coming north. A small band of them suddenly split off to the west. Through their field glasses, Cody and his commanding officer realized the splinter group was planning to intercept two mounted couriers. They devised a plan: Cody would take fifteen scouts and charge the Indian party just as they were about to attack the couriers, cutting them off from the main troop of Cheyenne.

Cody knew the battle was winnable. It was only a small group of Cheyenne, and they would be able to take them by surprise. In fact, he realized, it could be a sort of theatrical production—one he could dress for. In preparation for the ambush, Cody donned an outfit he often wore for his stage show, one a fellow cavalryman described as a "Mexican costume of black velvet, slashed with scarlet and trimmed with silver buttons and lace."[31]

They pursued the Cheyenne and saved the couriers. In the years to come, the events of the day would be exaggerated several times over, and many of the details—whether one Cheyenne warrior was killed, as the official Fifth Calvary report had it, or as many as six, as one cavalryman recorded in his diary—would be lost forever.[32] But the most basic and least-disputed version of the story was also the one that mattered most to Cody.

Clad in his show costume, Cody charged a Cheyenne warrior. They fired their guns. The other man's bullet missed; Cody's found its mark. Hurling himself on top of his adversary, Cody drew his knife and plunged it into the man's chest. Whether he realized it later or not, it provided a neat symmetry to the moment when his father had been stabbed for his status quo conservatism. But just then, he wasn't thinking of his father. He was thinking of Custer. Cody jerked the man's war-bonnet off his head. Then, with hardly a pause, he scalped him.

He thrust the man's scalp and bonnet into the air so everyone could see. "*The first scalp for Custer*," he shouted.[33]

Back at the Red Cloud Agency, Cody was told that the man he killed was named Yellow Hand. (He was actually named Yellow Hair.[34]) Cody sat down to write a short letter to his wife. It was the first time he would write the story, and he was brief, adding little embellishment: "I killed Yellow Hand a Cheyenne Chief in a single-handed fight," he wrote. Then he mentioned the scalp. "I have only one scalp I can call my own that fellow I fought single handed in sight of our command and the cheers that went up when he fell was deafening."[35]

In addition to Yellow Hair's scalp, Cody took nearly everything else from Yellow Hair's body that he could carry as souvenirs of the battle, including his war-bonnet, his guns, his ornaments, and other paraphernalia.[36] Yellow Hair's father offered Cody four mules to return his slain son's effects. Unmoved by the father's grief, Cody refused. He wanted them as props for his show.

That fall, Cody put together a stage play dramatizing the battle called *The Red Right Hand; or, Buffalo Bill's First Scalp for Custer*.[37] (It took its title from another one of Cody's dime novels, titled *Kansas King; or The Red Right Hand*, published several months before the fight with Yellow Hair.[38])

Though "Buffalo Bill" was a character shaped through a number of collaborations with other writers, actors, and show producers, Cody was himself a writer, and was likely responsible for at least the first draft of his own romantic narrative. By the time the Wild West show launched in 1883, Cody was claiming to have written thirteen novels himself.[39]

In the dime novels, the play, and later in his 1879 autobiography, Cody expanded on his fight with Yellow Hair, ratcheting up the dramatic tension. He also added some thrilling if obviously fictional scenes, such as a direct challenge shouted from a warrior. This challenge was supposedly translated by Cody from the Cheyenne, a language he did not speak. ("I know you, Pa-he-haska; if you want to fight, come ahead and fight me," Cody claimed to have understood one "war chief" to be shouting at him.[40]) But the expanded story of the battle forged Cody's national status as an American icon. Here was a dashing writer and raconteur: a charismatic man who had, somewhat incredibly, taken the "first scalp for Custer."

It was this sharp, sudden explosion of violence—more specifically, Cody's endless retellings and reenactments of that violence—that would propel him into the next, and most visible, stage of his career. He would become one of the most durable symbols of the romance and violence of the American west. In just over ten years, he would be performing before Queen Victoria. Much later, during Roosevelt's presidential administration, he would dine at the White House. By the end of his life, he would become a sufficiently durable American icon that Mark Twain could in 1906 pen a well-received novel, *A Horse's Tale*, written partially in the voice of Cody's *horse*.

Cody's fame was not just because he was a white man who had killed an Indian. Many had done that. And it was not even that he had claimed to be avenging Custer. It was the distinct manner in which he had taken Yellow Hand's life.

Scalping was a particularly vicious type of violence widely seen as reserved for Indians and whites. Some whites scalped Indians, as Cody did. And in popular newspaper accounts, scalping was often presented as a form of violence that whites suffered at the hands of Indians. This type of cruelty, which nearly always occurred in scantly populated outposts that most white Americans would never see and would likely have difficulty finding on a map, often became national news. Thanks to the transcontinental telegraph, Americans were able to learn about western violence in ways that had simply not been possible before the Civil War. Two months before Custer died at the Little Bighorn, a Connecticut journalist claimed that a family of Pennsylvania emigrants had been killed by Indians in southwest Kansas. "The family consisted of a man, wife, and two children," the article reported, "all of whom were brained with tomahawks and hatchets and then scalped."[41]

When Cody scalped Yellow Hand, it was an act of savage violence that many associated with Indians. It may have seemed that he was deliberately retrogressing, seeming to slide backward on the evolutionary track from savagery to civilization, in order to prove his dominance.

That year, America was celebrating its centennial. The death of Yellow Hair captured the imagination of a public hungry for big, mythic stories of American freedom. Cody gave them one: Custer had been avenged, and the west was once more a land for white men. *The first scalp for Custer.* This was the real accomplishment of Cody and his expanding crew of writers and actors: recognizing that a story of a western retrogression into savage violence—not just killing, but scalping—could also be a story of individual freedom in America.

Cody started putting Yellow Hair's scalp in storefronts to promote *The Red Right Hand*. The costume he had worn as a military uniform became a costume once again, so Cody could announce onstage that he was wearing the actual outfit used to avenge Custer. For his white audiences, Cody's plays were frontier melodramas acting out a simple, mythic conflict between good and evil, whites and Indians. And Yellow Hair's blood did much to smear the already blurry lines between myth and history.

Still riding the success of his battle with Yellow Hair, when Cody launched the "Wild West, Rocky Mountain, and Prairie Exhibition" at the Omaha fairgrounds on May 17, 1883, it was an instant success. Although the show was in many ways literally a circus, Cody didn't want his audiences to think of it as one. It was not some cheap spectacle, he insisted. It was an untainted slice of American history: "reality itself," as he put it. "The work done here is not the result of rehearsal; it is not acting," he proclaimed. Instead, "it is nature itself."[42] Strictly speaking, the show was never actually identified as a show at all. It was always and simply "Buffalo Bill's Wild West." The message was clear. The "Wild West" was not a show from or about the west. It simply *was* the west.

In that spirit, the show's programs included a number of quotations from westerners vouching for the show's realism and historical accuracy. One 1887 program contained an endorsement from General David J. Cook, a noted Denver lawman who proclaimed the show "the grandest realism ever presented." In his mind, the presentation was a "resurrection" of western life. Cook continued in this vein, adding that the "educational" experience would present things "just as they are," with no superadded romance or artifice, so that East Coast audiences could observe an authentic example of life in the west.[43]

Of course, it was nothing of the sort. By 1886, sharpshooters Lillian Smith and Phoebe Ann Moses—who by then had been performing under the name Annie Oakley for nearly a decade—had both joined the show. And while Smith's proficiency at hitting a plate thirty times in fifteen seconds with a Winchester .22, or Oakley's reported ability using the same gauge to hit a ten-cent piece from thirty feet away were arguably genuine, they certainly weren't authentic examples of everyday life in the west.[44] (Even in Dakota Territory, there weren't many plates or ten-cent pieces in need of killing.)

But along with many other exotic-seeming sights and stories, the show presented their acts as natural occurrences, not as what they actually were: as contrived artifice, theater. And in one sense, Cody was correct. The show wasn't just theater for its own sake. It had a political dimension.

In getting Cook to testify to the show's educational realism, Cody and Salsbury hoped that the show's perceived realism would benefit from Cook's reputation as a westerner. Unlike Cody, whose showmanship was based on scouting and whose scouting was based on showmanship, Cook was a well-known law officer. He had founded the Rocky Mountain Detective Agency in 1863 as a sort of far-west equivalent to the Chicago-based Pinkertons. He also served as sheriff of Arapahoe County and as major general of the Colorado militia.[45] Cody's show, Cook insisted, presented audiences "with the real heroes and heroines of the times that try the souls of men and that are fast passing away."[46]

Cook's endorsement summarized much of the allure of the show. As he acknowledged, part of the show's appeal had to do with nostalgia. Or, more precisely, with an odd kind of forward-looking nostalgia. The show was a "resurrection," as Cook put it, a chance to once more experience a mode of life thought to be long since lost. But if it was a resurrection, it was a temporary one, as it was also "fast passing away." In anticipating the show, audiences were also anticipating being nostalgic for having seen it while they still could. They were paying to look forward to the experience of looking backward.

As Cook suspected, many white Americans understood the show to be dramatizing history itself. For them, the show was about the inevitable eradication of primitive societies and the equally inevitable ascendance of Anglo-American civilization. As Cody's sister Helen Cody Wetmore later wrote, the show dramatized a theory of history in which "the inferior must give way to the superior civilization. The poetic, picturesque, primitive red man must inevitably succumb before the all-conquering tread of his pitiless, practical, progressive white brother."[47]

In other words, Buffalo Bill's Wild West was a unique opportunity for vicarious retrogression into the existential stakes of the country's Darwinian past. As one later program suggested, the show dramatized "the inevitable law of *the survival of the fittest*."[48] It was a chance to glimpse a different time and space—the resurrected old west—without leaving the comfort and safety of the Atlantic coast. It was, in this way, a kind of conservative experience.

But it was the show's allusion to writer Thomas Paine that made this political dimension explicit. Cook's promise that Wild West audiences would meet the "real heroes and heroines of the times that try the souls of men" would have been understood by many for its reference to an essay over a hundred years old: Thomas Paine's famous first line from *The American Crisis*, "these are the times that try men's souls."[49]

When Cook referenced Paine in order to make the case for the realism of Cody's Wild West, he was drawing parallels between the British colonies in the eighteenth century and the American west in the nineteenth. Both of those places, Cook implied, were battlegrounds of freedom. As Paine had it, the battle was a process by which "the Continent must in the end be conqueror," which meant that the land itself would dictate the nature of freedom in America.[50] It was not that settlers liberated the westward-spreading continent; it was that the continent liberated the settlers. In other words, both Paine and Cook—and, by extension, Cody—seemed to believe that freedom does not come *to* the west. Freedom comes *from* the west.

For audiences and for Cody alike, the Wild West show was no mere spectacle. It came freighted with ideas about the nation, about liberty, and even about science. Cody's west was, as the program proclaimed, about the supremacy of the "law of the survival of the fittest."[51] It also dramatized a new narrative of American freedom. If American political liberty was birthed during the times that try men's souls, those times could be recovered—"resurrected," as Cook put it—among the bison and the bowie knife and the bloody soil of the American west. In other words, the promise of Buffalo Bill's Wild West was an essentially retrogressive one: a conservative promise. A ticket bought you a glimpse not just at western scenes that were quickly receding into history, but a chance to renew the promises of an older, and more natural, frontier liberty.

NOTES

1. Qtd. in Reddin, 60.
2. Reddin, 59.
3. *Buffalo* [1884 Program], 18.
4. *Buffalo* [1884 Program], 13–15.
5. Reddin, 69.
6. Slotkin, 35–54.
7. Arthur 53–54; see also Russell, 305.
8. *Buffalo* [1884 Program], 13.
9. *Buffalo* [1884 Program], 13.
10. Cody *Life*, 18–20; Carter, 15.
11. Qtd. in Johannsen, 165.
12. Qtd. in Johannsen, 163, 280.
13. Qtd. in Johannsen, 287.
14. Cody *Life*, 28; Reddin, 54.
15. Cody *Life*, 20. Cody remembered his father serving in the state legislature, but there is no record of him having done so (Carter, 19).
16. Cody *Life*, 40–41.
17. Cody *Life*, 41.
18. Cody *Life*, 43. See also Warren, 10–12.
19. Cody *Life*, 44.
20. Cody *Life*, 34.
21. Cody *Life*, 110.
22. Reddin, 55.
23. Miles, 131.
24. Cody *Life*, 161–162.
25. Reddin, 56.
26. Cody *Life*, 324–326.
27. Cody *Life*, 327.
28. "Custer's," 4.
29. "Gen. Custer's," 1.
30. Cody *Life*, 341.
31. King, 42.
32. Russell, 229.
33. Cody *Life*, 344.
34. Russell, 234.
35. Qtd. in Russell, 230; Kasson, 36.
36. Cody *Life*, 347.
37. Kasson, 279.
38. Russell, 268.
39. Russell, 266–268; Kasson, 25.
40. Cody *Life*, 343.
41. "Indian," 3.

42. Qtd. in Reddin, 61.
43. Buffalo [1887 Program], 44.
44. Russell, 318; Buffalo [1887 Program], 47.
45. Cook *Hands*, 1–10.
46. Buffalo [1887 Program], 44.
47. Wetmore, 293.
48. "Buffalo" [1893 Program], 62.
49. Paine, 91.
50. Paine, 95.
51. "Buffalo" [1893 Program], 62, italics omitted.

Part II

THE EARLY HISTORY OF CONSERVATISM (1689–1880)

Chapter 8

The Nature of Freedom

For centuries, individual freedom has depended on our understanding of the laws of nature. In 1689, the English philosopher John Locke wondered what it would mean to have a civil society premised not on the divine right of kings but on the essential rights of individuals. For an answer, he tried to imagine what humans were like in a "state of nature."[1] He borrowed this idea partly from Thomas Hobbes, who had famously hypothesized that absent of the stabilizing force of the crown, life in the state of nature had been "solitary, poore, nasty, brutish, and short."[2]

But Locke didn't think the state of nature had meant lives of brief and relentless suffering. He thought it had been "a state of perfect freedom" in which men could "order their actions and dispose of their possessions and person, as they think fit, within the bounds of the law of nature; without asking leave, or depending upon the will of any other man."[3] In framing his hypothesis this way, Locke was referencing not just Hobbes, but a host of other thinkers stretching back to Aristotle. After all, Hobbes had also thought that the state of nature was a state of perfect freedom. But Hobbes thought it was a kind of bad freedom, tantamount to anarchy. As far as Hobbes had been concerned, the state of nature didn't mean perpetual freedom, it meant "perpetuall war."[4]

But Locke had quite a different vision of the state of nature. He didn't think it was anarchical. On the contrary, he believed "the state of nature has a law of nature to govern it," and the task of enforcing that law was "put into every man's hands."[5] Individuals had inherited the sovereignty of nature.

All this meant that when humans came together to form civil societies, the governments they formed could only be legitimate if individuals gave their consent—their power as executors of the law of nature—to that government.

This was an important realization. It meant that any civil society was predicated on a rational transfer of some of the freedoms of the state of nature from the individual to the government. Locke thought that government was necessary, but should only degrade the freedoms of the state of nature as much as was absolutely essential.

One problem Locke wrestled with was the question of private property. The Bible, he admitted, seemed to favor collective property ownership, not individual ownership. According to the Bible, economic inequality was unnatural. But Locke soon hit upon the principle of development, or what he called the rule of property. That principle said, in essence, that using human labor to develop nature transformed that nature into private property. That process then "excludes the common right of other men," because it took something that was commonly owned—nature—and made it privately owned.[6]

That was a crucial insight. Because people work differently—some are naturally faster or slower, more or less industrious—they accumulate property in varying amounts. As he explained it, "different degrees of industry were apt to give men possessions in different proportions."[7] The Bible seemed to have it backward: in the state of nature, *in*equality was natural.

Because it sanctified both individual freedom and individual property rights, Locke's view of nature was an appealing one. And one form of government that seemed to logically follow from that vision—a government made legitimate by, and tasked with ensuring, essential individual freedoms—was even more appealing, especially to a later generation of thinkers like Thomas Jefferson.

In the late 1770s, Jefferson was deeply committed to Locke's view of government, so much so that later historians would conclude that Locke's view of individual freedom essentially became America's view of freedom.[8] When the thirty-three-year-old Jefferson sat down to draft the Declaration of Independence in the summer of 1776, a number of Locke's pronouncements found their way into the document nearly word for word. Locke had written that individuals were born with all the rights of "the law of nature" including "life, liberty, and estate."[9] In Jefferson's draft of the Declaration, those ideas became the intertwined beliefs that "all men are created equal & independant [*sic*]" which granted the rights to "life, & liberty, & the pursuit of happiness."[10] These simple concepts—that governments should be premised on, and subordinate to, the inalienable natural freedoms of the individual—took root in America and, slowly, much of Europe.

In time, Locke's philosophy of government would come to be called liberalism. By 1859, the English writer John Stuart Mill could refer to the belief that "the rulers should be identified with the people" as "common among the last generation of European liberalism."[11] Yet what eventually blossomed into individual freedom had its roots in Locke's theory of the state of nature.

Of course, the state of nature was merely an idea. It offered a kind of philosophical origin story, a semi-secular Garden of Eden. But it was an idea that Locke had taken very seriously—so seriously that he didn't think the state of nature was merely an idea at all; he thought it had really existed. He thought it continued to exist, in fact, and made a point of noting that one could still find examples of it on the frontiers of America. He referred several times to the "woods of America" or the "wild woods and uncultivated waste of America" as examples of the state of nature.[12] To see America was to see civilization beginning anew. "Thus in the beginning all the world was America," he mused.[13] In his mind, America offered one last chance to grasp the original freedoms of the state of nature.

Both Locke and Jefferson believed that the American wilderness offered a tangible, real-life example of the mythical state of nature. For both, telling stories about freedom meant telling stories about American nature and the rights it granted. The American Revolution was at least in part about a government devoted to those natural rights. As the Declaration put it, the monarchy went against the "laws of nature and of Nature's God." One consequence of this focus on natural law and natural rights, though, was the suggestion that the rebellion wasn't really much of a rebellion at all, at least not in the normal sense of overturning an established historical order. Like Locke, Jefferson was careful to present freedom as something that did not originate in the normal course of history, but rather as something beyond the reach of history entirely, in the laws of nature. Freedom, American style, might be secured through politics or philosophy, but it didn't begin there. It began in nature.

But while this was a rhetorically savvy maneuver—it's rather hard to disagree with nature itself—Jefferson's emphasis on a nonhuman, nonhistorical freedom would create problems for a later generation of thinkers. In a nation birthed in Locke's shadow, anyone who wanted to be able to think about individual rights or individual freedom as political issues, not unchangeable natural phenomena, had their work cut out for them. After all, the laws of nature are static. They can be discovered, but not easily changed. If Locke's conception of freedom was governed by the laws of nature, that freedom could only be revised by discovering new laws of nature. By seeking to anchor individual political freedom to a natural realm far from flesh-and-blood individuals and nuts-and-bolts politics, Locke had painted himself into a corner. Jefferson followed him there.

Shortly after George Washington's presidential inauguration, a mob of insurgents stormed the Bastille in Paris, launching the French Revolution. A little over a month later, Gilbert du Motier, the Marquis de Lafayette, asked

Jefferson, then serving as minister to France, for his thoughts on France's own declaration.[14] Drafted by Lafayette and based on Jefferson's Declaration, the *Déclaration des Droits de l'Homme et du Citoyen* (or Declaration of the Rights of Man and of the Citizen) followed Jefferson and Locke in assuming that humans originated in a state of nature and were therefore born with certain "natural, inalienable, and sacred rights."[15] Lafayette referenced nature several more times in the *Déclaration*, writing that the aim of every government should be "the preservation of the natural and imprescriptible rights of Man."[16] Like the American Declaration, it enumerated what seemed like rational, enduring principles. Who could be against liberty and safety?

In early 1790, Edmund Burke was prompted to put down some of his thoughts on the French Revolution. The sixty-one-year-old Irish writer and parliamentarian had initially supported the French Revolution much for the same reasons he had urged peace with the American colonists in the buildup to the Revolutionary War: he admired the struggle for freedom. But Burke had begun to think the whole thing was dangerous. He wasn't opposed to liberty and property, but he was concerned about the view of nature that seemed to underlie everything about the revolution.

The revolution's emphasis on supposedly natural principles of freedom made him nervous. After all, it was easy to imagine someone who was at once perfectly free and perfectly ruinous to society. "Am I to congratulate a highwayman and murderer, who has broke prison, upon the recovery of his natural rights?" he smirked. "Is it because liberty in the abstract may be classed amongst the blessings of mankind, that I am seriously to felicitate a madman"?[17] Not only was he not sure that individual freedom was necessarily good, he wasn't sure that nature—at least as Locke, Jefferson, and others had imagined it—even existed.

Locke and other natural-rights philosophers had said that a government's legitimacy depended on the consent of its citizens, which came from the state of nature. But in Burke's view, this was exactly backward. It wasn't that individuals gave legitimacy to governments. It was that governments gave legitimacy to citizens. In England, he reasoned, freedom was an inheritance. It was an "*entailed inheritance* derived to us from our forefathers, and to be transmitted to our posterity; as an estate specially belonging to the people of this kingdom without any reference whatever to any other more general or prior right," such as those originating in the state of nature.[18] In other words, inheritance was what mattered, not nature.

An inherited monarchical government, he thought, was the real natural order. Rejecting it, as they were trying to do in France, was tantamount to an "usurpation on the prerogatives of nature."[19] Inheriting that established order, he concluded, meant following a "principle of conservation."[20] He wanted to conserve what was established, not overthrow it.

In short, Enlightenment-era debates about nature were also debates about individual freedom. In part due to his particular views on the role of nature in individual freedom, Burke's *Reflections on the Revolution in France* would in time come to be known as one of the earliest intellectual defenses of political conservatism. He departed from other Enlightenment philosophers in several ways, but the sharpest break was over the seemingly simple question of what was natural. Unlike most of his peers, Burke drew little distinction between nature, God, and government. Humans inherited all those things, all at once. In Burke's view, humans were part of a great, unbroken lineage. Civil society wasn't a human-built appendage to nature; civil society was a *part* of nature. Revolutions against governments were like revolutions against the natural order.

And operating from a "principle of conservation," as he put it, did not diminish human freedom. It made it better. For Burke, getting rid of the state of nature made humans more careful, more dignified, more connected to history. "Always acting as if in the presence of canonized forefathers, the spirit of freedom, leading in itself to misrule and excess, is tempered with an awful gravity," he wrote. "By this means our liberty becomes a noble freedom."[21]

A century earlier, Locke had located the origins of individual freedom in the pre-governmental state of nature, making governments a necessary corruption of that original freedom. Worthwhile freedom, Locke suggested, comes from knowing your origins in nature. But in locating individual freedom in an ancestral heritage of kings and noblemen, Burke was suggesting something very different. For him, worthwhile freedom came from knowing your place in that ancestry.

As the revolution dragged on, the tensions between the Girondins and the Jacobins lit the kindling that blazed into the Terror. Between 1793 and 1794, Maximilien de Robespierre and the Jacobins guillotined tens of thousands of people across France—according to current estimates, as many as 40,000—who were deemed enemies of the revolution.[22] In his early skepticism of the revolution, Burke looked increasingly prescient.

In America, Burke's thoughtful defense of monarchical stability didn't really translate. In a new country that tried to disentangle church from state and was all but founded on the civic theology of Locke, Burke's ode to the "principle of conservation" didn't make much sense. There was a relatively small number of Americans who wanted to return to the conservative stability of the monarchy.

In the early years of the French Revolution, the clergy and nobility had sat together on the right-hand side of the National Assembly. The representatives of the Third Estate, which included the peasants and the farmers, had sat on the left-hand side. It did not take long before "the right" began to be associated with the desire to preserve the established authority of the monarchy.

"The left" became associated with individual liberty, republicanism, and the revolution.[23] But the idea of a political right, in the European sense of the word, simply didn't exist in America. The whole system of an inherited aristocracy was anathema to a new nation founded on natural individual rights.

Yet natural rights didn't erase natural differences between individuals. In an 1813 letter to John Adams, Thomas Jefferson endorsed the idea that there was a "natural aristocracy among men." Some people were simply *better* than others: smarter, faster, stronger. He contrasted his idea of a natural aristocracy with an "artificial aristocracy, founded on wealth and birth," which he admitted was detrimental to good governance. But Jefferson was, at core, a different kind of democrat, and told Adams that a natural aristocracy was "the most precious gift of nature for the instruction, the trusts, and government of society."[24]

Even so, a natural aristocracy would be something new, not something old. Jefferson wasn't endorsing Burke's desire to conserve the trappings of England's inherited aristocracy; he was advocating something different altogether. Besides, America didn't exactly have an ancient political heritage to conserve. The Constitution was ratified by Rhode Island, the last state to do so, just six months before Burke's *Reflections*. The ink was barely dry.

The notion that humans had their origins in a mythical state of nature that conferred inalienable individual rights was a powerful one. It shaped America's core beliefs, what some would later call its national character. Freedom, to this way of thinking, did not exist for groups, and it did not emerge from Gods or kings. It existed for individuals, and it came from nature.

Because of this belief, Jefferson had assumed that America would be largely composed of individual, self-sufficient farmers. Farming, in Locke's view, had been the original way of creating property. Like Locke, Jefferson believed farmers were not dependent on anyone but their own industry, making them "the most independent, the most virtuous," the most "tied to their country, and wedded to its liberty."[25] (He didn't comment on the seemingly obvious irony that many wealthy farmers, including Jefferson himself, enjoyed that liberty largely because enslaved persons were doing the actual cultivation.) For Jefferson, freedom in American meant individual freedom, but it also meant having sufficient natural resources for individuals to farm. And as the eighteenth century rolled over into the nineteenth, the dream of a nation of autonomous, self-sufficient individuals spread, becoming something close to a national religion.

Of course, that individual freedom existed in tension with America's other great civic religion, democracy. Democracy assumed equality: that all men were created equal. (That such equality was actually wildly *un*equal— excluding, as it did, suffrage for nearly everyone who was not a white, property-owning male—should not go unremarked.) In contrast, Locke's natural freedom assumed inequality: through industry and opportunity some people would naturally acquire more property. But if Lockean freedom meant a certain kind of inequality, it also seemed to require sufficient natural resources to guarantee that such inequality was understood as the consequence of liberty. After Jefferson completed the Louisiana Purchase in 1803, dramatically expanding the western territories of the United States, the opportunity for certain individuals to seek out their own private state of nature, unrestrained by democratic ties to kith or community, only grew.

Two years after Jefferson's death, America elected its first western president. Then sixty-one years old, the slaveholding southerner Andrew Jackson won the presidency in 1828 in part based on his image as a rugged, frontier individualist. America's new age was clear to Alexis de Tocqueville, the French intellectual who toured America two years after Jackson took office. De Tocqueville, who found Jackson a man of "violent character and middling capacity," thought his grand tour of America would instruct other nations whose aristocratic traditions would eventually be upended by democracy.[26]

One thing that struck de Tocqueville about America in the age of Jackson was the relationship between democracy and individual freedom. The two things should be contradictory, after all. It was easy for democracy—the rule of many people generally—to be at loggerheads with individualism: the freedoms of any one person in particular. But de Tocqueville thought democracy actually fostered individualism. "Individualism," he concluded, "is of democratic origin." In aristocratic societies, he explained, "all the citizens are placed at a fixed post, some above the others."[27] In an aristocracy, he believed, humans were connected to other humans above and below them in the hierarchy, but they were not especially connected to humans in general.

In contrast, individuals in a democracy have a duty to their fellow citizens in the abstract, but not to one another in practice. He explained this disconnection by the fact that in a democracy, individuals are severed from precisely the sort of inherited responsibilities that Burke lionized. De Tocqueville concluded that in democracies, the claims of the past were unimportant. In America, history was always beginning anew.

In a conventional aristocracy, humans are bound by the legacies of their ancestors. But democracy, he concluded somewhat sadly, makes "every man forget his ancestors."[28] This detachment from history had been one of Burke's problems with the French Revolution. But it wasn't a problem unique to revolutions, de Tocqueville suggested. It was a problem endemic to democracy itself. Like Burke, de Tocqueville thought there was something melancholic and even alienating about the transition from aristocracy to democracy. Once, a person was born knowing his place. Now, he had to figure it out for himself.

De Tocqueville used the word "individualism" to refer to this new American belief that the individual, properly understood, was a free being, liberated from history and community. It was a brand new word, he admitted, "arising from a new idea. Our fathers knew only the concept of selfishness."[29] De Tocqueville's first translator wasn't sure how to render *individualisme* in English, and didn't try. "I know of no English word exactly equivalent to the expression," he wrote in a footnote.[30] Even in its genesis, individualism referred to *American* individualism.

De Tocqueville let his travels in America shape his understanding of the word. American individualism was a "sentiment," he wrote, that causes someone to isolate himself so that he "abandons society at large to itself."[31] This insight was something of a paradox. American society had been shaped by American individualism, but individualism meant, in large part, withdrawing from society.

De Tocqueville didn't think that was a good thing. His view of individualism was, like Burke's, fundamentally conservative: expressing a longing for community and certainty that simply didn't exist in the still-new nation of America.

NOTES

1. Locke *Second*, 19.
2. Hobbes, 84.
3. Locke *Second*, 18.
4. Hobbes, 151.
5. Locke *Second*, 19.
6. Locke *Second*, 29.
7. Locke *Second*, 37.
8. Hartz, 35–66; LeMenager, 1–22.
9. Locke *Second*, 53.
10. Qtd. in Helo, 112.
11. Mill, 7.
12. Locke *Second*, 23, 33.
13. Locke *Second*, 38.
14. Chinard, 135.
15. Qtd. in Kley, 1.
16. Qtd. in Kley, 1.
17. Burke, 7.
18. Burke, 29.
19. Burke, 29.
20. Burke, 42.
21. Burke, 30.
22. Hanson, 316.

23. Davies, 10.
24. Qtd. in Cappon, 388.
25. Qtd. in Randolph, 291.
26. De Tocqueville, 265.
27. De Tocqueville, 483.
28. De Tocqueville, 484.
29. De Tocqueville, 482.
30. De Tocqueville [trans. Henry Reeve], 104.
31. De Tocqueville, 482.

Chapter 9

Emerson's Great Man Theory of History

Around the time that de Tocqueville was exploring his faith in democracy, Ralph Waldo Emerson, a twenty-nine-year-old former minister, was suffering his own crisis of faith. He had been a Unitarian pastor, but his wife's 1831 death from tuberculosis left his religious belief so badly shaken that he felt obliged to resign his pastorate. He refused to continue to "worship in the dead forms of our forefathers," as he wrote in his journal.[1] He could no longer believe in something so outrageously outside himself.

Adrift, he traveled to Europe and met writers like Samuel Taylor Coleridge and Thomas Carlyle before eventually returning to America. It was then that he began the process of reinventing himself as something of a secular pastor. In March 1835, he gave a lecture on Edmund Burke in which he lauded "the superiority of his genius."[2] Six months later, he remarried. He was building a new life, a new self.

A thoughtful, reserved man with gentle eyes and a large nose, Emerson had never known a world in which individual freedom had not existed for white, property-owning men like him.[3] Jefferson had set down the principles of individualism decades before his birth. But Emerson was beginning to articulate a new, and uniquely American, view of the individual.

Emerson believed that humans acquired knowledge through the senses, but in the course of processing those sense impressions they shaped the knowledge. Our perceptions, in other words, are the only reality we know. This insight meant that "nature is not fixed but fluid," as he put it.[4] When two people perceive the same rose with a slightly different color, Emerson thought, they're actually shaping the reality of that rose, separately and with equal validity.

Even though Emerson had once called Burke one of his "wise masters," he was coming to a different conclusion about the natural world than Burke had.⁵ Nature, Emerson concluded, wasn't outside of humans, as Burke had thought. Nature was inside humans. We *were* the world we thought we were merely perceiving. This insight would have long-lasting implications for how Americans thought about the relationship between individual freedom and the state of nature. For Emerson, the world did not contain the individual. The individual contained the world.

Even though Emerson disagreed with Locke about whether the human mind was a blank slate at birth, he ended up agreeing with him about the centrality of the individual. He elaborated on this theory in an 1841 essay, "Self-Reliance," that would eventually come to serve as a kind of manifesto for the American individual.

Generations of scholars would later devote countless hours to understanding the essay's unique admixture of democratic aspiration and individualist striving.⁶ In it, Emerson sketched out what he thought was the ideal kind of individual. Such a person would be wholly independent, suspicious of governments, transformationally inventive, indifferent to the claims of history. This seemingly unusual type of individual was, in his words, simply "a man."

Such self-reliant men were detached from the claims of their ancestors, their nations, their creeds, their fellow citizens. "Every true man is a cause, a country, and an age," he wrote.⁷ To this way of thinking, self-reliant individualism was little more than a by-product of individual will.

This was a fairly short-sighted argument for him to have made, at least at a time in America when women could not vote and most Black people were not legally persons at all. Though he eventually became a committed abolitionist, at the time he was writing "Self-Reliance" he could sound complacent when it came to political freedom for people unlike himself. "[H]ow trivial seem the contests of the abolitionist," he said in an 1841 lecture. With the proper attitude—with the proper sense of divine individualism, perhaps—an enslaved person would not be a slave for long: "Give the slave the least elevation of religious sentiment, and he is no slave," he insisted.⁸ Emerson eventually abandoned such platitudinous thinking, however, and by 1850 he would be a committed abolitionist.

But he did not abandon his theory of self-reliance. Unlike a conservative like Burke, who valued a monarchy that ensured people knew their places in history, Emerson was interested in individuals who *didn't* accept their place in history. He was interested in men who were effectively indifferent to the claims of the past—men who remade history in their own image.

As far as he was concerned, a self-reliant person was like an earthquake: capable of suddenly and irrevocably redirecting the river of history. A "true man belongs to no other time or place, but is the centre of things," he explained. "Where he is, there is nature."⁹

Emerson was advocating a "great man" theory of history. To this way of thinking, history was a series of eras created by extraordinary individuals. Certain men did not merely move history forward; they reset it entirely. He had a number of examples of such self-reliant men, including Jeremy Bentham, John Calvin, and John Locke.

Emerson's individualism was curiously built. On the one hand, it was superficially democratic. Because everyone is different, everyone in principle had the capacity to be a world-transforming "true man." "That which each can do best, none but his Maker can teach him," he explained. "Where is the master who could have taught Shakspeare [sic]?"[10]

But even though such a philosophy was democratic in principle, it was aristocratic in practice. It was Jefferson's "natural aristocracy" by another name. Obviously, not everyone *would* be a Calvin, a Locke, a Shakespeare. Emerson was just pointing out that anyone *might* be.

Coupled with this implicit embrace of a natural aristocracy was a complicated attitude toward the past. Like Burke, he was suspicious of the idea of progress. "For every thing that is given, something is taken," he mused.[11]

With his natural-aristocratic embrace of great men and his ingrained suspicion of historical progress, Emerson was reinventing Burkean conservatism for the American nineteenth century. In the process, he was feeling his way toward something fairly original. He was trying to puncture the forward-looking myth of progress, the belief that newer things—newer inventions, newer belief systems, newer nations—were also better things. At the same time, he did not want to stumble backward into a romantic primitivism, yearning nostalgically for a pure and premodern world.

Emerson seemed to be wondering if were possible to harness the rugged virtues of the past in the interests of the future. The question had been nagging him for some years. He had already written that traveling into certain natural spaces was akin to traveling back in time. In the wilderness, he had written, man "casts off his years." In the woods was "perpetual youth."[12]

But in "Self-Reliance," he seemed to imply that such an odd temporal paradox—a kind of progress through retrogression—couldn't be planned in advance. It could only erupt organically. And more importantly, it could only come from individuals: from the type of world-transforming people he called "great men."

Emerson was advocating a type of individualism-as-revolution. When he said "self-reliant," he didn't mean someone who could put dinner on the table. He meant someone who moved through time and space like a comet sweeping up lesser bodies in its wake. The "reliance on governments which protect [property], is the want of self-reliance," he insisted.[13] Great men did not need governments. Governments needed great men. In a way, Emerson was looking backward in order to reinvent the present. He was forging a type of practical conservatism, one founded in a near-mystical faith in the individual.

It did not take long for Emerson to become established as the preeminent American intellectual. By the 1850s, people were already referring to "the Emersonian attitude" or "the Emersonian philosophy," confident that the phrase would be well understood.[14] There were detractors, of course, particularly in England. (One British magazine was baffled by the "Emerson mania" and sneered that the "American paradox-master" was little more than a "mighty phrasemonger."[15]) Another writer fretted about his emphasis on individual self-reliance, worrying that "the Emersonian attitude will confuse success with greatness."[16]

But for many, Emerson built a philosophical structure for talking about individualism—a word which had barely existed before de Tocqueville introduced it a few decades earlier—that was metaphysical but also perfectly logical. His essays and lectures amounted to a secular religion of American selfhood.

Despite his romantic and left-leaning embrace of individual freedom, Emerson continued to think that conservatism had not yet been investigated as well as it ought to have been. No one had really gotten it right. Those seeking to conserve the establish order had "better reason than is commonly stated," he thought. "No Burke, no [Klemens von] Metternich has yet done full justice to the side of conservatism."[17] Emerson was putting his finger on a problem that he had not yet resolved: what did it mean to be conservative in America?

Nine months after publishing "Self-Reliance," Emerson tried to clarify some of the connections between Burkean conservatism and self-reliant individualism in a lecture titled "The Conservative" that he gave at the Masonic Temple in Boston. He seemed to want to fuse European conservatism with American individualism, noting that "there is always a certain meanness in the argument of conservatism, joined with a certain superiority in its fact."[18] He thought historical change was inevitable, but because progress was a dubious proposition, such change had to be wed to a conservative disposition. For a "true man," he wrote, borrowing the phrase from "Self-Reliance," "both [reform and conservatism] must combine."[19] After all, he reasoned, progressive reformers had to be responding *to* something. "The past has baked your loaf," he declared to an audience of reformers, "and in the strength of its bread you would break up the oven. But you are betrayed by your own nature. You also are conservatives."[20]

He was saying that conservatism was an inextricable part of the historical landscape. It was impossible to *not* be conservative to some degree. "You quarrel with my conservatism," he explained, "but it is to build up one of your own."[21] His main concern was that conservatism, at least the way it had been understood up until that point, hadn't really been fused with American individualism. But again, he left his implicit question largely unanswered: What would American conservatism even mean?

Even though Emerson's essays rarely sounded like political tracts, they lent themselves easily to American politics, where it was all but impossible to talk about the individual without also talking about the government. (As late as 1901, the *Conservative Review* was lauding the "rugged practical teachings of Emerson."[22]) In 1850, a Swedish traveler named Fredrika Bremer experienced Emerson's political influence firsthand while in Boston attending a panel discussion hosted by the noted educator Bronson Alcott (who, years earlier, had taught the boy who would become Owen Wister's father).

The panel took questions from the audience. By degrees, Bremer recalled, "through the influence of Emerson," the conversation divided into two parallel streams, "which might in fact be called the two principal tendencies of the age":

> one [tendency] was Socialism, which seeks to perfect man and human nature by means of social institutions, and which seemed to have many adherents in the assembly; the second, under the guidance of Emerson, who would perfect society by means of each separate human being perfecting himself. The former begin [sic] with society, the latter with the individual.[23]

To adherents of individualism, society was like a species that developed only because of the actions of its members. Individuals, above all else, have the power to alter history and society. This was the view that had driven the left since the days of the French Revolution: the desire to augment the freedoms of the individual and decrease the power of the monarchy.

But as Bremer seemed to realize, around the middle of the nineteenth century a split was happening in America between individualists and socialists. Both of these ideas were arguably connected to what was called, in the aftermath of the French Revolution, the left. But because America had no monarchical tradition, and thus no political right, this became an increasingly significant division. The left's family tree was splitting, with liberal individualism on one branch and socialism on another. It was a crucial moment in the long process by which classical European liberalism would become American conservatism.

While Emerson was lauding the virtues of individualism, socialism, its apparent antipode, was hardly a new idea. In the late eighteenth century, Claude Henri de Rouvroy, the count of Saint-Simon—a young Parisian aristocrat who had followed the colonists' political agitations with great interest—had been inspired by the ideals professed by Jefferson and the other architects of the American Revolution. Like Lafayette, another French aristocrat-turned-revolutionary, Saint-Simon traveled to America and served in the army under George Washington.[24]

Saint-Simon returned to France even more committed to a democratic, non-hierarchical society. He eventually became one of the earliest proponents of a scientifically organized, centrally planned socialist economy. In their 1848 *Communist Manifesto*, Karl Marx and Friedrich Engels referred to Saint-Simon as one of the "founders" of the "Socialist and Communist systems."[25] By the end of the nineteenth century, Saint-Simon was often described with phrases such as "the first example of pure socialism" and "the first writer who gave form to its [socialism's] aspirations."[26] His ideas burned so quickly and so widely that it was easy to forget their kindling was first ignited because of his commitment to American-style individual freedom. The connection bears repeating: for Saint-Simon, what became socialism first began with a love of Jeffersonian liberty.

Charles Fourier, the other French thinker named by Marx and Engels as one of the founders of socialism, was a proponent of utopian communal societies in which people would live in what he called "phalansteries." Although his plans for a phalanstery in France never came to fruition, his socialist utopia did flower in America, if briefly. In the early 1840s, Emerson's friend George Ripley established a Fourierist cooperative community in rural West Roxbury dubbed Brook Farm. Nathaniel Hawthorne joined, later using the experience as the basis for his 1852 novel *The Blithedale Romance*. Emerson never joined, though he did profess admiration for what he called the "noble and generous" aims of Ripley and the other members of the community.[27] The socialist experiment began to fail almost as soon was it begun, though, and by the mid-1840s, it was essentially over.

Simply put, socialism had since its inception been bound up with American ideals, however indirectly. The language of left and right, of revolution and reaction, made sense in Europe, a continent burdened by centuries of monarchy and aristocracy. But those divisions didn't exactly apply to America. Even so, the country was hardly politically homogenous. In addition to the open wound of the slave system, which had institutionalized racial inequality for well over 200 years at that point, a much newer discussion over the nature of freedom had emerged. This was why Fredrika Bremer's midcentury realization that American political thought was splintering into two main classes—socialism on the one hand, Emerson's individualism on the other—was such an important one.

The two ideas were premised on two opposing ways of understanding society. Socialists, Bremer thought, wanted to improve "human nature by means of social institutions." Individualists, she wrote—men like Emerson and, earlier, Jefferson—wanted to focus on "each separate human being perfecting himself."²⁸ One group thought society was like an organism, a near-living thing that developed and progressed over time. The other group, people like Emerson, thought that society wasn't an organism at all, merely a collection of individuals. Perhaps without realizing it, Emerson had laid the intellectual groundwork for conservative individualism in America.

Emerson was writing at a moment when the word "conservative" was just beginning to settle into its modern usage. Before 1800, the term barely existed at all.

The use of the words "conservative" and "conservativism" to refer to certain political worldviews emerged out of the conversations that took place in the aftermath of the French Revolution. In France, the 1799 Constitution of the Year VIII established a conservative senate (the *Sénat Conservateur*), using the language of conservatism to paper over the upheavals of the revolution and suggest a broad sense of historical continuity.²⁹

This usage—equating "conservative" with aristocratic stability generally as well as anti-Jacobinism specifically—soon migrated across the Channel where it was applied to the English political scene. An 1816 article in the English magazine *The Antijacobin Review* defended the pro-royalist Pitt Clubs by praising "those conservative principles which all good men ought not passively to foster and cherish, but actually to promote."³⁰ *If you don't want blood running in the streets*, went the not-so-subtle implication, *then you must support the Crown*.

But it would take at least another decade before the word "conservative" began to imply something akin to a coherent worldview. In England, the Tory Party began to be recognized as the conservative party, spurred by an influential 1830 *Quarterly Review* essay. The essay proclaimed loyalty to "the Tory, and which might with more propriety be called the Conservative, party," which it felt contained the "most intelligent and respectable portion of the population of this country."³¹ After this essay, the word "conservative" quickly entered popular usage. Its basic meaning—to *conserve*, to *guard*, to *protect*—smoothed the reactionary edges from Toryism, and was implied to be synonymous with elite consensus, social stability, and with propriety of intellect.

Before 1830, no English language dictionaries included a clear political dimension to the word "conservative." After 1830, the word saw increasing usage in England, but it took longer to cross the Atlantic. In the 1830s and 1840s, Noah Webster's *American Dictionary of the English Language* noted no political connotations to the word "conservative" at all, defining it only as an adjective—not a noun—synonymous with "preservative." ("Having power to preserve in a safe or entire state, or from loss, waste, or injury."³²) But in an 1844 edition, Webster included a "Modern usage" that defined conservative for the first time as a noun: "One who aims to preserve from ruin, innovation, injury, or radical change; one who wishes to maintain an institution, or form of government, in its present state."[33] Conservative was no longer just an impersonal modifier. It was a person with particular ideas about government. It was something someone could *be*.

By the middle of the century, it was also something you could believe in. Without a legacy of feudalism and aristocracy, everyone in America could plausibly claim to be conservative. As Abraham Lincoln said in a speech to Republican party members in February 1860, before he announced he was running for president:

> You say you [southerners] are conservative—eminently conservative—while we are revolutionary, destructive, or something of the sort. What is conservatism? Is it not adherence to the old and tried, against the new and untried? [. . .] Consider, then, whether your claim of conservatism for yourselves, and your charge of destructiveness against us, are based on the most clear and stable foundations.[34]

In the years surrounding the Civil War, the word "conservative" could apply to any number of persons. "Conservative" could describe southerners, but it also could describe those seeking to conserve the Union. As Lincoln acknowledged, many people could plausibly claim to be conservatives. And perhaps, more importantly, many could plausibly claim the mantle of conserva*tism*.

Some of this linguistic flexibility would persist beyond the war. Throughout Theodore Roosevelt's life, for instance, he used the word "conservative" in different ways: sometimes as a term of opprobrium, a synonym for stubborn; at other times, he used it as a compliment, a synonym for thoughtful. He once joked that another man "made me feel like an elderly conservative."[35] Later, in a 1903 speech in Indianapolis, he proudly labeled Americans as "essentially a conservative people," emphasizing that of course he was referring to "the conservatism of good sense."[36]

In the years after the Civil War, "conservatism," like "conservative" before it, became a new addition to the American language. The 1865 edition of Webster's *American Dictionary* was one of the first to contain an entry for the noun "conservatism" as it pertained to political change. It was explicitly linked to a conservative mental state: "The disposition and tendency to preserve what is established; opposition to change; the habit of mind, or conduct, of a conservative."[37] Under the entry for "conservative," it included a new, secondary definition of the word: "One who holds intermediate or moderate opinions in politics; one who desires to maintain existing institutions and customs;—opposed to *revolutionary* or *radical*."[38]

In short, the idea of conservatism as a disposition was cemented by the mid-1860s. In the 1840s, a "conservative" was an individual who did certain things. But in the aftermath of the war, it also suggested someone who *believed* certain things. It implied an ingrained vision of historical change, of the good society, of human capacity for improvement.

This aesthetic, dispositional view of conservatives and conservatism continued through the end of the century. The 1897 *American Encyclopaedic Dictionary* explained conservativism as the result of certain "mental constitutions," noting that "at the close of the United States civil war, 1860–65, the people of the South were divided into two great parties—the conservatives, who were anxious for the restoration of the old order of affairs, and the radicals, who were in favor of a thorough regeneration and reconstruction of political institutions."[39] To be conservative, in short, was to long for the restoration of the old aristocratic order. And while the term implied a predisposition toward the historical past, it was also associated with a belief that inequality was an ineradicable and even desirable part of the natural world.

Many mid-nineteenth-century American conservatives, like Burke before them, would have been suspicious of any notion that the laws of nature commanded equality between individuals. But almost exactly at the time that the country was erupting into war, Charles Darwin published a book that eventually would provide a radical new way of thinking about history, social hierarchy, and the laws of nature. In time, a group of men would fuse Darwin's ideas about natural competition with Emerson's philosophy of individualism to produce a new way of thinking about conservatism in America.

NOTES

1. Qtd. in Perry, 57.
2. Emerson *Early*, 185.
3. Cooke, 193.
4. Emerson *Nature*, 55.
5. Qtd. in Rusk, 434.
6. Emerson's ideas about individualism and democracy are famously hard to pin down. West observes that Emerson is "neither a liberal nor a conservative and certainly not a socialist or even civic republican" (40). In general, most Emerson scholars emphasize how his writings lend support to the democratic project. As Cameron notes, nearly all modern critics agree that Emersonian self-reliance is not synonymous with simple self-interest (6). Richardson Jr. argues that Emerson's ideas support a larger project of "democratic individualism" (250). Cavell agrees that Emerson is a figure of democratic aspiration (*Emerson's*, 184). And Kateb makes the case that Emerson's theories of "democratic individuality" are opposed to the values of the aristocracy (19). However, most scholars also concede that

Emersonian self-reliance is also a call for the pursuit of individual greatness. Cavell underscores this close affinity between Emersonian individualism and Jeffersonian natural aristocracy (*Conditions*, 45). Rabiee argues that after "Self-Reliance," Emerson's "doctrine of natural aristocracy" became a kind of "neo-feudalism" (77–78). Similarly, Bercovitch admits that Emerson's individualism led him to invoke a "dream vision of laissez-faire" philosophy (336). Newfield extends this line of thinking, memorably describing Emerson's self-reliance as "corporate individualism," a philosophy emphasizing "individual merit" which allows for a "preservation of inequality" (5). More recently, Larson has concluded that much of Emerson's writing seems "either unmoved by or profoundly hostile to the core values of liberalism" (29). In sum, the view that Emersonian individualism, in "Self-Reliance," seems pitched to nudge individualism toward the political right is a view, while perhaps little-noticed, which is nonetheless an established component of Emerson scholarship.

7. Emerson "Self-Reliance," 156.
8. Emerson "Lectures," 13.
9. Emerson "Self-Reliance," 156.
10. Emerson "Self-Reliance," 168.
11. Emerson "Self-Reliance," 169.
12. Emerson *Nature*, 18. For more on wilderness, Emerson and western conquest, see Fresonke, 113–127.
13. Emerson "Self-Reliance," 170.
14. "Representative," 361; "Emerson," 139.
15. "Emerson," 139.
16. "Representative," 361.
17. Emerson "Lectures," 6.
18. Emerson "Lectures [II]," 182.
19. Emerson "Lectures [II]," 183.
20. Emerson "Lectures [II]," 186.
21. Emerson "Lectures [II]," 186.
22. Smith "Signs," 210.
23. Bremer, 233.
24. Booth, 5.
25. Marx and Engels, 99.
26. "[Review]," 123; Marshall, 153.
27. Qtd. in Beecher *Charles*, 498.
28. Bremer, 233.
29. Connelly, 201–207; Lockhart, 125–134.
30. "Pitt," 553.
31. "Internal," 276.
32. Webster [1830], 181.
33. Webster [1844], 952.
34. Lincoln, 122.
35. Roosevelt *Rough*, 185.
36. "President," 7. See also Thomas *Roosevelt*, 310–311.

37. Webster [1865], 278. The *American Dictionary* had begun adding definitions of "conservatism" as early as 1848, but defined it as a neutral practice roughly synonymous with preservation (Webster [1848], 216). It was not until the 1860s that the editors felt that conservatism involved an opposition to change.
38. Webster [1865], 278.
39. Hunter, 1069.

Chapter 10

Darwin Comes to America

By late 1859, it was clear to many Americans that the country was headed for some kind of schism. In October of that year, the abolitionist John Brown tried to instigate an armed slave revolt by leading a raid on the United States armory at Harpers Ferry, Virginia. On the first night of the raid, a party of Brown's men stole a pistol that Lafayette had given to George Washington nearly eighty years earlier.[1] Keenly aware of the symbolic battle he was waging, Brown issued his commands from Harpers Ferry while holding the weapon, seeming to view it as a talisman of freedom.

Its powers were apparently limited. Half of the men were killed during the raid, and most of the other half, including Brown, were captured a few days later by a detachment of Marines led by Colonel Robert E. Lee. Brown was eventually hanged for treason.

With his hand on the pistol that had been gripped by Lafayette and Washington, Brown must have felt that he was legatee of the revolution, a fighter for individual freedom. Many northerners agreed. Emerson, who by then had become a serious abolitionist, called Brown a hero and a "strict constructionist" who sought to limit federal overreach and preserve the union.[2] For Emerson, he was a kind of self-reliant hero: a conservative martyr to individual rights and small government.

A number of southerners didn't see it that way. Far from viewing him as a conservative, an editorial in the Richmond, Virginia *Whig* wasn't even sure he was entitled to due process. In the paper's view, Brown was a "miserable old traitor" who was "entitled to no trial at law."[3] Far from being a symbol of constitutionally protected freedom, Brown was for many southerners the vanguard of its destruction.

A war was in the offing. Less than a year after Brown was hanged, Abraham Lincoln was elected president. Five weeks after he took office, the Confederacy fired on Fort Sumter, sparking the Civil War.

A war of ideas was brewing, too. A month after Brown's raid, Charles Darwin, a little-known fifty-year-old English naturalist, published a book titled *On the Origin of Species*. It was a specialized scientific book, one that could hardly have been expected to attract an enormous audience. Yet to everyone's surprise, it sold out immediately, forcing his publishers to scramble to get a second printing into shops.

The book advanced the theory of natural selection. As Darwin explained it, natural selection was the idea that "individuals having any advantage, however slight, over others, would have the best chance of surviving and of procreating their kind," and that "any variation in the least degree injurious would be rigidly destroyed" over generations.[4] Darwin did not invent the idea of evolution, which most people still called the development hypothesis, out of whole cloth. In subsequent editions of his book, he made a point of tracing his intellectual forebears all the way back to Aristotle. It was commonly accepted that species evolved over time. Before Darwin, though, there was no scientifically plausible explanation for how species development actually worked.

At the beginning of the nineteenth century, the French naturalist Jean-Baptiste Lamarck had expanded on Erasmus Darwin's earlier theory of transmutation, hypothesizing that species development occurred through individual organisms' interaction with the environment. By midcentury, Charles Darwin did not think Lamarck was entirely wrong, but he didn't think he was entirely right, either. (In later editions of *On the Origin of Species*, he would actually give more credence to Lamarck's hypothesis, not less.[5]) In the fall of 1838, Darwin had read Thomas Malthus's forty-year-old *Essay on the Principle of Population*. In it, the English cleric and professor of political economy argued that the chief barrier to progress was population growth. Malthus reasoned that population was often kept in check by available food resources: it grew in times of plenty; it dropped in times of famine. Yet population was not a neutral reflection of resources. Left unchecked, it would grow until it threatened the supply of agricultural resources, producing catastrophic social instability.

Malthus's hypothesis that populations were governed by a constant struggle over a finite pool of resources became a crucial inspiration for Darwin's own development hypothesis. Malthus had thought that population and resources were precariously balanced, forever teetering on the brink of disaster. In his view, the competition for resources was a grim but unavoidable part of life, making perpetual progress all but impossible.

What Darwin realized was that that fierce competition between unequal individual organisms would, over many generations, naturally select for adaptive advantages. Individuals with variations which were somehow useful in the competition for resources would survive to reproduce themselves and those variations. Those individuals with unhelpful variations would be less likely to reproduce themselves and those variations. Over generations, populations naturally progressed so as to maximize adaptive advantages. Malthus, Darwin realized, had it almost exactly backward. Competitive struggle didn't hinder progress. Competitive struggle *drove* progress.

Darwin wasn't the only one working on the issue of population change. The English philosopher Herbert Spencer had anonymously published "The Development Hypothesis" in early 1852, seven years before Darwin. After Spencer read Darwin, his pithy summary of the theory of natural selection—that it was a "survival of the fittest"—would be so instantly memorable that Darwin borrowed it back from him, eventually incorporating it into the fifth edition of *On the Origin of Species* in 1869.

Eleven years Darwin's junior, Spencer was a clever polymath, a onetime civil engineer who wrote books that managed to be about politics, evolutionary biology, psychology, and philosophy, all at once. William James, who was one of Roosevelt's favorite professors at Harvard, admitted that although Spencer was not always respected among the intellectual class, he was nonetheless a thinker for "thoughtful laymen," the "philosopher whom those who have no other philosopher can appreciate."[6]

Spencer had read Emerson's *Nature* as a young man, and though he pronounced it "rather too mystical to please me," over time his estimation of Emerson grew.[7] Emerson's remark that nature was "the circumstance which dwarfs every other circumstance" stuck with him, and Spencer found his mind returning to the maxim from time to time.[8] He also shared Emerson's appreciation for nonconformity. Emerson had written that anyone who was a man must also be a nonconformist.[9] Spencer framed the issue somewhat differently. A "nonconformity to human authority implies conformity to something regarded as higher than human authority," he reasoned.[10] Spencer agreed that humans shouldn't conform to other humans. He just thought they had to conform to *some* authority. Nature was a force that superseded the petty regulations of human-created laws and governments.

Spencer was devoted to the belief that the greatest social good could be obtained by maximizing individual liberty and minimizing government. In his view, a laissez-faire principle of noninterference would bring the government in harmony with the laws of nature.

Unlike Emerson, who wasn't even sure that cumulative social development was even possible, Spencer was convinced that society was alive and evolving, just like any other animal. "Instead of civilization being artificial," he wrote, "it is a part of nature."[11] It was a "social organism."[12] If societies were natural and not human-built, he reasoned, they must have developed in accordance with the laws of nature.

And if society *was* an organism, it followed that the natural environment mattered immensely. For Spencer, certain environments could force individuals and even whole societies to regress backward on the evolutionary continuum. Individuals "retrograde on being placed in circumstances which call forth the old propensities," he wrote, noting that the western frontiers of America offered a good example of this principle. "The back settlers of America, amongst whom unavenged murderers, rifle duels, and Lynch law prevail—or, better still, the trappers, who leading a savage life have descended to savage habits, to scalping, and occasionally even to cannibalism—sufficiently exemplify it."[13]

Spencer was a committed Lamarckian. In his view, individuals deliberately enhanced and transmitted traits they had acquired through their own will. The most socially "fit"—which might mean physical strength, but also economic wealth, mental acuity, or any number of advantageous adaptations—would enhance that fitness through their own volition. They would become *more* fit, and transmit that fitness onto their progeny, who would continue the process. Because of this overlapping evolutionary cycle—individual evolution drove social evolution which in turn drove further individual evolution—individuals were never fully adapted to the modern social state.[14]

This developmental lag, Spencer thought, was partly what made government necessary at all. Because society was always more evolved than most of its inhabitants, humans needed a particular type of government: "Conservativism defends those coercive arrangements which a still-lingering savageness makes requisite."[15] Government should otherwise be regarded with no small amount of suspicion.

For Spencer, conservatism was necessary for the simple reason that the masses were never completely adapted to the modern social state. In Spencer's view, a good government—one that was built in accordance with the laws of nature—was not a utopian government. It was, as he put it, a conservative government.

Darwin's *On the Origin of Species* attracted immediate attention on both sides of the Atlantic, but it took a while for its ideas to gain widespread acceptance in America. There was a period of several decades in which writers, pastors, intellectuals, and philosophers publically auditioned his ideas: disseminating them, examining them, applying them to different issues.[16] During that time, many American intellectuals effectively reshaped those ideas, making natural selection their own. In the process, they created a kind of composite Darwinian philosophy: an American Darwin. After the Civil War, natural philosophers such as E. D. Cope, Alpheus Hyatt, and John A. Ryder began working toward a fusion of Darwin and Lamarckism that some called "the American school" of evolutionary theory.[17]

Adherents to the American school believed that species developed through the mechanism of natural selection, just as Darwin had advocated in *On the Origin of Species*. But they didn't let go of Lamarck, and in fact elevated a modified Lamarckian hypothesis to Darwin's level. Besides having the added benefit of fitting together nicely with Spencer's theories of social development, it's not difficult to see why the American school of evolution continued to emphasize Lamarck.

After all, Lamarck lent scientific credence to the national faith in individual improvement in a way that Darwin simply could not. To his adherents, Lamarck seemed to speak in a uniquely American tongue. The individual, Lamarck said, would always be at the center of things: the chief driver of development.

Such individualism was the distinguishing feature of the "American school" of evolutionary theory. But that individual-centered worldview didn't come from Darwin. For all the wide-ranging applications that Darwin's ideas went on to have—not just in the natural sciences but in virtually every field of human social knowledge, from economics to politics to city planning—he had remarkably little to say about actual humans in *On the Origin of Species*.

To correct this omission (which wasn't really an omission at all) and also to respond to Herbert Spencer and the American school, Darwin published *The Descent of Man* in 1871. In it, he tried to do what Spencer had been doing for nearly a decade: apply the development hypothesis to human development.

Humans were naturally social animals, he postulated. Civilized society wasn't something that was invented, tool-like, for human betterment; it was something innate. It was "almost certain that [man] would inherit a tendency to be faithful to his comrades, and obedient to the leader of his tribe," he wrote.[18] But while the human animal may be "obedient," Darwin didn't want to downplay the central role that competition played in natural selection. If a trait offered an adaptive advantage, the individual possessing that trait would be more likely to win the competition and reproduce. "There should be open competition for all men," he declared.[19] "Man is the rival of other men; he delights in competition."[20] Competition between unequal organisms, he stressed, was the key to natural selection.

Like many of his peers, Darwin thought that the competitions which drove human development were more readily observable in the younger nation of America. As is "generally admitted," he wrote in a Lamarckian-sounding aside, "the European settlers in the United States undergo a slight but extraordinarily rapid change of appearance. Their bodies and limbs become elongated."[21] He quoted Benjamin Apthorp Gould, an American scientist who thought that "residence in the Western States, during the years of growth, tends to produce increase of stature."[22] Simply living in the American west, Darwin seemed to be saying, produced durable changes in the human animal.

In other words, he seemed to agree that his own theories were somehow sharper, more vivid even, in the United States. To many readers of Darwin and other adherents of the "American school" of human development, the implication was clear: If you want to see the cold logic of natural selection at work in human civilization, you must come to America.

In the decades after *The Descent of Man*, Darwinism filled nearly all corners of American intellectual life. Scientists and scholars sought to discover the evolutionary principles underlying economics, sociology, law, history, and nearly every other field.

When it came to discovering an evolutionary science of political economy, perhaps the most prominent American thinker was William Graham Sumner. A dour man with a neatly trimmed mustache and an intense stare, one of Sumner's earliest interests was the relationship between America's western frontiers and its democratic values.

While still an undergraduate student, Sumner made the case that American democracy depended largely on its abundant available land.[23] In the early 1870s, he read Herbert Spencer for the first time. The experience was clarifying. Spencer "immediately gave me the lead which I wanted to bring into shape the crude notions which had been floating in my head for five or six years," he recalled.[24] Sumner became a professor of political and social science at Yale in 1872. Energized by his reading of Spencer, he returned to the subject of politics and the American west: "There are features of American democracy which are inexplicable unless one understands this frontier society," he wrote.[25] Competition on America's western frontiers, he believed, was what powered the American system.

Just as Darwin had argued that competition drove natural selection generally, Sumner believed that economic competition drove social evolution specifically. The strong—the industrious, the intelligent, the tenacious—would became wealthy and powerful; the weak—the lazy, the stupid, the indolent—would become poor and die. This was a central law of nature, he believed. Society could no more ignore it than it could ignore the law of gravity.

Although Sumner never identified himself as a "social Darwinist"—the phrase wouldn't be used at all until 1877, and wouldn't fully acquire its pejorative connotation for another several decades after that—it is worth remembering that for Sumner, as for most intellectuals, Darwinian development was science, not a bait-and-switch tactic for ensuring the supremacy of the elites. (That it did ensure the supremacy of the elites was more than a little convenient, but for Sumner, such a corollary simply meant those elites' status was already naturally sanctioned.) For him, the development hypothesis was just what it claimed to be: an explanation of the laws of nature. In Sumner's view, those laws were flouted at our peril.

Adhering to the development hypothesis in this way provided a natural justification for many things, including laissez-faire economic policy. "The millionaires are a product of natural selection," Sumner argued. And although they "get high wages and live in luxury," he continued, "the bargain is a good one for society," because creating optimum conditions for natural selection meant creating optimum conditions for social development.[26]

For Sumner, wealthy people got that way because they were more "fit," in a social or economic sense. And at a time when Lamarckism and Darwinism were given near-equal credence, it was easy to see wealthy people as having *become* fit through their own volition, a fitness they would pass on to their progeny, ensuring that America would continue to progress. For Sumner, a laissez-faire economic policy wasn't just good business sense. It assured the natural evolution of society.

In his view, America required an underpopulated frontier where individuals were dependent largely on themselves, not on social institutions. A frontier was necessary, he believed, because it allowed the dynamics of self-reliance and natural selection to play out without interference.[27] "If we do not like the survival of the fittest," he said in an 1879 lecture, "we have only one possible alternative, and that is the survival of the unfittest. The former is the law of civilization; the latter is the law of anti-civilization."[28] Following this law of nature, he felt, would allow for continuous social progress and safeguard the republic.

For Sumner, American social progress required the interlocking of two concepts: the "American school" of Darwinian natural selection and the colonization of the American west. It would not take long before many influential writers and thinkers began to agree.

Six years before the Civil War, the poet Walt Whitman had given voice to a growing democratic sensibility, identifying "the sign of democracy" as a "password primeval," as if democracy were the original animating word that gave life to American politics.[29] Yet, Whitman's valorization of democracy was actually something new, not anything "primeval" at all. James Madison had famously argued that direct democracy was a terrible idea. He thought the Constitution would work because it harnessed its horizontal democratic impulses to a vertical republican machine.

But while America was born with a republican, hierarchical system of government, after the Civil War, it increasingly liked to think of itself as purely democratic. In the aftermath of the war, a kind of sentimental rhetoric of democracy sprang up, glossing over the nation's republican, hierarchical heritage in a reconciliatory attempt to paper over the ravages of the war. New York abolitionist and clergyman Henry Ward Beecher liked to pepper his sermons with stirring references to democracy. Like Whitman before him,

Beecher was less interested in democracy as an actual system of governance than he was in the way that democracy made people feel.

It was in the middle of Reconstruction that Beecher most clearly articulated this reconciliatory view of democracy. "The value of all men, without regard to race or condition, is the essential, democratic American idea," he said in a sermon in his Brooklyn, New York, church. "The real democratic American idea is, not that every man shall be on a level with every other man, but that every man shall be what God made him," whether "born of Caucasian, or African, or Indian parents."[30] This, he assured the congregation, was what real democracy meant: not a horizontal system in which every man is "on a level with every other man," but instead just a vague type of personal freedom in which "every man shall be what God made him." Of course, this wasn't what democracy meant at all. Beecher was actually offering his congregation a dramatic redefinition of democracy.

This embrace of a new type of democracy was explainable at least in part by the fact that Beecher, like most of his educated peers, was an ardent defender of the Darwinian turn in American intellectual life. Darwin's theory of natural selection would, Beecher once said, "multiply the motives and facilities of righteousness, which was and is the design of the whole Bible."[31] Darwin helped propagate the "righteous" order of nature. And that order was one that simply needed unequal hierarchies. Hierarchies, for Darwin, were what made natural selection possible. After all, inequality—mutations and differences within a species—drove the process of evolution.

In the aftermath of the war and the push for reconciliation, men like Beecher began to offer stirring odes to democracy while pretending that democracy didn't require equality. At the same time, one of the most dramatic consequences of Darwin began to emerge: the idea that inequality was an ineradicable part of nature. For many this was a transformative idea, the sort of thing that later led Roosevelt to identify Darwin as "one of the chief factors in working a tremendous intellectual revolution."[32] And one consequence of that revolution was the widespread realization that certain types of inequality and hierarchy—the sort of thing that democracy was designed to negotiate—were in fact desirable components of the natural order.

As a result, for many people democracy stopped being an enemy of inequality and became its coconspirator. In the decades after the Civil War, for the first time one could embrace democracy and also, like Henry Ward Beecher, not worry about equality among men.

In the aftermath of the war, Darwin's ideas began to be seen by many as a central explanation for social progress. As Roosevelt later put it, the "rivalry that characterizes natural selection" was "one of the features in progress."[33] This was a crucial insight: *Social progress*, the thinking went, *is governed by the same natural laws that sanction inequality.* To this way of thinking, progress required inequality. Such a principle wasn't cruel. It was natural.

NOTES

1. See Geffert 41, *Life* 30, Reif AR38, *Report* 31.
2. Emerson "Remarks," 114.
3. *"Richmond,"* 257.
4. Darwin *Origin*, 601.
5. Russett, 10.
6. James, 104.
7. Spencer *Autobiography*, 278.
8. Spencer *Autobiography*, 310.
9. Emerson "Self-Reliance," 151.
10. Spencer *Autobiography*, 12.
11. Spencer "Evanescence," 13.
12. Spencer "Social Organism," 61.
13. Spencer "Social Statics," 21.
14. Spencer "Evanescence," 11.
15. Spencer "Social Statics," 27.
16. Lowenberg, 3; Russet, 10.
17. Ward, 59. See also Russett, 10–11; Wallace *Darwinism*, 420.
18. Darwin *Descent*, 171.
19. Darwin *Descent*, 414.
20. Darwin *Descent*, 380.
21. Darwin *Descent*, 271.
22. Darwin *Descent*, 62.
23. Parker, 359.
24. "Sketch," 266.
25. Qtd. in Parker, 360.
26. Qtd. in Hofstadter *Social*, 58.
27. See Sumner, 470–471; Parker, 360–361.
28. Qtd. in Hofstadter *Social*, 57.
29. Whitman, 30.
30. Beecher *Original*, 31.
31. Beecher *Evolution*, 52–53.
32. TR letter to Oliver Wendell Holmes Jr., 21 October 1904.
33. Roosevelt "Degeneration," 95.

Chapter 11

The Redeemers, the Socialists, and Conservatism After the Civil War

After the war, many intellectuals returned to the question Emerson seemed to be asking in the 1840s: What did it mean to be a conservative in America? One foundational conservative value was a general orientation toward the past. But it had been obvious for decades that Burkean conservatism, with its nostalgic longing for the stability of aristocracy and the monarchy, simply could not exist in America.

By the late 1860s, however, there was a recently vanished aristocratic tradition that more than a few thought worth conserving. The sentiment only grew after the end of Reconstruction in 1877. For one strain of American conservatism, it was a large and powerful lodestone: the system of white supremacy that lived in symbiosis with the system of slavery.

Like individualism, slavery was sustained in part by a set of beliefs about the laws of nature. Most white supremacists felt that racial privilege was sanctioned by those same natural laws. After the Civil War, a number of southern conservatives began building an intellectual edifice to support the belief that the war had been, as Virginia editor Edward A. Pollard called it in his 1867 manifesto, *The Lost Cause*. All that remained for the south, Pollard argued, was "the war of ideas."[1] Those ideas involved a number of overlapping issues, including political questions of federalism, philosophical questions of natural rights and individual freedom, and, above all, moral questions of racial inequality.

Conservative southerners like Thomas Nelson Page, who was barely twelve years old when the war ended, devoted themselves to "lost cause" mythology by spinning romantic tales of a chivalrous, genteel south.[2] Page was selling a nostalgic view of American history, one that carefully bowdlerized the horrors of the slave system and made racial inequality appear as natural as a summer thunderstorm. For a Virginian, he once explained, the "greatness of the past, the time when Virginia had been the mighty power of the New World [. . .] increased his natural conservatism."[3]

In a later book, Page continued to explore what he called "the Virginian character," which he said had been largely inherited from aristocratic England: a romantic heritage that he acknowledged seemed "feudal and aristocratic."[4] He praised what he saw as the kindly, paternal character of the antebellum slaveowners. For such men, he claimed, the Civil War hadn't actually been about slavery at all. It was instead about the tragic upending of a romantic, pastoral existence. For white supremacists in the south, he explained, Reconstruction sparked a kind of historical vertigo: an acceleration of the forward motion of history at exactly the moment when the former slaveowners wanted to slow the course of progress.

Needless to say, Page's ideas about historical change were inseparable from his opinions about white supremacy. "The Negro as a slave was an excellent laborer; as a freeman, at least under conditions which have existed in the country, he is not," he wrote, trying to explain why he felt Black liberation had been a detriment to the south.[5] At its core, his argument was straightforward, if exceedingly racist. He felt that slavery had been good for whites, good for the economy, and good for Black people. Since the war, everything had gotten worse. Like many conservative white southerners after the war, he longed for "the simplicity of the past."[6]

Following Burke, Page had particular beliefs about the natural laws governing society. Ideally, he explained, "progress moves on natural lines; nations rise and fall by natural laws."[7] His conservatism involved beliefs about nature, historical progress, and individual freedom, all built on a bedrock belief in racial inequality. But this type of conservatism was also unavoidably backward-looking. It suggested that days of prelapsarian wonder were hiding in the recent past, and to recreate that past was also to recreate that wonder.

Yet those days of wonder, it should go without saying, were hardly what he said they were. They were in truth days in which a racial hierarchy was keenly felt by every member of American society.[8] After the Fifteenth Amendment was ratified in 1870, prohibiting governments from denying the right to vote on the basis of race, an intellectual, political, and physical edifice sprung in the south up to safeguard against what was typically called "negro domination."[9] Unsurprisingly, the issue was understood quite differently in the north. "The North terms it simply the question of civil equality of all citizens before the law; the South denominates it the question of negro domination," as Page admitted.[10] Negro domination, in other words, was simply what conservative southerners called representative democracy.

Regardless, the "domination" did not last long. After 1877, when Rutherford B. Hayes was awarded the presidency by a single electoral vote in exchange for removing federal troops from the former Confederacy, whites began assuming control of elected offices at every level across the south, a process of disenfranchisement that many conservative white southerners called "redemption."

From the perspective of such self-appointed redeemers, their restoration was a resounding success. By the end of Reconstruction, about 2,000 Black men held federal, state, and public office throughout the south.[11] After the redeemers' so-called success, the number of Black elected officials declined precipitously. In 1875, there were eight Black Congressmen in the U.S. House of Representatives, all elected from former Confederate states. In 1885, there were two. In 1895, there was one. And by 1902, there were none at all.[12]

As the Black Mississippi congressman John R. Lynch dryly pointed out, southerners would cry "'Negro Domination' whenever the will of a majority of the whites would be defeated through the votes of colored men."[13] For white southern conservatives, the mere existence of Black suffrage made it seem as if democracy itself was crumbling.

And from their perspective, it was. Or rather, their specific definition of democracy, which mostly meant the rule of a popular majority of white, property-owning men, was crumbling. In the aftermath of the war, the only America they had ever known—an America entirely under the dominion of white men—had seemingly been upended by democracy writ large. They found themselves wanting almost exactly what Burke had wanted less than a century earlier: "An established aristocracy, and an established democracy, each in the degree it exists, *and in no greater*."[14] White southerners simply wanted their aristocracy back.

To give this age-old belief in racial inequality the gloss of modern scientific accuracy, some tried to make the case that white supremacy was supported by Darwin's development hypothesis. Shortly after the war, natural scientist Nathan S. Shaler argued that Blacks people had inherited certain characteristics that rendered them unfit for American liberal democracy. Using Darwin for intellectual cover, he claimed that Blacks had become evolutionarily distinct from whites. Whites had a responsibility to free "the negro" from "the instincts which the savage life of a hundred generations have planted in his blood," he wrote.[15] To his way of thinking, slaveowners had been on the cutting edge of evolutionary philosophy. Equal freedom simply wasn't natural.

But in general, the intellectual heft of Darwin was not required to defend the emerging postbellum southern conservatism. Southern conservatives could more easily and more honestly appeal to simple tradition. And that tradition, for men like Thomas Nelson Page, was one of genteel-sounding race-based aristocracy. It was common knowledge that after the Civil War, American conservatism acquired a significant racial dimension. As one writer put it in 1897, "upon the enfranchisement of the negro, it is hardly necessary to say that that race at once aligned itself with the radicals, while the whites were as a unit conservative."[16] But southern whites tended to see that conservatism in nostalgic terms: as an ancient dream of a romantic and honorable feudal society that proudly wrapped itself in the modern language of American democracy.

Postbellum southern conservatism, however, was not the only type of conservatism. On the coasts, a new generation of left-leaning economists and social scientists were, without realizing it, creating the intellectual space for a new generation of conservatives. While those progressive intellectuals were not themselves conservative, they did invent a modern, distinctly American socialism, requiring any conservatives who objected to respond in kind. Their eventual rejoinder would be a modern, scientific conservatism, one that wanted little to do with the southerner's desire to resurrect a racial caste system.

By the 1880s, the divide between socialists and Emersonian individualists—the same divide that travel writer Fredrika Bremer had noticed back in 1850—was widening into a chasm. Even in the early years of Reconstruction, there had been a gathering sense that the nation's laissez-faire financial systems were headed for some kind of crisis. Fueled by postwar inflation, rising interest rates, and rampant speculation in the railroad and real estate industries, the failure of the Philadelphia-based Cooke and Company bank in September 1873 had triggered a chain reaction of bank failures that led to a ten-day shutdown of the New York Stock Exchange. It was the worst financial crisis the United States had ever seen, and the first truly global economic depression.

Even then, some were already skeptical of the largely unregulated, individualist market economy. Earlier that year, Mark Twain and his friend Charles Dudley Warner had published a satire of the economic excesses of the day, a novel whose title would eventually come to signify the entire era: *The Gilded Age*.

Two years after the end of Reconstruction, one of the first intellectual salvos against the excesses of the Gilded Age appeared to little fanfare, a thick book titled *Progress and Poverty*. Self-published by an amateur economist from California, the left-leaning critique of American capitalism would eventually become one of the best-selling books of the final decades of the nineteenth century, catapulting its author to a level of acclaim and influence he scarcely could have imagined.

Born in Philadelphia, Henry George had gone west to look for gold as a young man. He didn't find any gold, but he did find work at a newspaper, where he started asking a question that would come to define his entire career: why, despite broad and ongoing economic progress, did poverty continue to exist? One day George had been riding his horse in the hills overlooking the bay when he was struck by sudden insight about nature and individual freedom. He found "the reason of advancing poverty with advancing wealth," as he later recalled. "With the growth of population, land grows in value, and the men who work it must pay more for the privilege."[17] For the first time, he felt he "recognised the natural order."[18]

Much like Locke, George decided that nature was a common inheritance. But unlike Locke, he concluded that this meant that land could only really be rented, not owned, by individuals. The solution to ongoing economic inequality, George argued in *Progress and Poverty*, was to abolish all taxes except for a "single tax" on land value. The value of land, George felt, was shaped by population growth, which meant that a significant portion of the wealth created on or by that land should belong to its populace.

In one of the book's earliest reviews, the *New York Herald* saw the book as a serious attempt to give American leftism some intellectual credibility. "Communism," the reviewer noted, "has made little headway in this country" in part because "the socialistic labor people have carefully avoided the use of brains." Yet unlike the socialists, the reviewer added, George "is a man of brains."[19] The reviewer thought his book could bring intellectual legitimacy to, and help create, a homegrown American left. *Progress and Poverty* eventually became the best-selling nonfiction book by a nineteenth-century American author, selling over two million copies in a dozen translations worldwide and making George the single most influential American economist of the late nineteenth century.[20]

After its publication, a number of journals and newspapers were founded to debate and promote what was called "Georgism," and eventually, several entire townships were founded to test his theories. A few years after his death in 1897, a young woman named Elizabeth Magie, who was a regular visitor to the single-tax township of Arden, Delaware, invented an early version of the board game Monopoly as a Georgist critique of unregulated laissez-faire capitalism.

Back east, a new generation of economists and social scientists was beginning to reject the Darwin-inspired individualism of Herbert Spencer and William Graham Sumner. Francis Amasa Walker, Sumner's colleague at Yale, wrote *The Wages Question* to make the left-leaning case that workers' wages were not, as the prevailing orthodoxy had it, paid out of a set fund of capital set aside for wages, but were created by workers' own labor. Sumner found Walker's left-leaning critique of individualist capitalism so unnerving that he maneuvered to have Walker fired from Yale.[21]

Undaunted, Walker moved to Johns Hopkins where he began mentoring a young intellectual named Henry Carter Adams. After earning Johns Hopkins's first doctorate in the social sciences in 1878, Adams studied abroad, where he had a small epiphany. "I am a socialist—to tell the truth," he confided to his diary.[22] He returned to the United States newly energized. He accepted a job offer from Cornell and set about building a community of like-minded thinkers.

These "ethical economists," as they were called, sought to lay the intellectual groundwork for socialism in America. The loose group included Adams, John Bates Clark, Richard T. Ely, Edwin R. A. Seligman, Walker, and others.[23] They wanted to decisively revise the individualist, Darwinian underpinnings of the Gilded Age economy, presumptions which had long been praised by established thinkers like Spencer and Sumner.

Inspired by his reading of Henry George, Columbia College professor John Bates Clark argued that individualism had long been tending toward socialism. "True socialism," he claimed, was widely misunderstood, and in fact was perfectly compatible with the individualism that drove America's "economic republicanism."[24] His radicalism was all the more clever for its commonsensical appearance. American economic individualism, he was saying, wasn't opposed to cooperative socialism at all. Seen from a certain angle, they were perfectly compatible.

Henry Carter Adams continued this line of thought. Echoing de Tocqueville's claim from a half-century earlier, he said that democracy had its origins in individualism, yet insisted the full freedom it promised could only be achieved by socialism. It was "the realization of coöperative economy which is to serve as the ideal of democratic peoples," as he put it. Of course, this would be a distinctly American socialism, the type that had its origins in individual freedom: "socialistic aims by individualistic means."[25]

Adams and Clark, like the rest of the ethical economists, posed a distinct threat to the Darwinian, individual-centered economic theories promoted by William Graham Sumner. Those theories, too, began with the centrality of the individual. But they concluded that American democracy meant not laissez-faire entrepreneurial capitalism, but something quite different: cooperative socialism.

In sum, by the mid-1880s a credible intellectual alternative to the rock-ribbed individualism of Ralph Waldo Emerson and William Graham Sumner was emerging. Henry George and the ethical economists offered a new theory of American progress, suggesting that American individualism tended not toward greater individualism but toward greater social cooperation. American freedom, they seemed to suggest, meant American socialism.

Seven years after the publication of *Progress and Poverty*, riding high on a groundswell of left-leaning sentiment among the working classes, Henry George would run for mayor of New York as the candidate of the Central Labor Union.[26] For a time, the race between George and the Democratic nominee Abram Hewitt was close, despite George having little support among the political elites and the mainstream press. Hewitt, like most conservatives, thought George was a dangerous foe of individualism. He raged that George wanted to "substitute the ideas of anarchists, nihilists, communists, socialists, and mere theorists for the democratic principle of individual liberty."[27] Backed by the Democratic machine of Tammany Hall, Hewitt ended up winning by a ten-point margin.

Still, George likely took some satisfaction in beating out the third-place finisher, an up-and-coming Republican who had recently been lured back from the west to run as the "cowboy of Dakota": a thirty-one-year-old named Theodore Roosevelt.[28]

By the final decades of the nineteenth century, one old truism about politics in America—that because America had no history of aristocracy, it had no political right, which also meant it could have no left—was starting to seem less accurate. The backlash against laissez-faire capitalism after the Panic of 1873 was significant, encompassing not just the emergence of new left-leaning intellectuals like Henry George and the socialist economists, but also a dramatic growth in labor organization. Trade union membership more than doubled in the last two decades of the nineteenth century, growing in power proportionally.[29] The number of labor strikes in the United States soared from under 500 a year in the early 1880s to over 1,500 a year in the early 1890s.[30] For many conservatives and indeed for much of the general public, socialism and unionism went hand in hand, a perception encouraged by the ethical economists themselves. There was a palpable sense that socialism was a viable option for America's future.

There was also something resolutely cheery about their leftism. George and the socialists suggested that they were looking forward to a brighter and more equitable future. They never completely forswore individualism, merely suggested they were trying to do something different with it.

In comparison, the southern redeemers didn't have a particularly good story at all. Their conservatism was grimly backward-looking, seeking to undo the postwar changes to the south and restore the racial hierarchy of the prewar years. Their conservatism was narrow and forbidding: a retrograde form of individual freedom tightly circumscribed by race.

The conservatism of William Graham Sumner did have a logical story to it, with the added benefit of being backed up with the latest research in social science. As one journalist put it at the time, Sumner "holds that men must do with social laws what they do with physical laws—learn them, obey them, and conform to them. Hence he is opposed to state interference and socialism, and he advocates individualism and liberty."[31] But those ideas, like Sumner himself, were hardly inspiring to the masses. As the journalist delicately added, the dour Sumner had acquired a "reputation for coldness and lack of what may be called 'humanitarianism.'"[32] Even if Sumner was correct that society was governed by Darwinian law, he was not the best salesman for the concept. His politics were all Malthusian alarm and apocalyptic survivalism. In his conservative story of America, there was no romance, no joy, no optimism.

But out west still lay an America that many continued to see as the fresh and abundant breast of a new world. By the 1880s, the idea that the west could serve as a kind of social safety valve—a way to release pent-up pressure from latent class conflicts in the east—was a well-established one. To this way of thinking, America had been able to avoid catastrophic class warfare through its ever-expanding western territory, most notably with the Louisiana Purchase in 1803 and the Treaty of Guadalupe Hidalgo in 1848. If eastern employment conditions grew intolerable, then instead of turning to the dynamite, a laborer could simply light out for the territories.

The west had long been seen as a way of starting over and escaping the claims of history. De Tocqueville sensed as much earlier in the century, writing that in "in the West one can observe democracy reaching its furthest limit. In those states, improvised in a way by fortune, the inhabitants arrived only yesterday [. . . and] each is ignorant of the past of his closest neighbor."[33] To move west was to unravel the warp and weft of the established America, with an opportunity to weave it anew on an individual's own terms.

Just a few years after the Panic of 1873, newspaperman Horace Greeley was already advising his readers to head west to escape the wreckage. He urged every working person to "go to the West," the "land of promise and of hope."[34] Over the course of the century, the notion that the west was a solution to the nation's economic ills became a near-mythic ideal. The concept was somehow both rational and romantic. If the struggles of eastern capitalism became too much to bear, an enterprising young man could always go west and grow up with the country.

By the end of the century, ideas about Darwinian competition, individualism, social progress, and the American west had begun to intermingle freely. The notion that Darwinism had political implications was widely accepted. As one late-century writer for the *Atlantic Monthly* noted, the "application of this general idea [of evolutionary theory] to political theory is obvious, and has been widely made" since the end of the Civil War.[35]

But what was new was the realization, made only by a few, that such political applications of Darwin represented a new American twist on Burkean conservatism. As that same writer continued, "Burke's entire political philosophy, from beginning to end, is a copious, powerful, and infinitely varied treatment of the doctrine of the survival of the fittest." This—Darwinism—"is the fundamental principle of his conservatism."[36] By the end of the century, Darwin offered a scientific anchor for American conservatism.

By the 1880s, as if spurred by the rise of Henry George and the "ethical economists," right-leaning intellectuals and social scientists were working to make laissez-faire individualism scientific. They believed in a political economy fully supported by the immutable laws of nature. Herbert Spencer's theories of social development, coupled with William Graham Sumner's Lamarckian applications of the "American school" of Darwin, offered a scientific explanation for the philosophy of American individualism that had been explained decades earlier by Emerson and, to a lesser degree, by Jefferson before that. These overlapping ideas boiled down to a set of simple beliefs about the natural laws governing social progress. Those beliefs held that unregulated competition would determine the superlative individuals—the "fittest," to use Spencer's phrase—that would drive American development. And where could such a dynamic unfold in its purest and most natural state? According to a growing chorus of voices, it was in the American west.

Not everyone thought such western Darwinism was a good thing, of course. One English writer had spent a year living on a Colorado ranch near the end of the nineteenth century. Unnerved by the seeming indifference of the western wild, she commented that "advocates of the doctrine of the 'survival of the fittest' should go on a western prairie in snow time to see it carried out with the utmost callousness and rigour."[37] Western Darwinism wasn't romantic at all, she concluded. It was brutal.

Another memoirist who had gone west, hoping to experience the "hurrah of the 'glorious free and boundless West,'" confessed that he had "no desire to repeat the experience. There was too much pure Darwinism in such a country—'natural selection and survival of the fittest.' The man who could not accommodate himself rapidly to poverty and hardships, had to die or emigrate."[38] These writers thought that the ruthless Darwinism of the west was about as far from the virtues of civilization as you could get. Having barely escaped the ravages of sickness and hunger, they had no desire to return.

But for a certain type of eastern man—white, wealthy, educated, bred to be a member of the American elite—such a stark view of the west wasn't terrifying. It was romantic. For them, the west represented a staging ground for a pure and authentic conservatism. This wasn't Burke's conservatism, though. There would be no simple nostalgic longing for the stability of God and king and country.

This was an American conservatism. It hinged on a simple belief that the west offered one last chance to select a natural aristocracy in America. Yet this class would not simply inherit their elite status. Instead, they would be selected for it, proving their leadership through Darwinian contests of merit on the culling fields of the American west. This idea updated Burke's conservatism for a new country and a new age, endowing it with the veneer of scientific accuracy. It held that the land west of the Mississippi would become the

Darwinian lists for discovering Emerson's "great men," Jefferson's "natural aristocracy." This was an idea just in its infancy. But when a young Theodore Roosevelt first ventured west, he could already sense its possibility.

NOTES

1. Qtd. in Blight, 51.
2. See Blight, 222–227.
3. Page *Old South*, 158–159.
4. Page *Old Dominion*, 312, 317
5. Page *Old Dominion*, 334.
6. Page *Old Dominion*, 336.
7. Page *Old Dominion*, 31.
8. See Bloom, 18–58.
9. Page *Old South*, 333.
10. Page *Old South*, 280.
11. Foner, xi.
12. See Middleton, xv–xx.
13. Lynch, 95.
14. Burke, 78, emphasis added.
15. Shaler, 59–60.
16. Hunter, 1069.
17. Qtd. in George Jr., 210.
18. Qtd. in George Jr., 229.
19. "Literature," 6.
20. Wenzer, xxxvi; Young, 97.
21. Cohen, 152–154.
22. Qtd. in Cohen, 158.
23. Cohen, 159.
24. Qtd. in Cohen, 161.
25. Adams "Democracy," 771.
26. Young, 95–107.
27. Qtd. in Young, 98.
28. "Republicans," 4.
29. Ulman, 19.
30. Sanial, 202.
31. "Sketch," 267.
32. "Sketch," 267–268.
33. De Tocqueville, 50.
34. Greeley, 361. See also Smith *Virgin*, 201–210.
35. Claghorn, 91.
36. Claghorn, 92.
37. "Cold," 420.
38. Beadle, 381, 382.

Part III

SELLING A DARWINIAN WEST (1884–1890)

Chapter 12

Equal to All Occasions

A year after Cody's Wild West debuted in Omaha, Roosevelt's new ranch house at Elkhorn was well on its way to completion. He went back and forth between New York and Dakota Territory several times over 1884, fulfilling his duties as an Assemblyman but returning to the west as often as he got the opportunity.

Located about thirty-five miles north of Medora, Elkhorn was a bigger and better cabin than the one he had built at Chimney Butte. Roosevelt had lured two old friends, Bill Sewall and Wilmot Dow, out to the Badlands to help run the ranch and build the cabin.[1] Roosevelt was immediately drawn to Sewall, his sister Corinne recalled, because Sewall was a kind of cowboy intellectual: a "simple, strong man of the woods" yet so "earnest a reader and so natural [a] philosopher" that he had a lasting influence on Roosevelt.[2] Both men were obsessed not just with living in the west, but with thinking seriously about what it meant to do so.

The new ranch house was a grand log cabin with a spacious study and an enormous fireplace where Roosevelt did much of his reading and writing and the ranch hands played chess by the firelight.[3] "I have managed to combine an outdoors life," Roosevelt marveled, "with a literary life also. Three out of four days I spend the morning and evening in the ranche house, where I have a sitting room all to myself, reading and working at various pieces."[4]

It was at Elkhorn, in between hours spent in the saddle and working on the books that would become *Hunting Trips of a Ranchman*, *Ranch Life and the Hunting Trail*, and *The Winning of the West*, that Roosevelt deepened his theory of how Darwin's development hypothesis pertained to the American west. He didn't want to believe that membership in the race of "frontier folk" was hereditary.[5] The Lamarckian in him believed that just as he had made his body, other people could make theirs.

After all, he pointed out, the same frontier that produced Daniel Boone had also produced some violent criminals. And for them, as for Boone, "the influence of heredity was no more plainly perceptible than was the extent of individual variation."[6] In other words, biological inheritance mattered, but not as much as individual determination.

He was coming to the conclusion that the American west was a proving ground for undiluted individualism. To this way of thinking, the individual was unencumbered—as well unadvantaged—by family history, circumstances of birth, social station, or economics. The west simply tested individual capacity. "All qualities," he concluded, "good and bad, are intensified and accentuated in the life of the wilderness."[7]

The logic was simple. If life in the western wilderness selected the fittest men, and if survival in that wilderness was determined by individual will—and not heredity or racial or class privilege—then the American west selected a natural aristocracy. Like the American school of evolutionary scientists, Roosevelt conflated the Lamarckian faith in individually acquired traits with the Darwinian development hypothesis. The west staged a sort of Darwinian contest through Lamarckian means. The west, in short, made aristocracy democratic.

Like many nineteenth-century writers and intellectuals, Roosevelt believed in a monolinear theory of civilizational advancement. He thought all nations and peoples were on various stages on a single, straight-line track progressing from "primitive" savagery to modern "civilization." This was a theory of history that borrowed from Darwin in that it presumed societies were constantly evolving. Yet Darwin's development hypothesis never suggested that species were evolving toward anything in particular. In contrast, the theory of civilizational advancement suggested that history was progressing toward a particular endpoint. Roosevelt, like many nineteenth-century intellectuals, held white American civilization to be that endpoint.

Part of the reason he found the Badlands so appealing was that he saw the region as a kind of experiment station for American history. It was a place to test his theory that individual merit that determined social and national supremacy. He was still in his twenties, newly widowed and alone. As he rode Manitou westward at a hard gallop, it was easy for him to believe only in the limitless potential of the individual.

"The first thing that a western plainsman has to learn is the capacity for self-help," Roosevelt announced a year after his cabin at Elkhorn was finished. Of course, he admitted, that plainsman should remember that "occasions may arise when the help of others will be most grateful."[8] (Such as in the construction of a certain cabin, perhaps.) But a westerner couldn't *count* on that help. A westerner could only really count on himself.

Roosevelt found this sort of self-reliance immensely comforting. It was a type of self-knowledge that seemed to come directly from the ascetic indifference of the land itself. *A western plainsman has to learn the capacity for self-help*, he wrote, as if half to himself. In the west, a man only needs himself. From there, it was easy to extrapolate: *America* needs men who only need themselves.

In the American west, Roosevelt thought, nothing was ever settled. Everything was up for grabs. "During the past century," he wrote at his desk at Elkhorn, "a good deal of sentimental nonsense has been talked about our taking the Indians' land." He admitted that violence was bound to occur whenever "brutal and reckless frontiersmen are brought into contact with a set of treacherous, revengeful, and fiendishly cruel savages."[9] But not only did he think such violence was necessary, he thought Indians never had any real ownership over the land in the first place.

For Roosevelt, rights—including property rights—were not necessarily absolute. They were subject to the laws of natural selection, meaning they existed only if they had been won through battle. Even before white settlers arrived, he explained, land disputes had been determined by war. This was the way of wolves and men alike. When those "brutal and reckless frontiersmen" went west, legal and political power was still determined by the same natural principle of supremacy through violence.

This was a key insight for Roosevelt. It meant that Darwinian natural law trumped human-created civil law. Any political claims based on ancestry or historical precedent did not ultimately matter. To think otherwise was not reasoning at all, merely "sentimental nonsense." What ultimately mattered was the basic Darwinian principle of competition.

Roosevelt thought of this conflict as "savage warfare," in the sense that it was a violent, asymmetrical struggle in which one group battled for existence with what it viewed as a less-evolved, more primitive version of itself.[10] For the forces of white civilization to lose such a war meant not just the loss of blood or treasure. It meant the loss of history itself. Anglo-Americans would roll backward on the track of civilizational advancement, regressing to a more primitive state.

Roosevelt thought that savage war—a "struggle between savagery and the rough front rank of civilization," as he put it—was the oldest and purest form of war. "It is primeval warfare, and it is waged as war was waged in the ages of bronze and iron," he wrote. In such wars, "all the merciful humanity that even war has gained during the last two thousand years is lost."[11]

But even though such retrogressions sounded disturbingly violent, Roosevelt didn't think they should be avoided. In his view, the wars that led to the acquisition of the western states and territories were the noblest, purest types of conflict. They selected the fittest and allowed for the continued march of civilization. "The most ultimately righteous of all wars is a war with savages," he later wrote. "The rude, fierce settler who drives the savage from the land lays all civilized mankind under a debt to him."[12] The dynamic that birthed American civilization, he was saying, was white settlers slaughtering nonwhite indigenes, proving their merits in a so-called righteous war that advanced civilization.[13] It only made sense for those individuals to be recognized as naturally superior rulers.

Roosevelt derived a simple principle of individualism from his years in the west. It said that individual merit could be decided through competition or war, and that merit was the chief determinant of one's place in the natural order. This principle assumed that the west was itself a leveling, democratizing force, and competitions held upon its plains were contests between equals. The outcome of those contests would produce a vertical, hierarchical society—which was inevitable; contests had winners and losers—but the contests themselves were horizontal and democratic, which was good. This was why Roosevelt's solution for virtually any social problem was to reduce it to the level of the individual—simply find out "the individual quality of the individual man," as he often put it—and act as if that individual was not shaped by a social or historical context.[14] For Roosevelt, history was a featherweight burden. Because he had been able to transform himself from a sickly boy into a barrel-chested horseman, he thought that others could as well. That, he thought, was the way it worked in the west. That was the way it worked in nature.

To this way of thinking, past inequities did not necessarily carry over into the present. Unlike England, he seemed to believe, America did not have a class of subjects who had inherited their aristocratic or peasant status. Instead, citizens had to constantly, relentlessly prove their status. As Benjamin Franklin had once put it, in America, people ask not *"what is he? but, what can he do?"*[15] It did not matter if your culture, lands, and family had been decimated by history. In the west, Roosevelt thought, the individual—regardless of race, wealth, nationality, or anything else—was completely free to survive or not survive, to fight or not fight, to thrive or perish. That ruthless freedom was the only thing that mattered. For Roosevelt, that was true equality.

This was a crucial dimension of his conservatism. He did not think that things should be *equitable*, reflecting fair opportunities or accounting for past injustices, so long as those opportunities were *equal*, or open to all. A footrace in which one participant is missing a leg yet given no staggered start or handicapping is terribly inequitable, yet at the same time perfectly equal. Roosevelt was fine with such a race. It was, after all, the way things worked in nature. Even though society might conceivably "pity the man that falls or lags behind in the race," he explained, "we do not on that account crown him with the victor's wreath." Instead, we "insist that the race shall be run on fairer terms than before, because we remove all handicaps."[16] Viewing the world in this way stripped the concept of fairness from the concept of equality, reducing equality to a simple formulation of *having the opportunity to demonstrate superiority*. This had the rigorous writ of natural law. And it seemed to make sense: an injured deer's opportunity to escape a hungry tiger was unquestionably equal to that of its uninjured herd. Nature brooks no petty human want of justice.

In 1884, Roosevelt tried to join a vigilante group organized in secret by the president of the Montana Stockgrowers' Association. The group wanted to round up and execute alleged cattle rustlers. Roosevelt wanted to help.

Granville Stuart, the president of the association, rebuffed him. He felt that Roosevelt was still untrained for frontier conditions. Perhaps more to the point, Roosevelt was from one of the most prominent families in the area. If any news spread of his participation, the raid could easily be spoiled.[17] Deemed yet a tenderfoot, Roosevelt did not get to join the vigilante group that would come to be called the "stranglers."

As he came to identify more strongly with the west, Roosevelt prided himself on a philosophy of unsentimental individualism. On his ranch, it was a "rule that [Indians] shall be treated as fairly as if they were whites," he wrote.[18] This did not mean that he had any special affinity for Indians; he didn't. He simply believed the best way to control people he considered undesirable was, paradoxically, through uncompromising equality.

He upheld this commitment to equality in his response to property crimes, proudly noting that his ranch was as devoted to "putting down horse-stealing from Indians as from whites."[19] He meant using extralegal means of determining guilt, innocence, and punishment. In trying to respond with equal force to any individual he felt wronged him—regardless of civil law or any mitigating historical factors—Roosevelt seemed to believe he was enforcing a timeless natural law that would inch the country toward a more evolved civilization.

A willingness to punish Indians in the same way as whites, he explained, "indicates rather an advanced stage of frontier morality, as theft from the 'redskins' or the 'Government' is usually held to be a very trivial matter compared with the heinous crime of theft from 'citizens.'"[20] For many of his fellow ranchers, the social hierarchy—who was a "citizen" and who was not—influenced their response to various struggles for power or resources. But Roosevelt had stumbled upon a democratic-seeming strategy that inverted this conventional wisdom. Instead of letting the social hierarchy determine the outcome of struggles for power or resources, he wanted to let struggles for power or resources determine the social hierarchy.

Competitive struggle, after all, was the way of nature. Power would flow to power.

By the summer of 1885, a year after he first tried to join a group of vigilantes, it was clear that the west had begun to change him. One reporter who saw him when he stopped in St. Paul in June marveled that "Roosevelt is changed from the New York club man to the thorough Westerner."[21] Roosevelt would have agreed. He told another reporter he enjoyed the ranch more than the city, because "on the frontier you find the noblest of fellows." The reporter pestered Roosevelt about the New York Assembly. "I am out of politics," Roosevelt responded in exasperation. He spoke as if he was rejecting politics absolutely, but he was really just discovering a new way of doing them. It wasn't just that there was "more excitement in the round-up than in politics," as he explained to the reporter. It was that ranch life was "far more respectable."[22]

From Roosevelt's perspective, that respectability was possible because men in the west were largely unconstrained by the norms of civil society. As Roosevelt said elsewhere, a westerner instead relied on "the ability to hold one's own."[23]

A few months after telling the reporter that ranch life was respectable, Roosevelt once again became associated with a presumably respectable group of vigilantes planning to lynch some alleged criminals outside the legal system. He didn't see this as some kind of hypocritical failing. He seemed to think vigilantism *was* respectable, in that it stripped away the trappings of civil society to lay bare the Darwinian struggle of the natural world.

In July 1885, Roosevelt, as chairman of the Little Missouri River Stockmen's Association, sent a posse north of the railroad between the Missouri and the Little Missouri rivers to hunt down alleged cattle and horse thieves.[24] This would become an eighteen-day journey to find and eliminate rustlers. Roosevelt had sent along Bill Sewall as his representative.[25] He was not conflicted about the decision. The rustlers "belonged to a class that always holds sway during the raw youth of a frontier community," he explained, adding that "putting down" such elements was "the first step towards decent government."[26] Vigilantism, he thought, was one of the normal stages in the progression from savagery to civilization.

Sewall, though not as ardent a defender of the practice as Roosevelt, likewise thought that vigilantism was basically a good idea. It imposed order on a range undivided by fences, a landscape that could easily slide into anarchy. "I don't like so free a country," he said. "Whare [sic] one man has as good a right as another nobody really has any right."[27] If everybody's claims were equal, he was saying, then the right to own property was equivalent to the right to steal it. What was needed, he seemed to suggest, was the opposite of such a country. What was needed was a country where some rights, and some people, had been proven to be simply better than others.

Sewall and the rest of the seven-man party on that particular trip did not end up catching any rustlers, let alone killing any. But the presence of the vigilantes was well known in the Badlands and was thought by some to exert a stabilizing influence on the region.[28] Roosevelt explained that the "vigilantes—locally known as 'stranglers,' in happy allusion to their summary method of doing justice—had made a clean sweep of the cattle country."[29] In his view, civil law would replace mob law only when the society had arrived at a certain waystation on its track toward civilization. Vigilantism was actually hastening the evolution of society.

Roosevelt knew that extrajudicial executions were legally questionable, at best. But he seemed to think that going west was like going back in time, to an earlier stop on the track toward modernity, and at such a station, vigilantism was necessary. Bill Sewall had said something similar about hunting for the rustlers the previous August, observing that most of his party seemed to think "they have gone back about 200 years."[30] The whole enterprise seemed, in a word, primitive.

Though Sewall didn't find the region nearly as agreeable as Roosevelt, he shared Roosevelt's view of the west's role in America's historical development. Both thought that going west meant a deliberative retrogression to an earlier point in America's development. And although Sewall was not fully convinced of the virtues of that retrogression, Roosevelt embraced it wholeheartedly. He thought that there was some idea of America that could be recovered by returning to an earlier age. This was the most durable of Roosevelt's conservative western dreams: the idea that going westward meant going backward. The west represented a chance to do it over. A chance, perhaps, to get it *right* this time.

That said, Roosevelt knew that the "stranglers" had occasionally, and maybe even frequently, executed the wrong men. At least "several of the sixty odd victims had been perfectly innocent men," he admitted.[31] He did not say how he knew that only "several" were innocent—and not dozens or half or even all of them—but he also knew that executing the innocent was the bargain of vigilantism. Without a society that agreed on the legitimacy of courts of law, guilt or innocence had to be decided by a class of property-owning men who appointed themselves lawkeepers, judges, and executioners. Men who own property have always made the rules about property ownership. Unencumbered by the civic legitimacy of the courts or elective office, one class of men with power and property had declared that another class of men without power and property were criminals. It was like a new feudalism.

Whether the vigilantes were correct in their judgments or not, the whole enterprise made for undemocratic politics. But Roosevelt did not see another way of helping society evolve. On balance, he concluded of the vigilantes, the "outcome of their efforts had been in the main wholesome."[32] Frontier justice seemed to require a frontier aristocracy.

One of the key political lessons Roosevelt seemed to glean from the vigilantes was that justice in the west was always subordinate to power. It almost didn't matter whether the vigilantes executed the specific people who had stolen the livestock, or even whether anyone had actually stolen any livestock at all. What mattered was that they kill *someone*.

Order, he felt, was the first requisite of a free society. A powerful group of men identifies a behavior it dislikes, tells itself such a behavior cannot be tolerated, and then punishes the behavior ruthlessly. Out of the primordial muck of such seemingly arbitrary violence, law and stability emerge.

"In any country where the power of the law is little felt or heeded, and where every one has to rely upon himself for protection," Roosevelt explained, men feel that to "submit tamely and meekly to theft, or to any other injury, is to invite almost certain repetition of the offense, in a place where self-reliant hardihood and the ability to hold one's own under all circumstances rank as the first of virtues."[33]

Despite the obvious class tensions the stranglers represented, Roosevelt thought the vigilantes were ultimately protecting individual rights. Society required order. Yet such order only had real legitimacy, he seemed to think, if its foundations were built upon a philosophy of "self-reliant hardihood" and "the ability to hold one's own."

In March 1886, about six months after Roosevelt sent Sewall after the cattle rustlers, the snow and ice began to melt upstream from Roosevelt's ranch, swelling the river. On the far side of the river, where Roosevelt and his cowboys kept their horses, was a range wedged between the river and some rocky ground. Roosevelt, Sewall, and Dow used a boat to ferry themselves across the river to the horses.

Every day, they would untie the boat from a tree, slide or carry it across the closest ice bank, lower it carefully into the rushing current, and then pole it across to the bank on the far side. One morning, one of the ranch hands returned to Elkhorn in shock. The boat was gone. He was carrying a length of rope from where it had been cut free, and a red mitten that had been dropped on the ice. The men were furious. Only one day earlier, a pair of mountain lions had eaten four deer carcasses the men had killed and hung to freeze in a thicket of cedars. Annoyed at the loss of the meat, and doubly irritated that they had lost the trail of the guilty mountain lions in an overgrown gorge, the theft of the boat was too much. It simply could not stand.

Roosevelt had little doubt who had stolen the boat. He immediately suspected three hard-looking men who lived in a shack twenty miles upriver. They had already been threatened by other ranch owners and were probably trying to escape the area, he observed, "as certain of the cattle-men had begun openly to threaten to lynch them."[34]

Roosevelt was forced to admit, though, that he didn't know if the trio had actually done anything or not. As he explained it, they had "long been accused—justly or unjustly—of being implicated both in cattle-killing and in that worst of frontier crimes, horse-stealing: it was only by an accident that they had escaped the clutches of the vigilantes the preceding fall."[35] But their presumed culpability as one class of criminals—horse and cattle thieves—had forced them into actual culpability as a different class of criminals: boat thieves.

This presented something of a philosophical problem. Whether the men had actually stolen any livestock or not, Roosevelt seemed to realize, their status as criminals had already been determined. If they had not stolen any livestock, and the cattlemen been declared criminals erroneously, then the absence of an impartial legal system that could exonerate them had all but forced them to become actual criminals by stealing a boat to escape the ranchers who seemed bent on their deaths. And if they *had* stolen the livestock, and the cattlemen were correct to declare them criminals, then their second crime of boat theft simply served as additional evidence of their primary crime of livestock theft.

In other words, it didn't actually matter whether they were "justly or unjustly" accused. They would inevitably be treated as if they were guilty. Once again, it was clear that the west, which seemed to be a land without laws, was in fact governed by a new type of aristocracy. Once a member of the property-owning elite identified someone as a criminal, that person's fate was sealed.

The leader of the trio was a stocky man named Finnegan. Roosevelt could identify his "wolfish" eyes and wild, long red hair that stuck out from under his broad-brimmed hat.[36] Like Roosevelt, Finnegan always wore a fringed buckskin shirt. Later, Roosevelt made a point of noting the men's ethnic backgrounds. Finnegan's Irish ancestry was obvious; the second man was a muscular "half-breed," and the last was an "old German."[37] In more ways than one, he seemed to believe, they were men with whom the ranchers could have neither security nor society.

The swollen river made it impossible to follow them on horseback, and the trio had taken both their own rickety scow as well as Roosevelt's. There was no other boat on the river. They must have been confident that Roosevelt would not pursue them.

They were wrong. Roosevelt, Sewall, and Dow set to work building a flat-bottomed scow to follow them.[38] According to the unwritten code of the land, they could not simply submit to the offense. Men like Dow, Sewall, and Roosevelt were, at least in Roosevelt's opinion, "tough, hardy, resolute fellows, quick as cats, strong as bears."³⁹ They were not prey. They were hunters.

Roosevelt and his men dressed as warm as they could, in heavy jackets and trousers topped with enormous fur coats. They armed themselves with rifles and a shotgun, packed enough flour, coffee, and bacon to last at least two weeks, and set off. After several days traveling down the river, breaking for camp each night, they came across the German man, unarmed, and surprised him. The other two were out hunting.

Roosevelt, Sewall, and Dow hid behind a bank near the camp and waited for the men to return. When the thieves were within about twenty yards of the camp, Roosevelt and his men rose, rifles cocked, and shouted for them to hold up their hands. The knees of the "half-breed," Roosevelt noted with satisfaction, were trembling with fear.⁴⁰ He surrendered immediately.

But Finnegan hesitated. Roosevelt advanced until he was within a few paces of him, keeping his rifle leveled at his chest the whole time. He repeated the order to raise his hands. For a few tense seconds, no one said a thing. Then, with a curse, Finnegan dropped his rifle and surrendered.

Having caught the thieves, Roosevelt and his men now had to figure out what to do with them. His fellow ranchers would have expected him to hang them. As Roosevelt well knew, vigilantism was the informal law of the land.

But Roosevelt didn't hang them. Instead, Sewall and Dow confiscated their weapons and the party set up camp for the night. The prisoners bedded down on one side of the fire, Sewall and Dow on the other. In the morning they would figure out how to get all six of them back upriver. But at least Roosevelt had his boat back. More important, he had not submitted meekly to the loss of his property.

At sunrise they made a plan to travel downstream before doubling back to Elkhorn. But they soon realized they were effectively trapped by masses of drifting ice, making their pace excruciatingly slow. Roosevelt kept a nervous eye on their dwindling food supplies. After several days, they were reduced to eating unleavened bread made with river water. Roosevelt's unwillingness to hang the thieves was beginning to seem an unsustainable luxury.

They at last worked their way about thirty miles downstream, where they came upon several ranches. The ranch hands would be certain to help them, Roosevelt reasoned, because of the same class interests that had led to the creation of the stranglers the year before. It was "a stock country," he explained, seemingly meaning both *a land filled with stock* as well as *a nation governed by stockmen*. And in such a country, "all make common cause against either horse-thieves or cattle-thieves."⁴¹ A rancher near Killdeer Mountain who lent him a wagon was utterly baffled, as Roosevelt recalled, as to "why I took so much bother with the thieves instead of hanging them off-hand."⁴²

On the morning of April 12, 1886, they finally reached Dickinson. Exhausted, Roosevelt handed the men over to the sheriff.[43] (The territorial judge the men would eventually face was an eastern transplant with the improbably resplendent name of Western Starr.[44]) Roosevelt had not slept in close to thirty-six hours, but still took a moment to write a letter to his sister and tell her he "took the prisoners [sic] on to here overland," admitting he had been "pretty well done out with the work, the lack of sleep and the strain of the constant watchfulness."[45] On balance, the experience had been exhilarating.

Roosevelt had brought Tolstoy's *Anna Karenina* along on the trip. (Finnegan and the other men had brought their own books, a stack of dime novels detailing the exploits of outlaw Jesse James.[46]) Roosevelt admired what he saw as Tolstoy's moral neutrality. He "simply narrated," Roosevelt explained, "putting the facts before us that we ourselves might judge them."[47] The individual reader became the magistrate.

Trudging through the muck to deliver Finnegan and his conspirators to the sheriff, Roosevelt appreciated how *Anna Karenina* seemed to have little use for a law that transcended individual judgment. One of the novel's protagonists, the nobleman and farmer Konstantin Levin, at one point endorses just such a principle of individualism: "there can be no durable activity if it is not founded in individual interest: this is a general, a philosophical truth."[48] Roosevelt began to see the hunt for the thieves as an act of such individual interest, an adventure in Emersonian self-reliance.

If nothing else, Roosevelt, who had claimed for himself the natural right to hang or not hang the thieves, would have appreciated *Anna Karenina*'s epigraph from Deuteronomy: "Vengeance is mine, I will repay."[49]

Almost from the moment he first discovered the theft, Roosevelt began viewing it in grand, mythic terms. He rarely identified the men by the crime they actually committed against him, a boat theft. Instead, he emphasized their alleged history of livestock theft, crimes he admitted he couldn't substantiate.

"I got the three horsethieves in fine style," he wrote a few days after returning to Medora.[50] A month later, he was still referring to the incident as the "horsethief hunt."[51] In his mind, he wasn't only punishing an offense that he could substantiate with evidence—a boat theft—but also punishing a class of persons that symbolized something undesirable: horse thieves. Like everything else in the west, the incident quickly became about establishing a hierarchy: lawmakers above lawbreakers, owners above takers. He was already beginning to spin the story into something romantic. When his account of the incident appeared in *Century* magazine two years later, Remington did the illustrations.

As Roosevelt admitted, whether the accusation of livestock theft had been made "justly or unjustly" was immaterial. The Irish Finnegan, the "vicious" German, and the muscular "half-breed" had all been prejudged by the ranch owners to have committed those crimes.[52] So when the boat theft provided a pretext for their capture, Roosevelt leaped at the opportunity. He wasn't just after men who had stolen his boat. He was after men who had been marked as horse thieves.

Tracking and capturing the men established his place above them in the natural order. Just after remanding the men to the sheriff, he jotted a quick letter to his sister Corinne to capture his thinking on the matter. He told her he was "as brown and as tough as a pine knot and [now] feel equal to anything."[53]

Roosevelt was employing a centuries-old use of the word "equal" to mean *adequately strong*, as in "equal to the occasion." But the context in which he was using the word—seeking to punish citizens for crimes for which they had not been tried—illuminated an important part of his beliefs about the west. *Equal*, of course, can mean both *adequately strong* as well as *having the same rights or privileges*. Roosevelt's blasé summary of the previous year's hangings as being "in the main wholesome" was not the words of someone who thought Finnegan and the other alleged thieves had the same rights as he did. Based on his knowledge of Darwin as well as his observations of the American west, Roosevelt seemed to have concluded that proof of natural supremacy was proof of ontological superiority: that might makes right.

In capturing Finnegan's gang, Roosevelt had arrived at a paradox. He said he felt equal to anything, but that sense of equality came by demonstrating that Finnegan and the others were *not* his equals. He had felt the rush of absolute freedom when he held three men's lives in his hands. And it was only then, at the moment when he had most clearly proven his superiority, did he at last announce he felt equal to all things.

NOTES

1. Morris, 277.
2. Robinson *Brother*, 111.
3. Hagedorn, 240; Roosevelt *Hunting*, 11–12; Vollweiler, 39.
4. TR letter to Corinne Roosevelt Robinson, 12 May 1886.
5. Roosevelt *Winning Volume I*, 101.
6. Roosevelt *Winning I*, 130.
7. Roosevelt *Winning I*, 131.
8. Roosevelt *Hunting*, 42.
9. Roosevelt *Hunting*, 18.
10. Roosevelt *Winning II*, 239.

11. Roosevelt *Winning III*, 46.
12. Roosevelt *Winning III*, 46.
13. For an overview of Roosevelt's complicated attitudes toward race in general and Indians in specific, see Dyer, 1–20, 69–88.
14. Roosevelt "Message" [1905], 629.
15. Franklin, 606.
16. Roosevelt "Degeneration," 108.
17. Hagedorn, 144–147.
18. Roosevelt "Sheriff's," 39.
19. Roosevelt "Sheriff's," 39.
20. Roosevelt "Sheriff's," 39.
21. Qtd. in Hagedorn, 308.
22. Qtd. in Hagedorn, 309.
23. Roosevelt "Sheriff's," 44.
24. Hagedorn, 323–324.
25. Di Silvestro, 315–316.
26. Roosevelt "Sheriff's," 42.
27. Qtd. in Hagedorn, 307.
28. Hagedorn, 323.
29. Roosevelt "Sheriff's," 43.
30. Qtd. in di Silvestro, 183.
31. Roosevelt "Sheriff's," 43.
32. Roosevelt "Sheriff's," 43.
33. Roosevelt "Sheriff's," 44.
34. Roosevelt "Sheriff's," 42.
35. Roosevelt "Sheriff's," 43.
36. Roosevelt "Sheriff's," 46.
37. Roosevelt "Sheriff's," 43. See also Hagedorn, 365–386.
38. TR letter to Henry Cabot Lodge, 16 April 1886.
39. Roosevelt "Sheriff's," 44.
40. Roosevelt "Sheriff's," 46.
41. Roosevelt "Sheriff's," 50.
42. Roosevelt "Sheriff's," 51.
43. TR letter to Corinne Roosevelt Robinson, 12 April 1886.
44. Hagedorn, 385; Lawson, 427.
45. TR letter to Corinne Roosevelt Robinson, 12 April 1886.
46. Roosevelt "Sheriff's," 50.
47. TR letter to Anna Roosevelt, 19 June 1886.
48. Tolstoï [II], 14.
49. Tolstoï [I], 1.
50. TR letter to Henry Cabot Lodge, 16 April 1886.
51. TR letter to Henry Cabot Lodge, 20 May 1886.
52. Roosevelt "Sheriff's," 43.
53. TR letter to Corinne Roosevelt Robinson, 12 April 1886.

Chapter 13

Cody and the Queen

By the mid-1880s, Cody had fully transformed into the character of Buffalo Bill. He cut a dashing figure. He was around six feet tall, and his 170 pounds of lean muscle were carefully concealed by his fringed buckskin shirt and trousers tucked into knee-high leather boots.[1] His curly hair hung around his shoulders, and his long, thick mustache curved upward above his goatee, making him look perpetually amused. In the language of the show's promotional materials, an iconic portrait of Cody emerged: a man who had harnessed the values of the American past.

As the show's 1887 program announced, he was "the representative man of the frontiersmen of the past."[2] But what made him such a unique character was that the past hadn't rendered him unsuited to modern life. On the contrary; his mastery of what the show called "primitive existence" was exactly what made him an exceptional leader and businessman. Exposure to that primitive life, the program concluded, had revealed his innate superiority as a "natural gentleman."[3]

But he was a new sort of gentleman. Not the idle aristocracy of England, but the superior man of America's naturally selected elite. He had not inherited a kingdom; he had scouted his own. In a phrase the show used more than once to describe him, he had established himself as a "knight of the plains."[4]

The show shilled his individualism relentlessly, emphasizing that his self-creation made him naturally superior. That he was "full of self-reliance" made him "a leader among the manly pioneer battle between civilization and savagery."[5] Perhaps most importantly, those qualities had been validated by the modern marketplace. He made sure that audiences knew he owned a large cattle ranch in Nebraska.[6] In other words, audiences knew that Cody was a leader in the "manly pioneer battle" for civilization largely because he was a landowner and a cattle king. This depiction was the lynchpin of the show's conservative vision of the American west. Westerners like Cody were like explorers of a faraway land from long ago, hardened by experiences that had established them as natural leaders of men.

Despite his well-publicized history as a killer of Indians, Cody was by most accounts a good employer of them. He made a point of treating his Indian performers well. In interviews he tended to say that Indians were "kind and truehearted people," calling for them to be "properly treated by whites."[7] But this attitude was rarely reflected in the show itself, which overwhelmingly cast Indians as savage aggressors and whites as brave defenders of civilization.

By the mid-1880s, the show featured as many as a hundred Indian performers. It regularly included a reenactment of Cody's killing of Yellow Hair, what the show's announcer called "the first scalp taken in revenge of Custer's fate."[8]

The act began with white actors (playing cavalrymen) and the Indian actors (playing Indians) galloping toward each other. The actor playing Yellow Hair would shout a challenge to Cody. *I know you, Pa-he-haska; if you want to fight, come ahead and fight me.* Cody would respond in kind, and the two men would turn, gallop their horses toward each other, and fight. Much of the audience knew the story already, of course, and understood that the scalp was supposed to avenge Custer's death at the Little Bighorn, when he had been defeated by a confederation of tribes led by Crazy Horse and inspired by the great Hunkpapa Lakota chief Sitting Bull.

So it was a coup for Cody, and provided a pleasing degree of theatrical and historical symmetry, when he was able to hire Sitting Bull for the 1885 season. Sitting Bull's name was almost as well known in the United States as Cody's, and Cody tried to make his appearance into a moment of reconciliation. He and Sitting Bull even shared a pipe together. (In front of reporters, of course.) The program tried to help the show's white audiences understand Sitting Bull's stature in the Lakota nation, identifying him the "Napoleon of the Indian Race." Cody presented his appearances with Sitting Bull as a truce between two old, eminent warriors. Audiences were told that Sitting Bull had joined the show out of a desire to meet the great Buffalo Bill, the cavalryman who had "contributed so largely to his defeat in 1876."[9]

Sitting Bull did not perform in the show, but he did appear in parades and was available to the press. His much-vaunted reconciliation with Cody was all part of the show, though, and he was soon tired of life on the road. The constant badgering from reporters for lurid details from the Battle of the Greasy Grass (what the Lakota called the Battle of the Little Bighorn) seemed to exhaust him.[10] Near the end of the season, he announced he was done with the show. Cody gave him two parting gifts: a white hat like Cody's, as if to symbolize that they were now both on the same side, and one of the trained ponies from the show: a tall white-gray horse with a beautiful bridle and saddle.[11]

The next season, Cody was eager to get Sitting Bull to return, but was met with resistance from Indian agent John McLaughlin, who thought Sitting Bull was a dangerous revolutionary. Unlike the other performers, Sitting Bull did not appear in the actual show; he was more of a ceremonial figure. But this was exactly the point. Cody always insisted that the show was reality itself and not a show at all. Having Sitting Bull associated with the Wild West show lent it legitimacy as an institution of American history.

Regardless of its accuracy, the show did offer a particular narrative of American history. It papered over the violence of the Indian wars, turning death into spectacle. Thanks to Cody's show, the shocking violence of a man's scalp being cut from his skull had been turned into an applause prompt. Sitting Bull's presence lent credence to that version of the past.

Yet the Indian wars were still ongoing. Various battles between Indian tribes and the U.S. government would continue, in different places and with different tribes, throughout the show's over thirty-year run. But Cody's show, and especially Sitting Bull's association with that show, made the violent conflicts of the west seem like ancient history.

This illusion—that history was, well, history—was part of Cody's theatrical genius. Even in the show's earliest days, Cody had emphasized the show's nostalgic value. One early program had referred to bison as the "fast-disappearing monarch of the plains," and described the "scarred and weather-beaten" stagecoach used in the Deadwood robbery act as an "old relic."[12] Like the rest of the show, the coach was described as something that was a romantic part of the past, not the modern world. In Cody's show, history wasn't something that was still *with* America, actively creating the present. It was something that was over and done with, useful only when men like Cody wanted it to be.

To his way of thinking, in the American west history was always beginning anew. Cody was simply dramatizing the most recently completed iteration of that history. Sitting Bull's presence made it clear that that phrase of history was over, exactly as white American audiences wanted it to be. Despite its promise to faithfully recreate the past, Cody's Wild West enacted nothing so much as a theater of modernity, one in which the past didn't really matter at all. All battles were theatrical recreations of conflicts that had long since been forgotten. Now, everyone was wearing a white hat. Everyone was on the same side.

At the end of 1886, Cody brought the show to New York's Madison Square Garden. It was an enormous triumph. Almost 19,800 people saw the show in two performances on Thanksgiving Day alone.[13] By 1887, the show was officially a worldwide success. Mark Twain reportedly saw the show twice in a row, and was moved to tell Cody that the show reminded him of his first trip to the far west in 1861, when he had accompanied his brother Orion to Nevada Territory. Cody's show was "free from sham and insincerity," Twain wrote, and "the effects produced upon me by its spectacles were identical with those wrought upon me along [sic] time ago by the same spectacles on the frontier." He pronounced it a "distinctively American" phenomenon.[14]

It was a phenomenon the Queen of England was keen to see. Cody was invited to bring the show to England to take part in Queen Victoria's Golden Jubilee, celebrating her fiftieth year of reign. At the end of March, he packed up the show—200 performers and 250 animals including burros, elk, deer, and 35 bison—and boarded the *State of Nebraska* for what would ultimately become a six-year tour. Between 1887 and 1893, "America's National Entertainment" became a worldwide phenomenon, traveling to England, France, Spain, Italy, Australia, Germany, and Holland.[15]

England embraced Cody's romantic vision of the west. London's bookshops featured the works of the long-dead James Fenimore Cooper, who had made famous the sort of buckskin shirt Cody wore. Novels featuring his frontier hero Natty Bumppo suddenly began to sell thousands of copies, despite being over sixty years old.[16]

In the early summer of 1887, Cody and Salsbury brought the Wild West to Queen Victoria in a private command performance for the prince and princesses of Battenberg, the Marquis of Lorne, the Queen, and others. By custom, such performances were typically done at the palace; however, Cody proudly noted, "the Wild West was altogether too colossal to take to Windsor, and so the Queen came to the Wild West."[17]

Near the start of the show, a horseman galloped around the performance arena carrying an American flag. The announcer emphasized the show's American nature while downplaying any overt nationalism for the foreign audience, describing the flag as "an emblem of peace and friendship to all the world."[18] But Cody watched in amazement, he later wrote, as the Queen slowly rose and bowed in the direction of the flag. The rest of the court party then rose, too, and the women bowed, the noblemen removed their hats, and the generals saluted.[19]

Cody's troupe roared its approval. For Cody, the moment was heavy with significance, and spoke to the potent symbolic power of the American west. His romantic vision of the west was, he realized, a type of political currency. It had purchased America a new standing on the world stage. Here, he thought, "was an outward and visible sign of the extinction of that mutual prejudice" that had long been felt between the two nations. "We felt that the hatchet was buried at last and the Wild West had been at the funeral," he recalled.[20] To master the story of American western history was to master no small amount of political and cultural power.

NOTES

1. Russell, 478.
2. Buffalo [1887 Program], 5, 6.
3. Buffalo [1887 Program], 5, 6.
4. Buffalo [1887 Program], 9, 44.
5. Buffalo [1887 Program], 6, 9.
6. For more on Cody's ranching interests in the west, see Bonner, 3–126.
7. Qtd. in Reddin, 74.
8. Qtd. in Reddin, 76.
9. Qtd. in Reddin, 79.
10. Reddin, 80.
11. Lemons, 70.
12. Qtd. in Kasson, 7.
13. Reddin, 84.
14. Qtd. in Buffalo [1887 Program], 48.
15. Reddin, 90–91.
16. Cody *Story*, 730.
17. Cody *Story*, 734.
18. Cody *Story*, 735.
19. Cody *Story*, 735.
20. Cody *Story*, 737.

Chapter 14

The Cowboy of Dakota

One year earlier, around the time that Cody was performing his sold-out shows at Madison Square Garden, Roosevelt was completing his book on Thomas A. Benton and beginning to look for a new challenge. Earlier that year, an army captain had been killed while pursuing Geronimo in Mexico, just south of Arizona Territory. Tensions between the United States and Mexico had run high for a few months, and Roosevelt, seemingly energized by his vigilantism with the boat thieves and long since transformed from an asthmatic New Yorker into a deadshot westerner, thrilled at the possibility of putting his body to the test.

He wrote to Secretary of War William Endicott offering to raise a few companies of cowboy rifleman in the event of a war with Mexico. Concerned that his isolation in the west was causing him to miss important developments, he instructed Henry Cabot Lodge to telegraph him at once if war seemed imminent.

He was starting to fret about where, exactly, his cowboy life was taking him. Worrying that his "chance of doing anything in the future worth doing seems to grow continually smaller," he vowed "to grasp at every opportunity that turns up," including war. "I think there is some good fighting stuff among these harum-scarum roughriders out here," he wrote to Lodge, adding that "whether I can bring it out [of them] is another matter."[1] Those rough riders just needed someone to lead them. Someone had to harness the beliefs and practices of the westerner, he mused, and show those on the East Coast those beliefs could be put to use. He was beginning to agree with Cody: it wasn't just that western lands had value. Western ideas did, too.

But his cowboy company, which he had seemed to envision as a sort of international crew of wide-brimmed vigilantes, panned out. And a few months later, when the Republican Party bosses visited him to talk about running in the New York mayoral race, he was willing to listen. By early fall, he had returned to New York and was busily preparing for the 1886 mayoral campaign, where the thirty-one-year-old ran as "the cowboy of Dakota."[2]

He lost the mayoralty, badly. New York Democratic politics were still run out of Tammany Hall, led by Richard Croker ever since William Kelley wrested control from William "Boss" Tweed in the early 1870s. Backed by the Democratic political machine, Abram Hewitt beat out the Independent candidate, Henry George. Roosevelt came in third.

George, the upstart left-leaning economist, had been making the Republican and Democratic bosses nervous. The runaway success of his book *Progress and Poverty* marked him as a fierce critic of economic inequality. Even though Roosevelt was nervously telling friends in mid-October that the "George vote will be very large," he was still annoyed that he had to defend himself against what he saw as George's bizarre ideas.[3]

One of George's prominent supporters had declared that Roosevelt and Hewitt were both members of the "landlord class, whose interests are best served when wages are low and rents are high."[4] Roosevelt tried out his theory of western individualism in his rebuttal. At Elkhorn ranch, he declared, economic woes "can only be gotten over through that capacity for steady, individual self-help which is the glory of every true American." This was not merely his opinion, Roosevelt stressed; it was a law of nature. You could no more fix economic problems through legislation than you could "by passing an act to repeal the laws of gravitation."[5] George's noisy leftism did not just go against common sense, Roosevelt groused. It went against nature itself.

After losing the election, Roosevelt went off to Europe for three months to nurse his wounds. In December he suddenly remarried in London, wedding his childhood friend, Edith Kermit Carow. He had kept the engagement a secret from even his closest friends.[6]

In the spring of 1887, he returned to the west. This time, it would not be for long. Roosevelt had been absent for one of the worst winters that anyone could remember, and the herd had been near-decimated. Between November and February, blizzard after blizzard had pounded the land. With their thicker coats, the hardier native cattle were able to withstand the cold, but still starved for lack of food. The new stock that had been driven north from Texas simply froze to death.[7]

In March, the snow softened enough for Merrifield to ride out and survey the damage. "I got a saddle horse and rode over the country," he recalled, "and I'm telling you, the first day I rode out I never saw a live animal."[8]

When Roosevelt arrived in April, he felt sick. The previous summer, he had optimistically calculated that he would be able to sell between 200 and 300 head of steer and dry stock that year, and would garner a good return on his initial investment.⁹ No longer. Now, he just wanted to figure out exactly how much he had lost. He dashed off a series of letters trying to describe the devastation. The losses were "even worse than I feared," he wrote his sister Anna.¹⁰ "Everything was cropped as bare as a bone," he told Sewall. "The sagebrush was just fed out by the starving cattle. The snow lay so deep that nobody could get around; it was almost impossible to get a horse a mile. In almost every coulee there were dead cattle."¹¹ A few days later, he wrote Henry Cabot Lodge that there had been a "perfect smashup all through the cattle country of the northwest," and the "losses are crippling."¹² He found himself hoping he would lose only half of the $80,000 he had invested up to that point. That was the best-case scenario. Worst-case, he had lost everything. He was, he wrote his sister Anna grimly, now "planning how to get out of it."¹³

Whether due to the monetary losses or to the fact that Edith was pregnant and due in September, Roosevelt was unhappy in the west. "For the first time I have been utterly unable to enjoy a visit to my ranch," he wrote, sounding surprised. It didn't even feel like home anymore. "I shall be glad to get home" to New York, he confessed.¹⁴

As he often did, he extrapolated from his own experience to the entire nation. When biography becomes history, life becomes mythic. In his mind, it was not just that he had left the west inconsequentially, the way one might leave a hotel. It was that the west itself had changed. Its glory days, he told himself, were quickly passing away.

For the first time in a long while, he seemed confused about western identity and self-reliance in America. After the destructive winter, he mused the following year, most ranchers had lost money. This was not surprising. "This is especially true," he wrote, "of the numerous Easterners who went into the business without any experience and trusted themselves entirely to their Western representatives." He paused, as if remembering that *he* was once again an easterner, and then changed course: "although, on the other hand, many of those who have made most money at it are Easterners, who, however, have happened to be naturally fitted to the work."¹⁵ The spiritual energy and economic potential of the west, he seemed to decide, had been best harnessed by easterners who went west and then went back east, reborn by the new skills they had acquired and the new codes by which they had learned to live. That is, by men exactly like him.

But the real point he was trying to make was that the west, not just as a space but as an *idea*, was quickly fading into history. "The best days of ranching are over," he concluded with finality.¹⁶ The west was becoming a site for nostalgia: not just a place of rocks and scrub grass and cattle, but a place of memory. It was now a place to ponder America's past in order to figure out its future.

By the late nineteenth century in America, the word "nostalgia" was just beginning to acquire its modern definition of a general and sentimental longing for the past. Prior to this shift in meaning, it referred specifically to a sickness for a particular homeland. The word comes from the Greek words *nostos*, meaning a homeward journey—a word the ancient Greeks used to refer to the return home after the Trojan War—and *algia*, or pain. But *nostalgia* is not a term from antiquity. Its earliest English use dates only from the mid-eighteenth century.

Nostalgia, to put it slightly differently, was invented about the same time that progress was invented. Prior to the industrial revolution—and its accompanying assumption that technological change, civilizational progress, and the passage of time all flow together in a single unwavering direction—for most people, circumstances did not change that much from year to year. Before the late 1700s, for example, it took nearly 300 years for the daily wage of a European worker to double.[17] Generations tended to stay in a single place, doing a single type of work. There was comparatively little visible change over time. Later generations would eventually call such societies *primitive*. But after the twin engines of industrial revolution and liberal democracy accelerated the fan blades of modern capitalism and civilization, many people began to feel a type of motion sickness brought on by the whirl of modernity. This longing for a simpler time became conflated with a longing for a simpler place, and so the word "nostalgia" was born.

For Americans, the idea of nostalgia was an odd one. In the early days of the republic, there was hardly a long-missed homeland for anyone to long for. In 1830, Noah Webster's third edition of the *American Dictionary* didn't include a listing for *nostalgia* at all, even though the word had already been in use in England for nearly eighty years. But then came the dramatic transformations of the middle of the century, when the end of the Mexican-American War produced the modern American west in 1848 and then the Civil War nearly tore the country apart thirteen years later. The onslaught of rapid change and the accompanying suspicion that things used to be simpler, if not better, suddenly proved attractive. By the middle of the century, Webster had added a definition for the word: "a species of melancholy, resulting from absence from one's home or country."[18]

After spending three years in the west, Roosevelt found himself trying to articulate a new type of nostalgia, one that fused its original definition—a longing for a place—with an attitude toward history: a longing for a place in the *past*. For him the "species of melancholy" Webster described came from a fear that the best and freshest days were quickly receding into history. Yet even if those days were lost forever, individuals and nations could still recover their spirit by a pilgrimage to the western frontiers of America, the original fount of that nostalgia.[19]

Two years after the publication of *Hunting Trips of a Ranchman*, Roosevelt was working on a follow-up, to be called *Ranch Life and the Hunting Trail*, and trying to explain his conservative attitude toward history. His was a new conservatism, divorced from the old Burkean certainties. He did not want to conserve the past in the sense of repeating it. For his entire life, he believed in the forward progression of history. But he also thought that civilizational progress worked best if it was driven by certain foundational values and beliefs. Certain values, he seemed to think, existed in their purest form in the mythic history of the American west: things like self-reliance, the unshakable freedom of the individual, the idea of a society of men governed by the best and strongest. In his mind, these values were not just old. They were *true*. But Roosevelt, like many Americans, also believed that time and space were interwoven. To move spatially—to go west—was to move temporally: to go, in a sense, back in time. This was why words like "primitive," words that conjured chronological associations, leaped to his mind so readily when he was in the west.

He once mentioned to his sister Corinne that the west, with its "loneliness and freedom," spoke to something deep inside him. "I am greatly attached to the Ranch and the life out here," he wrote. "It is in many ways ideal; we are so very rarely able to, actually and in real life, dwell in our 'hero land.'"[20] He did not mean that the west was ideal only in the sense of being superlative. He was suggesting that it was literally an *idea*, a romantic "hero land" that would otherwise exist only in the realm of storybooks and dreams.

Roosevelt was not the first to conflate longitudinal change with temporal and mental change. But he was one of the first to suggest that primitive values, if briefly assumed in the west by eastern men like himself, could, once transported back east, become a civilizational accelerant. His conservatism was wedded to a belief in the give-and-take between west and east, between the time-tested values of the past and the requirements of modernity. In other words, old things from the west could drive new things in the east.

As his friend and future secretary of state John Hay said a few years later, Roosevelt's trajectory began in the "cloistered life of American college boys, sheltered from the ruder currents of the world by the ramparts of wealth and gentle nurture," but "he passed, still very young, to the wild and free existence of the plains and the hills. In the silence of those vast solitudes men grow to full stature, when the original stuff is good. He came back to the east, bringing with him, as Tennyson sang, 'the wrestling thews that throw the world,'" and he "has gone rapidly forward and upward."[21] He had, as he promised his father decades earlier, finally "made his body," far out in the prairies and looming skies of western America.

Roosevelt worried that America's frontier days were fading fast. He was a young man who had already lost most of his loved ones. The fact that all living things wither and die was never far from his mind. It was a natural truth he transmuted into a political truth: Civilization moves forward by briefly looking backward. It does so at the behest of strong men of iron grip, men who can hold fast to the best and oldest things even as time's ratchet tries to wrench them from their grasp. Even in the brief time he had spent in the Badlands, he sensed that what he thought was a true and authentic west, an older west, was rapidly slipping away.

In his view, America, like all civilizations, progressed from primitive to advanced conditions. "Stock-raising, as now carried on, is characteristic of a young and wild land," he explained in *Ranch Life and the Hunting Trail*. "As the country grows older, it will in some places die out, and in others entirely change its character." This transformation was inevitable. "The great free ranches, with their barbarous, picturesque, and curiously fascinating surroundings, mark a primitive stage of existence as surely as do the great tracts of primeval forests, and like the latter must pass away before the onward march of our people."[22]

As he prepared to leave the west after the blizzards, Roosevelt seemed to console himself with the thought that the west was no longer what it once was. There would no longer be the sort of raw individualism that had once characterized the region. People like himself, he wrote, who had exulted in ranching's "abounding vigor and its bold, restless freedom, will not only regret its passing for own sakes, but also feel real sorrow that those who come after us are not to see, as we have seen, what is perhaps the pleasantest, healthiest, and most exciting phase of American existence."[23]

Years later, this nostalgia for the Badlands only deepened. In his autobiography, he recalled that the region was "still the Wild West in those days, the Far West, the West of Owen Wister's stories and Frederic Remington's drawings." That wilderness had vanished into the ether of memory and myth. "That land of the West has gone now," he continued, "'gone, gone with lost Atlantis,' gone to the isle of ghosts and of strange dead memories."[24] This elegiac note, first struck when his new marriage and the losses from the harsh winter of 1886–1887 had soured him on the Badlands, would hardly waver at all in the years to come.

Yet, despite his melancholy tone, Roosevelt didn't actually believe that the changing Badlands were a symbol of the inevitable decline of American individualism. Read one way, the loss of a "primitive stage of existence" would seem to mean a loss in "bold, restless freedom." But Roosevelt was coming to believe that such primitive experiences could be found again and again, and that they could be used each time to renew American liberty. This was what made his youthful conservatism not just a disposition, but something closer to an applied political philosophy. Returning to a primitive stage, of course, required finding what he saw as a primitive place: somewhere like the

Badlands. But he didn't want to regress to a primitive stage only to stay there. He wanted brave men like himself to return to a primitive stage temporarily, in order to extract useful ideas. Such men would then return to apply those ideas to modern society, ensuring that the civilization would remain, as in one of Roosevelt's favorite phrases, a "progressive civilization": a civilization moving ever forward on the linear track of historical advancement.[25] What was unique about the American imagination, he was coming to suggest, was that it required a regression to primitive conditions in order to enable further advancement into modernity.

NOTES

1. TR letter to Henry Cabot Lodge, 10 August 1886.
2. Ratifying Roosevelt's nomination, Thomas C. Acton urged his fellow Republicans to "[m]ake the cowboy of Dakota next Mayor" [sic] ("Republicans" 4).
3. TR letter to Henry Cabot Lodge, 20 October 1886.
4. Qtd. in Morison [Vol. I], 114.
5. TR letter to Denis Donohue, Junior, 22 October 1886.
6. TR letter to Henry Cabot Lodge, 1 November 1886.
7. Hagedorn, 435.
8. Qtd. in Hagedorn, 438.
9. Robinson *Brother*, 136.
10. TR letter to Anna Roosevelt, 16 April 1887.
11. Qtd. in Hagedorn, 440.
12. TR letter to Henry Cabot Lodge, 20 April 1887.
13. TR letter to Anna Roosevelt, 16 April 1887.
14. TR letter to Henry Cabot Lodge, 20 April 1887.
15. Roosevelt *Ranch*, 24.
16. Roosevelt *Ranch*, 24.
17. Van Zanden, 181.
18. Webster [1857], 679.
19. For analyses of nostalgia's progressive elements, see Ladino, 1–50 and Lowenthal, 18–32.
20. Robinson *Brother*, 138.
21. Hay, 223.
22. Roosevelt *Ranch*, 24.
23. Roosevelt *Ranch*, 24.
24. Roosevelt *Autobiography*, 93. The reference to Atlantis is from Rudyard Kipling's poem "Philadelphia."
25. Roosevelt "Degeneration," 104.

Chapter 15

Remington's Great White West

In 1887, Roosevelt got in touch with Poultney Bigelow, the editor of *Outing* magazine. Roosevelt liked the work of *Outing*'s young western illustrator, whose drawings he'd been seeing there and in other magazines. He wanted to talk to Bigelow about that illustrator, who, conveniently, was also Bigelow's old friend from Yale, Frederic Remington. Roosevelt ended up hiring Remington to do the illustrations for his second book, *Ranch Life and the Hunting Trail*, which would be serialized in *Century* magazine the following year. It was a big job. The assignment called for sixty-four illustrations for the magazine and another nineteen for the book, which would be published later in 1888.[1]

Roosevelt and Remington had much in common. Both had lost their fathers at a relatively early age: Roosevelt when he was nineteen and his father was forty-six; Remington when he was eighteen and his father was also forty-six. Both had gone west very soon after losing their fathers. Both had tried ranching, although Roosevelt had always been more successful at it.

Over the last few months of the year, Remington worked feverishly on the illustrations for Roosevelt's book. Though he was happy to get the commission, it was a lot of work. That one job for Roosevelt, to be published in 1888, would be equivalent to his entire published output for 1887.[2] On top of that, Remington also had to finish some illustrations for Cody's new book, *Story of the Wild West*, also forthcoming in 1888. Like everything like Cody did, the book was carefully designed to bolster the Buffalo Bill myth by connecting Cody's own colorful life story to a long history of buckskin-shirted frontiersmen: the "renowned pioneer quartette, Boone, Crockett, [Kit] Carson, and Buffalo Bill."[3]

Remington would keep in touch with Roosevelt for virtually his entire life, but at the start, something about Roosevelt's aloof manner bothered him.

Perhaps Roosevelt, a Harvard man, looked askance at a Yale Art School dropout. Or maybe Roosevelt, who carefully tended his image as a range-riding cattleman, learned that Remington was trying to pass himself off as an experienced rancher, when he had really just co-owned a sheep ranch for a few years. Roosevelt had always thought that sheep ranching was disgracefully unmanly. ("Cattle-men hate sheep," he had sneered a few years earlier. "No man can associate with sheep and retain his self-respect."[4])

But whatever it was, when Remington was done illustrating *Ranch Life* in November 1888, he complained to a friend that "my opinion [of Roosevelt] is that he is a g——d_____," and "that is all I have got to say about it in public."[5] (As a teenager, Remington had thought that swearing was his "weak point," and had to "look my letters over carefully to see if there is any cussing in them."[6] For the rest of his life, he edited his cursing in letters.) Yet he seemed to get over it quickly, as it was not long before Remington was telling friends that of all his published work, "the thing which I like best is a holiday book by Roosevelt."[7]

Even if Roosevelt wasn't treating him like a peer, it was clear why he hired him. Remington was becoming the standard-bearer for popular illustrations of the American west. As one critic noted around that time, Remington's best work endowed the west with "a glamour of romance." Remington's four trademark subjects, the critic continued, had become instantly recognizable. "In one group are his Indians, especially the type of the Sioux; in another are his soldiers; in a third are the cow-boys; and in the fourth are the horses."[8]

Yet despite the regular appearance of those western subjects, few of his drawings depicted western landscapes in any actual detail. Generally, his pictures would foreground a small group of men (and they were nearly always men: he once joked that he "had never drawn a woman—except once and then had washed her out") with one or more horses set against a large expanse of empty space. In his drawings, the actual west was mostly a stark white blankness.[9] He liked the clarity of midday in his drawings, and once told Wister, not entirely in jest, to make sure that no scenes in his stories were set at night.[10] His backgrounds included only the faintest hints of trees or mountains against the horizon.

Nearly always, his westerners were tasked with standing in for the west itself. The usual image was a lanky cowboy, Indian, soldier, or horse set against a stark, almost lunar backdrop. "There is in general," the same critic added of Remington's work, "the same setting and background for one group as for the other three."[11] Another contemporary critic of Remington's observed "the absence of detail of background" in his work.[12] Yet Remington seemed totally unbothered about the easy conflation of a wester*ner* with the actual landscape of the west itself. For Remington, the individual dictated the nature of the region. Not the other way around.

The expanse of white space that frequently stood in for sage and scrub grass was still rich with symbolism. Remington was, after all, increasingly recognized as one of the great popular illustrators of the west. For many easterners unable to brave lengthy journeys on the railroad or stagecoach lines, Remington's drawings of the west were, in essence, *the* west. As one journalist noted at the time, "Eastern people have formed their conceptions of what the Far-Western life is like, more from what they have seen in Mr. Remington's pictures than from any other source."[13] For many Americans, Remington's work was the closest they would ever come to seeing the west with their own eyes.

This duty made his choices in depicting the landscape all the more notable. Like Muybridge's Zoöpraxiscope, Remington's west was a kind of negative space: a white screen onto which he and his audience could project their dreams of ceaseless motion and rugged individualism. In most of Remington's illustrations, the west appeared as a kind of white-draped stage, recognizable only as "the west" chiefly because it was home to his own theater of Indians, soldiers, cowboys, and horses. Western nature, his pictures suggested, was not really natural at all. It was instead a kind of anti-nature, a barren whiteness in which men in well-worn clothes were busy birthing civilization from the abyss of an empty land.

Yet that empty west was exactly what Americans wanted to see, and it made Remington successful in a way that he had never dreamed possible. In December 1889, he and Eva bought an enormous house in New Rochelle, New York. It was a three-acre estate on a hill, replete with tennis court, stables, and a boat dock. He named it "Endion," after an Ojibwe word meaning "my home."[14]

In 1890, *Harper's Weekly* began promoting Remington as a kind of artist-adventurer, a hybrid illustrator and writer devoted to documenting the west. Remington had expanded from drawing into writing in part to burnish his reputation as a visual journalist, but also to ensure there was a healthy market for his illustrations. There were a limited number of writers doing western work who needed artwork, but if he could also write those stories, then the market for his illustrations was limited only by himself. According to *Harper's*, he was someone who did not merely represent the idea of the west, but a scholar who "perfects the history which his pictures illustrate" and whose illustrations captured the west in "virile and masculine style."[15]

In the former Dakota Territory, a new religious movement was uniting a number of different tribes. The millennial "Ghost Dance" permitted its practitioners to go into a trance to see long-dead ancestors, and at the same time promised to expel whites from historically Indian lands.[16]

Given that the dance was quickly becoming a multi-tribal practice, the Indian agents and military experts in the area were convinced it presented a problem. Major General Nelson A. Miles thought the dance portended an uprising. James McLaughlin, the agent at Standing Rock agency in North Dakota, agreed, and was sure the dance was a mass political movement orchestrated by the leader Sitting Bull, who had long since left Cody's Wild West show to reestablish himself as a leader of his people.[17] McLaughlin loathed Sitting Bull. He thought him a "fraud" as a leader, a "physical coward" as a warrior, and in possession of a quality that made McLaughlin more nervous than anything else: a "thorough hater of the whites."[18] He wanted to stop the Ghost Dance as much as Miles. He just wasn't sure how, or when.

Remington had been thinking about empire a lot recently—what it meant for a nation to grow, to stretch its arms over the globe—having recently read Rudyard Kipling's stories about the British Raj. Kipling's stories of British India had been recently republished as his first book *Plain Tales from the Hills* and were getting wide attention. In a letter to a friend, Remington remarked that Kipling reminded him of "a second Bret Harte," the western writer whose romantic stories about the frontier west had once made him the highest-paid writer in America.[19] Remington clearly saw a link between the American west and the American course of empire.

He got to see that linkup close in the fall of 1890, when he traveled to the Pine Ridge Agency in South Dakota for *Harper's*. He planned to meet up with Miles, whom he had first met in Arizona when he was reporting on the hunt for Geronimo. Miles had been promoted to major general earlier that year, and the two men greeted each other warmly. As usual, Remington had nothing but gushing admiration for the military, describing them in formation near the Crow Agency looking "natty and trim—as straight as a sapling, with few words and no gestures."[20] They were the very model of the western hero, he thought approvingly. Lean and hard and silent, like leather riding quirts. In private, he was even more effusive, telling a friend that "Miles is the biggest man in America."[21]

Riding with the cavalry spurred him to think about different types of conservatism. Complaining about the contract system by which cavalry horses were procured for the army, Remington opined that the problem could be solved by basic self-reliance. He thought one inefficiency could be fixed by allowing the officers to buy their own horses. But this solution, which was conservative in the sense that it returned governmental authority to the individuals, would never be adopted because it conflicted with another sort of conservatism, one that Remington didn't like at all: a bureaucratic conservatism. Nothing is ever really fixed in the modern army, he complained, "because a lot of nice old gentlemen in Washington are too conservative to do anything but eat and sleep."[22]

This bureaucratic conservatism, he thought, was just a reflexive embrace of the status quo. It was old men hanging on to familiar ways. It wasn't modern conservatism, in the sense of embracing a Darwinian system of strenuous competition where, as he put it, "any abatement of vigor is rewarded by being shelved." The army, like many government bureaucracies, had its hierarchy upside down. The "ambitious young men"—what might be called the fit, in the Darwinian sense—"have to wait patiently for their retirement, and in process of waiting they, too, become old and conservative."[23]

Publicly, Remington proposed no solutions to this other than to suggest it was a problem for the economists to solve. Privately, though, he thought this sort of inverted conservatism—trusting established bureaucracy instead of unestablished individualism—was intractably stupid. He grudgingly admitted that a rigid organization like the army probably needed a dense hierarchy, whether it was inefficient or not. But he didn't like it. "It may be all right, all the long way round, of doing business—it's the conservative way—it has always been so—but its god inspired idiocy just the same," he grumbled.[24]

Riding with Miles, Remington toured the battlefield near Lame Deer Creek. It was there in 1877 that Miles and his troops had defeated Lame Deer and his band of Miniconju Lakota in an early morning surprise attack. Except for Sitting Bull's band of Hunkpapa Lakota, who were still at large, Lame Deer's band had been the last remaining portion of the group that had defeated Custer at the Little Big Horn. Remington quoted Miles remembering that he had "kicked them out of their blankets in the early morning." And now, Remington opined, over twenty years later, the "Indians recognize him as their conqueror." In Remington's mind, they had accepted their rightful role as mere objects of America's military conquest. "One old chief," Remington wrote, "pointed to the stars on his [Miles's] shoulder-strap, and charged him to remember that they helped to put them there."[25] He had made the western landscape an empty whiteness in his drawings, and now he seemed similarly ready to erase its actual denizens. In Remington's imagination, Indians were a conquered people living in the twilight of existence. It was just that not all of them knew it yet.

When he got back to New York, Remington spent some time reviewing the article with Fred B. Schell, his editor at *Harper's*. Telling Schell about the story behind the story—the kind of thing writers would talk about privately, but wouldn't print—Remington talked about the tensions that had been set simmering by the Ghost Dance, speculating that "we are going to have an Indian War." He thought the evidence was pretty obvious. "Miles wouldn't order troops from Arizona unless he thought so," he noted.[26]

He was right. Before the year was out, Sitting Bull and hundreds of Lakota would be killed in one of the worst single-day massacres of the centuries-long conquest of the west.

NOTES

1. Samuels *Frederic*, 92.
2. Samuels *Frederic*, 92.
3. Cody *Story*, front matter.
4. Roosevelt *Hunting*, 120–121.
5. FR letter to William A. Poste, 11 November 1888.
6. FR letter to Scott Turner, 1877.
7. Samuels *Frederic*, 93.
8. Jones, 186, 187.
9. Qtd. in White *Eastern*, 57.
10. FR letter to Owen Wister, 12 April [1894].
11. Jones, 187–188.
12. Qtd. in Splete, 181.
13. Coffin "American," 348.
14. Bright, 144.
15. Qtd. in Samuels *Frederic*, 135.
16. Utley *Last*, 85.
17. Qtd. in Russell, 356, 357.
18. McLaughlin, 99, 141, 210.
19. FR letter to Lt. Powhatan Clarke, 13 September 1890. For more on Harte and the west, see Penry, 74–82; Scharnhorst *Bret*, 3–69; and Witschi, 15–42.
20. Remington "Chasing," 55.
21. FR letter to Lt. Powhatan Clarke, 27 January 1891.
22. Remington "Chasing," 51.
23. Remington "Chasing," 51.
24. FR letter to Lt. Powhatan Clarke, 12 January [1893].
25. Remington "Chasing," 53.
26. FR letter to Fred B. Schell, [Nov 1890].

Chapter 16

Natural Inequality and the Course of Progress

After the devastating losses from the blizzards, the newly remarried Roosevelt knew he wouldn't be coming back to the Badlands quite as often as he used to. In the fall of 1889, he told Sewall that he would probably close Elkhorn the following year, as he would "never make good my losses" from the snowstorms.[1] But he didn't stop thinking about the role that the American west would play in the country's national imagination, nor about the claims that scientifically determined natural law made upon modern free societies.

In the thirty years since Darwin had published *On the Origin of Species*, popular interest in evolution had only grown. Roosevelt could not help but notice that the American public was particularly taken by writers who seemed to be churning through the wake left by William Graham Sumner and Herbert Spencer, trying to understand society, politics, and economics in accordance with the new laws of nature that had been set down by Darwin.

One such writer was Benjamin Kidd, a young British civil servant who wanted to use modern evolutionary science to solve social problems. Kidd was trying to discover a scientific, evolutionary basis for public policy, while navigating between the Scylla of Spencer and the Charybdis of Marx. He thought the "two diametrically opposite camps of individualists and collectivists into which society is slowly becoming organized" were insufficiently guided by science. Much as Fredrika Bremer had concluded that the problems of the nineteenth century were polarized by Emersonian individualism on the one hand and socialism on the other, Kidd thought that individual liberty had been secured, but the question of inequality was still unresolved. "It is a grand thing to be free and sovereign," he mused, "but how is it that the sovereign often starves?"[2] Kidd agreed with Roosevelt's old mayoral opponent Henry George that modernity and poverty should not so easily coexist. Ultimately, Kidd thought that the individualism of Herbert Spencer wasn't really supported by Darwinian natural law, but neither was the collectivism of Marx.[3] He had concluded that resting social inequality on a bedrock of political equality would make for a shaky house. He thought that evolutionary science could help firm up the foundation.

After Roosevelt read Kidd's book *Social Evolution*, he saw an opportunity to explain his own thoughts on the relationship between Darwin and social policy, and did so in a lengthy article published in *The North American Review*. Roosevelt generally agreed with Kidd, but thought that some of his conclusions—especially those about the relationship between individualism and equality—seemed wrongheaded. Roosevelt wanted to wade into the country's ongoing debates about individual freedom and the laws of nature and to set down in print, more clearly than he ever had before, his own ideas about Darwin, nature, and individual freedom.

Some of those principles were obvious, in his view. It went almost without saying that human society was governed by natural laws. Human progress "can only have been made under and in accordance with certain biological laws," Roosevelt pointed out. This, in turn, meant that Darwin "largely govern[s human] progress." More importantly, the principle of natural selection had political implications. For Roosevelt, progress didn't just refer to a simple change over time. It meant social or civilizational advancement. Darwinian natural selection governed the advancement of societies as readily as it governed the evolution of any other organism.

Roosevelt also thought that Kidd, like Spencer and Sumner before him, was correct in adapting the Darwinian principle of competition to the social scene. Roosevelt had personally seen this principle at work in the Badlands. "Competition and selection must not only always accompany progress, but must prevail in every form of life which is not actually retrograding," he argued.[4] If the process of natural selection governed social advancement, then competition was the engine powering that process.

But Roosevelt wanted to clarify that Darwinian competition, properly understood and applied to society, shouldn't mean a literal struggle for life and death. Individuals should compete for sales bonuses, not bread. Of course, a nonlethal economic contest could easily lead to bankruptcy or debilitating illness that would, in turn, have lethal consequences. But it didn't really matter. Roosevelt was not particularly interested in the unexceptional individuals who would lose such competitions. He was interested in the exceptional individuals who would win them.

One area where Roosevelt disagreed with Kidd was over the value of individualism in society. In Kidd's view, individual interests and social interests were usually at odds. But Roosevelt's unique admixture of *noblesse oblige* and western individualism led him to disagree with rationalists like Kidd who thought that individualism was synonymous with simple selfishness.

Instead, Roosevelt believed that abstract virtues like duty, honesty, tenacity, and bravery—qualities he usually just called "character"—could be cultivated and put to work, just as individualism could. Like Kidd, he was deeply suspicious of left-leaning reformers. Many of the "social plans advanced by would-be reformers," he thought, "are entirely destructive of all growth and all progress." Both he and Kidd thought such plans were "supra-natural," part of a misguided attempt by well-meaning individuals to play God and control the forces of nature.[5]

But unlike Kidd, he thought that human history contained a number of examples of pro-social individualism, such as the military, police, or fire departments. "In the process of evolution men and societies have often reached such a stage that the best type of soldier or citizen feels infinitely more shame," he wrote, "from selfish abandonment of the interests of the organism of which he is part, than can be offset by the gratification of any of his desires."[6] Individualism, in other words, was malleable. Self-reliance could be harnessed to benefit the individual and society simultaneously.

Roosevelt argued that socialism was not just bad policy, but actually contrary to the laws of nature. "A state of retrogression must ensure," he thought, "if all incentives to strife and competition are withdrawn."[7] In his view, socialism meant devolution. Yet he also believed there was a role for an active governmental hand. That role just wasn't what the liberal reformers like Henry George or socialists like Henry Carter Adams thought it should be.

Roosevelt envisioned a minimal, Darwinian government that would select for what might be called social individualism while deselecting for antisocial individualism, finding ways to, as he put it, "weed out" such individuals.[8] In a sense, it was a policy that Roosevelt himself had pursued with the boat thieves. If society was a perpetual struggle for dominance and rights and resources—a ceaseless battle to determine the "fittest"—then it was crucial for Roosevelt that such a struggle determine the fittest in an ethical sense, not merely in a physical or economic sense.

But the way to accomplish that goal, Roosevelt decided, was to make sure that two requirements were met. First, it was important that social competition not be a Hobbesian battle for life itself. It was true that creating an unequal hierarchy and providing incentives for ascending that hierarchy was what allowed society to evolve. But in the social arenas, it should be a figurative competition to determine the "survival of the fittest," not a literal one. (In advanced societies like America, Roosevelt thought, a life-or-death "rivalry of natural selection" actually "works against progress," not for it.[9])

And second, it was important that social competitions resemble their natural counterparts. That meant that social competition should not be handicapped to account for historical inequalities. The competition itself should be equal, in the sense of being open to all. Yet the outcomes of such competitions should be unequal, in the sense of producing winners and losers. Ensuring such equal competitive opportunities, Roosevelt concluded, was the natural function of the government.

Such a theory of society was by no means perfect. First, the emphasis on competitions that did not adjust for past inequality would, over time, magnify disparities in the population. Over the course of generations, the successful would grow more successful; the weak would grow weaker. Roosevelt admitted that his philosophy required a "certain proportion of failures" in each generation.[10] And second, even decades after Spencer, the notion that society was a natural organism subject to Darwinian law was at least debatable. The U.S. Constitution famously located its power to in a contract among "We the People," not in nature. According the Constitution, society was not a natural organism, like a colony of ants; it was a human invention, something more like a printing press.

But Roosevelt had thought about his ideas and had answers for both these critiques. First, the possibility that his plan would eventually make the strong even stronger was not a flaw in his theory at all. It was the entire point. Roosevelt wanted to find a scientific grounding for what he called a "progressive" society, a civic and economic engine that moved relentlessly forward on the track toward civilization. The doctrine of natural selection held that over time, populations acquire traits that present adaptive advantages and discard traits that do not. Individual inequality and a "proportion of failures" were simply part of the gear train required to make it all work. Over time, Roosevelt hypothesized, such inequalities would produce a stronger, smarter, wealthier society.

And second, unlike many of his fellow Americans, Roosevelt's knowledge of natural history seems to have led him to reject the idea that humans are somehow divided from the natural world. The romantic myth that humans and human-built things somehow stood apart from nature had been, scientifically at least, discarded. If humans were natural, and society was a human creation, then society was natural.

Besides, the idea that society should enact particular natural truths was hardly a new one. Thomas Jefferson had emphasized what he thought were the natural origins of human freedom. Unlike the later Constitution, which said that liberty existed because of a contract, Jefferson's Declaration professed that freedom was granted to each individual by the "Laws of Nature and of Nature's God." For Jefferson, like Locke before him, individual liberty and the social contract were built on natural principles.

Roosevelt was merely updating Jefferson's nature for the age of Darwin. He believed that social advancements were the result of competition between individuals. Such a struggle wasn't a Malthusian battle for ever-scarcer resources, but a social competition that *created* resources. This was the dynamic he had seen in the west, where individualism had completely transformed the city of Medora in just a few years.

Fifty years earlier, Henry David Thoreau had thought that it would create an "advantage to live a primitive and frontier life, though in the midst of an outward civilization."[11] Roosevelt concluded that such an advantage wasn't merely philosophical, but practical. When an individual temporarily retrogressed to a "primitive and frontier life" in order to advance modern society, he created conditions that were uniquely suited to the type of competition that determined superior individuals and moved society forward.

For Roosevelt, advancing society in this way required a specific role for government. He concluded that "the true function of the State, as it interferes in social life, should be to make the chances of competition more even, not to abolish them." In other words, government should be a neutral referee, not an interested handicapper. "We wish the best men," he continued, "and though we pity the man that falls or lags behind in the race, we do not on that account crown him with the victor's wreath." In his view, if society would "remove all handicaps," and not attempt to eradicate inequality but rather to *encourage* it, society would prosper. The point of a competition is, after all, to produce an unequal outcome, not to produce a tie. Such a government would create "a test of the real merits of the victor."[12] It was the perpetual selection of such "victors" that he believed would ensure the continued progress of society.

This was the core of Roosevelt's western conservatism. It was a rigorous and, in his mind, scientific explanation for why social inequality was not just necessary, but even good. Inequality, to this way of thinking, was the animating spark for all subsequent progress.

Though the word would not exist for another six decades, Roosevelt was envisioning a meritocracy. (The term would eventually be coined by the British sociologist Michael Young in his dystopian 1958 satire *The Rise of the Meritocracy*). A meritocracy would be a system of governance in which power is meted out on the basis of merit—by skill or character or intelligence or strength—as opposed to on the basis of inheritance or caste or even popular approval. In Roosevelt's imagination, such a system of government would need to discover its naturally superior citizens through Darwinian contests of merit. This basic idea—that competition produced inequality, which was a naturally progressive force for society—was transformative in Roosevelt's political imagination.

Such a system, he realized, would ensure a class of superior individuals. But at the same time, it would not produce a traditional aristocracy. It would instead produce a quintessentially American class of rulers. Roosevelt's theory of meritocracy was democratic, in the sense that its competitions would be open to all comers. It also would be scientific, in the sense that it would stage fair and open contests to determine the "fittest" members of various social scenes. And what made it conservative was that it relied on what he believed were timeless, natural principles. It was the scientific realization of Jefferson's hope that America might be ruled by a "natural aristocracy."

Roosevelt's theory of American civilization—which was simultaneously a theory of Darwinian social evolution and theory of individualism in the west—emerged in small asides in his books about ranching in the west as well as in a series of shorter essays such as his review of Kidd's *Social Evolution*. It had a bracing clarity to it. But one complication was that it required frontiers, and frontiers were not just located in space, but also in time.

Roosevelt's experiences in the west had taught him that civilization required perpetual competition. The competitions that characterized natural selection were really a kind of war. For the same reason, historical progress was also a kind of war. There was a linear quality to history, he thought, in that it went in one direction at a time, like a railroad line making stops in an unvarying sequence. Competition—war—made the train run.

Later, Roosevelt tried to explain this theory in greater depth, explaining that to "conquer a continent, to tame the shaggy roughness of wild nature, means grim warfare."[13] He did not see trying to "tame" nature as repudiating Darwin's ideas, but rather as enacting them. Organisms seek adaptive advantage through competition, even if that advantage is sought over nature itself. Americans, he thought, achieved progress by seeking out so-called primitive spaces suitable for conquest. But seeking such conditions required a kind of conservative temporality, as they involved a past that only existed in the warm glow of myth and memory. "To conquer the wilderness," he continued, "means to wrest victory from the same hostile forces with which mankind struggled in the immemorial infancy of our race."[14] Going into that wilderness means walking a trail first trod in man's "immemorial infancy." In other words, finding a wilderness suitable for conquest requires a fantasy of retrogression: a belief that by moving geographically one is also moving chronologically.

A journey to a wilderness like he had found in the Badlands meant a journey to what he called "primeval conditions." Those conditions changed an otherwise-civilized person, as they "must be met by primeval qualities."[15] Sometimes, he thought, individuals needed to briefly retrogress to such primeval conditions, taking up its primeval qualities in order to drive further progress. As Roosevelt had seen in the Badlands, the presence of white and wealthy easterners changed those primeval conditions. Their presence, he seemed to think, forced those conditions to evolve.

One outcome of this line of thought was the belief that America was spurred by a sort of evolutionary imperialism. Eastern men who had gone to western spaces were, in a sense, soldiers. They had set in motion a sequence of events, like warriors for history who returned to the original fount of individual freedom—the primeval state of nature—in order to advance modern civilization.

The American west, Roosevelt began to believe—just as John Locke had 200 years earlier—recreated the original freedoms and conditions of the state of nature. As Roosevelt put it, the west magnified "all the good qualities and all the defects of an intense individualism."[16] Gentlemen of the east rode the train of progress backward when they went west, retrogressing to an earlier and more intense individualism. And when the moment of retrogression was complete, they rode the train forward again, this time at a dizzying pace. "The pioneer days pass; the stump-dotted clearings expand," he later wrote, and then some of the men who had been the "heralds and harbingers of an oncoming civilization" return to modern society in order to lead it.[17]

Roosevelt would later wax lyrical about the type of westerner who would gamble on his own individual might, only to be rewarded with the sort of success that drove American progress. In parts of the west, he said in a letter to his sister Corinne, natural superiority was equated with economic superiority. The west was a place where "every prominent man is a millionaire, a gambler, or a labor leader, and generally he has been all three," Roosevelt wrote. Those westerners had "worked, and striven, and pushed, and trampled, and had always been ready, and were ready now, to fight to the death in many different kinds of conflicts." And in doing so, they had "built up their part of the West."[18]

Thinking about the American west as a primitive place of conquest, or the birthplace of an "intense individualism," as he liked to put it, was not just a philosophical exercise. For Roosevelt, such a belief also had practical consequences. "To the hard materialism of the frontier days," he wrote, "succeeds the hard materialism of an industrialism even more intense and absorbing than that of the older nations."[19] When men sought out "primitive" western spaces, it sparked a primeval individualism that poured coal on the engine fires of modern civilization, helping to make American industrial output better than that of "older nations." Retrogressing to primitive conditions—to a land of fierce Darwinian struggle—was, Roosevelt concluded, one of the chief drivers of American progress.

NOTES

1. TR letter to William Wingate Sewall, 13 October 1889, Theodore Roosevelt National Park [Collection], Dickinson State University.
2. Kidd, 2, 3.
3. Kidd, 291.

4. Roosevelt "Degeneration," 95.
5. Roosevelt "Degeneration," 99.
6. Roosevelt "Degeneration," 100–101.
7. Roosevelt "Degeneration," 108.
8. Roosevelt "Degeneration," 103.
9. Roosevelt "Degeneration," 97.
10. Roosevelt "Degeneration," 98.
11. Thoreau, 11.
12. Roosevelt "Degeneration," 108.
13. Roosevelt "Citizenship," 138.
14. Roosevelt "Citizenship," 138.
15. Roosevelt "Citizenship," 138.
16. Roosevelt "Citizenship," 139.
17. Roosevelt "Citizenship," 138–139.
18. Qtd. in Robinson *Brother*, 152, 153.
19. Roosevelt "Citizenship," 139.

Chapter 17

The Ghost Dance

In November 1890, Cody took a break from touring his Wild West around Europe and traveled back to the United States.[1] Almost as soon as Cody arrived in New York, he received notice that General Miles had requested a meeting with him in Chicago. Miles was convinced that the Ghost Dance meant that Sitting Bull was planning a war, and asked Cody to go to Sitting Bull's camp. "He knew," Cody later said of Miles's request, "that I was an old friend of the chief, and he believed that if any one could induce the old fox to abandon his plans for a general war I could." If Cody couldn't dissuade him, however, Miles wanted Cody to try to delay him until U.S. troops arrived. The idea, Cody claimed, was "to prevent a horrible massacre of the defenseless white settlers, who were already in terror of their lives."[2]

Cody was certainly willing to talk with Sitting Bull. But somewhat incredibly, Miles deputized Cody—who was, technically, little more than a professional entertainer—to arrest Sitting Bull and deliver him to the nearest commanding officer.[3]

James McLaughlin, the agent in charge of the territory, was appalled at Miles's recklessness. Miles was asking Cody, who had no standing military authority whatsoever, to arrest an Indian on Indian land. McLaughlin was certain that "any attempt by outside parties to arrest Sitting Bull would undoubtedly result in loss of life."[4] If necessary, McLaughlin pointed out, he could simply have Sitting Bull arrested by the agency police. There was no need to turn the whole operation into more fodder for Cody's circus.

From Miles's perspective, there was a certain logic to sending Cody. It was as if he had concluded that the issue was, on its surface, a cultural dispute. A number of tribes were engaging in a religious act—the Ghost Dance—that the U.S. military felt had dangerous political implications. Seen one way, the Ghost Dance was a performance that contained a story about a retrogression into the past. It reanimated long-lost customs and long-dead people, and it promised to use that reanimated history to bring the age of white America to an end. In a sense, the dance was the inverse of Cody's own Wild West show. Cody's show also contained a story about a retrogression into the past. The difference was, the Wild West show's story was useful to white Americans, not Indians.

When it came to white American civilization, Cody's show celebrated its ascendance. The Ghost Dance looked forward to its decline. Given that Cody was the creator of the show that had once employed Sitting Bull, perhaps it made sense to General Miles to send an old fellow performer to try to resolve the dispute, and hope the resolution took care of the underlying social problem.

Cody left for Sitting Bull's camp with a small party on the morning of November 28.[5] But McLaughlin soon received the response from Washington he'd been hoping for: a rescission of Miles's order. Relieved, McLaughlin sent a rider out to catch Cody before he got too far. McLaughlin later congratulated himself on averting a battle and saving the life of "a royal good fellow and most excellent showman."[6]

Miles was furious that McLaughlin had interfered to stop Cody. Cody was simply exhausted. He had traveled almost nonstop from Europe to New York to Chicago to North Dakota. With nothing left to do, he submitted a bill for $505.60 to cover his transportation costs and retired to North Platte to rest up for his return to Europe.[7]

Yet Miles remained convinced that a battle was imminent. He had convinced himself that the only option was to put "those large powerful warlike tribes, that have been for years a terror to the north-west States and Territories, entirely under military control, and at once."[8] For his part, McLaughlin continued to think that it "would not do to allow so cunning and malignant a leader as Sitting Bull to put himself at the head of these frightened or desperate people."[9]

On December 12, McLaughlin received an order to arrest Sitting Bull. He arranged for Lieutenant Bull Head from the Standing Rock police to make the arrest. He also stationed over 100 soldiers from the Eighth Calvary nearby, in case they became necessary.[10] On McLaughlin's orders, Bull Head and his colleague Sergeant Shave Head mustered a party of thirty-nine Indian policemen and four informally deputized relatives to arrest Sitting Bull.[11]

Early on the morning of the 15th, Bull Head placed Sitting Bull under arrest. He reportedly agreed to go peacefully, and asked that his best horse—a tall white-gray horse that may have been the one gifted to him by Cody five years earlier—be saddled so he could ride it to the agency. As he got dressed in his cabin under the watch of the police, the camp slowly began to wake and gathered in protest around Sitting Bull's cabin.

When Sitting Bull stepped outside and prepared to mount his horse, the Ghost Dancers opened fire on the police, sparking a battle that killed six Standing Rock policemen, including Bull Head and Shave Head. Eight Ghost Dancers were also killed; another five were wounded.[12] As the sun continued its upward path, Sitting Bull's horse, which would miraculously survive, still stood waiting for its rider.[13] By the time the gunfire ceased, Sitting Bull had been killed as well.

Two weeks later, the death of Sitting Bull led indirectly to an even graver incident on Lakota lands. After Sitting Bull had been shot and killed, a group of Hunkpapa Lakota fled and joined a group of Miniconju Lakota near Wounded Knee Creek, on the Pine Ridge reservation. On December 29, 1890, at least 150 men, women, and children were killed by members of the Seventh Calvary Regiment under the leadership of Colonel James W. Forsyth. Many others were wounded and would die later. The regiment, in contrast, suffered losses of twenty-five soldiers.[14]

It was a devastating and bloody massacre with no obvious catalyst. In the aftermath, no one was exactly sure what had sparked the violence. By some accounts, it was because one or more of the tribesmen started doing the Ghost Dance.[15]

What later was called the Massacre at Wounded Knee signaled, for many white Americans, the end of the centuries-long Indian Wars. Even though in the coming decades there would continue to be battles in the southwest, the sheer scale of the violence at Wounded Knee seemed to signal the end of something.

Cody seemed ambivalent about the massacre. After all, he mused, it would mean the end of "one of the most picturesque phases of Western life—Indian fighting." Nevertheless, he remained proud of his own role in that violence, proclaiming that "in the time I spent on the Plains, Indian warfare reached its greatest severity and its highest development."[16]

Cody seemed to take the Ghost Dance as little more than a cultural event much like his own show, a "dance" in the same way that the polka was a dance. Why else would he conclude that the conflicts over the Ghost Dance, culminating in the deaths of hundreds of Lakota, were regrettable largely because they represented the end of something "picturesque"?

For Cody, the deaths seemed to have more signaling power than anything else. They were literally picturesque: like pictures, not people. The signs and symbols of the American west had become almost entirely divorced from any real-life western referents. "Soldiers" and "Indians" had become like ideograms from a language of pure symbols, where the words didn't refer to anything with heft or blood or shade at all. After all, he was only playing at being a scout. Why would he not conclude they were merely playing at being Indians?

In the aftermath of Wounded Knee, Remington traveled back to South Dakota to interview some of the soldiers and try to understand what he euphemistically called the "Sioux Outbreak in South Dakota." He was struck, as he often was, by the soldiers' taciturn professionalism. In many ways, Remington was still the boy who loved to collect drawings of soldiers. He had not yet outgrown the sort of romantic veneration of the military that is most often seen in civilian men.[17]

He spoke with one reflective officer who was smoking a pipe. They agreed the episode was a testament to the ferocious bravery of the American military. There "is one thing which I learned," the officer mused, "and that is that you can bet that the private soldier in the United States army will fight. He'll fight from the drop of the hat anywhere and in any place, and he'll fight till you call *time*."[18]

There was a brutal logic to this that Remington found appealing. For the officer, Wounded Knee was not about politics or land or contracts or anything else. It was about simple Darwinian superiority. Who lived, who didn't. For him, war had a self-justifying morality. It didn't matter what the U.S. army would fight *for*, he seemed to think, so long as it would fight, anywhere and in any place.

For Remington, the real significance of Wounded Knee had little to do with the dramatic and overwhelming loss of Lakota life. And to a degree it was not really about the losses to the American military forces, either. The event was instead about testing a battle-hardened manliness. It was a Darwinian tool for culling the strong from the weak. This brutal battle for dominance was, for Remington, what American history was all about.

Remington recalled once chatting with a journalist who claimed he did "not like American history; it is brutal—crude—lacking in *finesse*." The reporter preferred the history of Germany, France, or Italy. Remington thought about this, and decided that the journalist was probably right in his appraisal of American history. But that was exactly why Remington liked it in the first place. "I do," he decided, "like American history." For him, America did not evolve despite its brutality; America evolved because of it.[19]

Unsurprisingly, Remington's dim view of Indian life—the way he seemed to view the deaths of hundreds as mostly useful for measuring the evolutionary fitness of the U.S. army—tended to make its way into his art. One contemporary critic complained that Remington was "least satisfactory in his Indians. Pick up any random of his Indian pictures, and the chances are that about every Indian, even in the minutest details, is like every other one. These Indians are invariably grotesque, exaggerated, and often on the border of caricature."[20]

But many others thought that typological sameness—that seeming inability to draw Indians with diversity equal to whites—was what made Remington's drawings great in the first place. As Wister wrote admiringly, Remington had "pictured the red man as no one else, to my thinking certainly, has pictured him. He has told his tragedy completely. He has made us see at every stage this inferior race which our conquering race has dispossessed, beginning with its primeval grandeur, and ending with its squalid degeneration under the influence of our civilized manners. [. . .] Remington is not merely an artist; he is a national treasure."[21]

At the encampment, Remington met one soldier who had been shot in the hip. The young man was limping around in the sunshine with the help of a crutch, glad to be once again outdoors. Once he healed, "I'm going to re-enlist," he said. "I hope I'll get back here before this trouble is over." The young man apparently did not realize there were not many of that particular group of Lakota left to fight. "I want to get square with these Injuns," he insisted, as if he suffered an individual affront that demanded restitution.[22]

Remington acknowledged that the army's "professional interest in the military process of killing sometimes rasps a citizen's nerves." (He meant civilian, not citizen, but the slip, which suggested that the military stood above other citizens, was nonetheless revealing.) To a soldier, he continued, "everything else was a side note of little consequence so long as his guns had worked to his entire satisfaction." And the young soldier who sought to "get square" by fighting until there was literally no one left to kill was simply voicing a natural human desire. "You see," Remington noted with approval, "there was considerable human nature in this man's composition."[23]

To put it in a different way, for Remington, Wounded Knee (which as early as 1896 would begin to be known as it is today, as a "massacre") served two purposes. It furthered what Remington called the "professional" knowledge of battle, providing a vigorous opportunity for gunfire and bloodshed, a field where, as he wrote admiringly, the "Springfield carbines worked so industriously."[24] But it was also, Remington suggested, a literal force of nature: a place for the display of the "considerable human nature" deep inside all men fighting in the west. The west, again, offered an opportunity to realign society according to older, and truer, natural forces. It was human nature to test oneself on the field of battle. It was human nature to want to "get square" with a foe. And it was human nature to want to vanquish that foe until nothing of him remained. This, Remington thought, was the promise of the Indian Wars. This was the promise of the west.

After the deaths of Sitting Bull and the Lakota at Wounded Knee, men like Remington and Cody took it upon themselves to make sense of the episode, to write it into the larger narrative of Anglo-American history. Remington wrote articles and drew pictures. Cody, for his part, made an offer to purchase Sitting Bull's horse. Upon returning to Europe, Cody promptly put the horse in the show the following season. And when the show made its triumphant return to America three years later, Cody would have yet another one of his brilliant ideas. He staged the Battle of the Little Bighorn with the actor playing Custer riding Sitting Bull's actual horse.[25]

The crowds loved it.

NOTES

1. Kasson, 185; Russell, 351–352.
2. Cody *Autobiography*, 305.
3. Russell, 359.
4. McLaughlin, 210.
5. Utley *Last*, 125.
6. McLaughlin, 211.
7. Utley *Last*, 126.
8. Qtd. in Utley *Last*, 126.
9. McLaughlin, 213.
10. Andersson, 115.
11. McLaughlin, 218.
12. Andersson, 109–118.
13. A number of sources have repeated the claim that Sitting Bull's horse was a gift from Cody that had been cued to perform by gunfire. The horse, according to these claims, commenced its trained performance from Cody's show when it heard the gunfire that killed Sitting Bull. No contemporaneous accounts support this story. See Lemons, 64–74 and Andersson, 350.
14. Utley *Indian*, 257; Andersson, 94.
15. Andersson, 92.
16. Cody *Autobiography*, 312–313.
17. Remington "Sioux," 68.
18. Remington "Sioux," 68.
19. Remington "Toro," 120.
20. Jones, 188.
21. Wister "Remington," 15.
22. Remington "Sioux," 69.
23. Remington "Sioux," 69.
24. Remington "Sioux," 68.
25. Lemons, 74.

Part IV

IN SEARCH OF A PRACTICAL HISTORY (1890–1895)

Chapter 18

The Johnson County War

In the late afternoon of April 5, 1892, a party of over fifty men boarded a private train in Cheyenne. Many were wealthy ranchers who had just come from a meeting of the Wyoming Stock Growers' Association. They had arranged for a special six-car train to transport them and their supplies in an all-night trip to Casper.

The expedition was led by Wister's old friend Frank Wolcott, the Kentucky-born manager of the VR Ranch. The group included Hubert Teschemacher and Frederic de Billier, in whose ranch Roosevelt was an investor. In all, there were twenty-one wealthy ranchers, seven private detectives, two journalists, one surgeon, and twenty-two mercenaries with over five thousand rounds of ammunition. The purpose of the excursion was to defend the interests of the stock growers against the perceived threat of smaller businesses.

The best way to do this, everyone on the train agreed, was to round up and execute seventy alleged cattle rustlers.[1]

The trip was supposed to be the deciding battle in the ongoing conflict that would come to be known as the Johnson County War. It had its roots in a simple labor conflict. Twenty years earlier, wealthy Wyoming ranchers had confederated to consolidate their power and landholdings, forming the Laramie County Stock Association in 1873. By the early 1880s, the ranchers were drawing starker lines between employers and employees. In 1883, Thomas Sturgis, secretary of the Wyoming Stock Growers' Association, proposed and passed a resolution making it impossible for any member of the association to employ a cowboy who owned his own cattle.[2] He thought cowboys could not have enough money to purchase their own cattle—they certainly weren't being paid very much—and concluded that any cowboy who owned a cow must have stolen it. Any potential business threat was cast as a criminal threat. This lent a legal asymmetry to the existing class asymmetry. Stockmen who owned cattle were businessmen; cowboys who owned cattle were thieves.

There was a pleasing circularity to this that sustained the interests of the ranch owners. In essence, the law was whatever they said it was. "Rustler" was no longer a legal finding but a term of art, with pretensions. Any individual who did not accept his place in the social order—who aspired to, say, buy cattle or start a ranch of his own—was deemed a rustler. Those rustlers were in turn marked for extrajudicial execution. By the late 1880s, local newspapers had started using the phrase "reign of terror"—a phrase that had been birthed in the blood of the French Revolution—to describe the actions of the cattlemen.[3]

But the hanging spree the stockgrowers hoped would be their moment of triumph failed. On April 9, they killed Nick Ray and Nate Champion at the KC Ranch, the first of the seventy they planned to execute. They didn't get a chance to kill again. The local community reacted swiftly, and 200 citizens cornered the vigilantes at the TA Ranch near Buffalo.

The Johnson County War was partly an economic conflict in which businessmen tried to consolidate their power by spurning civil procedure in favor of a "lynch law" that would let them maintain, through fear and intimidation, a ready supply of employees drawn from a perpetual laboring class. Much like Roosevelt's own earlier interest in vigilantism had suggested something about his political worldview, the actions of the ranchers revealed something about their own conservatism. A group of elites had held itself and its economic interests above the democratic body politic and civil law.

When Owen Wister heard about the conflict, he immediately began planning to turn the real-life reign of terror into a series of articles and short stories. Eventually, he would dramatize the conflict in his novel *The Virginian*. Wister felt the story had all the stuff of good fiction—high conflict, a sweeping setting, a clear villain.

Unlike the local newspapers, though, Wister didn't side with the ranchers. The real heroes, he seemed to think, were the wealthy vigilantes who took the law into their own hands in order to protect their economic interests.

Whether due to the hospitality shown to him by Frank Wolcott or a natural inclination to sympathize with the powerful, Wister had long been on the side of the ranchmen. One of the early skirmishes in the Johnson County War happened in 1889 in the Sweetwater River valley, about three miles east of Independence Rock on the old Oregon trail. Homesteaders James Averell and Ella Watson had both staked claims that later ended up in the middle of a vast tract of land controlled by wealthy stockman Albert J. Bothwell. Bothwell reportedly had tried to buy out their claim, but was rebuffed. Bothwell and his associates eventually decided Averell and Watson had stood in their way long enough, and accused them of being cattle rustlers. Once the accusation had been made, it in effect became true. On July 20, 1889, Averell and Watson were hanged from a pine tree on a cliff overlooking the river, about five miles from Averell's homestead.[4]

Bothwell and five others were arrested. They immediately made bail and the charges were subsequently dropped. In a sign of the close relationship between big cattle interests and western vigilantism, three of the men accused of executing Averell and Watson were later appointed to the executive committee of the Wyoming Stock Growers' Association.[5]

Shortly after their arrest, Wister, who was on one of his trips west, wrote in his diary that he had "sat yesterday in smoking car with one of the gentlemen indicted for lynching the man and the woman [at Sweetwater]. He seemed a good solid citizen, and I hope he'll get off."[6] Merely knowing that the accused was a fellow "gentleman" trumped any concerns about due process or the rule of law. A shared moment of genteel bonhomie was enough to convince Wister that the extrajudicial execution must have been justified, if the charges weren't fabricated altogether. After all, the gentleman seemed like Wolcott, Teschemacher, de Billier, and even Roosevelt: wealthy, white, an all-around "good solid citizen."

Wister's support for such vigilantism did not wane after the Sweetwater incident. Less than two weeks after the surrender of Wolcott and the other vigilantes, Wister wrote an essay titled "Among the Cow-Boys" in which he explained that extrajudicial executions were sometimes necessary. Democratic institutions like a jury trial, he thought, were not unmovable cornerstones of civil society. They were instead more like optional decorative touches that could be added later.

The problem, he explained, was that easterners had "no very clear notion of the real West," a place where "a life as primitive and archaic as the patriarchs of the Old Testament comes into continual collision with the latest thing in modern civilization." In other words, the west was at a different place on the evolutionary track that led from primitive conditions to civilized modernity. Old Testament conditions required Old Testament punishments: what he called a "war of extermination." He conceded that while lynching may "seem shocking to Eastern traditions of law and order," it was necessary, as "there are no policemen on top of the Rocky Mountains." Ultimately, he wrote, the "extermination of thieves was most wholesome." After all, it protected the interests of the wealthy ranchers, and "stock raising was left in peace."[7]

(Perhaps without realizing it, in describing the executions as "most wholesome," Wister was echoing Roosevelt's earlier description of vigilante executions, when he had characterized them as "in the main wholesome."[8] Both men were eager to present extrajudicial executions not just as legally unproblematic, but as conducive to society's general well-being.)

Later that year, encouraged by the favorable response to his essay defending western vigilantism, Wister sent two western short stories, accompanied by a letter of introduction from Dr. Silas Weir Mitchell, who had first sent him west seven years earlier, to Henry Mills Alden, editor of *Harper's* magazine. Alden liked what Wister was trying to do and paid him $175 for the stories. Wister's first western story, "Hank's Woman," was published in an August issue of *Harper's Weekly*; "How Lin McLean Went East" would appear in the December issue of *Harper's Monthly*. In June of the following year, Alden offered Wister a contract for a series of western sketches at a rate of $250 each.[9]

Alden wanted those sketches to focus on what he believed was the real, unadorned west: the brutal battle between strong and weak. Each of Wister's stories, Alden instructed, should be grounded in a "real incident," adding that lynching was specifically the sort of thing he wanted. "We wish in this series to portray certain features of Western life which are now rapidly disappearing with the progress of civilization," Alden explained. "Not the least striking of these is that of the appeal of lynch law, which ought to give capital subject for one of your stories."[10]

With the Johnson County War, Wister had found his great theme as a writer. From that moment, he was rewarded with prestige and financial remuneration for telling stories about tough westerners doing things at the margins of the law.

In October 1892, Wister traveled to the Methow Valley in north-central Washington state to visit Guy Waring and his wife. To welcome his old Harvard friend, Waring had constructed a makeshift Porcellian Club flag, but the chilly rain preventing him from flying it.[11] They went hunting and Wister toured the Big Bend Country where the Columbia River turns south around the Selkirks. It was a grain country, growing a crop in the west that was shipped east for the nation's sustenance—a metaphor that was not lost on Wister. Like seemingly everyone else in America, he was looking forward to the World's Fair in Chicago the following year, where, as he wrote in his journal, "innocent gazers" would get to marvel at the "huge specimens of wheat and other grain grown 'In the Big Bend Country.'"[12] The fair promised to bring the American west to the world. It was almost exactly what Wister wanted to do with his writing.

The train that took Wister back east rumbled through the huge expanse of the former Dakota Territory. A week after saying goodbye to Waring, Wister noticed that an army officer in his car was reading the Christmas issue of *Harper's* containing "How Lin McLean Went East." Wister felt a little thrill.

The officer left the magazine on the seat opposite him and Wister picked it up and pretended to thumb through it idly. He noted to himself that his story had been well illustrated by William Thomas Smedley. "This looks like a good number," Wister said to the officer, with all the casual indifference he could muster. "I read a story in there," the man commented.

Wister could barely contain himself. He asked what the story was about.

"Oh, it's a cowboy," said the officer, adding, "Lin McLean. That's it. He went East." And the jovial officer proceeded to recount the plot of Wister's story in detail. "Oh, it's a good cowboy story," he concluded with a grin.[13]

Wister tried to keep his cool—he wanted to stay "incognito," as he put it—but inside he was fairly vibrating with excitement. It was only his second western story ever published, and here was proof that people were reading it and actually liking it. It was a small gift grown in the west and sent to the east, like the Big Bend grain he imagined traveling to the World's Fair.

As the view of the landscape rushed from east to west out his car window, Wister must have felt like he was flying on his own power. He calmly told the man that the story sounded good; he would have to read it sometime. They talked about other matters.

But later that night, in the privacy of his journal, he exulted, "There's encouragement for you, O Wister!"[14] He was on his way.

NOTES

1. Smith *War*, 189, 196, 226, 194.
2. Smith *War*, 26–27.
3. Smith *War*, 180. See also McDermott, 20–35.
4. Smith *War*, 121–125. See also Mokler, 264–272.
5. Smith *War*, 129–133.
6. OW journal, 12 October 1889.
7. Wister "Among," 65, 67.
8. Roosevelt "Sheriff's," 43.
9. See Payne, 122–124, 138; Wister *Owen*, 165–166.
10. Qtd. in Payne, 138.
11. OW journal, 13 October 1892.
12. OW journal, 25 November 1892.
13. OW journal, 2 December, 1892.
14. OW journal, 2 December, 1892.

Chapter 19
The World's Columbian Exposition

A month after the violent end of the Johnson County War, Cody brought his own wild west fantasy to London. He also renamed the show, giving it the grandiloquent name of "Buffalo Bill's Wild West and Congress of Rough Riders of the World" in preparation for its triumphant return to America at the World's Fair the following year. The new name, as Cody's sister Helen Cody Wetmore recalled, suggested a desire to show the world "a representation of the cosmopolitan military force," with a name that was "at once ethnological and military."[1]

Cody never explained exactly why he chose the new name, but it did contain a piece of long-established, if obscure, horseman slang. Several years earlier, Roosevelt had spoken approvingly of the "harum-scarum roughriders" he had met in the west.[2] Before that, during the Civil War, an Illinois cavalry regiment was called the "rough riders."[3] Although the phrase would later be indelibly tied to Roosevelt's military adventures in Cuba, Cody always insisted he made it up for his show. The "expression 'rough riders,' which afterward became so famous, was my own coinage," he claimed, incorrectly.[4]

In addition to the white American westerners and the Indians, Cody added cavalrymen from Germany and France, vaqueros from Mexico, gauchos from Argentina, and warriors from the Cossack nations in Russia. Opie Read, the southern writer and humorist, thought that Cody had "made the warriors of all nations join hands."[5]

Remington, who saw the show in London that summer, thought Cody was actually staging an international cowboy tournament. "The great interest which attaches to the whole show," he wrote in a review for *Harper's Weekly*, "is that it enables the audience to take sides on the question of which people ride best and have the best saddle. The whole thing is put in such tangible shape as to be a regular challenge to debate."⁶ The show had become a way to determine the fittest horse- and gunmen in the world.

Remington joked that when the show made its homecoming at the World's Columbian Exposition the following year, the "Sioux will talk German, the cowboys already have an English accent, and the 'guachos' [sic] will be dressed in good English form." But even though the show had expanded, it had remained true to its roots as a rough-hewn performance of the cowboy philosophy of the American west.

It continued to symbolize the aggressive self-reliance associated with the western states and territories, he wrote. With its international cast of cowboy warriors, the show represented "a poetical and harmless protest against [. . .] the slavery of our modern social system," when men were "wastes of uniformity—where the greatest crime is to be an individual."⁷ In Remington's view, the show was an international testament to the Emersonian self-reliance of the American individual.

Despite its promise of military uniformity, the Congress of Rough Riders would continue to thrill audiences with performances of American-style nonconformity and self-reliance. It was precisely this sturdy individualism that most of Europe and America had, thanks to Cody's tireless touring, come to associate with the faded romance of the American frontier west.

Cody returned to the United States a far bigger celebrity than he had left. As the European tour was coming to a close, many genteel Americans who might otherwise have dismissed him as an uncouth westerner recognized that Cody had, without any of his countrymen ever quite realizing it, been approved by the highest levels of European aristocracy. Although his "fellow-citizens in the United States have never taken him quite seriously," one reporter commented, the Europeans' love of his show led them to "finally look upon the Colonel as one of the characters of the age."⁸

His grand homecoming would be the 1893 World's Columbian Exposition in Chicago. International expositions were then still relatively new events. The first had been the Great Exhibition in London in 1851. There were then several more in Europe before United States held one in Philadelphia in 1876, in celebration of America's centennial.⁹ It was there that French sculptor Frédéric Auguste Bartholdi unveiled the massive, torch-holding copper right arm of the statue he was working on, *Liberty Enlightening the World*. To guarantee its structural viability, Bartholdi had turned to a forty-seven-year-old civil engineer who designed an intricate iron skeleton. That engineer, Gustave Eiffel, later used a similar truss to build his 1,063-foot-tall *Tour Eiffel* for the 1889 World's Fair in Paris, held to commemorate the hundredth anniversary of the French Revolution.

Expositions had become showcases for their host nations' wealth and sophistication. And many Americans wanted to make sure that their upcoming exposition, held to celebrate the quadricentennial of Columbus's journey to the New World, would loudly announce the significance of the United States on the global stage. The 1893 World's Columbian Exposition, or the Chicago World's Fair, would be only the fifteenth international fair. More importantly, it would be America's second time hosting. And the country had changed since the last time.

The nation was increasingly coming to see itself as a bustling, urbanizing nation of businessmen. The population, which had been 47 million at the end of Reconstruction in 1877, had grown to 67 million by 1893. In the minds of many Americans, but especially many of its westerners, the city of Chicago best represented this transformation. It was a former western outpost that had seemingly overnight reinvented itself as an urban metropolis, having more than doubled its population between 1880 and 1890.[10] As one advocate for holding the fair in Chicago put it, the "marvelous growth of Chicago from a frontier camp to the active city of more than a million souls" would "best typify the giant young nation."[11] Chicago was fast becoming, as one advertising booklet had it, the "Metropolis of the West."[12]

Once Chicago had been chosen, the World's Columbian Exposition Corporation had to decide what the fair should look like. One of their first steps was to hire Frederick Law Olmsted's landscape architecture firm.[13] Olmsted was already well known as the landscape architect who, with Calvert Vaux, had designed New York's Central Park along with a number of other parks along the Atlantic coast, including the Chestnut Hill Reservoir where Theodore Roosevelt first met Alice Hathaway Lee.

Visually, the fairgrounds embraced a conservative temporality, gesturing at the future by embracing a romantic past. In practice, this meant an odd mix of cutting-edge futurism, gleaming white faux-classical architecture, and western Americana. The grounds were anchored by the Great Basin, a 2,500-foot long stretch of water featuring Daniel C. French's 100-foot tall classically inspired statue *The Republic*.[14] The entire fair was dotted with similarly massive sculptures, including statues of buffalo, moose, bear, and other western animals. Two of the most striking were Colorado sculptor Alexander Phimister Proctor's massive pair of equestrian statues *The Cowboy* and *The Indian*, located just outside the Transportation Building.[15]

Proctor had modeled *The Indian* on the famed Lakota chief Red Cloud. Twenty-five years earlier in the Powder River basin, Red Cloud had successfully led a devastating series of attacks on the U.S. cavalry that became known as Red Cloud's War. His son, Jack Red Cloud, eventually joined Cody's show as a performer.[16] Yet when Red Cloud was memorialized by

Proctor, audiences seemed to forget he was once widely seen as a terrifying menace to white America. One observer thought *The Cowboy* and *The Indian* were equally "spirited and successful" and confused Red Cloud with his son, reporting that he was just another "one of Buffalo Bill's Indians."[17]

The Midway Plaisance boasted the fair's answer to the Eiffel Tower: the instantly iconic, 268-foot tall rotating amusement wheel that made inventor George Washington Gale Ferris famous overnight.[18] North of the Midway were the galleries and buildings devoted to the individual states of America. On June 8, Cody was on hand for the dedication of the Nebraska building. As for most of his public appearances, Cody wore his beaded buckskin suit and brought along performers from his show. After the massacre at Wounded Knee, Cody's presence served as a kind of symbolic assurance that the Indian wars were indeed over and white American civilization would proceed apace.

To prove it, Cody hired one of the survivors of the Wounded Knee massacre for the show. In mid-April, he had finally gotten permission from Hoke Smith, secretary of the interior, to take 100 Indians to the World's Fair as performers.[19] Smith had, according to one reporter, "finally decided that the influences of the Wild West combination upon the Indians were civilizing."[20]

In a grimly appropriate turn, Cody's performer claimed to have neither family nor name. "Johnny Burke No-Name," one reporter wrote, was the lone "surviving member of his family" after the Seventh Cavalry Regiment had struck the "band of Indians at Wounded Knee like a cyclone." The man was presented as a relic of a quick-receding past: a vanquished enemy, rescued from oblivion and transformed into a harmless theatrical curiosity. At the opening of the Nebraska building, Cody's new employee was, the reporter noticed, much "petted and highly caressed by the good people of Nebraska, who occupy his forefathers' lands."[21]

But the main attraction of the fair was not Cody's show, and it wasn't the Ferris wheel. It wasn't even the dazzling display of electric lights, a technology that most Americans had never seen. It was the buildings themselves. Dubbed the "White City" for their gleaming white finish, the Beaux-Arts buildings were neoclassical wonders, adorned with countless sculptural columns and cornices and crown moldings. After touring the fairgrounds, architect Peter B. Wright noted that the architecture alone was sufficient to "take this down to history as *the* Great Exposition."[22]

Of course, that architecture did not exactly look like contemporary America. It was more like a revival of a time that never existed, a conservative yet imaginary attempt to lend America some of the lost beauty and grandeur of antiquity. A number of observers compared the architecture to ancient Rome; for others, it was the "Venice of the Western World."[23]

But it was all stagecraft. The architecture, like the fair's imposing statuary, was meant to be thrown up quickly and then to degrade even faster. What appeared to be gleaming marble and granite was actually made of "staff," a plaster made of fibrous powdered gypsum. The buildings let the architects' imaginations run wild. With staff, they could work quickly, grandiosely, and with little concern for cost.

The buildings were an American spectacle, meant to evoke the grandeur and permanence of some ancient civilization, thrown up in weeks and then decaying in the summer sun.[24] One reporter, visiting while the buildings were still under construction, marveled at the illusions spun by the "papier mache workers" and their "stage made city." It was amazing, he reported. The "very things which appear most massive and substantial are really the flimsiest of the flimsy."[25]

Of course, Cody would have been indignant at any implication that his show, like the rest of the fair, was flimsy stagecraft. Cody's Congress of Rough Riders was not invited to perform at the fair itself, so they leased a space between 62nd and 63rd Streets just opposite the fairgrounds. The show was a highly visible, if unofficial, addition to the fair: Cody was an honored guest at the opening ceremonies, he met regularly with the press, and the show location was even included on the official fair map.[26]

The advance notices proclaimed that Cody had put together a kind of international cowboy army, peopled by "primitive horsemen, as well as the representatives of the most prominent military nations of the earth," all "legitimate representatives of the irregular soldiers of past and contemporaneous history."[27] Although he would have scoffed at the comparison, his show was rather like the buildings and the fair itself: the best of the past, hand-selected and presented to the future. Audiences loved it. Cody ran two performances a day, rain or shine.[28] By the time he closed for the season, he had made as much as a million dollars in profit.[29]

Cody again created a theater of the American frontier west that ingeniously pretended not to be theater at all. His show told a story in which the freedoms of the present had been created by the conquests of the past. But like the other elements of the fair—Proctor's sculpture, Johnny Burke No-Name, even the buildings themselves—that past was always presented as a benign, romantic past, like a family heirloom. For Cody, the past was an object of entertainment and curiosity; not something that made claims upon the present.

He also seemed to think that the west was a kind of Darwinian sorting ground. He promoted the Chicago show as "the first time of the coming together of these various [international] riders" on American soil, with the implication that those riders would, on some level, be competing: "the contrasts should afford interesting study as well as lively entertainment."[30] In Cody's mind as well as, perhaps, in the minds of thousands of fairgoers who saw his show, the winners of the American west were also the winners of history.

Chapter 19

NOTES

1. Wetmore, 273.
2. TR letter to Henry Cabot Lodge, 10 August 1886.
3. Russell, 370.
4. Cody *Autobiography*, 316.
5. Qtd. in Wetmore, 273.
6. Remington "Buffalo," 847.
7. Remington "Buffalo," 847.
8. Qtd. in Kasson, 90.
9. Burg, xi–xii.
10. Burg, 3.
11. Qtd. in Higinbotham, 9.
12. *Chicago*, vii.
13. Burg, 76–77
14. Burg, 120.
15. Burg, 181. Proctor met Roosevelt at the fairgrounds and later sculpted Roosevelt on horseback. The enormous bronze was dedicated in Portland, Oregon, in 1922; two copies were subsequently dedicated in Mandan and Minot, North Dakota, in 1924.
16. Russell, 377.
17. White and Igleheart, 383.
18. Snyder, 272.
19. "Short," 1.
20. "Nubs," 8.
21. "Nebraska," 7.
22. Qtd. in Burg, 114.
23. Burg, 115.
24. Burg, 151–152.
25. Graves, 6.
26. Kasson, 99.
27. "Amusements," 6.
28. Kasson, 100.
29. Russell, 375.
30. "Amusements," 6.

Chapter 20

The Boone and Crockett Club

On June 15, 1893, Roosevelt and Wister sat down for a private dinner with a group of friends in a rustic, single-room log cabin outfitted with hunting rifles, bear furs, and unhewn log furniture.[1]

The cabin looked at least a hundred years old. In fact, it had been built only a few months earlier, on the fairgrounds of the World's Columbian Exposition, just a few blocks from the newly established University of Chicago.

The men had gathered to celebrate the accomplishments of the Boone and Crockett Club, the hunting and conservation group that Roosevelt had founded six years earlier. Roosevelt had appointed Wister and four other men to oversee the planning of the cabin—"Hunter's Cabin," they called it—and it had been erected on the south end of Wooded Island, just across the bridge from the fair's electricity building.[2]

It was a one-room cabin anchored by an enormous stone fireplace. Crossed over the fireplace was a pair of bentwood snowshoes; above the snowshoes was a ten-point elk rack supporting two rifles. Blankets and hides were draped over a settee and a set of bunk beds, both of which were fashioned of rough, unfinished logs. Outside, another enormous elk rack was mounted above the front door. An ancient prairie schooner parked just beside the entrance added to the general effect.[3]

Even though the Boone and Crockett Club was six years old at that point, the dinner at Hunter's Cabin represented something of a coming-out party. The club had acquired national prominence. In four months it would publish a book titled *American Big-Game Hunting: The Book of the Boone and Crockett Club*. It was the first of what would become seven books of essays, featuring contributions from Wister, Roosevelt, and others. But the cabin was by far the most visible and certainly the most expensive publicity campaign the club had ever undertaken. Even with its rough furnishings—all carefully arranged to look like the makeshift home of a destitute mountain man—the cabin had somehow ended up costing the club $2,500.[4]

At the private dinner, Roosevelt, Wister, and the other club members welcomed a number of dignitaries connected to the fair as their guests.[5] Wister commented that they dined "well and simply, [in] camp fashion."[6] But the apparent shabbiness of their surroundings didn't quite match the dinner. The men had eaten planked whitefish, steak, and salt pork, replete with waiters, fine silverware, and champagne.[7] It was, Wister concluded fondly, a "lively dinner."[8]

In a way, the theatricality of the dinner—real champagne in a fake hunting cabin—served to encapsulate the conservatism of many of its members. As it often was for Wister and Roosevelt, time and space were conflated: for them, going west was like taking a deliberate step back in time, one where you could bring selected trappings of the future with you. (Or at least a bottle of champagne.) Conflating time and space in this way was a cognitive error, albeit an understandable one. After all, a western log cabin built in 1893 and an eastern luxury hotel built in 1893 are equally old. It is only cultural biases about time and space and progress that mark one structure as more "primitive" or "historical" than the other.

The cabin was intended to memorialize that harbinger of modernity, the white western settler. "The club felt very strongly," Roosevelt explained, "that the life of the pioneer settler, the life of the man who struck out into the wilderness as part of the vanguard of civilization, and made his living largely in warfare with the wild game, represented a phase of our history so characteristic and yet so evanescent that it would be a mistake not to have it represented at the Chicago Exposition. There is nothing in the history of any other nation which quite corresponds to it."[9] For Roosevelt, Wister, and others, the cabin wasn't just a cabin. It also allowed its inhabitants to actually experience an earlier "phase of our history," as Roosevelt put it.

This was the real reason the Boone and Crockett Club had come to the fair. Not just to promote themselves, but to cultivate the sort of conservative temporality that allowed for the very possibility of historical and natural preservation. They wanted to keep the past alive so it could continue to be useful. After all, if the western settler was the "vanguard of civilization," it was crucial that the west itself—its land, its game, its folkways—be conserved, so that American civilization could perpetually renew itself.

Roosevelt had founded the Boone and Crockett Club six years earlier with George Bird Grinnell, the New York naturalist and editor of *Forest and Stream* magazine. Grinnell was nine years older than Roosevelt, but the two had much in common. Like Roosevelt, Grinnell had been born to wealthy New York parents, and like Roosevelt, he had shown an unquenchable early interest in animals and the outdoors. Before Roosevelt had matriculated into Harvard, Grinnell had already graduated and gone west with Colonel George Custer to explore the Black Hills in 1874. (And that was not even his first trip beyond the Mississippi River. In 1870, the year he graduated from Yale, Grinnell had accompanied one of his professors on a paleontological expedition to Nebraska where he first met William F. Cody, then still working as an army scout.[10])

By the time Roosevelt went to Dakota, Grinnell had finished his doctorate in zoology and become the publisher and senior editor of *Forest and Stream* magazine.[11] Grinnell had more knowledge about the geography, flora, and fauna of the American west than almost anyone else in the world. So he was somewhat amused when he read Roosevelt's first western book, *Hunting Trips of a Ranchman*, in 1885. It struck him as the credulous work of a wide-eyed tenderfoot.

In his review of the book for *Forest and Stream*, Grinnell tried to put the matter delicately. Roosevelt's "experience of the Western country is quite limited," he explained politely, as he "has not become accustomed to all the various sights and sounds of the plains and the mountains." More of a problem was the book's uncritical rehash of many old hunting yarns that Grinnell simply knew weren't true. Roosevelt hadn't been a westerner long enough to know any better. All the same, Roosevelt's book was charming in its noviitate sense of wonder. If nothing else, Grinnell wrote, the book had a few nice pictures, even if one drawing of an elk did resemble nothing so much as a "hydrocephalous dwarf."[12]

Shortly after Grinnell's review appeared in the July 2, 1885, issue of *Forest and Stream*, Roosevelt marched down to the magazine's offices at 40 Park Row, just next to the New York Times Building across from City Hall. Roosevelt was undoubtedly annoyed, but Grinnell recalled that after discussing some of the problems of the book, Roosevelt "at once saw my point of view."[13] As they spoke, the two men realized they had much in common. Besides their privileged Manhattan boyhoods and early infatuation with natural history, both had loved the western novels of Mayne Reid as children. Reid's novels, such as *The Scalp Hunters*—featuring a young protagonist who felt his body grow stronger in the demanding environment of the American southwest—had thrilled the young Roosevelt. Reid's stories "had appealed to my imagination" as well, Grinnell recalled.[14]

And both men, of course, were avid hunters. Grinnell tried to get Roosevelt to understand that story of big game hunting in the west was at its core a story of loss. They talked about Montana, where the destruction of small game for hides was beginning to be a problem. That process, he said, echoed the earlier slaughter of the bison. The "last of the big [bison] herds," Grinnell mused, "had disappeared."[15]

Over the next several years, Roosevelt and Grinnell had a number of conversations about the killing of western big game. At the time, Grinnell admitted, they had little understanding of "the attempts that would at once be made to turn into money all our natural things."[16] For too many hunters, western big game meant big money. More money would lead to more hunting. More hunting would lead to even more money and so on until the land and its wildlife were completely destroyed. It all boiled down to an existential and ecological paradox: the fact that people wanted to hunt big game seemed to predestine a future in which there would be no big game to hunt.

In other words, they were talking about conservation. They were not necessarily using that particular word, but they were obsessed with the idea it represented. The term was then still fairly new; just a few years before they met, no one would have heard it used in that way. Yet Grinnell and Roosevelt developed an increasingly firm conviction that wildlife needed to be preserved. At the time, their goals were almost entirely recreational: they wanted to be able to hunt. As Grinnell put it, they were at first interested in game preservation "chiefly with the idea that it should be protected in order that there might still be good hunting which should last for generations."[17] In place of the hunting ethic practiced by many of their peers, in which sportsmen killed as much as they wanted, wherever they wanted, Grinnell and Roosevelt envisioned a kind of dialectic of destruction, in which game would be preserved in the present so it could be killed in the future.

Their enthusiasm for hunting got them thinking about history and temporality in interesting ways. The goal, as they began to conceive of it, should not be simply preserve the current amount of game. Instead, they wanted someone to lead a restoration of the earlier, more abundant, stocks of game. Their sportsmen's sensibilities led them to a tentative, still unformed philosophy of wildlife conservation. And that philosophy, in turn, was built on bedrock of their conservative temporality.

They wanted to act in the present to build a future that was just like the past.

In the fall of 1887, Roosevelt first had the idea of starting some sort of hunting club. He knew that naturally the club would be made up of men like Grinnell and himself: members of the American gentry who had learned to hunt and track on the proving grounds of the far west. As Grinnell put it, the club should be full of "men of social standing, whose opinion is worth regarding and whose influence is widely felt in the best classes of society."[18]

In December, Roosevelt proposed the idea to a few of his hunter friends at a dinner he hosted on Madison Avenue. He liked the name Boone and Crockett Club, after Daniel Boone and Davy Crockett. They were men, Roosevelt proclaimed grandly, who "served in a certain sense as the tutelary deities of American hunting lore."[19] (Boone and Crockett were also the names of the driving horses owned by his maternal grandparents on their Georgia plantation.[20])

The men drew up a constitution. Roosevelt was chosen as president. Grinnell, Wister, and several others were named to the executive committee. The chief objects of the club, they declared in their constitution, were fivefold: to promote "manly sport with the rifle"; to promote travel "in the wild and unknown" parts of America; to work for "the preservation of the large game of this country"; to promote the study of natural history as it pertains to wildlife; and to promote "the interchange of opinions and ideas" about hunting, travel, rifles, and the like.[21]

The earliest purpose of the club was simply to articulate an ethics of hunting. They wanted to set down a code of behavior for the type of man who liked to think of himself as what Grinnell and Roosevelt called a "true sportsman."[22] For them, it was not enough to kill. The killing had to be done in the right sort of way and by the right sort of people. Their constitution forbade specific hunting practices, including trapping, shooting an animal in water from a boat, "crusting" (bogging down a quarry in snow while the hunter is advantaged by snowshoes), and "fire-hunting" (using the light from a fire pan to temporarily stun deer at nighttime).[23]

(Given that the Boone and Crockett Club from its inception renounced fire-hunting, it bears noting that according to one book with which Roosevelt might have been familiar, Daniel Boone himself used to go fire-hunting as a young man.[24])

However, Grinnell and Roosevelt didn't want to forbid certain practices only among the club's members. They wanted to start a cultural shift. They wanted the American elite to model certain behaviors in hopes that those behaviors would trickle down to the population at large.

For Roosevelt, one way of working toward that goal was to suggest that crusting, fire-hunting, and the rest of the banned practices were insufficiently masculine. The club was made up of gentlemen hunters, he argued, but they weren't flabby aristocrats. They were men who believed that for "true sportsmen," the "harder and manlier the sport is the more attractive it is."[25]

In one of the club's earliest public manifestos, Grinnell acknowledged that the club's members had hardly been known for their environmental stewardship. "In the past the worst enemies that the great game of the West has had," he wrote, "have belonged to just this class" of well-off men. Some hunters guilty of such herd decimation were at least motivated by material gain—they wanted to sell skins or meat. But other hunters had no such excuse. The "wealthy hunter," he admitted, "did his slaughtering in pure wantonness."[26]

However, he promised, under the Boone and Crockett Club's guidance, such indiscriminate killing would come to an end. For one thing, the club's hunting ethics were for everyone, not just its members. "This club discountenances the bloody methods of all game butchers without regard to occupation, wealth or social status," he declared. Two years after the club's founding, Grinnell claimed, its influence could already be seen in a "considerable change of sentiment." Now, it was "becoming a recognized fact that a man who wastefully destroys big game, whether for the market, or only for heads, has nothing of the true sportsman about him."[27]

Needless to say, the criteria implied by the phrase "true sportsman" were debatable at best. The hunters who Roosevelt and Grinnell derided as "game butchers"—the men who sold hides and meat to put food on their tables and shelter over their heads—likely didn't care if they counted as sportsmen at all. Yet, in fairly short order, Roosevelt and Grinnell were able to impose a set of rules, a system of ethics, and even something of an aesthetic framework on an activity that had long characterized the frontier west.

At the time, hunting was hardly the highly regulated activity that it would eventually become. There was no federal agency tasked with fish and game management. Barely one year before Roosevelt proposed the Boone and Crockett Club, the U.S. Department of Agriculture had first established its Division of Economic Ornithology and Mammalogy. But that division was tasked with researching the effects of wildlife on agriculture—and mostly just birds, at that point—not on regulating wildlife populations. The first state hunting licenses would not be issued until 1895. And although by 1893, as Grinnell and Roosevelt acknowledged, "many of the States have good game laws," it didn't matter much, as "in very few [of those states] are they rigidly enforced."[28]

Yet through Roosevelt and Grinnell's efforts, hunting—an activity that for centuries had been either a necessity for survival or an unthoughtful exercise of individual freedom—was, seemingly overnight, turned into an informally regulated social behavior subject to the norms of modern gentility. It was no longer enough to kill a bear, whether for survival or fun or profit. Now a person had to do so in a socially acceptable way. Or at least in a way that was socially acceptable to men like Roosevelt and Grinnell.

Though the club had its origins in hunting, it did not take long for it to embrace a philosophy of environmental conservation. Decades later, Grinnell would write that "no single thing that [Roosevelt] did for conservation has had so far-reaching an effect as the establishment of the Boone and Crockett Club."[29]

In 1872, Congress had established Yellowstone as the first national park in America, which also made it the first national park in the world. One of the earliest proposals for a national park had come in the 1830s from artist George Catlin, whose traveling shows would later inspire Remington and

Cody alike. He was one of the first to suggest the federal government take steps to create "*A nation's Park*, containing man and beast, in all the wild and freshness of their nature's beauty."[30] A quarter century later, Henry David Thoreau made a similar call for the creation of "national preserves."[31]

On March 1, 1872, President Ulysses S. Grant signed a bill to set aside a tract of land near the headwaters of the Yellowstone River "as a public park or pleasuring-ground for the benefit and enjoyment of the people."[32] Yet, because the bill also gave the secretary of the interior the power to preserve timber deposits and grant building permits, the nature of what the first national park would actually become—a wildlife reserve, a reserve of natural resources to fuel private business, a site for commercial tourist development, or something else entirely—remained unsettled.

Because the park was so remote, the question of how the nation's first national park should be managed remained unresolved for nearly a decade. By the 1880s, though, the Northern Pacific Railroad's lines had reached the edges of the park.[33] The Yellowstone Park Improvement Company was able to harvest timber, game, and geyser formations, and because there was no enforcement law, it could not be punished for doing so. Grinnell thought the company was effectively hijacking public property: "seizing and converting to its own use time, game and other valuable things within the Park."[34]

By 1891, one of the Boone and Crockett Club's chief interests had become the question of Yellowstone's management. In the short term, they wanted to convince Congress to keep the railroads out of the park. But in the longer term, Grinnell wanted to set a precedent that would shape America's vision for what a national park should be. After initially believing that a railroad might be beneficial to the park, Roosevelt had come around to Grinnell's view. "I am glad to hear that Roosevelt is going to stand back on the question of railways in the Park," Grinnell commented.[35]

Roosevelt did more than just stand back. In 1892, he wrote an article for *Forest and Stream* expressing his outrage. "It is of the utmost importance that the Park shall be kept in its present form as a great forestry preserve and a National pleasure ground, the like of which is not to be found on any other continent than ours; and all public-spirited Americans should join with *Forest and Stream* in the effort to prevent the greed of a little group of speculators, careless of everything save their own selfish interests, from doing the damage they threaten to the whole people of the United States, by wrecking the Yellowstone National Park," he wrote with breathless indignation.[36]

The Boone and Crockett Club threw its full support behind a Senate bill that would prohibit the Montana Mineral Railway from building a rail line to Cooke City, Montana, through the park.[37] They succeeded: the bill failed. Two years later, Iowa Republican congressman John F. Lacey's 1894 "Lacey

Act" became law, finally giving the Department of the Interior authority to prosecute poachers and other lawbreakers in the park. The Boone and Crockett Club had quietly become one of the most influential lobbyists for American environmental conservation.

NOTES

1. Wister *Roosevelt*, 36; Bold *Frontier*, 17.
2. Grinnell "Boone" [1893], 49.
3. Arnold, n.p.
4. Bold *Frontier*, 17.
5. Roosevelt and Grinnell *American*, 336.
6. Wister *Owen*, 164.
7. Bold *Frontier*, 18.
8. Wister *Owen*, 164.
9. Roosevelt "Boone," 267.
10. Punke, 11–13.
11. Punke, 116–123.
12. Grinnell "Hunting," 451.
13. Grinnell "Introduction," xv.
14. Qtd. in Punke, 5.
15. Grinnell "Introduction," xv.
16. Grinnell "Introduction," xvi–xvii.
17. Grinnell "Introduction," xvii.
18. Grinnell "Boone" [1889], 513.
19. Roosevelt "Boone," 267.
20. Roosevelt *Autobiography*, 12.
21. Grinnell "Boone" [1893], 49.
22. Grinnell "Boone" [1893], 49; Roosevelt "Boone," 267.
23. Roosevelt and Grinnell *American*, 338.
24. Flint, 26.
25. Roosevelt "Boone," 267.
26. Grinnell "Boone" [1893], 49.
27. Grinnell "Boone" [1893], 49.
28. Roosevelt and Grinnell *American*, 12.
29. Grinnell "Introduction," xviii.
30. Qtd. in Eisler, 109, italics in original.
31. Qtd. in Reiger, 126.
32. Forty-Second Congress, 32.
33. Reiger, 132.
34. Grinnell "Brief," 447. See also Cutright, 174.
35. Qtd. in Reiger, 157.
36. Qtd. in Cutright, 175–176.
37. Reiger, 158.

Chapter 21

Environmental Conservation and Political Conservatism

Shortly before the World's Fair, still flush with the club's recent success in defeating the railroad, Grinnell wrote with pride that the club had "not spared time nor trouble in advocating beneficial legislation, and opposing injurious measures, in Congress." Overall, they had done "much to impress upon many classes in the community the importance of preserving our National Parks, our forests and our game."[1] The club wasn't just a genteel collection of wealthy hunters, he realized. It was actually *doing* things. What began as a code of ethics for gentleman's hunting club began, in short order, to be a loose philosophy of conservation that shaped America's parks policy.

Or as Grinnell put it, the club's original purpose was soon "reversed." Even though the organization started "as a club of riflemen, apparently concerned only with their own recreation," he explained, "it early discovered that more important work was to be done in the field of protection than in that of destruction."[2]

As a political idea, though, conservation remained fraught. It was predicated on a kind of temporal prisoner's bargain. And for the bargain to work successfully, everyone had to enter into it, whether they actually wanted to or not.

The bargain of conservation worked like this: Individuals living in the present had to accept limits on certain freedoms—the freedom to kill what they wanted and to build what they wanted—so that over time, select parts of the American landscape would look as they did in the past: fewer rail lines and hotels, more trees and wildlife, and so on. All this was done so that other individuals, living at some point in the future, could enjoy similarly curtailed freedoms. This, in its most basic sense, was the logic at the beating heart of Roosevelt's early philosophy of conservation. And that philosophy, in turn, was built atop his long-standing conservative disposition.

For it to be any other way, the two men worried, was to sever any continuity between past and future. During Grinnell's lifetime alone, he had seen the wild bison herds almost eliminated for the simple reason that Americans were exercising their natural right to hunt. The same thing could happen to other species, to forests, to rivers. To *not* limit certain freedoms—to allow men to exercise their natural liberty to cut down as many trees and kill as much game as the market could withstand—was essentially to doom America to a future impoverished of resources and of wonder. In more ways than one, the country would be poorer.

Yet there was no getting around the plain fact that even the smallest effort to conserve wildlife infringed on someone's individual liberty. This presented a problem. If one thread of western conservatism emphasized Emersonian self-reliance—the idea that individuals are makers and masters of themselves—then any philosophy of conservation would seem to be less than conservative. It was awkward but unavoidable: the Boone and Crockett Club advocated limits on individual freedom. As they saw it, when it came to natural resources, individual freedom had to be tempered in the present so that it would exist at all in the future.

Grinnell appreciated the irony. The club had been formed to guarantee individual freedoms on the hunting grounds of the American west. But almost immediately after, it began trying limit those same freedoms. "No sooner had the Club been organized and begun to consider the subjects which most interested it," he observed, "than it became apparent that on all hands the selfishness of individuals was rapidly doing away with all the natural things of this country, and that a halt must be called."[3] They had organized to indulge their interests, only to realize that if everybody indulged those interests, there would be a problem.

(Of course, when non-club members pursued those interests, or at least didn't pursue them in the same way, the club didn't think their actions equal to those of gentleman sportsmen. They saw instead the "selfishness of individuals" and decided "a halt must be called.")

Even so, Roosevelt and Grinnell seemed to sense that conservation, on some level, simply looked bad. It involved a group of wealthy individuals trying to limit the freedoms of the less fortunate and saying it was for the greater good. From this perspective, conservation seemed to require a hierarchical society. Conservation needed some kind of aristocracy to say to the public, *No, don't hunt like that; instead hunt like this: like a gentleman.* It left the unavoidable impression that in the Boone and Crockett Club resided a small and powerful group of wealthy men seeking to curtail everyone's freedom.

The concern that conservation would be seen largely as the pastime of aristocrats was perhaps why Roosevelt and Grinnell went to such lengths to make the Boone and Crockett Club's brand of wildlife conservation appear democratic. The best way to do that, they decided, was to appeal to the idea of the American west. More than once, Grinnell claimed that the west had magically endowed Roosevelt with an inalienable democratic spirit.

When Roosevelt had first gone west, Grinnell explained, an "old-time independent spirit still prevailed, and one man was just as good as another." Even though relationships between individuals were unequal, each man possessed an equivalent and unassailable core of individual liberty. Roosevelt recognized this attitude, Grinnell noted, "which at first must have astonished him, as it did other Eastern men," and quickly adopted those western values as his own. Roosevelt "sympathized with the independent spirit and adjusted himself at once," he concluded.[4]

Even so, that "independent spirit" wasn't necessarily a democratic one. Individual freedom and democratic politics are only occasionally compatible. Something might be perfectly democratic, in the sense of reflecting the general will of the people, yet at the same time perfectly ruinous to the freedom of a particular individual.

However, instead of simply acknowledging the tension between liberty and democracy, Grinnell wanted to make a more complicated case. He wanted to suggest that the west had bred in Roosevelt a philosophy of individual freedom and self-reliance. But he also wanted to suggest that that philosophy was compatible with democratic equality, not opposed to it.

Roosevelt's conservatism, informed by his reading of Darwin, had long been built on a bedrock of social inequality. For him, the relationship between social development and inequality was simple: competition between unequal individuals drove social development. Some individuals were faster than others, smarter than others, braver than others. That was simply the way of nature. It was inequality—the unceasing series of competitions to determine the best—that propelled American development.

But environmental conservation complicated this principle. For hunters given sufficient time and energy, the principle of competition and the incentives of the marketplace would lead inexorably to species extinction. Left unchecked, the principle of competition would make future competition unfeasible. When it came to harvesting natural resources, the victor would also be the last one standing.

So what Grinnell and Roosevelt needed to do was to make the counterintuitive case that western individualism was synonymous with western democracy. That way, the Boone and Crockett Club would appear to be urging conservationist measures not because they were quasi-aristocrats who sought to bend the masses to their desires, but rather out of a spirit of democratic fellowship. They would be merely trying to protect the freedoms of future citizens.

In addition to his embrace of the west's "independent spirit," Grinnell explained, Roosevelt's early experiences in the west were also where "he learned his first lessons in real democracy, for he was constantly associating with men of various classes and types, each one of whom was in his own estimation as good as any one else."⁵ Elsewhere, Grinnell conflated individual freedom with democratic values even more explicitly. When Roosevelt went west, he wrote, "he made for himself a position as a man, and not as a master." Such Emersonian self-reliance was, he proclaimed, part of Roosevelt's "democratic spirit."⁶

Put differently, the Boone and Crockett Club was attempting something that Roosevelt was becoming quite good at. They were trying to make aristocracy seem democratic. A group of powerful, well-born men wanted, for thoroughly honorable reasons, to restrict the freedoms of a certain class of people in order to recreate the conditions of times long gone. And they thought that desire was perfectly in service of those people.

What made such conservation truly conservative, though, was the way that Roosevelt tried to suffuse it with a certain temporality. Americans need to "preserve [wilderness], not only for the sake of this generation," he wrote, but "above all for the sake of those who come after us." In many ways, this sentiment represents an excellent distillation of an animating spirit of American conservatism. Roosevelt wanted the citizens of today to imagine that the citizens of tomorrow would want to be more, and not less, like the citizens of yesterday.

Above all, wilderness preservation couldn't look like the maneuverings of a cabal of elites. "The work of preservation must be carried on in such a way as to make it evident that we are working in the interest of the people as a whole, not in the interest of any particular class," Roosevelt insisted. It was imperative that Americans believed that wilderness conservation was "essentially a democratic movement in the interest of all our people."⁷

There was a certain logic to their emphasis on democracy. As Grinnell pointed out, the wealthy and the well-born had always owned game preserves, going back at least to eleventh-century England. If necessary, they could own them again. But "unless the State and Federal Governments establish such reservations," he insisted, "a time is at hand when the poor man will have no place to go where he can find game to hunt. The establishment of such refuges is for the benefit of the whole public—not for any class—and is therefore a thoroughly democratic proposition."⁸

Ultimately, the Boone and Crockett Club was dedicated to two sets of ideas. First, that men like them knew the best way to manage natural resources for the future. They had long felt that when it came to wildlife and timber, the best future was one that didn't resemble the present, but rather the past. And second, they wanted that philosophy of practical conservatism to be democratic—by, and for, the people. However, they were not the first to fuse ecological conservation, political conservatism, and the appearance of a democratic ethos. One prominent new member of President Cleveland's cabinet had been doing it for years.

In 1893, Julius Sterling Morton had just been appointed secretary of agriculture by President Cleveland. But the midwestern newspaperman and founder of Arbor Day had long been interested in the political ramifications of environmental conservation.

After planting a number of seedlings in Nebraska Territory as a young man, Morton felt that tree planting had an important temporal and political component. Trees represented time and possibility, he wrote on the first Arbor Day in 1872, and were available to everyone regardless of class or creed. "Trees grow in time," he wrote. The trees "planted by the poor man [will] grow just as grandly and beautifully as those planted by the opulent." There was a social lesson in the "unswerving integrity and genuine democracy of trees, for they refuse to be influenced by money or social position." In short, "[t]here is no aristocracy in trees."[9] Morton created Arbor Day in part to make the Jeffersonian case that trees were the products of American individualism: If someone were willing to plant and tend them, they would grow.

Alongside his work as secretary of agriculture, Morton developed a reputation as an individualist and an amateur political philosopher. Like Roosevelt and Grinnell, he used the natural world to hypothesize about the future and to root it deeply in the past. (Despite being a lifelong Democrat, Morton would nonetheless go on to be a supporter of Roosevelt's. His son, Paul Morton, would later serve as Secretary of the Navy during Roosevelt's presidency.) Roosevelt returned his admiration, later describing Morton as having "qualities of sturdy manhood, of courage, fearlessness, broad-mindedness and absolute integrity" that were connected to his sense of time: for Roosevelt, Morton was a man "far-sighted enough to realize the great need of tree culture."[10]

Morton's conservative thinking was not limited to matters of horticultural, though. He was an advocate of lower taxes to encourage private forestry management, a supporter of the gold standard, and an enthusiastic promoter of the Jeffersonian ideal of a limited government for a nation of self-reliant farmers and foresters.[11] Given his lifelong conservative individualism and support for arboreal conservation, few could have found it surprising that after President Cleveland's second term came to an end, Morton would return to Nebraska and devote his energies to editing a weekly journal he called *The Conservative*. Its first issue contained a kind of editorial manifesto written by Morton, one that tied environmental conservation to political conservatism. The journal was devoted to conservatism broadly stated, which included a government driven by a "merit system" to determine the fittest and the best.[12]

Morton published an occasional column called "Conservatisms," authored by veterinary scientist Frank S. Billings, which collected pithy slogans explaining the journal's modern brand of conservatism. In keeping with Morton's unwavering belief in absolute self-reliance—in matters arboricultural as well as matters political—many of the sayings praised the American belief in individual ability and denigrated the European aristocratic focus on family lineage: "Family pedigree is a rotten crutch for inability," read one slogan. "Conservatism is the acme of intelligent self-preservation, individual or national," went another.[13]

But many simply emphasized the conservative thinking that held that democratic contests of Darwinian merit would determine America's natural aristocracy—its best and bravest. "Weakness and unfitness are identical," one aphorism noted, making the straightforward Darwinian case that strength meant fitness. Another connected natural fitness to natural freedom: "The weak are invariably slaves."[14]

Still others emphasized the conservative logic that Darwinian science, applied to democratic politics or the marketplace, would determine America's natural elite: "True kingship is leadership by natural selection through popular election."[15] The reasoning was identical to Jefferson's dream of a "natural aristocracy," updated for the age of Darwin.

The subscription list for *The Conservative* eventually climbed as high as 15,000.[16] Although the founding of the journal was still some years off when Morton became secretary of agriculture, the intellectual germ of the journal—the notion that thinking seriously about natural conservation went hand in hand with thinking seriously about political conservatism—was already in place by 1893, the year of the World's Fair.

And even though Roosevelt and Grinnell's wildlife conservation was not precisely the same thing as Morton's arboreal conservation, both types nonetheless sought to build a future that would be firmly tethered to the past. Conservation, Morton stressed, was not just the domain of a wealthy elite. It was important to him that both political conservatism and environmental conservation be understood as essentially democratic—open to all—even if, in practice, certain groups would benefit more than others. For conservation to work, he reasoned, people needed to believe in the "genuine democracy of trees."[17]

One of Roosevelt and Grinnell's earliest attempts to present conservation as democratic was their 1893 book *American Big-Game Hunting*. It was the first of seven books that would eventually be published by the Boone and Crockett Club. Roosevelt and Grinnell edited and financed the book themselves, using Roosevelt's money and Grinnell's *Forest and Stream* publishing arm.[18] Many of the short essays in that book, written by Roosevelt, Grinnell, Wister, and other members of the club, displayed a buoyant conservativism—a belief that slow-vanishing things can still be useful, a kind of pragmatics of loss—and sought to marshal support for building a future that would usher in a new American Eden.

Of course, when Roosevelt was talking about wildlife, he was rarely *only* talking about wildlife. In their introduction to the book, Roosevelt and Grinnell made clear that they thought hunting—and, by extension, resource conservation—would foster certain conservative-individualist virtues. Hunting is "a sport for a vigorous and masterful people," Roosevelt wrote. The hunter needed "manliness, self-reliance, and [the] capacity for hardy self-help."[19] Without sufficient big game for hunting, he thought, there would not be a self-reliant, self-helping people. Losing big game meant losing American individualism.

For Roosevelt's contribution to the book, he penned a memory of hunting for pronghorn antelope on horseback accompanied by a pack of braying hounds. The scene was a direct visual echo of aristocratic coursing—the only thing missing was Roosevelt blowing a horn and bellowing "tally ho!"—and continued a line of thought that Roosevelt and Wister had been cultivating for several years: that the cowboy or hunter, seen correctly, was a kind of natural aristocrat, and the opportunities for practical retrogression into the aristocratic-seeming past afforded by the American west allowed him to prove his superiority.

Hunting prongbuck, Roosevelt wrote, presented one such opportunity for retrogression. He thought that prongbuck "represent on our prairies the antelopes of the Old World."[20] (At one point, Roosevelt attributed not just his own motivations but his *horse*'s to the pleasures of such retrogression, proclaiming in a fit of romantic speculation that his pony was perhaps "overcome by dim reminisces of buffalo-hunting in his Indian youth" as it chased a doe.[21]) Roosevelt was gesturing not just toward an earlier moment in a temporal sense, but to an earlier moment in a developmental sense. Conserving the animal meant conserving the experience of hunting it, which for Roosevelt meant conserving the dream of the Old World.

In Grinnell's chapter, wistfully titled "In Buffalo Days," he wrote of the "relics of the past" that were the American bison. "Of the millions of buffalo which even in our own time ranged the plains in freedom," he declared with apocalyptic drama, "none now remain." Although the essay was nominally an occasion to reminisce on successful bison hunts, for Grinnell, it was really a chance to pontificate about time, history, and American wildlife. For him, bison had become symbols of a quick-receding history—"mementos of the past"—and a reminder of a lost abundance that he longed to see again. But absent some sort of intervention, a phase of American life would conclude once the "buffalo passed into history."[22]

However, he stressed, bison were not doomed irretrievably to the fog of nostalgia. There were things Americans were already doing to encourage conservation, and they could do more if they wanted to. National parks, he explained, were excellent examples of a conservationist impulse. "In the Yellowstone National Park, protected from destruction by US troops, are the only wild buffalo which exist within the borders of the United States," he claimed.[23] In his view, conservation was the cure for temporal dislocation. Through conservation, bison could be brought out of the past and into the future.

In his contribution to the book, Wister wrote about a hunting trip he had taken to Washington State in search of white goat. He wrote about wildlife in a way that yoked it to a fast-receding past, as if there were just enough time to snatch those animals back from the brink of annihilation. Venturing that far west, he wrote, had been like traveling back in time. Out among the "primeval dust" and the "primeval mud," his hunting party initially found no goats. The animals seemed like ghosts of history.[24]

Wister's party eventually found only a few isolated goats, leading him to marvel that it was as if the goats "had retired from society, and were spending the remainder of their days in quiet isolation."[25] Although the trip had begun with Wister feeling that he had ventured back into the "primeval" past, by the end, it was clear to him that goats still existed in the present, if in much-diminished numbers. The few lonely goats they stumbled on were like forgotten hermits, left behind by the acceleration of modernity.

But like Grinnell and many of the other members of the Boone and Crockett Club, Wister wanted to make clear that there was something people could *do*. Even though he never used the word, the latent tension between conservatism and conservatism seemed clear in his mind.

Because conserving wildlife meant restricting individuals' freedom to hunt it, it was difficult to reconcile the Emersonian self-reliant strand of conservatism with the Boone and Crockett Club's nascent conservationism. Wildlife conservation and individualist conservatism were, it seemed, at odds.

However, Wister thought he had finally figured out how to reconcile them. "The pervading spirit of the far West as to game, as to timber, as to everything that a true American should feel it is his right to use and his duty to preserve for those coming after is—'What do I care, so long as it lasts my time?'" he wrote. The insinuation was unmistakable: in order to guarantee wildlife to "those coming after," the American political ethos must expand beyond caring only if it "lasts *my* time." The first step, he suggested, wasn't a change in individual freedom but in individual will. By the end of the trip, Wister explained, he had "willingly decided to molest no more goats" by deciding to eschew the trophy-driven value system that governed most recreational hunting.[26] Yet this shift wasn't driven by a new awareness of animal life, but instead by a new awareness of time and ecology.

Wister was pointing toward a new way of thinking about temporality. It was no longer enough for an individual, living in the present, to care only if something "lasts my time." For a person to value practical retrogressions into the American "past" for purposes of social regeneration (and to assume that future citizens would also value such retrogressions), that person also needed to value wildlife conservation. Simply put, being a conservative meant conserving nature.

This shift in thinking wasn't about curtailing individual liberty, but rather reorienting the object of that liberty away from destruction and toward preservation. After all, if the elite of the past required rugged, self-reliant hunting experiences as proofs of their masculinity, then it stood to reason that the elite of the future would as well. In that light, ecological conservation would become the safeguard of political conservatism.

NOTES

1. Grinnell "Boone" [1893], 49.
2. Grinnell "Brief History," 490.
3. Grinnell "Brief," 490.
4. Grinnell "Introduction," xix.
5. Grinnell "Introduction," xix, xx.
6. Grinnell "Theodore," 18.
7. Roosevelt "Wilderness," 24.
8. Grinnell "Big-Game," 448–449.
9. Qtd. in Olson, 165.
10. Qtd. in "Personal," 5.
11. Lora, 29–33.
12. Morton, 1.
13. Billings "Conservatisms," (2.3) 12, (2.12) 11.
14. Billings "Conservatisms," (2.6) 13.
15. Billings "Conservatisms," (2.3) 12.
16. Lora, 26.
17. Qtd. in Olson, 165.
18. Bold *Frontier*, 38.
19. Roosevelt and Grinnell "Boone," 14.
20. Roosevelt "Coursing," 129.
21. Roosevelt "Coursing," 133.
22. Grinnell "Buffalo," 155, 210, 158, ibid.
23. Grinnell "Buffalo," 210.
24. Wister "White," 29.
25. Wister "White," 53.
26. Wister "White," 58.

Chapter 22

The Science of Western History

A few years before the World's Fair, Herbert Baxter Adams, a professor of history at Johns Hopkins University, had an unusually good student named Frederick Jackson Turner. Adams was a leading advocate of the idea that history was a scientific discipline. He modeled his history seminars after scientific laboratories, saying the classes were "laboratories where books are treated like mineralogical specimens."[1] History, he taught his students, was beholden to the same Darwinian laws as evolutionary biology. Adams was a proponent of the "germ theory" of history. To his way of thinking, civilization reproduced somewhat biologically, spreading like a germ, which in part meant that a civilized nation needed a certain type of racial makeup.[2] It was a simple law of science, he seemed to think: for the same reasons that *Panthera leo* reproduced more lions, American Anglo-Saxons, descended from Germanic tribes by way of England, reproduced more civilized nations.

His student Turner did not think this was exactly correct, but he did not think it was entirely wrong, either. After earning his doctorate, Turner returned to his home state of Wisconsin and became a history professor at the University of Wisconsin. He kept in touch with Baxter over the years, and in late 1892 sent him an article he had written arguing that historians needed to think more about geography. Baxter urged him to write a similar paper to present at the summer meeting of the American Historical Association, to be held in Chicago to coincide with the World's Fair.

Many serious historians thought that summer's meeting would be a joke. Justin Winsor, who had been a founding member of the association nine years earlier, complained to Adams that the list of participants was "pitiful," because any real historian could see that the conditions hardly made for a "creditable show for American scholarship."[3] The meeting was, after all, going to be held a short walk from a Ferris wheel and Buffalo Bill's circus.[4]

Turner was the last of five speakers scheduled to speak at the Art Institute Building for an evening session on July 12, 1893. His paper was long, and the audience had already heard four other speakers that session. But though the immediate reception of his paper was politely restrained, his central argument—that the wilderness of the North American west had essentially invented what it meant to be American—would gain traction in the years to come. In time, the thirty-one-year-old historian's talk, "The Significance of the Frontier in American History," would come to dominate the way virtually everyone thought about American history.[5]

After completing his doctoral work at Johns Hopkins, Turner had been happy to return to his home state of Wisconsin. He was born in Portage in 1861 and graduated from the University of Wisconsin in 1884.[6] Like many of his fellow undergraduates, Turner was captivated by the idea that modern evolutionary theory would eventually provide a scientific explanation for society, government, and even history itself. In a notebook he kept as a student, he wrote that Darwin and Spencer had "given us a new world." And that new world meant that "evolution & its accompanying features is now in the intellect" of all educated men.[7]

He knew that he had a unique moment at his disposal. Scientists were using Darwin to remake their understanding of the world, and that same knowledge would soon be applied to society. "We have a new system of nature," he wrote in his notebook. "We must now obtain a new theory of society."[8] He dreamed of writing something great, something that could be seen as "using Evolution etc as text."[9] After completing his undergraduate degree, he decided to stay at the university to pursue a Master's. He wanted an opportunity to think more deeply about the legacy of the American west.

In the summer of 1887, Turner made a trip to Boston. Far from home, he thought about the often-hidden influences that a region had on a person. Westerners, he hypothesized, lived "among the advance guard of new social ideas and among a people whose destiny is all unknown. The west was looking to the future, the east toward the past."[10]

In 1888, Turner finished his master's and moved to Maryland to study with Adams. Like his mentor, Turner was interested in the idea of natural systems, particularly the idea that society itself was an organism evolving independently of humans. When he was hired as a professor at the University of Wisconsin in 1890, he began working in earnest to fuse his interest in the American west with his conviction that society was an organism.

He carefully studied the first volume of Theodore Roosevelt's *The Winning of the West*, which had been published the previous year. In his copy, he carefully marked Roosevelt's lines about "the vast movement by which this continent was conquered and peopled."[11] Inspired, he wrote a draft of an essay titled "The Hunter Type" that he never published, realizing it was basically work that Roosevelt had already done.[12]

Like Roosevelt, he continued to be interested in the relationship between the American west and its inhabitants. In February 1891, he gave a lecture on what he said was the central drama in American history: the colonization of the west. "What first the Mediterranean sea and later the New World was to the Aryan peoples, breaking the bond of custom, and creating new activities to meet new conditions, that the undeveloped West has been to the American descendants of these Aryans," he wrote.[13] Much as Roosevelt had first suggested in *The Winning of the West*, Turner began to think that the frontier west had forged a new race of Americans.

Two months later, he was struck by a new report issued by Robert P. Porter, the superintendent of United States Census. The census had always used a simple formula for determining the unsettled territory of the country: anything fewer than two inhabitants per square mile meant the land was, for census purposes, classified as "unsettled." In the report, Porter observed that from the first census in 1790 until the tenth in 1880, the United States had always had a clear "frontier of settlement": a western section of the map dominated by unsettled territory. But with the 1890 census, for the first time in history that was no longer true. "Up to and including 1880 the country had a frontier of settlement," Porter concluded, "but at present the unsettled area has been so broken into isolated bodies of settlement that there can hardly be said to be a frontier line."[14] As a result, the notion of westward movement could no longer have a place in census reports. This was a momentous declaration, and even Turner had to have been a little surprised the first time he read it. America, which had been pushing westward for centuries, had officially declared the end of the frontier west.

While he chewed over this new development, Turner kept studying the natural laws he thought underpinned society. "Society is an organism, ever growing," he wrote in an 1891 paper he delivered to an audience of Wisconsin schoolteachers. "History is the self-consciousness of this organism."[15] Like his mentor Adams, he believed that all nations were at various points on a single line of evolutionary development. He and Adams both believed that this developmental track was leading toward ever-greater consolidation, and that America was, as Adams put it, "an organic part of a larger organism now vaguely called the World-State."[16] However, the study of particular regions revealed that the evolutionary historical model was complicated. This type of region-based historical study, Adams said, had a "wholesome conservative power in these days of growing centralization."[17]

Turner's career would turn on discovering such "wholesome conservative power." He continued trying to invent a unified historical theory of America and the west. In late 1892, he sent an article exploring those ideas titled

"Problems in American History" to Adams, who liked it quite a bit. Adams, who was serving as the secretary of the American Historical Association that year, suggested that it would make a good basis for a paper Turner could deliver at the Association's meeting in Chicago. Turner thought so, too.[18]

On the evening of July 12, 1893, near the end of a blazing summer day, the young professor gave his paper. Turner looked even more youthful than he actually was. He was slightly under medium height, with an athletic frame and a powerful, deliberate stride. His hair was parted neatly to his right, and he had a close-cropped mustache and bright blue eyes.[19] There had been already been four papers delivered that night, and Turner had yet to speak. But to some members of the tired audience, the vigorous young man must have looked like exactly what he was: the future of the American past.

As usual, Turner had been rewriting his paper almost up until the moment he gave it. (He had passed up an invitation to attend Cody's Wild West that day, choosing instead to finish revising his paper.[20]) But he had been thinking about such a paper for years, trying out the ideas in lectures to literary clubs or in small student journals. And although the paper hardly changed the world overnight, and afterward only garnered a few polite responses from his fellow historians, "The Significance of the Frontier in American History" would slowly come to have a long and lasting influence on the way people thought about the history and development of America.

Frontier was something of a vexed word. It was originally an Old French directional term that simply meant "front." In the early fifteenth century, it acquired a military usage referring to the front line of an army. Around that same time, it also began to be used as a general synonym for border, or the part of a state facing another state. But it wasn't until the seventeenth century in America that the word began to be used to refer to the border facing outward from the settled or inhabited regions of a country.

When Turner used the term, he was using it in its newer, American sense. But its earlier militaristic connotations were still carried in the history of the word. Later, Turner tried to explain his use of the word in greater detail, writing that "of course Frontier and West are not identical but I used Frontier as (so to speak) the barometric line that recorded the advance of settlement, the creation of new Wests, not merely as the area of Indian fighting, vigilantes, annexations, etc."[21]

Turner began his talk by referencing the census report declaring the closing of the American frontier. But it didn't take long for him to segue into his main idea, which he would spend the rest of the paper—and arguably the rest of his career—pursuing. Turner was an experienced lecturer, and his pleasant voice likely commanded the audience's attention as he announced that he had figured out the chief forces driving American history. "The existence of an area of free land, its continuous recession, and the advance of American settlement westward, explain American development," he declared.[22]

One striking feature of Turner's lecture was the way it conflated geography and economics. Turner began by speaking about land in an economic sense, as unclaimed property: "free land." But then he immediately began speaking about it in a geographic sense, suggesting that unclaimed property had been subject to "continuous recession" for centuries, as if by erosion. Of course, he didn't mean the land was literally receding, but he wanted to make the case that the shifting boundaries of land that had been claimed by Anglo-Americans was, in some sense, an unstoppable force of nature. Nonwhite-owned property had been receding, as persistently and irreversibly as a river carving its pathway through solid rock.

He emphasized this natural view of American history by referring in general terms to "the advance of American settlement westward," without specifying who, or what, was causing that settlement. He didn't reference particular laws or policies that made it possible; for him, the expansion of America had been always inevitable.

Turner spoke this way because he thought this way. He believed American history was something that was subject to the laws of nature, which meant it could be studied with the same scientific inquiry. The west, he thought, was a like a world unto itself, one that changed those who encountered it. And those who encountered it changed the west in turn. His hypothesis was that this dynamic explained the development of America.

Turner had been steeped in the linear-progressive model of history. To this way of thinking, a "primitive" society is primitive in the comparative sense that it has not progressed to the level of an "advanced" society. This was model of history heavily influenced by the popular Darwinism of the day. It suggested that history was teleological, or proceeding toward a particular endpoint. Advanced societies were closer to that point; primitive societies were farther from it. History, it was widely agreed, was the story of societies progressing toward that endpoint, which was commonly called "civilization."

Needless to say, the linear-progressive model was not the only way of thinking about history. It had logical flaws that were readily apparent. Progress, for example, isn't assured. Change may be inevitable, but not all change is necessarily beneficial. The linear component of the model, too, was not as settled as Turner made it seem. It assumed that there was only one ultimate outcome for societies: that all societies, everywhere, were evolving toward a particular point. But this was debatable, to say the least. One society might simply be different from another without being any more progressive or advanced.

But arbitrary differences are not the stuff of sweeping theories, and a sweeping theory was what Turner was hunting. Early in his paper, he acknowledged this conventional, linear-progressive developmental view of history. Citing the "evolution of institutions," he checked off the obvious steps in historical development: "the rise of representative government; the differentiation of simple colonial governments into complex organs; the progress from primitive industrial society, without division of labor, up to manufacturing civilization."[23]

But that, he continued, wasn't the whole story. He argued that America's historical evolution hadn't been a single, unbroken event. It had actually occurred a number of times. Turner thought historians could track, like Darwinian natural scientists, "a recurrence of the process of evolution in each western area reached in the process of expansion." In other words, the linear-progressive evolution had happened several times: once with each successive iteration of America's western borders. Turner was arguing that moving west longitudinally was tantamount to retrogressing chronologically. "American social development," he announced, "has been continually beginning over again on the frontier."[24] The western edges of American settlement had been like a renewable Eden—"like Genesis," as Owen Wister had noted nearly a decade earlier—that ceaselessly regenerated, beginning ever anew as it slowly crept from east to west.

This theory of progress would eventually be dismissed by later generations of historians. But at the time, Turner saw himself as a kind of historical scientist, trying to uncover the unchanging natural rules governing social and historical change. And in his view, history was progressive and linear. Just as surely as bows and arrows were replaced by rifles and a market economy replaced the barter system, so would the so-called civilized east would replace the primitive west.

Yet it wasn't simply that there was a linear progression toward civilization and each region experienced it at different times, Turner explained. It was that to a large degree, progress happened in the east by retrogressing into the wilderness of the west. America's unique historical trajectory, he argued, was characterized by "perennial rebirth." That perpetual renewal was possible in large part because of western expansion, which in turn ensured that the country remained in "continuous touch with the simplicity of primitive society." It was that contact with primitive society, he concluded, that created the "American character."[25]

This wasn't just a theory of history. It was a theory of national selfhood. Americans took two steps backward into the primitive conditions of the frontier in order to launch into a dramatic leap forward into modernity. In Turner's view, the main narrative of American history was the story of white settlers traveling into the so-called primitive west, developing the land, and then enjoying the benefits of that development in the east. It was that cycle of retrogression, he suggested, that enabled the forward march of eastern civilization.

Seen in this light, the real steam engine that had been powering American development was not the east at all. "The true point of view in the history of this nation is not the Atlantic coast," he announced dramatically, "it is the Great West."[26]

This was one of the first conservative theories of American history. It certainly was not a rejection of the idea of evolutionary progress. Turner's whole purpose, after all, was to understand what made progress happen in the first place. And it wasn't an instinctive preference for the tried-and-true over the new and untested, either.

Instead, Turner was envisioning a practical conservatism, a usable past. And for Turner, a certain type of western space—one that allowed for a deliberate and temporary retrogression into the frontier west—was the chief driver of American civilization. If one definition of conservatism was simply the philosophy of preserving the mythic individualism of an earlier age, then one conclusion of Turner's was unmistakable: conservatism was what made the future happen.

NOTES

1. Adams *Methods*, 103.
2. See Ostrander, 258–261 and Cunningham, 261–275.
3. Qtd. in Jacobs, 2.
4. White "Frederick," 7–66.
5. Limerick, 20–23.
6. Jacobs, 6–7.
7. Qtd. in Jacobs, 9.
8. Qtd. in Jacobs, 10.
9. Qtd. in Jacobs, 9.
10. Qtd. in Bogue, 35.
11. Jacobs, 4.
12. Jacobs, 4. For more on the origins of Turner's thesis, see Billington. For analysis of Turner's rhetoric and regionalism, see Cronon, 73–101 and Steiner, 103–135.
13. Qtd. in Bogue, 83.
14. Porter "Distribution," 4. See also Richardson *How*, 115.
15. Qtd. in Bogue, 79.
16. Qtd. in Bogue, 79.
17. Qtd. in Bogue, 474.
18. Bogue, 91.
19. Jacobs, 15.
20. Faragher *Rereading*, 2.

21. Qtd. in Jacobs, 163.
22. Turner "Significance," 199.
23. Turner "Significance," 200.
24. Turner "Significance," 200.
25. Turner "Significance," 200.
26. Turner "Significance," 200.

Chapter 23

A Practical Conservatism

Turner spent the remainder of his lengthy presentation offering historical examples of his theory. He wanted to overturn the conventional linear-developmental model of history and substitute a conservative-developmental model that was specific to America. American frontiers, he explained, were fundamentally different from European frontiers. European frontiers were akin to military borders. But in America, the frontier was "the meeting point between savagery and civilization." It was a kind of jagged temporal gulf—dividing past from present, primitive from civilized—lying "at the hither edge of free land."[1]

Like a host of others, including Roosevelt and the entire United States government, when Turner said "free land," he meant land that was available for development by white settlers. When he noted that the far edge of the frontier was already populated—by Indians—yet at the same time freely available for settlement, he didn't see it as a contradiction.

Turner shared his understanding of Indians with many educated Americans at the time. He believed that although Indians were likely capable of being civilized, they were not civilized at the present. In his view, an Indian tribe was little more than the result of an unsuccessful attempt at modernity. This is why it was perfectly reasonable to him that land occupied by Indians was also freely available for annexation by white Americans.

Like many other nineteenth-century intellectuals whose worldview perpetuated a host of racial prejudices, Turner often conflated Indians with wilderness, savagery, and the historical past. The concepts tended to blur together. In his mind, wilderness was an ancient, savage space filled with ancient, savage Indians. Yet he also thought that wilderness and Indians, both of which he associated with the past, had been enormously important to the development of American history. Retrogressions into that so-called primitive past, he believed, had birthed the American man.

In this belief he was breaking with his mentor Herbert Baxter Adams. Adams had thought that the social and political institutions that enabled modern civilization had originated in Germany and then spread, germ-like, to England before migrating to America. But it was actually America's own usable past, Turner concluded, not Germany's—America's looming wilderness, its native populations—that produced its government and its unique conception of the individual. "The frontier," he announced, "is the line of most rapid and effective Americanization."

> The wilderness masters the colonist. [. . .] Before long he has gone to planting Indian corn and plowing with a sharp stick; he shouts the war cry and takes the scalp in orthodox Indian fashion. In short, at the frontier the environment is at first too strong for the man. He must accept the conditions which it furnishes, or perish, and so he fits himself into the Indian clearings and follows the Indian trails. Little by little he transforms the wilderness, but the outcome is not old Europe. [. . .] The fact is, that here is a new product that is American.[2]

Turner was envisioning an overlapping series of conquests. The white settler attempts to conquer the primitive wilderness but is initially conquered by it. For Turner, this conquest was also a retrogression. The colonist had left the modernity of the east and surrendered to a primitive wilderness. Eventually, that retrogression fired the engines of progress to build something new and distinctly American.

Progressing in this way—that is, by retrogressing—had had lasting effects on America, Turner thought. It had put something in the soil, ensuring that every subsequent crop bore the fruits of that original moment of conquest. As Turner put it, advancing along the frontier meant "a steady movement away from the influence of Europe, a steady growth of independence on American lines."[3] In trying to view American history as a scientist, he had come to the Lamarckian conclusion that acquired traits could be transmitted to subsequent generations. The traits acquired in the western "past"—in so-called primitive conditions—would be transmitted into the future, ensuring ongoing historical development.

Turner was making a mental leap that no historian had made at that point. He was suggesting that environment played a large and unacknowledged role in the social and political makeup of a nation. But he didn't think environment mattered in the way that someone like Herbert Baxter Adams thought it mattered. Adams had thought that people made the world. He had concluded that civilization was a heritable value, something that had been transmitted through the Anglo people over the course of centuries. Those carriers of civilization, Baxter thought, made England, made America.

Turner thought it was actually the opposite. It wasn't that people made the environment. It was that the environment made people. This was a theory of history that made much better use of Darwin's insights into how the environment shaped populations. American ideas about freedom and civilization and justice couldn't be traced solely to some ancient Anglo-Celtic heritage, Turner thought. He didn't think ethnic heritage was completely irrelevant, of course. Elsewhere, Turner echoed Roosevelt's Anglo-centric theory that America's very first westerners came from "non-English stock, Scotch-Irish and German" that "constituted a distinct people" of "frontiersmen."[4] But he did think that racial heritage simply wasn't as significant as the cumulative force of the western experience.

This emphasis on regional history, rather than racial heritage, meant that the lines of longitude stretching across the continent were a kind of evolutionary text. "Line by line as we read this continental page from west to east," Turner said, "we find the record of social evolution."[5]

It was the theory that the west had determined America's social and political evolution that would be Turner's greatest breakthrough. He concluded the west had effectively selected what it meant to be an American. The frontier, he argued, "promoted the formation of a composite nationality for the American people." It took easterners and immigrants and made them western. And in making them western, it made them American. "In the crucible of the frontier," he continued, "the immigrants were Americanized, liberated, and fused into a mixed race."[6]

If his audience was listening carefully, they might have realized that Turner was updating Roosevelt's hypothesis, first explored in *The Winning of the West*, that America's western frontiers had birthed a new race entirely. These "frontier folk," as Roosevelt put it, were examples of an "intensely American stock who were the pioneers of our people in their march westward."[7] But Turner believed that the western experience hadn't only made a new people. It had also decisively revised the nature of freedom in America.

At the same time that western lands were cultivating a new type of American, they were spurring the growth and power of the federal government. Best exemplified by the Louisiana Purchase, which, as Turner noted, had been "called out by frontier needs and demands," the dream of a small federal government began to die at the exact moment the western borders of America began to grow.

As Turner pointed out, westerners in the nineteenth century wanted land. With land came demands for political power. And those demands ultimately led to the creation of new states by a growing federal government. Turner borrowed a quotation from Lucius Q. C. Lamar, the Mississippi judge who had recently retired from the Supreme Court: "In 1789 the States were the creators of the Federal Government; in 1861 the Federal Government was the creator of a large majority of the States."[8] It was simply unavoidable, Turner concluded, that the government had grown along with the west.

The west had long functioned as a force that changed the states and the federal government. Yet what was most surprising about Turner's theory was that it suggested those western-led changes occurred because of an underlying conservatism. The central dynamic of American history was a repeated return to circumstances associated with the past. It was this continual retrogression that created progress.

And even though that retrogression ultimately led to a larger federal government, the government, at least in his view, hadn't been the chief driver of that retrogression. Individuals were. The frontier, he said, "is productive of individualism."[9] Turner thought that America's western frontiers had created a particular type—a representative American—that propelled the wheels of progress, driving America forward by pushing back ceaselessly toward the past. This was the American individualist: the type of person who understood freedom to be measurable by the degree to which he could exercise his will in the world.

This didn't happen by magic, of course. To Turner, the logic was clear: individuals clamored for public land to be made available for private ownership, which encouraged individuals to own and develop the land. That ownership in turn led to a political culture emphasizing individual rights. "So long as free land exists," he said, "the opportunity for a competency exists, and economic power secures political power."[10]

Nearing the end of his paper, Turner began cataloguing the unique intellectual traits the western frontiers had bred. That new "American intellect," he explained, was "lacking in the artistic" yet had "coarseness and strength" along with "acuteness and inquisitiveness," a "practical, inventive turn," a "masterful grasp of material things," and so on. These, he concluded, "are the traits of the frontier."[11]

Like all transformative insights, Turner's seems inevitable in retrospect. *Yes*, portions of his audience may have thought. *Of course those are American traits.* But he was working at the cutting edge of historical knowledge. He wanted to understand American society in a more rigorous, scientific way. He wanted to study America less as a nation than as a species, charting its evolution just as Darwin would have. The conclusion he reached—essentially, that individual freedom came from the American west—was as clear as it was jarring.

By that point, Turner had had been speaking for a very long time. He was the last of five speakers, and his audience was likely exhausted. (The published version of his paper was around 10,000 words.) But he closed by offering something of a warning. Now that the Census Bureau had declared the frontier closed, it would be foolish to expect the expansive character of Americans to simply change. On the contrary, he cautioned, a nation of westerners will always be in search of a new and broader west. The "American energy," he warned, "will continually demand a wider field for its exercise." But finding such a field would not be easy, for "never again will such gifts of free land offer themselves."[12] The implication was clear: for America to keep being America, it would have to continually search for new and better wests.

It was inevitable, he thought, that Americans would continue to seek out new lands for conquest. The forward momentum of American history was propelled by individualists retrogressing into a primitive past. And the frontier, Turner concluded, "did indeed furnish a new field of opportunity, a gate of escape from the bondage of the past."[13] The west, in other words, allowed for an escape from the sclerosis of eastern modernity, from the tyranny of the recent past, with an opportunity to begin anew by delving into an older and more authentic history.

The audience received Turner's speech politely and then filed out into the summer Chicago night. Most of them were probably eager to get to sleep. Tomorrow there was another lengthy morning session scheduled for the final day of the conference.

Though his paper was summarized extensively in the meeting's proceedings, the larger reaction to his paper was muted. It would take years before one historian who had elected to go see Buffalo Bill's Wild West instead of listening to Turner's paper admitted he had made the wrong decision.[14] Over the next few decades, "The Significance of the Frontier" would be republished innumerable times. Much later, Turner would use it as the first chapter of his book *The Frontier in American History*. But in 1893, its transformative influence was hardly apparent. Turner sent out copies of the paper to writers and intellectuals who he thought might be interested, including Roosevelt, whose *Winning of the West* had been such a formative influence for Turner.

Roosevelt, likely noticing Turner's debts to his own book, politely responded that he was "greatly interested" in the paper, noting that "I intend to make use of it writing the third volume of my 'Winning of the West.'"[15] He added, in a somewhat backhanded compliment, that he thought Turner seemed to "have put into definite shape a good deal of thought which has been floating around rather loosely."[16]

Other readers were hardly more effusive. Francis A. Walker, the economist who had written an aggressive critique of Henry George's single-tax theory, wrote that the subject seemed "fascinating," but admitted he hadn't actually read the essay yet.[17] John Fiske, the philosopher and historian who was one of the preeminent Darwinians of the day, thought that Turner's essay was "admirable," but couldn't resist adding that he had already been working from a similar perspective. Edward Everett Hale, the influential Boston Unitarian clergyman, merely acknowledged receiving this "curious and interesting paper."[18]

Although Turner was no hardline reactionary, he did believe that American history was essentially conservative. Real development could only come through a kind of retrogression. As he later insisted, political problems had to be understood in their historical context so that "history may hold the lamp for conservative reform."[19]

His was a new theory of American history. In his view, the western frontier bred a culture of practical conservatism, full of individuals eager to briefly retrogress into an ostensibly primitive past while professing scorn and indifference to the tyranny of the present. If Turner was correct, then America was a land in which a better, older freedom was perpetually waiting over the western horizon, just waiting to be torn from the clutches of the past by rugged men in leather breeches.

NOTES

1. Turner "Significance," 200.
2. Turner "Significance," 201.
3. Turner "Significance," 201.
4. Turner "Problem," 289–290.
5. Turner "Significance," 207.
6. Turner "Significance," 215, 216.
7. Roosevelt *Winning I*, 101, 103.
8. Turner "Significance," 218.
9. Turner "Significance," 221
10. Turner "Significance," 223.
11. Turner "Significance," 226–227.
12. Turner "Significance," 227.
13. Turner "Significance," 227.
14. Bogue, 98.
15. TR letter to Frederick Jackson Turner, 10 February 1894.
16. TR letter to Frederick Jackson Turner, 10 February 1894.
17. Qtd. in Bogue, 113. For more on Turner and George, see Lough, 4–23.
18. Qtd. in Jacobs, 3–4.
19. Turner "Social Forces," 226.

Chapter 24

The Evolution of a Cowboy

The year before the World's Fair, Poultney Bigelow had dragged Remington to Europe on an ill-begotten adventure. He had an audacious proposal. They would travel to Europe by ship and then paddle a canoe from St. Petersburg to Berlin along the Gulf of Finland. Bigelow wanted to try to get a book out of it, and in addition to the company of his old college friend, he wanted Remington to do the illustrations.[1]

Remington accepted. He needed a break from an increasingly fractious America. "Things are badly out of joint in the U.S.," he wrote Bigelow. "The West and South and the East are fighting each other in Congress." After making gains among southern and western Democrats in the 1890 elections, the Populist Party had been formally created in May 1891. The left-leaning Populists were critical of modern laissez-faire capitalism, particularly the big banks and railroads. Remington, who was perhaps most responsible for artistically representing the people and politics of America's western section to its east, thought that such "sectional difference is inevitable and will increase." Western populism, he added ominously, "has danger in it to the Republic."[2]

So in the early summer of 1892, Bigelow and Remington had set off for their brief and disastrous European adventure. Remington immediately regretted leaving America. They got into trouble with the Russian police and had to abandon their canoes. In haste, they took a steamship down the Neiman River before eventually arriving in Germany. Remington was greatly relieved to finally arrive in London at the end of the month.

He got a taste of home by taking in Buffalo Bill's Wild West show near the Thames. He reviewed the show positively for *Harper's Weekly* and became friendly with Cody. (Cody eventually started including Remington's review in the show programs.[3]) He thought the show would teach audiences around the world about the western origins of American individualism. The Wild

West show was, he wrote, a poetical "protest" against a time when it often seemed like "the greatest crime is to be an individual."[4]

When Remington returned to America, he started planning for a lengthy trip through the west and Mexico that would culminate with a visit to the World's Fair. When Poultney Bigelow complained he hadn't seen him, Remington crowed, "I told you I was off for the Wild West."[5] He had had enough of Europe. "[Damn]—Europe—the Czar," he wrote. "I go to the simple men—men with the bark on—the big mountains—the great deserts and the scrawny ponies."[6] He finally made it to Chicago, where he saw the Fair and took in another viewing of Cody's show. He liked it even better when he saw it in America. Afterward, he said the show had "renewed his first love"—the west.[7]

Late that summer, Remington traveled to Yellowstone. It was there that at last he met Owen Wister, who had been following his career for quite some time. Remington knew who Wister was, too. He had just finished illustrating one of his stories. With "Hank's Woman" and "How Lin McLean Went East" both published in *Harper's* the previous year, Wister was beginning to make a name for himself as a writer of short stories about cowboys and the west.

Like Remington, Wister had been reading Rudyard Kipling's recent stories about the British Raj. There was something in them that reminded him of the American west. Remington already thought that Kipling was like "a second Bret Harte," but for the frontiers of India, not America.[8] Reading Kipling had spurred Remington to consider the many links between settlement and empire.

If Kipling was a second Bret Harte, Wister thought there ought to be a second Kipling, as well—an American one. After an earlier trip to Wyoming, Wister had wondered why there "wasn't some Kipling saving the sage-brush for American literature," before it all vanished.[9] He rose to his feet, suddenly resolved, and went up to the library and worked until after midnight on the story that would become "Hank's Woman." He thought he could be that new American Kipling.

After a chance meeting in Yellowstone, it wouldn't take long before his new friend Remington would think so, too.

Earlier that summer, when Wister had met with Henry Mills Alden at *Harper's* to discuss additional work for the magazine, Alden had suggested a series of firsthand articles on the west and offered to pay $250 for each. He then offered something else that made Wister feel as if he was about to get his big break. What if he were to send Remington along with Wister, to do a whole western adventure in fiction and illustrations?[10]

For some time, Wister had been following Remington's blossoming career as he tried to cultivate his own. Like seemingly everyone else, Wister thought

Remington's western illustrations were the very best. He couldn't believe his good fortune. One thing "I plainly see," Wister realized, amazed at Alden's offer, is "that one of my dreams—to have Remington as an illustrator[—]is likely to be realized in a most substantial manner."[11] That dream came true sooner than he thought. By early September, Wister had toured the World's Fair with his mother. They likely saw the fifteen Frederic Remington illustrations on exhibition at the Liberal Arts Building, and Wister had dinner in the Boone and Crockett Club's cabin, where he also worked on a new western story.[12] After touring the fair, Wister put his mother on a train back home and continued on through Yellowstone.

It was on September 8, at the very end of his trip, that Wister ran into Frederic Remington at lunch in the Norris Basin at Yellowstone Park, which the Boone and Crockett Club had successfully lobbied to protect just a few years earlier.[13] Remington was nearly as happy to meet Wister as Wister was to meet Remington. He had just finished the illustrations for Wister's "Balaam and Pedro," a story which would eventually be published in the January, 1894 issue of *Harper's*.

(Roosevelt would later castigate Wister for the unalloyed violence of "Balaam"—which featured a horse's eye being gouged out—saying that "there's nothing masculine in being revolting."[14])

Remington and Wister dined together at the Mammoth Hot Springs Hotel near Fort Yellowstone, where they soon found they shared a common sensibility. Both men held a conservative set of beliefs about America. As Remington had complained to Poultney Bigelow a few months earlier, he thought that the America of his birth was fast slipping away. He blamed the recent waves of immigrants, among other things. "It is no longer the America of our traditions," he concluded bitterly.[15]

For his part, Wister was impressed to meet another student of the American west who agreed with him about "the disgrace of our politics, and the present asphyxiation of all real love of country." They both thought that the "continent does not hold a nation any longer," but was now "merely a strip of land on which a crowd is struggling for riches."[16] And they both seemed to believe that even though the country had begun to go off the rails at some time in the recent past, it could nonetheless be set aright through the individualist virtues of the American west.

They were an odd-looking pair. Wister was tall but seemed smaller than he actually was, and Remington was by that point up to 240 pounds. He struck Wister as a "huge rollicking animal." But Wister was eager to get to know the artist whose work he had enjoyed for so long, and it didn't take long before they found a kind of comfort in each other. Wister sometimes worried that his conservatism was just melancholy in disguise. He had to try to "compel myself to see the bright side of things, because I know the dark side impresses me unduly," as he confided in his journal after their meeting. But Remington, a jocular, gregarious bear of a man, expressed a similar conservatism. To "hear him more caustic in his disgust and contempt at the way we Americans are managing ourselves than I have ever been," Wister marveled, "was most unexpected."[17]

Theirs was not an unalloyed pessimism, though. What distinguished their conservatism was a warm, swift undercurrent of optimism. Lurking under their disgust with congressional bickering and the rise of populism was a persistent belief in the possibility for renewal. For both of them, the American future could be rejuvenated by the history of the frontier west.

They so enjoyed each other's company that at their first meeting, they decided to spend a leg of their respective trips back east together. Before going their separate ways in St. Paul, they spent the train ride discussing future collaborations. Remington even read a few pages of a draft of a new story Wister was working on.

From then on, Remington and Wister kept in touch. Remington liked his company, and with Wister's growing collection of stories and sketches for *Harper's*—all illustrated by Remington—Wister also provided him with a steady stream of work. After their first few collaborations, Remington began to realize that Wister's talent was something special. He started offering him substantive notes on his drafts.

"Dear Nerve-cell," he wrote, trying out a nickname after reading a draft of Wister's 1894 story "Little Big Horn Medicine." He suggested adding a "squaw interpreter" and changing an Indian character's name. The one Wister had originally used—"Young-man-afraid-of-his-mustache"—was, Remington thought, a stale joke.[18] Wister agreed and made both changes. After reading the manuscript of another story, "Specimen Jones," Remington found a plot hole: "why don't the white fellows run away," he wondered. They were on horseback, and "the Injuns on foot." He suggested revising to make it clear they could not retreat. "Change, so that they are *surrounded*."[19] Wister agreed again, revising the story so that the white characters were, as Remington suggested, entirely surrounded.

As time went on, Remington began trying to shape Wister's work before he had even started on it. His suggestions were partly driven by economics—"I want M.S. [manuscripts] to illustrate," he wrote in April, joking that "I am starving"—but also partly by ideas.[20] Unlike drawing, writing did not seem to come easily to Remington. The large grammatical and syntactical difference between his private letters and his published work suggested that his articles and books benefited from a heavy editorial hand. But with his new friend, Remington seemed to briefly imagine Wister as a kind of intellectual appendage, the kind of writer he had always wanted to be. He thought America was ready for a Kipling for the American west—a bard for America's rugged course of empire. The country needed a new Bret Harte, or maybe a new James Fenimore Cooper. He began pestering Wister to write something about "a South Western Natty Bumpo [sic]."[21]

Soon, his article suggestions to Wister grew more specific. There was, he speculated, "[g]reat & rising demand for—a cow-boy article." He even had a title in mind: "The Evolution & the Survival of the Cow-boy."[22]

He had a standard list of requests that he thought made for good illustrations: "Put every person on horse back and let the blood be half a foot deep," he had joked to Wister in April. "Be very profane and have plenty of shooting. No episodes must occur in the dark."[23] But Remington was serious about tracing the evolution of a certain kind of westerner. After the global success of Cody's western show, the figure of the cowboy was fast becoming the prototypical westerner, and even the prototypical American. He wrote to Wister again in the fall, requesting that he "please—make me an article on the evolution of the [cow]puncher."[24]

The emphasis on "evolution" was not coincidental. Remington had long had a casual interest in Darwinian evolution. He held the common view that Indians had not attained the "highest evolution of civilization," even though he was otherwise sympathetic to pleas for Indian rights.[25] And after viewing the masses of people thronging the Midway at the World's Fair, he had joked that a "composite photograph" of "humanity in all its dissimilitude" might be "a goat or something else dear to the Darwinian heart."[26]

By the mid-1890s, he was beginning to think that he had witnessed to the evolution of what he called "a new type"—the cowboy. He dashed off some suggestions to Wister. While visiting a New Mexico ranch, he wrote, he had viewed the "Mountain Cow-boy," a type he said had emerged from Texas between the end of Civil War and the end of Reconstruction.[27] But after the crash of the cattle boom, he thought that particular strain of cowboys was worth documenting for posterity.

Like Roosevelt, Wister, Turner, and others, Remington was realizing that when he spoke about cowboys, he wasn't speaking about a job. It was instead something closer to an ethnic category: a "type," as he put it. The cowboys he knew personally were all Texans of Mexican origin. In fact, he told Wister, cattle "country is deserted by whites—a great waste." He dashed off some points of reference to help Wister better get a sense of the figure he was talking about: "Cheyanne [sic] saddle—fine chaps—$15 hats—Fringed gloves—$25. boots," and so on. He suggested a few jokes and a scene in which a horse's rope gets caught, saving it from flying over a cliff. "Well go ahead," he said, pressing Wister to write the article. "Will you do it"?[28]

He insisted on one thing. The cowboy, he stressed, "did not exist as an American type" originally. He was instead a mix of southern Scotch-Irish stock with the Spanish conquerors, "a combination of the Kentucky or Tennessee man with the Spanish." During the Civil War, he continued, the cowboy "sold cattle to Confederate Armies," or perhaps "was a soldier in Confed army." Eventually, Remington thought, the big cattle companies spelled doom for the small, independent-contractor cowboy.[29]

Remington did not have any historical or documentary evidence of any of this, of course. He was merely synthesizing what he had heard from old ranch hands with what he had seen and read in the newspapers. But he was obsessed with the idea that there was a particular Darwinian type that the American west had birthed, and he wanted to study it like a scientist, a historian, and a political philosopher, all at once.

Or at least he wanted Wister to do it for him. Four days after Christmas, as he planned a trip up to Canada, Remington dashed off a quick letter to Wister, reminding him to keep working on the cowboy evolution article. "How is the cow-boy article coming on?" he asked.[30] By early 1895, he finally had his answer.

A few months after Canada, Remington had traveled to Florida, where he eagerly read a draft of Wister's article. It wasn't what he had been expecting. Writing from the Hotel Punta Gorda, Remington tried to find the right words to tell Wister he hadn't written the article that Remington had hoped for. "The 'Cow-boys' are all right," he began gingerly. But he wanted Wister to do more with it. "Tell of the settlement and decline of the cattle business and of the *survival*—such as we find in the mountains," he suggested, repeating some of his earlier ideas.[31] Though Wister had apparently agreed with him that the cowboy was a type whose evolution could be charted, Remington thought he had gotten the genealogy wrong.

Over the years, he had gotten closer to Wister. He started by framing his notes as off-handed suggestions Wister was free to disregard, sprinkled with qualifications like "I only 'throw it out causually' [*sic*]," as he wrote after reading a draft of one story.[32] But after two years of exchanging letters, Remington thought they had become good friends, and even collaborators.

Once he got back home to New Rochelle from Florida, Remington put his finger on what had been bothering him about Wister's "evolution of the cowboy" article. It was Wister's insistence that cowboys had to be white. "Strikes me there is a good deal of English in the thing," he wrote. Wister hadn't taken his advice about the ethnic origins of the American cowboy. "I never saw an English cow-boy," Remington added dryly. He'd "seen owners" that were English, though.

Remington thought Wister hadn't given enough credit to the nonwhite cowboys. "You want to credit the Mexican with the inventing the whole business," he advised.[33]

But Wister didn't budge. He wanted the history of the cowboy to be a white history. In the final version of the article, Wister insisted that when "the English nobleman" encountered Texas, "the slumbering untamed Saxon awoke in him."[34]

Nonetheless, Remington and Wister were not as far apart as Remington seemed to think. Both thought that the cowboy was a new American type, and both were keen to trace the genealogy of that type. Both, too, thought that the cowboy was connected to certain conservative undercurrents in American history. For Wister, this was a long-hidden connection to an Anglo-Saxon aristocracy; for Remington, it was a possible allegiance to "Confederate Armies" during the war.

Besides, Wister wasn't trying to be dishonest. Like Remington, he was merely playing armchair ethnologist. For Wister, it was likely just a straightforward calculation. If the cowboy was forming a new aristocracy in the American west, then of course he would have been Anglo-Saxon. Wister could hardly conceive of it otherwise.

After all, he had a sense of having descended from an aristocracy himself. Prior to the war, his family had owned slaves for generations. His great-great-grandfather had signed the Constitution for South Carolina. He was always dimly aware of how nationality, racial background, and family legacies intertwined for America's ruling classes. He just never had to consciously think about them. They were simply there, humming in the background of his mind like a telegraph wire.

Remington was born to none of that. Despite his brief turn at Yale and his current status as one of America's wealthiest and most well-known illustrators, Remington was always on the periphery of the loose westerner's club formed by Roosevelt, Wister, and others. He never really felt accepted by Roosevelt. And though he may have come to feel that he and Wister were close friends while he was advising Wister on drafts of "The Evolution of the Cowpuncher" in the spring of 1895, he soon came to realize that Wister, too, had been keeping him at arm's length.

In the early spring of 1895, Remington was looking forward to a dinner Roosevelt was hosting. Roosevelt, then serving on the Civil Service Commission, had invited Remington and Wister, along with John Hay and a few others, to his house in Washington on April 5 for a dinner in honor of Rudyard Kipling. Remington, Roosevelt, and Wister were all great fans of Kipling's, who had recently published his collection of children's stories peppered with Darwinian references to the "law of the jungle."[35] In a few years, he would write his racial ode to American imperialism titled "The White Man's Burden."

Despite being an English subject, Kipling was living at the time in Vermont, where he wrote *The Jungle Book* and did most of his best-known writing. Remington liked this about him. "All the best men are in America," he told Poultney Bigelow, looking forward to the dinner.[36] In the days leading up to the dinner, it seemed like the American west was on everyone's mind. Wister's story "The Second Missouri Compromise" had just been published in March (Roosevelt had already read it and pronounced it "capital").[37] And Roosevelt had finally reached out to Frederick Jackson Turner. Turner had reviewed the three volumes of *The Winning of the West* in *The Nation* magazine the previous month, and Roosevelt had been pleased with the favorable review.[38]

"It is not ordinarily my habit to write to reviewers," he wrote to Turner, but he wanted to compliment Turner on how "thoroughly conversant" he was with that period of western history. Roosevelt made a show of asking about an obscure source that might be found in a Canadian archive, but he was really just writing to cultivate Turner's friendship. After Roosevelt's polite but cool acknowledgement of Turner's World's Fair speech a few years earlier, Turner seemed to have finally impressed him.[39]

Going back to their Harvard days, Roosevelt had always called Wister by his childhood nickname, "Dan." (Wister's father had wanted to name him Daniel and persisted in calling him that even though he was ultimately named Owen.[40]) It was a genuine version of the kind of chummy familiarity that Remington tried to affect with his many nicknames for Wister, like "Nerve-Cell" and "War Eagle." But Remington had never heard anyone call Wister "Dan." So he was shocked and a little mystified when he received Roosevelt's invitation to the dinner and saw his reference to a "Dan Wister." He sat down to write a letter to Wister, intending to ask him if he wanted to meet in Philadelphia and share a train down to Washington. (Despite Remington living in New Rochelle, New York, less than a day's journey from Wister's home in Philadelphia, the two rarely saw one another in person.) But he couldn't help but bring it up the nickname. "I am going to Washington Friday morning to dine with Theo. Roosevelt," he wrote. "He said Dan Wister was coming—are you Dan"? He seemed to be barely trying to hide his hurt feelings. "If so you have been trifling with me."[41]

Remington did not, in the end, attend the dinner. Whether it was the truth or not, he told Poultney Bigelow he had gotten sick.[42] Afterward, Kipling wrote Remington a short note thanking him for doing the illustrations for one of his stories for *Cosmopolitan* magazine and saying he missed him at the dinner. "It was great fun at Roosevelt's dinner," Kipling wrote, "but I had counted a good deal on your being there."[43]

Remington soon got over his hurt feelings, or at least acted as if he did. Since the beginning of 1895, Remington had been half-secretly working on a new project, one that would allow him to rely less on the slow, laborious writing of articles that he could then quickly illustrate for cash. Remington never fully embraced oil painting, which was slow and difficult to reproduce. And his magazine illustrations, while lucrative, depended on the production—usually by others—of western- or military-themed stories. He didn't want to have to rely on other people. So over the course of 1895, he began experimenting with a new type of art that came relatively easily to him, didn't depend on plodding or flighty writers, and could be easily and endlessly reproduced. Once he hit on it, it seemed obvious. He couldn't believe he hadn't tried it before. "All other forms of art are trivialities," he proclaimed exuberantly. He was obsessed with sculpture, or, as he liked to call it, "mud."[44]

NOTES

1. Splete, 135; Samuels *Frederic*, 170.
2. FR letter to Poultney Bigelow, 5 January 1892.
3. Samuels *Frederic*, 257.
4. Remington "Buffalo," 847.
5. FR letter to Poultney Bigelow, 10 April [1893].
6. FR letter to Poultney Bigelow, 29 January [1893].
7. Remington "Gallop," 112.
8. FR letter to Lt. Powhatan Clarke, 13 September 1890.
9. Wister *Roosevelt*, 29.
10. Payne, 122–124, 138; Wister *Owen*, 165–166.
11. OW journal, 28 June 1893.
12. Samuels *Frederic*, 196.
13. Scharnhost *Owen*, 56.
14. Wister *Roosevelt*, 34.
15. FR letter to Poultney Bigelow, 27 May [1893].
16. OW journal, 8 September 1893.
17. OW journal, 8 September 1893.
18. FR letter to Owen Wister [before June 1894].
19. FR letter to Owen Wister [before July 1894].
20. FR letter to Owen Wister 12 April [1894].
21. Splete, 251.
22. FR letter to Owen Wister [September 1894].
23. FR letter to Owen Wister 12 April [1894].
24. FR letter to Owen Wister [September or October 1894].
25. Remington "Appeal," 95.
26. Remington "Gallop," 111.
27. FR letter to Owen Wister [September or October 1894].
28. FR letter to Owen Wister [September or October 1894].
29. FR letter to Owen Wister [20 to 30 October 1894].

30. FR letter to Owen Wister [29 December 1894].
31. FR letter to Owen Wister [February 1895].
32. FR letter to Owen Wister [before June 1894].
33. FR letter to Owen Wister [February 1895].
34. Wister "Evolution," 603.
35. Kipling, 33. Kipling first referenced the "Law of the Jungle" in 1894. For more on Darwinian competition and individualism in Kipling, see Mackie, 455–464.
36. FR letter to Poultney Bigelow [1895].
37. TR letter to James Brander Matthews, 6 April 1895.
38. Turner "Roosevelt's," 240–242.
39. TR letter to Frederick Jackson Turner, 2 April 1895.
40. Payne, 8–9.
41. FR letter to Owen Wister [31 March 1895].
42. FR letter to Poultney Bigelow [1895].
43. Qtd. in Splete, 270.
44. FR letter to Owen Wister, 24 October [1895].

Chapter 25

The Bronco Busters

When it finally appeared in the September 1895 issue of *Harper's Monthly*, Wister's essay on the "Evolution of the Cow-Puncher" had changed considerably from Remington's original idea for the article. But it offered a grand and sweeping vision of the relationship between social evolution and the American west. It was also the clearest articulation of Wister's western conservatism to date.

Wister had been publishing short stories for several years, and he had already decided he wanted to do something longer. As early as 1892, he had considered writing a longer book on the west titled *The Course of Empire*.[1] More recently, he had weighed the possibility of writing a history of the western bank Wells Fargo called *The Romance of a Corporation*. ("No one has yet made a Corporation his hero" in a book, Wister observed, not incorrectly.[2])

With "The Evolution of the Cow-Puncher," Wister sketched a history of what he thought was a superior American "type." He brought together strands of speculative history, political philosophy, and Darwinian development to weave a story of American racial and social inheritance. Though the essay was nominally historical, Wister was already thinking of how its lessons could be applied to the series of short stories he had been working on since 1891. They starred his unnamed western cowboy who went by "the Virginian," an appellation that seemed to obliquely signal he was born to the American aristocracy. Wister kept working on and adding to those stories, which would eventually coalesce into a novel. But he first needed "The Evolution of the Cow-Puncher" to lay the philosophical groundwork.

In the essay, Wister made the case that the modern cowboy wasn't particularly modern at all. The cowboy instead represented, he argued, the reemergence of the European aristocrat, now refitted for life in America. In the "flannel-shirted democracy" of the west, he wrote, you hear "only good concerning this aristocrat born and bred."[3]

The essay in part seemed a response to Frederick Jackson Turner, whose talk on the frontier at the World's Fair had, much like Roosevelt's *Winning of the West*, sought to explain the west's role in America's historical development.

Unlike Turner, though, Wister thought that western settlers were not a new type of people, but rather a reemergence of an old and noble tribe. Originally, he wrote, the cowboy was "no new type, no product of the frontier," but was merely an atavistic return of a long-lost genteel "medieval man." For Wister, the cowboy was the latest iteration of an aristocratic lineage stretching back to medieval England. "Directly the English nobleman smelt Texas," he imagined, and "the slumbering untamed Saxon awoke in him."[4] A cowboy was neither a reborn European nor an uneducated manual laborer, but a knight-errant in a Stetson.

Wister had been thinking about the American conservatism and the cowboy for some time, well before Remington had begun prodding him to write the article. The year before, Wister had been traveling from Tucson to Los Angeles when Eugene V. Debs led the American Railway Union on a strike against the Pullman factory in Illinois. Over the summer of 1894, the strike spread throughout the west. Wister initially supported the strikers, but when he realized the strike would prevent him from getting the first-class cabin he had paid for, he grew bitter. What had the workers really hoped to achieve? Equality? Science taught that equality was impossible. Darwinian development required the opposite to spur the sort of competition necessary for natural selection. "It is our destiny to demonstrate the eternal lie of equality," he mused darkly as he made his way back east. "Dogs and horses are not equal. Why shall men be?"[5]

Mentally, he began to contrast the strikers—a force he blamed on the "deluge of immigrants [that] is diluting our Anglo-Saxon race"—with what he thought were real, native-born Americans: cowboys.[6] He later recorded in his journal his admiration for some cowboys he had met in New Mexico, writing that they were "of the manly, simple, humorous, American type which I hold to be the best and bravest we possess and our hope in the future." These westerners, he thought, were heirs to the truest, the hardest, the best America. "They work hard, they play hard, and"—unlike the labor agitators—"they don't go on strikes."[7]

Wister concluded that the cowboy, that American-born neo-aristocrat, had the power to transform politics in America. For him, the cowboy was at his core a political figure. Remembering Oliver Wendell Holmes Jr.'s interest in the common law, Wister wrote that the cowboy "cuts the way for the common law and self-government, and new creeds, polities and nations arise in his wake."[8] The common law—that primeval, lumbering, self-evolving force that members of the elite were constantly learning more about—was able to make its way west thanks to the cowboy, Wister wrote. For him, America's democratic traditions were really transplanted aristocratic traditions, rebaptized in the icy streams of the mountain west.

Wister's efforts to establish himself as the great bard of the American west were paying off. The year before, Roosevelt, unprompted, had recommended Wister's stories and essays to the Columbia drama professor James Brander Matthews.[9] But "The Evolution of the Cow-Puncher" offered the clearest and most vigorous explanation of his conservative theory of American individualism. For him, the west's legal and political inheritance had been bequeathed by displaced aristocrats.

This was a different conservatism, though, in that it didn't as much conserve old things as it instituted new things that merely pretended to be old. In Wister's theory of history, Anglo-Saxon westerners had inherited both an aristocratic spirit and an unwavering commitment to individual freedom. That individualism, in turn, was what marked them as naturally superior. Their "independence of spirit or mind or body," he explained, was "the cardinal surviving fittest instinct that makes the Saxon through the centuries conqueror, invader, navigator"—and now cowboy.[10] In other words, they were naturally selected rulers, fitted by ancient principles and Darwinian law to lead America into the future.

Wister's story of the west, in short, was one in which a long-lost tribe of American aristocrats came west and became cowboys. In his mind, the self-reliant westerner had drafted America's future through a lineal connection to an Anglo-Saxon past.

Remington's newfound interest in sculpture, or "mud," had been sparked the previous fall, when he had been sketching out ideas for one of Wister's stories at his large upstairs studio at his house in New Rochelle. The playwright Augustus Thomas, who had come to visit while Remington worked, watched as Remington sketched a scene and then, changing his mind, cleaned off the charcoal lines and turned the arrangement of the scene by 270 degrees, putting a figure who had been at the far left into the background and bringing the background characters to the front. Thomas was impressed by how easily he was able to do this.

"You're not an illustrator so much as you're a sculptor," Thomas had told him. "You don't mentally see your figures on [just] one side of them. Your mind goes all around them." He called that ability "the sculptor's degree of vision."[11]

By 1895, Remington could see that Wister was headed for great things. The Virginian character he had been using in a number of his stories was destined to become an American classic. In his friendly competition with Wister, Remington framed his turn toward sculpture as a turn toward permanence. For him, this was a kind of conservatism: an embrace of one of the oldest and most durable art forms. Other types of art were evanescent, Remington decided, but sculpture was forever.

He announced to Wister that he had stumbled on "a receipt for being *Great*—everyone might not be able to use the receipt but I can." Remington was excited about trying something new, but more than that, he was keen to create durable relics, stuff that would remain for the future as a permanent reminder of the American past. "My oils will get old and watery," he mused, "my water colors will fade—but I am to endure in bronze."[12]

The subject he had chosen for his new venture would not have surprised anyone. "I am doing a cow boy on a bucking broncho and I am going to rattle down through all the ages," he told Wister.[13] He knew what the public wanted. As he admitted to Poultney Bigelow, "Cowboys are cash" when it came to Frederic Remington.[14]

The final bronze statue stood twenty-three and a half inches tall.[15] It depicted a western horseman riding a bronco reared back on its hind legs. The mustachioed cowboy was raised off his saddle, pitching forward to maintain his center of gravity. His left foot barely held the stirrup. The brim of his sombrero was flipped upward, exposing a look of intense, brow-furrowed concentration. The sculpture seemed to capture a moment of wild, barely contained energy, a tug-of-war between man and nature.

In mid-October, the statue went on sale for $250 at Tiffany and Company in New York. The jeweler where Theodore Roosevelt had bought his bowie knife over a decade earlier would now sell a work of art commemorating that same sort of adventure.

"The Bronco Buster" was well-reviewed in the popular press. The *Century* praised it as "purely American."[16] The *New York Times* declared that it presented Remington "in a new and unexpected light." William Dean Howells told Remington that "you are such a wonder in every way that it would be no wonder if sculpture turned out to be one of your best holds."[17]

By late October, Remington was so excited about the completed sculpture that he was ready to make up with Wister. "My dear 'Dan,'" Remington wrote. (He used the name "Dan," he explained with what seemed like an audible smirk, because "that seems to be the only way I can identify you with your friends.") He was thrilled about the kind of artistic permanence the sculpture promised. "It dont decay—[. . .] I am d—— near eternal if people want to know about the past."[18] Sculpture was akin to carving one's will into the very building blocks of the earth. In Remington's mind, sculpture—unlike textiles, writing, drama, painting, or anything else—was forever.

Wister, as if trying to apologize for never telling Remington to call him "Dan," promptly wrote Remington and declared his intention to buy one. "I am going to own the Broncho Buster," he promised.[19] He wasn't planning to view it eventually, he specified. He was going the very next day.

Wister liked the piece, but he was also keenly aware of how much he still needed Remington. Remington was, after all, the preeminent western artist, and Wister was fast becoming the preeminent western writer. By then, Wister planned for his stories featuring the Virginian to become a novel, and he wanted Remington to do the illustrations.[20] Remington knew how much Wister needed him. In extolling the permanence of his statue to Wister, he had been unable to compare it to the evanescence of Wister's chosen media. "D—— your *'glide along'* songs—they die in the ear," he wrote, referring to Wister's youthful dream of becoming a musician. And he had a similar opinion of the durability of Wister's current cowboy protagonist: "your Virginian will be eaten up by time—all paper is pulp now."[21]

Wister didn't think this was true, but he also knew that Remington was a much bigger figure than he was. Even if he didn't want to admit it to himself, Wister knew that at least some of his success was because his name had been so often linked to Remington's. When *Bookman* magazine printed a "geographical map of American Literature" three years later, assigning different regions of America to different writers—western New York went to James Fenimore Cooper, the central Mississippi River to Mark Twain, and so on—the entire southwest was assigned to Remington and Wister.[22] Wister needed Remington, and they both knew it.

So in vowing to buy the "Bronco Buster," Wister could not resist prefacing his promise with a nervous inquiry as to whether Remington would, in fact, continue to work in pen-and-ink for publication. "Only once in a while you'll still wash your hands [of sculpting clay] to take hold of mine I hope," he wheedled. "It would be an awful blow to one of this team if bronze was to be all, hereafter."[23] (Wister must have breathed a sigh of relief when in one of Remington's next letters he said he was still busy "illustrating talky-talky stories."[24])

For his part, Roosevelt loved "The Bronco Buster" too, although he did not exactly promise to buy one. "I never so wish to be a millionaire [. . .] as when you have pictures to sell," he wrote Remington after the opening of one of his shows, less than a month after the sculpture went on sale.[25] At the time, Roosevelt was living in New York City and serving as the president of the Board of Police Commissioners. His office was less than a mile and a half from Tiffany. Despite being a wealthy man, Roosevelt never did buy any of Remington's paintings or sculptures, and his copy of "The Bronco Buster" would only come, three years later, as a gift.[26]

It would come as the culmination of a theater of western retrogression, when Roosevelt, seemingly in search of yet another west to conquer, would once again don hat and stirrups, borrow the name "Rough Riders" from Buffalo Bill Cody, and ride off to put the new theory of western conservatism to the test, to see if western Anglo-American individualism did, indeed, anoint the winner in the battle for survival of the fittest.

NOTES

1. Vorpahl *My*, 35.
2. Qtd. in Scharnhorst *Owen*, 62.
3. Wister "Evolution," 603.
4. Wister "Evolution," 610, 603.
5. Qtd. in Scharnhorst *Owen*, 75.
6. Scharnhorst *Owen*, 75.
7. OW journal, 8 June 1895.
8. Wister "Evolution," 604.
9. TR letter to James Brander Matthews, 29 June 1894.
10. Wister "Evolution," 604.
11. Thomas "Recollections," 361.
12. FR letter to Owen Wister [January 1895].
13. FR letter to Owen Wister [January 1895].
14. FR letter to Poultney Bigelow [1895].
15. Samuels *Frederic*, 225–226.
16. Coffin "Remington's," 319.
17. Qtd. in Samuels *Frederic*, 228, 227.
18. FR letter to Owen Wister, 24 October [1895].
19. Vorpahl *My*, 166.
20. Wister *Roosevelt*, 59.
21. FR letter to Owen Wister [January 1895].
22. "Chronicle," 468.
23. Qtd. in Vorhpahl *My*, 166.
24. FR letter to Owen Wister [late October 1895].
25. TR letter to Frederic Remington, 20 November 1895 in Splete, 278.
26. Samuels *Frederic*, 235.

Chapter 26

Progress, Populism, and the Lure of War

Frederick Jackson Turner liked to keep a close watch on new political developments in the west. During the first presidential campaign after the Panic of 1893, he tried to connect his conservative theory of American history to the new rise of the Populists.

Influenced by Henry George's theories of western lands and economic inequality, the Populists had mustered a left-leaning critique of eastern bankers and political leaders that gripped many in the west and south. For the election of 1896, the Democratic Party would choose William Jennings Bryan, the young congressman from the first district of Nebraska, as their presidential nominee. He would be soundly defeated by Ohio Republican William McKinley.

Bryan had built his presidential bid on a platform of bimetallism, or the theory that making both silver and gold legal tender would bring greater prosperity to the west. Bryan and the Populists were opposed by the railroad companies and the eastern financial establishment, who benefited from the gold standard and would lose from the inflation that bimetallism promised. Roosevelt didn't think the issue should belong solely to the Populists, and expressed his hope that "the Conservatives will do something for international bi-metalism; it would help us [Republicans] out greatly."[1]

Even so, the rise of Bryan made Roosevelt nervous. "Not since the Civil War has there been a Presidential election fraught with so much consequence to the country," he wrote his sister Anna. The Populists "who are behind Bryan are impelled by a wave of genuine fanaticism."[2] Wister was similarly anxious. Bryan's popularity struck him as a "very dark omen for our democracy."[3]

By the time the election rolled around, Roosevelt was disgusted. Populism, his view, had become little more than intellectual cover for the radical left: a shelter for "all the men who pray for anarchy, or who believe in socialism," or simply "want to strike down the well-to-do."[4]

Bryan's campaign culminated at the Democratic National Convention in Chicago, where he delivered his famous "cross of gold" speech. He divided the country between its eastern financial elites and its western and southern farmers.[5] He claimed that the issue was fundamentally one of freedom, telling the rapt crowd that it "is the issue of 1776 over again."[6] One journalist commented that Bryan had given birth to a "radical new party."[7]

But Turner wasn't convinced Bryan was quite as radical as many seemed to think. The western Populists, Turner explained in an essay in the *Atlantic Monthly*, chose to pursue left-leaning policies, but they did so to solve what were essentially conservative problems: the passing of a traditional way of life. Seen this way, Bryan and the Populists represented a reemergence of one of the oldest strains in America: the frontier individualist. "In the arid West these pioneers have halted and have turned to perceive an altered nation and changed social ideals," he explained. "They see the sharp contrast between their traditional idea of America, as the land of opportunity, the land of the self-made man, free from class distinction and from the power of wealth, and the existing America, so unlike the earlier ideal."[8] It was these westerners, he thought, who held the lamplight for Emersonian self-reliance. Whether or not they were correct to do so, they turned to Bryan from a sense that the "traditional idea of America" had been somehow left behind.

And while Turner acknowledged the Populists seemed radical, he insisted it was mostly because they had migrated westward against the tide of progress. "The story of the political leaders who remained in the place of their birth and shared its economic changes differs from the story of those who by moving to the West continued on a new area the old social type," he explained.[9] In other words, western settlers had propelled themselves by seemingly paddling against the current of history, progressing by continually pursuing old ways in even older lands.

Far from being straightforwardly radical, he concluded, the Populists were actually tapping into an old conservative wellspring. Their ideas only seemed new, largely because their motivations and ways of life were so old. But the larger point was the same one he pursued several years earlier at the World's Fair: in America, continuous development required deliberate and temporary retrogression into the past. For Turner, American progress was always conservative.

Turner's belief that progress required constant regeneration on the fertile fields of an older world was a principle that Remington felt personally. He was feeling old, and he longed for the grit and vigor of his youth.

Remington had always been a big man, but as he approached his middle thirties he began to worry that he was becoming soft. He took up bicycle riding and wrote an article for *Harper's Weekly* on the new fad.[10] Bicycling invigorated him: he felt more like his younger, healthier self.

The general fear of decline was part of his conservative disposition, much in the same way it was for Wister. But Remington didn't only fear the loss of national greatness. He also had a visceral fear that his body was slowly failing him. He resolved, as he did many times throughout his life, to quit drinking. Bicycling seemed to be working against that resolution, though, as it was also "the greatest thing to produce a thirst for beer."[11]

(Remington likely didn't see this as a contradiction, as "drinking" for him really just meant hard liquor. He once told his uncle that he hadn't had a drink in years, at least if one didn't count "anything stronger than claret or beer."[12])

Remington's desire to recover a younger, fitter body was linked to his desire to recover a younger, fitter America. Even with all his success, some small part of him never stopped believing that he had been denied one inheritance of his father's America.

He was reasonably happy. He was certainly wealthy, with his enormous estate in New Rochelle. But something was missing. He wanted to be a part of something grand and important and world-changing, something he felt had been denied to his generation of Americans. "I have only one ambition," he confided to Poultney Bigelow, "and that is to see a war."[13]

Remington, Cody, Roosevelt, Turner, and Wister belonged to a peculiar generational cohort. Born too late for the Civil War and having known relative peace, they spent their professional lives telling stories that seemed to belong to an earlier and more vigorous age of conflict. As the only son of a Civil War hero, a respected newspaperman, and a powerful New York Republican Party leader, Remington had been born in a very long shadow. At a young age, Seth Remington had proven himself on the field of battle. Later, he applied that bravery by establishing himself in the masculine worlds of journalism and politics. His son, in contrast, left military school for an art program he never completed. His father made a name for himself in a bloody war to keep the nation from bursting at the seams. His son made a name for himself drawing pictures of soldiers and cowboys cavorting on the desert tundra of the west. Though Remington had made his own way in the world, his father's death had forever denied him the chance to see if he measured up in his father's eyes.

The loss of his father's appraising gaze is one thing he shared with Roosevelt. If boys learn to be men at their father's knees, one lesson Remington could have learned was also the lesson most vigorously denied him: that the world of men is a world of war. He had been influential in military matters, in his own way. General Nelson Miles seemed to understand that he and the rest of the military benefited from Remington's flattering depiction, and went out of his way to make himself available to Remington. In 1894, the Massachusetts militia debuted new slouch hats as part of their standard uniform, a choice the press attributed to Remington's influence. His "long series of pictures of regulars in the West has filled the public mind with a new type of soldier—a rather rakish and roughish person in appearance," declared the Boston *Transcript*.[14] *Harper's Weekly* agreed, writing that the Remington-inspired hat had a certain "manly grace" and that "Mr. Remington deserves to make his mark on the contemporary soldier."[15]

Remington may have been pleased at the compliment, but it was not enough. His father had been a brevet colonel in the Civil War, and the best he could do was inspire some jaunty new slouch hats? By comparison, the accomplishment must have seemed thin indeed. The following year, Remington began voicing his desire to see a war. He knew he was not strong enough to actually fight in one. But it was also no longer enough to tour around, sightseeing the final lingering conflicts of the Indian Wars. He wanted his own war.

War increasingly must have seemed like an inheritance denied. His parents—like the parents of Roosevelt, Wister, Turner, and everyone else his age—had witnessed firsthand the horrors of the Civil War. Many of their parents were old enough to have heard stories about the Mexican-American War, which gave birth to the modern west. For Remington's parents' generation, war *did* something. Whatever its awful human toll, its legacies could be seen on every map. War had been not just how young men tested themselves; it had been how America became itself.

As Roosevelt later put it, "we of this generation do not have to face a task such as that our fathers faced." They may be "the children of the men who proved themselves equal to the mighty days," he added, but they were not yet the men themselves.[16]

It would have been easy for Remington to look at the men of his father's generation and conclude, not unreasonably, that nothing he would ever do could have that same significance. This was, of course, a romantic view of war. But it was a view of war that was easy to acquire if one had never fought in one. Had Seth Remington lived, he might have concluded his son was living in a time of unimaginable peace and prosperity, and perhaps been unsettled by his wide-eyed hunger for war.

Conflict, for Remington, was the spark animating America's forward progress. This was a core part of his conservatism, in the sense that it assumed that evolutionary progress was the consequence of beneficial adaptations. Conflict and competition were the way that those adaptations were recognized. Part of the reason Remington had made it his life's work to document the west was that it was widely viewed, rightly or wrongly, as a region where foundational conflicts between the strong and the weak were still resolved with ruthless efficiency. He and his friends had come to a rough consensus: that the American west was an opportunity for Darwinian sorting. And war was the ultimate sorting mechanism.

For Remington, the culling fields of the American west were at best a poor substitute for the unsentimental competition of pure war. Shortly after "The Bronco Buster" sculpture was unveiled, Remington wrote to Wister to brag about the sculpture and muse on the inevitability of war. "I think I smell *war* in the air," he wrote. "When that comes to the Wild West we'll have passed into History and History is only valuable after the lapse of 100 years and by that time you and I will be dead."[17]

War, in his mind, was history's thresher. He seemed to think that the type of war he wanted would again come "to the Wild West." Perhaps he thought it was a force like Haley's comet that only came around once a century. It had devastated the Indian populations of the American west, and in time, it would come around again to devastate another population. Or perhaps he thought that centuries of the western Indian Wars somehow simply didn't count as war. But whichever it was, war had been seen up close by his father's generation, and he believed it had not yet been glimpsed by his.

War was in the air.

NOTES

1. TR letter to Henry Cabot Lodge, 8 August 1895.
2. TR letter to Anna Roosevelt Cowles, 26 July 1896.
3. Wister *Roosevelt*, 50.
4. TR letter to Cecil Arthur Spring Rice, 8 October 1896.
5. Cherny, 59.
6. Kazin, 61.
7. "Mr. Bryan's," 391–392.
8. Turner "Dominant," 442.
9. Turner "Dominant," 442.
10. Remington "Colonel," 468–469.
11. FR letter to Poultney Bigelow [1895].
12. FR letter to Robert Sackrider [Spring 1899].
13. FR letter to Poultney Bigelow [1895].
14. Qtd. in Martin, 1114.
15. Martin, 1114.
16. Roosevelt "Strenuous," 6, 5.
17. FR letter to Owen Wister [early November 1895].

Part V

CUBA AND THE NEW WEST (1896–1902)

Chapter 27

The Rush of War

On May 30, 1895, Wister's friend and mentor Oliver Wendell Holmes Jr. had given a Memorial Day speech to Harvard's graduating class. Holmes had been wounded in the Civil War over thirty years earlier, and, like Roosevelt, thought that conflict and competition was the chief engine of American progress. For many people, Holmes said in his speech, it seemed that "war is out of fashion." People tried to prevent suffering and pain in any number of ways, he pointed out, including labor unions and socialism. But the Darwinian "struggle for life," he continued, "is the order of the world." No matter how much you tried, you couldn't escape it: man's "destiny is battle."[1] War was not done with man, nor man with war.

Holmes didn't want to romanticize battle, of course, but he wanted the students to understand that war wasn't an aberration in the natural order; war *was* the natural order. It offered a clarity and a certainty absent from civilian life. The very point of existence, he explained, was "to ride boldly at what is in front of you, be it fence or enemy; to pray, not for comfort, but for combat; to keep the soldier's faith against the doubts of civil life."[2] *Pray for combat*. This was a Darwinian view of war, one that held that struggle was the organizing principle of existence.

Afterward, Roosevelt exclaimed, "by Jove, that speech of Holmes' was fine; I wish he could make [anti-imperialist activist] Edward Atkinson learn it by heart and force him to repeat it forwards and backwards every time he makes a peace oration."[3] Roosevelt believed in the elucidating, redemptive powers of war. Holmes had it right. War had a brutal clarity that simply didn't exist in civil politics. In a later speech, Roosevelt would propose that "no triumph of peace is quite so great as the supreme triumphs of war."[4] In a way, he had been longing for combat for years: probably since Alice died and certainly since he tried to join the vigilance group organized by the president of the Montana Stockgrowers' Association back in 1884.

But now he could glimpse an opportunity on the horizon. After the failed Cuban War for Independence in 1878, Cuba had become an important trading partner for the United States, but remained under Spanish control. In the early 1890s, the Cuban intellectual, writer, and revolutionary José Martí began agitating for Cuban independence. Influenced by the left-leaning ideas of Henry George, Martí became a key voice for Cuban home rule.

For many in the United States, Roosevelt included, the Cuba question was the Monroe Doctrine redux. If it was up to him, Roosevelt explained, "every foot of American soil, including the nearest islands in both the Pacific and the Atlantic, should be in the hands of independent American states."[5] The United States was the natural authority in the Americas, to this way of thinking, and any Spanish interference was an affront.

When Martí was killed in a May 1895 uprising near Palma Soriano, the rumblings for Cuban independence within the United States grew steadily louder. It was more than a little convenient, of course, that the dream of Cuban independence aligned neatly with the dream of a Western Hemisphere dominated by the United States.

Soon, Roosevelt was musing that it was getting "very difficult for me not to wish for a war with Spain."[6] By January 1897, Roosevelt admitted he was becoming a "quietly rampant 'Cuba Libre' man," and wished that President Cleveland would send a fleet.[7] A few months after Cleveland left office, he found himself in a position to do something about it.

Fifteen years after he wrote *The Naval War of 1812*, Roosevelt was appointed assistant secretary of the U.S. Navy by President McKinley. He had gone from a wealthy young writer to a rancher to the corridors of federal power in two decades. After two years of service as New York's police commissioner, he resigned his position and moved to Washington.

For his part, Remington felt that Cuba would be his last shot to witness the kind of military glory that had long been an inheritance denied. He tried to get Wister excited about it, too. He told him, "[w]e are getting old, and one cannot *get* old without having seen a war."[8] But Wister didn't agree.

Wister was one of the few people Remington knew who was still unmarried at his age. Instead of seeking the romance of war, Wister pursued romance of a different sort. He was courting Mary Channing, who everyone called Molly, a distant cousin he had known for years and a descendant of William Ellery Channing, a good friend of Ralph Waldo Emerson's.[9] On April 21, 1898, the day Congress declared war on Spain, Wister would marry Channing in Philadelphia.[10]

The narrative that Cuba was in need of liberation coalesced in the popular imagination. Remington tried to explain this line of thought to Wister, using shocking language he seemed to think Wister would appreciate: "*Cuba Libre.* It does seem tough that so many Americans have had to be and have still got to be killed to free a lot of d—— niggers who are better off under the yoke. There is something fatefull in our destiny that way. This time however we will kill a few Spaniards instead of Anglo Saxons which will be proper and nice."[11]

In his own way, Remington was trying to explain something he could barely explain to himself. He was arguing that liberation was the destiny of men like him and Wister, even though in his view liberation had been pointless in America, as onetime enslaved persons had been "better off under the yoke."

The racism of his letter only concealed its incoherence. The point didn't even make sense. If it was better for enslaved people to be "under the yoke" than out of it, why try to free them at all? But in however ignorant a manner, Remington was explaining his faith in America's mythic, romantic destiny. As far as he was concerned, war was simply *good.* He saw war much as he saw the now-vanishing myth of the American west: as a primal, regenerative force that made history happen.

In December 1896, newspaper magnate William Randolph Hearst sent Remington and journalist Richard Harding Davis to Cuba to report on the conflict for his *New York Journal.* War was good for the newspaper business. An apocryphal story began to circulate that Hearst had sent Remington off with a sardonic set of instructions: "You supply the pictures, and I'll supply the war."[12]

Remington was initially thrilled to go, but once he got from Key West to Cuba, it didn't take long for the excitement to subside. There was no poetry in the thing. The best he could do was to sputter a list of travesties to Poultney Bigelow: "small pox—typhoid—yellow jack—dishonesty—suffering beyond measure."[13]

But the experience didn't blunt his desire to see a war. In the summer of the following year, as Remington was finishing up the illustrations for Wister's first western novel, *Lin McLean,* Roosevelt invited Remington and two journalists to come observe the naval fleet. He wanted them to observe some of the White Squadron conducting maneuvers off Hampton Roads, Virginia. Roosevelt, who said he was having a "bully time" as assistant secretary of the navy, seemed to see a connection between his current military preparations and his earlier western adventuring.[14]

After the excursion, Roosevelt told Remington that while he wished he could be with him out west, "among the sage brush," he wanted Remington's help to "make the American people see the beauty and the majesty of our ships, and the heroic quality which lurks somewhere in all those who man and handle them."[15] It was as if he wanted Remington to help him find some way of affixing the majesty of the frontier west to the iron mass of American nautical might. The same heroic quality that could be found in ranchers and cowboys could also, he suggested, be found in the captains and sailors of the navy.

Afterward, he expanded on this line of thought. Remington had sent Roosevelt a copy of his new book of illustrations *Drawings*, for which Wister had written the preface. (Roosevelt loved the book, particularly "Fox Terriers Fighting a Badger," which included a Roosevelt lookalike watching the titular scrap.[16]) When Roosevelt wrote back to thank him, he again prodded Remington to begin to think of the sea as he had once thought of its western plains. Try to "care for the ship" as "you do for the horse," he urged. The sailor, like the horseman, "is simple and honorable; and he works hard, and if need be is willing to die hard."[17] The implication was clear: a sailor was a cowboy by another name.

Roosevelt seemed to want every inch of the globe to be shaped in some way by his expansive vision of the American west. Earlier, with Cuba clearly on his mind, he had written to Frederick Jackson Turner and told him he thought it would be "a good thing for this country when the West [. . .] grows so big that it can no more be jealous of the East than New York is now jealous of Boston."[18] In an indirect way, the war in Cuba would be a way to grow another west.

By the end of 1897, Roosevelt seemed to be revising his opinion of Remington. If their relationship had at times been coolly professional, the time they spent together observing the White Squadron seemed to bring them closer. Roosevelt mentioned to an assistant postmaster general that several of Remington's illustrations would make excellent postage stamp art.[19] Remington received a copy of Roosevelt's *The Winning of the West* from his wife for Christmas. (It did seem odd, he admitted, that he didn't own the book yet).[20] Beyond that, Roosevelt had been deeply impressed with Remington's recent story in *Harper's*, "Masai's Crooked Trail." Roosevelt had known Remington could draw—everyone knew that—but he was somewhat amazed that he could write, too. "Are you aware, O sea-going plainsman," he wrote him—as if still trying to make sure Remington knew that America's next great western adventure would be overseas—"that aside from what you do with the pencil, you come closer to the real thing with the pen than any other man in the western business?"[21] Remington, reading the letter, must have fairly glowed with pleasure.

Remington's work—his illustrations, his sculpture, and now his fiction—would, Roosevelt predicted, persist and help shape "the cantos in the last Epic of the Western Wilderness before it ceased being a wilderness."[22] Both men seemed to think that the glory days of the American west, the romantic days of combat and conquest, seemed to at last be coming to a close.

Wister felt it, too. His debut novel *Lin McLean*, which was stitched together from stories that had appeared over the years in *Harper's* and other publications, seemed to mourn the fading youth of the west. The book was published on December 7, 1897, and within a week, Roosevelt had written Wister to tell him how much he liked it, praising it as a "historic document for one phase of the life of endeavor in our race's history which is as evanescent as it is fascinating."[23] That west had been, Wister wrote in the novel, a "raw, hopeful, full-blooded cattle era, which now the sobered West remembers as the days of its fond youth."[24]

That era had also been an era of radical equality, a Darwinian Eden in which no living beings had any advantages save those proofed through contests of might or merit. "For one man has been as good as another in three places—Paradise before the Fall; the Rocky Mountains before the wire fence; and the Declaration of Independence," Wister wrote in the novel.[25] And now that wild, democratic arcadia was fading into oblivion.

But there remained yet another wilderness. Another west. For many, Cuba represented what the American west had once represented: a new state of nature. It offered yet another fount of untapped freedom, a place ripe for settlement and civilization. In a book published in the run-up to the war, writer James Hyde Clark opined that "not a little of the interior [of Cuba] was left in a state of nature."[26] Another writer, tabulating Cuba's untapped natural resources, agreed that most of the island was "still in a state of nature."[27]

Since the time of John Locke, the "state of nature" had been a mental exercise in milling the raw materials of freedom from an untamed wilderness. It was the same dynamic Wister, Turner, Roosevelt, and countless others had glimpsed in the American west. To dream of a western "state of nature" was to dream of renewing the American social compact, with gentleman westerners like Roosevelt as a new generation of founders. And now, in Cuba, it was happening all over again.

By 1898, both Remington and Roosevelt were eager for a war. Roosevelt was resolute: "If there is a war I, of course, intend to go," he announced to a friend. He didn't mean he wanted to go in a supervisory capacity as assistant secretary of the navy; he wanted to go fight in it, as a soldier.

He thought his experiences in the Badlands were good training. He had "acted as sheriff in the cow country" when he apprehended the boat thieves, he continued, an experience he thought would make him "of some use with the President" when it came to Cuba.[28] The rough-and-tumble of the American west was the purest training a man could hope for.

On February 15, 1898, the battleship *Maine* exploded off the coast of Havana, killing most of its crew. Though the cause of the explosion was unknown, Roosevelt was instantly sure that Spain was at fault. It was an "act of dirty treachery on the part of the Spaniards *I* believe," he wrote the next day.[29] He began quietly campaigning to join a regiment in Cuba.

For most people, it would have been an audacious thing to do. Roosevelt was thirty-nine years old, with a stable job and six young children and a wife. And now he wanted to quit the job to go chase adventure. His friends thought it was madness. His boss, Secretary of the Navy John D. Long, thought Roosevelt had "lost his head to this folly of deserting the post where he is of the most service and running off to ride a horse."[30] But ever since college, running off to ride a horse was what Roosevelt did.

By late April, Roosevelt had been offered a lieutenant colonelcy in a Cuba-bound cavalry unit that journalists quickly dubbed a "cowboy regiment."[31] After accepting, the first person Roosevelt contacted was his old ranch hand from Medora, Sylvane Ferris. He told him he was raising a regiment of westerners.[32] He wanted Ferris to join.

When the New York *Sun* reported that Roosevelt was rounding up such a regiment, it used an old bit of horseman slang that had become widely known ever since "Buffalo Bill" Cody had begun using it earlier that decade. Roosevelt would, the paper reported, be heading up a "regiment of rough riders."[33]

The regiment came together quickly. Roosevelt ordered a lieutenant colonel's uniform from Brooks Brothers. He received a Waltham pocket watch from his sister Corinne and her husband Douglas. He also received a .38 Colt revolver that had been salvaged from the wreck of the *Maine* from his other sister, Anna, and her husband William.[34]

He received permission to enlist 1,000 men. Many were southwestern horsemen, but some were what the press snidely dubbed the "Fifth Avenue Boys," mostly Harvard and Yale men, a few of whom reportedly showed up with polo mallets and golf clubs.[35] The idea was that the eastern elite would serve alongside the western adventurers. Rank would be decided not through heredity or society, but through merit. "Let the best man win," as Wister would later say. The Rough Riders would enact a kind of Darwinian selection on a military scale.

Yet despite the public's interest in what Roosevelt called the "Harvard contingent," Roosevelt wanted people to know that the elite young men of the eastern seaboard only made up a small fraction of the regiment. The bulk of the volunteers came from the American west. Roosevelt seemed to view those men as living embodiments of the philosophy of practical conservatism that he had developed since moving west fourteen years earlier. To him, the men were throwbacks to an earlier, hardier age. As he explained it, the westerners came "from the lands that have been most recently won over to white civilization, and in which the conditions of life are nearest those that obtained on the frontier."[36] By conserving certain values from the frontier past, those values could, if properly harnessed, plow the soil for the future of "white civilization."

In articulating his vision for the Rough Riders, Roosevelt was referencing a set of ideas which had by that point become commonplace for him. As far as he was concerned, the logic was simple: the men's value as soldiers stemmed largely from the fact that they came from a region characterized by older, seemingly obsolete modes of life. He was testing the value of a usable past. The Rough Riders would use America's frontier past to conquer a new state of nature—Cuba—so that it, too, could be won for white civilization.

After all, the cold-eyed individualism of the west, in which no living thing is given reflexive preference over any other living thing, was precisely the type of equality that led to useful distinctions between men. The westerners "had their natural leaders," Roosevelt pointed out. Such leaders were distinguished naturally, by fitness or merit. They were "men who had shown they could master other men, and could more than hold their own in the eager driving life of the new settlements."[37] This was an opportunity to test Roosevelt's grand theory: that superiority in the American west was not just about the west. It signaled something important about status in a much larger ontology. To this way of thinking, cowboys from Wyoming were not just rulers of cattle. They were rulers of men.

Among newspapermen, excitement over the so-called Rough Riders was burbling. Roosevelt, who had been a writer before he had been almost anything else, recognized a good story when he saw one. As Poultney Bigelow once snidely put it, "whatever he [Roosevelt] did after leaving college was luridly retailed by himself in whatever magazine offered him the largest pay per word."[38]

Roosevelt initially professed to dislike the name "Rough Riders." The official title of the regiment, he pointed out, was simply the First United States Volunteer Calvary.[39] Yet once the military began to use the phrase in official communications, the regiment gave up and started using it themselves. And for good reason. As Roosevelt seemed to sense, the name conjured just the sort of conservative story of America that he, along with Remington, Wister, and Turner, had made his bread and butter.

The whole enterprise sounded like a scene out of Wister's stories: cowboys from the past, fighting to secure the future of freedom. It was the type of thing that seemed deliberately staged to gallop into history books and dime-store

264   Chapter 27

novels. Before he even departed, the Frederick A. Stokes publishing company approached Roosevelt about publishing a book about his new venture. Roosevelt politely declined.

He had already sold the book rights to Scribner's.[40]

NOTES

1. Holmes Jr. "Soldier's," 87, 88.
2. Holmes Jr. "Soldier's," 92.
3. TR letter to Henry Cabot Lodge, 5 June 1895.
4. Roosevelt "Washington's," 244.
5. TR letter to William Astor Chandler, 23 December 1897.
6. TR letter to Anna Roosevelt Cowles, 9 March 1896.
7. TR letter to Anna Roosevelt Cowles, 2 January 1897.
8. Qtd. in Vorpahl *My*, 215.
9. Bell Jr., 501.
10. Wister *Roosevelt*, 56.
11. FR letter to Owen Wister [early April 1896].
12. Qtd. in Vorpahl *My*, 230.
13. FR letter to Poultney Bigelow, 28 January 1897.
14. TR letter to Frederic Remington, 18 August 1897, in Splete, 220.
15. TR letter to Frederic Remington, 15 September 1897, in Splete, 221.
16. Splete, 287.
17. TR letter to Frederic Remington, 26 October 1897.
18. TR letter to Frederick Jackson Turner, 15 December 1896.
19. TR letter to John A. Merritt, 23 December 1897.
20. FR letter to Theodore Roosevelt, 25 December 1897.
21. TR letter to Frederic Remington, 28 December 1897, in Splete, 288.
22. TR letter to Frederic Remington, 28 December 1897, in Splete, 288.
23. Scharnhorst *Owen*, 11; TR letter to Owen Wister, 13 December 1897.
24. Wister *Lin*, 109.
25. Wister *Lin*, 109.
26. Clark *Cuba*, 275.
27. Foord, 360.
28. TR letter to C. Whitney Tillinghast, Second, 13 January 1898.
29. TR letter to Benjamin Harrison Diblee, 16 February 1898.
30. Qtd. in Samuels *Teddy*, 12.
31. "Cowboy Regiments," 1.
32. TR letter to Sylvane M. Ferris, 24 April 1898.
33. "Roosevelt Accepts," 5.
34. TR telegram to Brooks Brothers, 2 May 1898; TR letter to Douglas Robinson, 3 May 1898; Roosevelt *Rough*, 137. See also Samuels *Teddy*, 19, 30.

35. Samuels *Teddy*, 18.
36. Roosevelt *Rough*, 18.
37. Roosevelt *Rough*, 19.
38. Bigelow *Seventy*, 280.
39. Roosevelt *Rough*, 11.
40. TR letter to Robert Bridges, 21 May 1898.

Chapter 28

The Cowboy Regiment Abroad

In May, the unit dispatched to San Antonio for training. The cowboy regiment seemed rife with romance, just the sort of thing newspapermen loved. The Washington, DC, *Evening Star* breathlessly heralded the "distinguished bad men" who made up the Rough Riders. The reporter described a number of them: "'Rocky Mountain Bill' Jenkins, from Montana," along with "'Broncho' George Brown, from Arizona, who lives in Skull Valley," and of course "'Dead Shot' Jim Simpson from Albuquerque," who can put a "bullet through a jack rabbit's eye at a distance of a thousand yards while riding a wild horse." In truth, the reporter let his imagination run away from him. No men with those names heralding from those locations appeared on the muster rolls. Still, the reporter was correct that the regiment unified the disparate regions of the west. "The different contingents of cowboys, plainsmen and mountaineers from widely separated sections of the great west," he wrote, had made the whole thing rather "like the meeting of delegations of politicians from distant states."[1]

One thing was perfectly clear: Roosevelt's cult of individual merit reigned. Eastern universities, lineages, and social clubs held little currency. The *Star* reporter concluded that the cowboys tolerated the "'dudes' from New York," but were unimpressed by their school affiliations and financial status. "Brawn and daring are the only qualities that claim respect in this military camp," he concluded.[2]

The men stayed in San Antonio for about a month. It was, in a way, the culmination of some of Roosevelt's earliest fantasies of the west: a place where an individual's abilities were all that mattered. Roosevelt was tickled by the sight of cowboys and ranchers commanding the Harvard men. "You would be amused," he wrote to a friend, to see the "Knickerbocker club men cooking and washing dishes for one of the New Mexico companies." Eager to show that his philosophy of individual merit wasn't limited to whites, he added that there were also "a score of Indians," who he thought were "excellent riders and seem to be pretty good fellows."³ It was true that there were a number of nonwhite, non-Protestant Rough Riders: members of the Pawnee, Chickasaw, and Cherokee tribes, Roman Catholics, men of Irish descent, Jewish men, and Latinos.

In other words, Roosevelt saw the Rough Riders as a chance to test many of the ideas he had long held about the west and the value of strenuous competition. He believed the west was a perfect place to test how to best produce a hierarchical society through democratic means. It offered equality without equitability. If a nonwhite westerner should prove himself a better rider or rifleman than his white, eastern counterpart, then it was only natural that the westerner should be the easterner's superior.

It was this dynamic—discovering and recognizing the best men—that pulsed beneath the surface of the Cuban conflict. Many Americans had a vague, uneasy sense that modernity was making its young men soft and weak. Roosevelt himself worried about the new "over-civilized man" who retreated from vigorous competition with the world."⁴ Chauncey M. Depew, the former president of the New York Central railroad, said the Rough Riders were testing the idea that "under the slouch hat of the cowboy, and the imported tile of the [Ivy League] dude, is the same American manhood when American manhood is needed." The Rough Riders represented the reemergence of American manhood, Depew concluded, the "union of the buckskin and the broadcloth."⁵

On May 29, the Rough Riders began loading up for the trip from San Antonio to Tampa, where they arrived on June 3. On the train, Roosevelt read French intellectual Edmond Demolins's book *Anglo-Saxon Superiority: To What It Is Due*.⁶ Demolins made the case that political and economic philosophies were linked to ethnic heritage.

Anglo-Saxons' global dominance, Demolins argued, was a result of their long-standing embrace of individualism and rejection of socialism. "The social group which is at present in advance of all the others, the Anglo-Saxon group, owes that advance to the development of individual activity," he asserted. "Socialism is, therefore, in contradiction with the actual march of progress."⁷ But in the same way that Roosevelt and Turner both thought the American west had shaped an entirely new American type, Demolins thought that individualism was not simply a lineal inheritance; it could be learned. It was a trait that, once acquired, could lead to national triumph.

At bottom, Demolins was making a simple case that individualism was a scientific and civilizational good. What he saw as Anglo-Saxon superiority had its roots, he explained, in moral individualism. "In the sweat of thy face shalt thou eat bread," he wrote, referencing Genesis.⁸ This was a moral principle—*for whatsoever a man soweth, that shall he also reap*—but it was also a loosely Darwinian principle.

To this way of thinking, individual striving led to increased offspring. As Darwin had observed of "primeval man," individuals who were "the most sagacious, who invented and used the best weapons or traps, and who were best able to defend themselves, would rear the greatest number of offspring."[9] For similar reasons, Demolins concluded, individualism assured national progress; socialism would doom it. For him, socialism wasn't just a bad idea. It was "an anachronism," one that went "against the forward motion of the world."[10] Consequently, he concluded, a forward-looking individualism was the surest path to national superiority.

Roosevelt liked Demolins's book very much, although he quibbled with his contention that the military deadens individualism. Not in America, Roosevelt thought, as the train made its way east to Tampa.[11] In this country, he concluded, military prowess had long been a function of individualist westerners. Now he was headed to Cuba to put that notion to the test.

Remington was going, too. He wrote Wister in June to try to give him one last chance to come along. He apologized for having missed Wister's wedding, but congratulated him as one of the last of his friends to get married. "I didn't think you would be caught," he wrote, joking that Molly "wants to keep a rope on you," which would be hard to do, as he had "been [like a] *broncho* for so long." At any rate, if Wister should manage slip the hobble, Remington promised an outrageous spectacle of violence in Cuba: "Say old man there is bound to be a lovely scrap around Havana—a big murdering—sure."[12]

Wister didn't take the bait. Instead, he took his new wife on a camping trip to the Pacific Northwest.[13] But Roosevelt and Remington were desperately eager to, as Remington said, "see a war." So along with Richard Harding Davis, Frank Norris, and a few other correspondents, Remington found himself aboard General Shafter's flagship *Segurança*, waiting to depart Tampa for Cuba.[14] It was Remington's first time meeting Norris, the twenty-eight-year-old western writer who, just four months earlier, had published his shocking breakthrough novel *McTeague*. Remington had gone to Cuba with Davis already, when Hearst's *Journal* commissioned them to go and report on the brewing tensions two years earlier. Davis's book on the experience, *Cuba in War Time*, had been published the previous year with illustrations by Remington. All the men were eager to be underway.

At the time, it was the single largest seagoing invasion of another country in America's history. They were part of a fleet of 32 transport ships, protected by 14 warships, transporting 12,000 soldiers. As Davis observed, the seven-mile-long flotilla brought to mind the Spanish Armada.[15] Going to

Cuba didn't just mean war. It meant empire. And Roosevelt and Remington couldn't wait.

Not all Americans supported the war, of course. And few of those that did would have made the case that invading Cuba was anything resembling a conservative course of action. One writer for J. Sterling Morton's journal *The Conservative* thought the war was a terrible idea—unnecessary for American interests and promising steep costs in blood and treasure.

Yet even though the *Conservative* felt the war was not conservative in the least, it still framed the war's conservativism as a correlative of its Darwinism. In an article on "The Spanish-American Imbroglio," the *Conservative* writer noted that "Darwin and Spencer have told us that the survival of the fittest and perishing of the unfit were among the most manifest works of Nature." He continued, asking, "[i]f survival of the fittest is the law by which God works, is it not doing that work to strengthen and multiply the fit rather than the unfit?" In other words, culling the weak and bolstering the strong was not just natural, but moral. The *Conservative*'s case against the war was that it was trying to rig Darwin's laws: helping the unfit—Cubans, in this case—rather than hastening their demise. In interfering, the writer worried, the United States was going against "natural law."[16]

Champ Clark, the Democratic congressman from Missouri, was willing to be persuaded that Cuba might safely be conquered and annexed. To him, the island seemed much like Texas or California in an earlier age: part of the "natural frontier" of America. Nevertheless, he worried that a war might change what he considered America's fundamentally conservative spirit. As he wrote in an essay on the war in *The Conservative Review*, "yesterday, we were a happy, conservative, self-contained people; today we are the most feverish, reckless, ambitious adventurers known among men."[17] Even for supporters of the war, it was hardly settled whether it was a conservative or unconservative course of action.

Yet, at the same time, as Clark's easy assumption that Cuba was part of America's "natural frontier" suggested, many people saw the war as a part of America's ongoing history of western adventuring. And to this way of thinking, violent frontier conquest wasn't a repudiation of the American spirit. It *was* the American spirit. Even if he didn't realize it, Clark was referencing Frederick Jackson Turner's argument, from five years earlier, that temporary retrogression into "frontier conditions" had been the chief driver of American development.

And it was by this newer, Darwinian definition of conservativism— understanding conservatism not as a stodgy preference for aristocracy but as a deliberate retrogression to establish a modern hierarchy governed by the "fittest"—that the war in Cuba was perfectly conservative. It involved men traveling west—by clothing and affect, if not by compass—and retrogressing to frontier conditions: learning from, as Roosevelt put it, the "wild riders and riflemen of the Rockies and the Great Plains."[18]

The conflict symbolized a retrogression into a wild past. It promised a kind of absolution from modernity, another baptism in freedom. In this way, it was completely, utterly conservative. The war represented a chance to find yet another state of nature, to drink once more at the original fount of freedom.

In more ways than one, people saw the American invasion of Cuba as a continuation of its centuries-long conquest of the west. As Richard Harding Davis put it, referencing Emmanuel Leutze's massive 1861 mural of manifest destiny, "Westward the Course of Empire Takes Its Way," when it came to Cuba, the "course of empire to-day takes its way to all points of the compass—not only to the West."[19]

Robert P. Porter, the former superintendent of the Census who eight years earlier had declared the American frontier closed and inspired Frederick Jackson Turner's revolutionary new theory of American history, shared this view. "Just as the restless and hopeful population of the Eastern States has migrated westward, and to some extent southward, in our own country," Porter wrote, "so it would find its way to Cuba if conditions allowed of extensive settlement and homemaking."[20] In other words, Cuba was simply *next*. The west had long been viewed as a primitive proving ground for America's future leaders. Now that the continental frontier had been declared closed, those same unsettled conditions were available again overseas.

Viewing the invasion as the logical continuation of the settlement of the American west typically meant understanding the war as something governed by the Darwinian laws of nature. "The accidents which led to the war," one writer explained, "merely precipitated a result inevitable as the law of the survival of the fittest. The consequent territorial expansion is the necessary outcome of the inevitable process."[21] For a century before there was even an American nation to speak of, the American west had been viewed as an example of the mythic freedom exemplifying the "state of nature." And since Darwin's development hypothesis had spread to all corners of the intellectual and political firmament, it had become common to romanticize the American west not just as a state of nature of boundless freedom, but also as a space in which that freedom allowed for the sort of democratic, wide-open competition that would certify society's "fittest." Now that same logic could be extended to Cuba.

Seen in this way, imperialism wasn't warmongering; it was a conservative enactment of the immutable laws of nature. In a statement supporting the war, New Hampshire congressman Cyrus A. Sulloway declared that history itself was governed by Darwinian principles. "The Anglo-Saxon advances into the new regions with a Bible in one hand and a shotgun in the other," he said. "It is but another demonstration of the survival of the fittest."[22]

And the participation of a romantic group of western horsemen lent that Darwinian enterprise a mythic resonance. Seen in that light, the invasion was no cheap squabble over America's hemispheric authority. It was about cowboys fighting a Darwinian battle for freedom. Trumbull White, who was churning out a book on *Our War with Spain for Cuba's Freedom*, spoke about the Rough Riders as if they were the last gasp of a species rapidly headed for extinction. The "cowboy is a rapidly passing type," he mused. In Cuba, the cowboy "has made what may prove to be his last stand, as a soldier."[23]

In sum, Roosevelt was not alone in viewing the Rough Riders as important players in this new Darwinian battle for supremacy. Viewed one way, the project was not conservative in the slightest. After all, it wasn't trying to conserve the established political order in Cuba at all; it was trying to intervene in it. But viewed another way, it was a manifestation of a newer, forward-looking conservatism: one that tried to use the mythic trappings of a frontier past in order to advance the cause of individual freedom in a way that brought it more fully in line with the evolutionary laws of nature.

From the quarterdeck of the *Segurança*, Remington watched the troops disembark on the beach at Daiquirí Bay on June 22, his sketchbook ready. This was the war he had been waiting for. It was the culmination, as he put it, of a "life of longing to see men do the greatest thing which men are called on to do"—fight in a battle.[24] But the war didn't look very glorious. It was morbidly hot, with thick clouds of smoke from the fires burning in Daiquirí. The men were overdressed in their wool uniforms and overcoats, carrying heavy camp blankets. Remington watched as the soldiers loaded into launch boats and made their way to shore.

There was some muted gunshots, some shouts, and then, after a time, the American flag was run up the pole at a blockhouse. Remington exhaled and went ashore with the rest of the correspondents and the Sixth Cavalry. The Sixth was still waiting for orders, so Remington shouldered his pack and hiked off toward Siboney, about six miles to the east. Everywhere he looked, he saw the soldiers' blue coats and gray blankets, abandoned in the stifling heat. They dotted the landscape like an alien species of plant. "It was all so strange, this lonely tropic forest, and so hot," he thought.[25]

He fell in with a group of cavalry orderlies and met a number of Cubans along the way, some of whom were picking up the abandoned uniforms. The correspondents traded wild rumors they had picked up from the wounded: that the Rough Riders had been ambushed, that Colonel Wood had been killed.[26] None of them were true. That night, Remington and a few other correspondents, including fellow *Harper's* correspondent and novelist John Fox Jr., slept under a mango tree outside Siboney, listening to the shuffle and clank of marching troops.[27]

At least some of that noise was from the Rough Riders, who finally marched into Siboney early the next morning. Roosevelt was happy to be on a horse again. He chatted ebulliently and pointed out unfamiliar trees and birds, speculating on the quality of hunting in the area. One would have guessed, Richard Harding Davis thought, that it was a "hunting excursion in our West." It still seemed not quite real, more like playing cowboy than being at war. It seemed "impossible to appreciate," the men agreed, "that we were really at war—that we were in the enemy's country."[28]

A few hours later, their jubilation was muted when they were caught in a fierce firefight with the Spanish troops. They crawled in the dense jungle while bullets, shot from an unseen enemy, picked off soldiers as if by chance. Davis observed that the westerners seemed prepared for the fight. "It was easy to tell which men were used to hunting big game in the West and which were not," he thought. Unlike the easterners, the western men "slipped and wriggled through the grass like Indians."[29]

By the end of the battle, a dozen Rough Riders had been killed or fatally wounded, and another sixty were injured. The grass became matted with blood as the men dragged the wounded back to camp and then buried their dead in a trench. Roosevelt realized with a kind of sinking horror that the undergrowth was full of enormous land crabs, some as big as rabbits. Once things had quieted, the crabs emerged, claws clicking, and gathered in gruesome rings around the dead.[30]

Back at camp, Remington saw the first wounded Rough Riders come in. He had missed the fight completely, and vowed not to let it happen again. He and Fox shouldered their packs and hiked on. The weather didn't let up. Since disembarking at Daiquirí, none of the men had been dry for longer than a few minutes. Remington and Fox bummed soggy crackers and coffee from sympathetic officers and slept in their ponchos. Fox fretted about malaria.

Remington had acquired a nasty cold he worried would turn into bronchitis. "Can you suggest any remedy?" he asked.

"The fare to New York," Fox muttered.[31]

By June 30, the American troops and supplies had been consolidated for the march on Santiago. Remington was still isolated from the fighting. He felt tired and increasingly ill. He had come all this way to see a war, but now he was soaking wet and catching cold. And there was nothing to see.[32]

Late that afternoon, Roosevelt and the rest of the cavalry division received orders to march on San Juan Heights, north of their position and east of the ultimate target of Santiago. The Rough Riders followed the First and Tenth Cavalry. Finally, they climbed El Pozo hill, where they camped for the night. In the morning the mood was tense. No one talked much. At least, Roosevelt observed, he finally found some sugar for his coffee.[33]

The infantry division was ordered to take the village of El Caney. Roosevelt and the rest of the cavalry were supposed to help by creating a diversion with the artillery from El Pozo.[34] Just after six on the morning of July 1, before they had left the campground, Roosevelt heard a "peculiar whistling, singing sound" zipping through the air, followed by an explosion immediately overhead.[35] Before the day even started, shrapnel from the shelling had wounded four Rough Riders. Roosevelt leaped on his horse and led his men down the hill and into the underbrush toward the San Juan hills.

The plan had already gone awry. They were supposed to reconnoiter with the Second Division, but now there was no chance of that happening. It was deliriously hot. Sweat poured into the men's eyes, making it hard to see the sights of their guns. They still couldn't see exactly who were shooting at them, but at last they were able to discern that a half mile away, Spanish forces were entrenched on the upslope of the San Juan hills.[36]

Remington, there to document the war for *Harper's*, would miss nearly all of it. When the shelling started, he was terrified. It was, he later said, as if he was "in a trance." The sound of the Spanish Mauser rifles was not at all what he had been expecting. The barrage made a far-off rustling noise, like a walking stick striking a pile of leaves. "I wanted the roar of battle," he admitted, which "I never did find."[37]

Remington made his way through the troops with a vague sense that he should get to Santiago. A bullet zinged past his head. He dove into the tall Guinea grass and crawled toward the American soldiers studding the mango trees, only later realizing that he'd lost his sketchbook in the process.[38] He caught a brief glimpse of San Juan Hill, then quickly ducked back from the storm of bullets. He heard the war, but he couldn't see it. And he also couldn't draw it.

Below El Pozo hill, the African American Ninth Cavalry Regiment was in front of Roosevelt and the Rough Riders. The First was to his left. They advanced on what they later dubbed Kettle Hill, after a large cauldron they found at the summit.[39] The Third and Sixth, along with the Tenth Calvary Regiment, were split between Kettle Hill and the larger hill to the left, which held the San Juan blockhouse.

The Ninth and Tenth were the two African American cavalry regiments that had been created in the aftermath of the Civil War. While the regiments' officers were nearly all white (early on, a young George Custer had refused a lieutenant colonelcy with the Ninth), the regiments nonetheless offered opportunities for African American employment and advancement. By 1867, the Ninth and Tenth had moved west, where they would serve for nearly twenty years in the southwest and Great Plains.[40] (Remington had spent time with the Tenth back in 1888 and was impressed with the rugged individualism of the cavalry, noting a number of "episodes [which] prove the sometimes doubted self reliance of the negro."[41]) It was in Kansas that they were first dubbed the "buffalo soldiers" by the Cheyenne.[42]

In Cuba, the Black regiments would have ordinarily been separate from the white units. But in the thick of battle, Roosevelt observed, the regiments "completely intermingled—white regulars, colored regulars, and Rough Riders" alike.[43] Roosevelt liked this. It was the sort of race-blind test of individual merit that he had long championed.[44]

Roosevelt saw a captain commanding a troop from the Ninth Cavalry and told him the Rough Riders had been ordered to support the regulars in the assault on the hills. As far as Roosevelt was concerned, that meant rushing the hills. The captain replied that he had received no such orders. His orders had been to keep his men where they were.

Roosevelt looked around for Colonel Wood, the commanding officer, but he was nowhere to be seen. This seemed like exactly the sort of opportunity for the individual initiative he was always talking about. "Then I am the ranking officer here and I give the order to charge," he announced, effectively declaring himself in charge of the operation.[45] The captain hesitated. He had, after all, received his orders from the colonel, not the lieutenant colonel.

"Then let my own men through, sir," Roosevelt said impatiently, as if he was not in the middle of a war but back in Cambridge, hindered by some oaf blocking the doors of the Porcellian.[46] He rode through the lines, followed by the grinning, swaggering Rough Riders. And then, somewhat incredibly, members of the Ninth and Tenth followed after. The Rough Riders, one troop of the African American Tenth, a few troops of the First, and another few troops of the African American Ninth charged Kettle Hill.[47]

When Roosevelt later described it, he made it sound as if it were a wild, hilarious adventure, the sort of romp he'd had back in Dakota Territory. The men looked "delighted," he recalled. They were shouting and cheering, thrilled to be caught up "in the spirit of the thing."[48]

But leading his men uphill into a hailstorm of gunfire was a desperately risky thing to do. To some, it surely looked less like bravery and more like cockeyed indifference to the lives of hundreds. Astride his horse, cheering his men along, Roosevelt must have seemed for a moment like the sort of naive young man who equates bravery with death.

As one writer pointed out the following year, when "Roosevelt rode up that fatal hill, no one of all his followers expected him to finish it alive."[49] The Spanish held the high ground, and Roosevelt was galloping head-on into an entrenched and better-equipped army that he couldn't even see. Yet he didn't make it seem like a capricious hazard. Instead he made it seem like it was the only thing he could do—the rousing culmination of an asthmatic boy who had spent years mastering his own body and dreaming of adventures in the

American west. Astride his horse, he waved his hat like a cowboy and gave the order to charge the hill.[50]

There were not many Spanish forces on Kettle Hill to begin with. San Juan Hill, about 400 yards to the southwest and the tallest hill in the San Juan Heights, was better defended. Fewer than 500 Spanish soldiers in total defended the two hills.[51] The Spanish forces in the heights had already been pushed back considerably by the Ninth and Tenth Cavalries.

All the same, it was a scrambling, disorderly affair. Roosevelt, the only one on horseback, galloped part of the way, only to be stopped by a barbed wire fence and forced to continue on foot.[52] Throughout, the bullets didn't cease. Roosevelt gave an order to one soldier only to see him promptly collapse, shot through the head.

At the crest of the hill, the Ninth, the Tenth, the Rough Riders, and others continued firing on the Spanish entrenchments until they had driven them back entirely.[53] Roosevelt tried to lead the infantry over to assist in the fight at San Juan Hill, but then received orders to hold the hill at all costs.[54] By nightfall, the gunfire died down. Kettle Hill was held. To the southwest, the infantry had taken San Juan Hill, too.

Roosevelt had killed a man during the charge. "Did I tell you that I killed a Spaniard with my own hand," he wrote to Henry Cabot Lodge a few weeks after the battle, sounding uncharacteristically flat. "Probably I did."[55] As if to help the whole story pass quickly from history into legend, he later added that he had used the Colt revolver that had been recovered from the wreck of the *Maine*. It lent a pleasing symmetry to his presence on the island. Here was a Colt revolver—the gun that helped conquer the west—recovered as a relic of Spanish aggression, now repurposed for vengeance.

After San Juan Hill was taken, Remington briefly wandered up there and surveyed the dead. Even though he had lost his sketchbook, he tried to commit the sights to memory. He still had a war to cover, although he must have been wondering what kind of story he was going to get out of it. He hadn't seen the battles of San Juan or Kettle Hill. His eyes lingered on the Spanish soldiers, lying dead in their trenches. Most had been shot in the head. The sight of their teeth glinting through their lips was, he later recalled, horrible. Then he heard gunfire starting again and he retreated back down the hill. He felt feverish, desperate for sleep. Whatever he had been expecting, it wasn't this. The nausea of war mixed with a creeping fever that had been brought on by the damp and filthy conditions. On top of everything else, he had hardly eaten in days.

The next day, Remington was too sick to move. He lay in camp and thought about the war he'd seen. He began to feel that he couldn't explain it, couldn't even draw it without making himself complicit in some kind of lie. "All the broken spirits, bloody bodies, hopeless, helpless suffering which drags its weary length to the rear, are so much more appalling than anything else in the world," he mused. The whole experience resisted language itself: "words won't mean anything to one who has not seen it."[56]

From boyhood, Remington had loved pictures of tall, brave soldiers. But the reality of war seemed to kill his taste for such things. When the time came to illustrate his coverage of the war for *Harper's*, he submitted no pictures of military valor. Instead, most of his subjects were wounded men. He submitted paintings of soldiers crossing a bloody San Juan River; wounded men in tattered clothes being treated at a field hospital; seemingly lifeless soldiers sprawled facedown in the tall grass. War was perhaps not so straightforwardly the "greatest thing which men are called on to do," as he had once put it.[57] It was instead something dirtier, something sadder. Remington returned to Siboney and secured passage to New York on a hospital ship. By July 10, he would be home in Endion.[58]

After Kettle Hill, Roosevelt's fight was essentially over. His war, though, was not. For weeks, he and his men were first garrisoned and then quarantined, weak from malnutrition and sick with yellow fever. On July 16, Spain formally capitulated. Three days after that, Roosevelt was still more or less where he'd been on July 1—on the San Juan Heights. Although he was personally able to avoid the fever, "our condition is horrible in every respect," he wrote grimly.[59]

It was apparent that one could easily survive a gun battle yet still die in the war. He began a letter-writing campaign to get his men released from quarantine. On August 3, Roosevelt got all of the brigadiers general and majors general to sign a letter he drafted to General Shafter affirming their conviction that continuing the quarantine would be deadly. "This army must be moved at once, or perish," they stressed.[60]

Two weeks later, Roosevelt was finally on his way home.

NOTES

1. "Rough," 11.
2. "Rough," 11.
3. TR letter to Henry Cabot Lodge, 19 May 1898.
4. Roosevelt "Strenuous," 8.
5. Qtd. in "Editorial," 440.
6. Roosevelt *Rough*, 48.
7. Demolins, viii, 303.
8. Demolins, 305.
9. Darwin *Descent*, 201.
10. Demolins, 304.

11. Roosevelt *Rough*, 49.
12. FR letter to Owen Wister [June 1898].
13. Scharnhorst *Owen*, 115.
14. Samuels *Frederic*, 272.
15. Davis, 89.
16. Billings "Spanish," 8, 10.
17. Clark "American," 82, 84.
18. Roosevelt *Rough*, 10.
19. Davis, 360.
20. Porter "Future," 421.
21. "British," 562.
22. "Grand," 1.
23. White *Pictorial*, 376.
24. Remington "With," 962.
25. Remington "With," 964.
26. Davis, 132–133.
27. Remington "With," 964.
28. Davis, 140.
29. Davis, 165.
30. TR letter to Corinne Roosevelt Robinson, 27 June 1898.
31. Remington "With," 966.
32. Samuels *Frederic*, 279.
33. Roosevelt *Rough*, 113–114.
34. Davis *Cuban*, 196–199; Roosevelt *Rough*, 115.
35. Roosevelt *Rough*, 116.
36. Davis, 203.
37. Remington "With," 970.
38. Remington "With," 972.
39. Roosevelt "Rough," 433.
40. Leckie, 8, 18.
41. Remington "Scout," 25.
42. Leckie *Buffalo*, 27.
43. Roosevelt "Rough," 434.
44. Roosevelt *Rough*, 128.
45. Roosevelt "Rough," 430.
46. Roosevelt "Rough," 430.
47. Washington et al. *New*, 56.
48. Roosevelt *Rough*, 129.
49. Handford, 124.
50. Roosevelt "Rough," 430.
51. Smith "Spanish-American," 47.
52. Roosevelt *Rough*, 130.
53. TR letter to Leonard Wood, 4 July 1898.
54. Roosevelt "Rough," 435.
55. TR letter to Henry Cabot Lodge, 19 July 1898.

56. Remington "With," 974, 975.
57. Remington "With," 962.
58. Samuels *Frederic*, 284–285.
59. TR letter to Henry Cabot Lodge, 19 July 1898.
60. TR letter to William Rufus Shafter, 3 August 1898.

Chapter 29

Rewriting a Legacy

Once he returned home, Roosevelt immediately began crafting the story of the Rough Riders' cowboy-warrior valor. To him, the war had demonstrated the utility of western individualism. His men, he wrote, were "hardy, self-reliant, accustomed to shift for themselves in the open under very adverse circumstances."[1] Those were the qualities that had led to victory abroad; those were the qualities that would lead to greatness at home. The war, he decided, had been the test of individual fitness he had hoped it would be. And he had passed that test.

Unlike Remington, Roosevelt had a grand time in Cuba. Robert H. Ferguson, a family friend and fellow Rough Rider, wrote that the battle had surpassed Roosevelt's old dreams of violent western adventure. "No hunting trip so far has ever equaled it in Theodore's eyes," he observed. Roosevelt "was just reveling in victory and gore."[2]

Leaving his post as assistant secretary of the navy to volunteer for the war had been a risky gambit. Charging up Kettle Hill had been riskier still. But now those risks were beginning to pay dividends. His western conservatism—staging a retrogression into a so-called state of nature to test his fitness—resonated with the public. Even before he returned home, some in the New York Republican Party began pushing for Roosevelt to be their nominee in the 1898 gubernatorial race. In early September Roosevelt acknowledged, with some false modesty, the "vociferous popular demand to have me nominated for Governor."[3] As if worried he would be accused of doing it all for political gain, he added he would "rather have led this regiment than be Governor of New York three times over."[4] Nevertheless, Roosevelt hatched a canny plan to pit a group of Independent parties against the Republicans and secured the Republican nomination. On November 8, just over four months after he rode his horse up Kettle Hill, he narrowly beat Democratic candidate Augustus Van Wyck and was elected governor of the state of New York.

He also began telling and retelling the story of the Rough Riders. His early discomfort with the theatricality of the name had melted away. His story of the experience, *The Rough Riders*, appeared serially in *Scribner's* magazine between January and June 1899, and then, lightly revised, was republished as a book in December. Like any writer, Roosevelt emphasized the parts of the story that he thought most important. But in doing so, he was molding his western conservatism into a much smaller vessel.

Roosevelt initially emphasized the heterogeneous, multiracial aspect of the charge up Kettle Hill. It was as if he saw the war as proof of his long-standing dictum to treat everyone the same, regardless of race. Out west, he seemed to imply, America's history of racial hierarchies simply didn't matter. There was more than a little historical naiveté in this, of course. The failure of Reconstruction was hardly an ancient memory. Hardy self-reliance should have seemed a laughably small-bore weapon against centuries of institutionalized oppression. Nonetheless, it was a weapon Roosevelt believed in. He thought that in the west, individuals were unshackled from America's social hierarchies. They were free to test themselves and find their place within an older, more durable, and—most importantly—a natural hierarchy.

Roosevelt initially extended this logic to the frontier of Cuba, suggesting that it had been a place where individuals of different races could test their mettle largely unburdened by America's history of racial discrimination. On October 14, a month after returning, Roosevelt spoke to an African American audience at the Lenox Lyceum music hall in New York. He declared that the Cuban campaign had proved the importance of individual merit. He had always endeavored, he said, to "treat a man for what he shows himself to be as a man, neither favoring him nor opposing him for anything unconnected with the qualities he really possesses." The crowd cheered.[5]

Roosevelt also acknowledged the contributions of the African American Ninth and Tenth Cavalry regiments, not just to the larger campaign, but to his own existence. The Rough Riders would likely have been slaughtered on that hill had the Ninth and Tenth not saved them. He cast the charge as a collective enterprise in which all men, Black and white, became cowboy individualists bound by a common cause. The "Ninth and the Rough Riders went up [Kettle Hill] absolutely intermingled, so that no one could tell whether it was the Rough Riders or the Ninth who came forward with greater freedom to offer up their lives for their country," he declared, to more applause.[6]

Many of the Black cavalrymen agreed with this inclusive view of the Rough Riders. One writer later recounted how a white Rough Rider had shook the hand of a soldier from the Tenth with vigorous gratitude, saying, "We have you fellows to thank for getting us out of a bad hole." The cavalryman grinned. "That's all right," he had said. "It's all in the family. We call ourselves *The Colored Rough Riders!*"[7]

Roosevelt waxed philosophical about the apparent paradox by which the Darwinian drama of war—a literal life-or-death struggle to determine superiority—naturally brings men together. Hierarchies of merit were the only hierarchies that mattered, because they were the only hierarchies that were natural. "I don't think there is a man in the Rough Riders who will forget the tie of friendship between them and the Ninth and Tenth Cavalry," he said. He explained the relationship between the different regiments in glowing terms:

> We didn't feel it [camaraderie] for the Ninth and Tenth because they were colored any more than we felt it for the Third and Sixth because they were white, but because they showed themselves brave men, worthy of respect. And now in civil life it should be the same way. [. . .] I want to see every American citizen treated on his merits as a man, so that he can rise or fall according as he does or does not show himself worthy.[8]

Race was irrelevant, Roosevelt was saying, so long as an individual was treated strictly according to merit. As far as he was concerned, the way in which the white Rough Riders fought shoulder to shoulder with the Ninth and Tenth proved this principle. He recalled that after the battle, several Rough Riders had said that the "Ninth and Tenth are all right; they can drink out of our canteens."[9] The audience roared its approval of the image. He made sure they knew he saw the entire cavalry in Cuba, Black and white alike, as informal members of his multiracial cast of Rough Riders. All were "brave men, worthy of respect."

Roosevelt wasn't exaggerating the Rough Riders' embrace of the Ninth and Tenth. As Texan Rough Rider Carl Lovelace put it in a letter written two weeks after the charge on Kettle Hill, "get it out of your head that negroes can't fight. They can. That Tenth cavalry. Will I ever forget one charge I saw them make." He added that "I've got more respect for the colored soldier and citizen than I ever had before. [. . .] The negro soldier is the equal of any."[10] Another Rough Rider, Alexander H. Wallace, said that "there is not a Rough Rider in the regiment who will not take off his hat to the Tenth Cavalry—a colored regiment—as fighters. They do not know fear. Excellent shots, gritty and ambitious in the extreme."[11]

Roosevelt concluded that the war had overcome the men's prejudice. The case he seemed to be making was straightforward. Proofs of innate individual merit trumped habits of acquired race prejudice. Nature beat nurture.

However, if the story of multiethnic western individualism was the first Rough Riders story that Roosevelt told, the story he began telling in 1899, first in the pages of *Scribner's* and later in the book *The Rough Riders*, was slightly different. As time went on, he introduced a theme that was entirely absent from his or his fellow Rough Riders' contemporaneous accounts, one that was, by all available historical evidence, demonstrably false: that the Black soldiers were less brave and less skilled than their white comrades. Whereas in 1898, he had unambiguously acknowledged the valor of the Black cavalry, in 1899 he said they were, "of course, peculiarly dependent upon their white officers." Occasionally, he continued, there were Black officers "who can take the initiative and accept responsibility like the best class of whites; but this cannot be expected normally." In an even more surprising turn, he also insinuated that some of the Black infantrymen were cowards. "None of the white regulars or Rough Riders showed the slightest sign of weakening," he wrote, "but under the strain the colored infantrymen (who had none of their officers) began to get a little uneasy and drift to the rear." As a result, Roosevelt claimed, he had to draw his revolver on them, after which there were no other problems with desertion. That "was the end of the trouble."[12]

Unsurprisingly, scores of African American soldiers and civilians were appalled at Roosevelt's allegations, especially since he had seemed to say exactly the opposite not six months earlier. Sergeant Presley Holliday from the Tenth gave a detailed, careful rebuttal to the *New York Age*, one of the preeminent Black newspapers, in which he explained that everyone who actually "saw the incident knew the Colonel was mistaken about our men trying to shirk duty." More to the point, Roosevelt himself recognized he had been in error, as the following day he had gone to the Tenth and apologized, saying he "had seen his mistake and found them [the soldiers he thought were going to the rear] to be far different men from what he supposed."[13]

And now, long after everyone had gone home, Roosevelt had revived the insinuation that the Black infantrymen were cowards. He had said it. And no matter how many Black soldiers protested otherwise, people would believe it. "Roosevelt has said they shirked," Holliday mused with resignation, "and the reading public will take the Colonel at his word and go on thinking they shirked."[14] Although there were ample accounts suggesting the Rough Riders were saved by the Ninth and Tenth—and not the other way around—by the time *The Rough Riders* was published as a book in late 1899, Roosevelt was conflating the Cuban campaign no longer just with cowboy individualism, but with *white* cowboy individualism. In response, author and educator Booker T. Washington devoted several chapters of the book *A New Negro for a New Century* to chronicling the many ways in which the work of "Afro-American soldiers was minimized or slurred over" in the war coverage.[15]

Washington had good reason to be offended. But Roosevelt's aspersion was doubly unfortunate because he and Washington shared something of a conservative temperament and a belief in the redemptive power of individual effort. Roosevelt felt that America's history of racial inequality was essentially irrelevant, so long as an individual was "treated on his merits as a man."[16] Washington felt basically the same way. He would later write that "mere connection with what is regarded as an inferior race will not finally hold an individual back if he possesses intrinsic, individual merit." It was a "great human law," Washington continued, that "merit, no matter under what skin found, is, in the long run, recognized and rewarded."[17]

Seeming to recognize that they held similar beliefs about self-reliance, Roosevelt tried to arrange a meeting with Washington. As early as March 1899, he was telling T. Thomas Fortune, editor of the *New York Age*, that he wanted to meet Washington.[18]

(He eventually invited Washington to dinner at the White House on October 16, 1901, the first time an African American man had ever been hosted in the executive mansion. It was an act which incensed many white southerners as well as Owen Wister who, in one of his more explicitly racist moments, complained about the spectacle of a Black man dining in the White House, earning a sharp rebuke from Roosevelt.[19])

Roosevelt's belief that individual self-reliance found its fullest bloom in the American west may have rubbed off on Washington, who, shortly after meeting Roosevelt, began using an old horseman's idiom in a way that completely changed the way Americans speak.

A few decades earlier, a new western-inflected metaphor—"pulling yourself up by your bootstraps"—had emerged as a way of describing something that was obviously impossible. As the president of Drury College observed in 1877, "Men do not raise themselves over high fences by pulling at their bootstraps."[20] As late as 1898, it was used to satirize Roosevelt's own ambitions. One "Wit and Humor" column in the run-up to the Cuban campaign said that Roosevelt's promotion to lieutenant colonel "explodes another old theory," namely "that a fellow can't raise himself by his own bootstraps."[21]

But eventually the metaphor drifted free of its original meaning. Pulling oneself up by the bootstraps slowly stopped being a ludicrous physical impossibility and started being associated with something akin to Emerson-style western individualism. Booker T. Washington was one of the first people to use the phrase in this new way. He trumpeted the achievements of Black workers who had "simply lifted themselves by their bootstraps," having "risen from a low to a higher level in their occupation and in American civilization" through individual effort.[22] After Washington, what had once been synonymous with a subversion of the laws of nature came to refer to a timeless American value: the natural self-reliance of the individual.

Although Washington would eventually make his peace with Roosevelt, in 1899 he was furious at Roosevelt for his slur on the bravery of America's Black soldiers. He was right to be angry. But whether the affront was born of deliberate contempt or political expediency, Roosevelt was inarguably building a narrative that he felt would be useful.[23] And that narrative was not just about the war, but about the west.

It was similar to the way, four years earlier, that Wister had ignored Remington's insistence that cowboys were originally Mexican. Instead, Wister had claimed that cowboys were the evolutionary heirs of Anglo-Saxon knights. Remington had been correct, of course. Many cowboys were Mexican. Many were Black. (By some estimates, as many as one in three cowboys were Black.[24]) Vanishingly few were actually Anglo-Saxon. But thanks in part to the stories of Wister, Roosevelt, and Remington, the perception of America's multiracial west began to change.

It was appropriate, then, that after the Spanish-American War Roosevelt became a figure similar to Wister's Anglo-Saxon cowboy: the gentleman cowboy warrior. As one reader of Richard Harding Davis's book put it, "Colonel Roosevelt is a splendid, heroic figure, a romantic warrior, a veritable knight of old."[25] He became something of an atavistic aristocrat—a gentleman borrowing the romance of the past in order to conquer the present.

On September 13, 1898, the Rough Riders, who until then had been quarantined at Camp Wikoff on Long Island due to yellow fever, fell into formation and waited with barely concealed excitement. They were finally mustering out.

They also had a surprise for Roosevelt. A few of the men led Roosevelt to a small table on which an object was hidden by an old blanket. One of the troopers gave a short speech and then the blanket was whisked away, revealing a gift that the men thought perfectly symbolized their leader and their fight in Cuba: Remington's sculpture "The Bronco Buster."[26]

Roosevelt, overcome, stood for a moment taking it in. The bronze rider's brow was furrowed in concentration, his mouth invisible under his thick mustache. His right foot had slipped from the stirrup and the brim of his campaign hat flipped upward dramatically, as if blown back by the lurching horse. Every muscle, every ounce of concentration possessed by the rider seemed to try to bend wild nature to his will. Animal and man seemed frozen between disaster and mastery. With the mustache, the expert horsemanship, and the keen intensity of the rider's expression, the Rough Riders must have wondered if the unnamed Bronco Buster didn't look a little like Roosevelt.

Roosevelt looked up. "Nothing else could have possibly happened to touch and please me as this does," he said. "I am proud of this regiment beyond measure, because it is typically an American regiment. The cow-puncher was the foundation of this regiment, and we have got him here in bronze."[27] The statue seemed to perfectly capture Roosevelt's view of the war.

The Rough Riders regiment had from the beginning been intertwined with Roosevelt's own sense of western history and national destiny. The statue, which originally captured a split-second of random cowboy valor, now seemed to symbolize an entire war. The statue sheared the jagged violence from the centuries-long project of American settlement, sanding it into a story about rugged men and the romantic days of the old west. The cowboy was "the foundation" of this "typically American regiment," Roosevelt declared. America was a cowboy nation. This had been a cowboy war.

Roosevelt sent a short letter to Remington voicing his appreciation for the sculpture. "It was the most appropriate gift the Regiment could possibly have given me," he wrote.[28] The sculpture recast one emblem of the west in another context, suggesting new frontiers for a new age of American empire.

Remington acknowledged the symbolism the statue seemed destined to assume. "The greatest compliment I ever had or ever can have was when the Rough Riders put their brand on my bronze," he told Roosevelt, unable to hide his emotion. "After this everything will be mere fuss."[29]

Roosevelt wanted to put that "brand" anywhere he could. When it came time to publish *The Rough Riders* as a book, he put the Rough Riders' stamp on an earlier generation of western writers by including an old western poem for the book's epigraph. He chose an extract of "The Reveille," the poem that Bret Harte, the godfather of western American literature, had written for an 1862 meeting intended to drum up Californians' support for the Union cause in the Civil War.

Roosevelt quoted the first three verses of Harte's poem, in which men are summoned to war as a way of settling their ledgers with the past. "Come, / Freemen, come! / Ere your heritage be wasted," the narrator proclaims.[30] The poem surely attracted Roosevelt for its romantic and proudly western view of battle. But the poem was also, in its way, an early example of a new kind of conservatism. Its soldiers have to draw on the past as a down payment, in blood, on the future. So as not to let their "heritage be wasted," they had to go to war.

This emphasis on heritage continued elsewhere in *The Rough Riders*. Heritages, Roosevelt suggested, have to be proven. And it was tests of war that plucked from those heritages America's naturally selected leaders. In praising Colonel Leonard Wood in the book, Roosevelt emphasized that he was "a natural soldier."[31] War was perhaps the purest form of natural selection. In Roosevelt's view, Wood was good at fighting because he had been made—or, in Lamarckian fashion, had made himself—for it. To use Harte's word, his "heritage" was war.

And as for Roosevelt's heritage? It was, as his stories of the Rough Riders seemed designed in every instance to suggest, to be a gentleman soldier-cowboy. And to be a ruler of men.

Remington had been hired by *Scribner's* to provide a painting for Roosevelt's essay on "The Cavalry at Santiago." The magazine was counting on his skills as a documentarian—he had, after all, been in Cuba to cover the war. It was to be a striking image of the dramatic culmination of the Rough Riders' story: their charge, along with the Ninth and Tenth Cavalry units, up Kettle Hill.

The final painting depicted a loose mass of around fifty white Rough Riders—the Ninth and Tenth are nowhere to be seen—clutching hats and rifles as they stream up a slight incline. In the foreground, two Rough Riders have been cut down by bullets. Two Spanish soldiers lie on the ground, presumably dead though their white uniforms are still pristine. Leading the charge in the middle ground, on the far left of the painting, is the lone figure on horseback. None of the men's faces are distinct. It was published with the title "Charge of the Rough Riders at San Juan Hill."[32]

Roosevelt was somewhat perplexed when he saw it. He noted that Remington "does not give the individual faces," drolly adding—as if the blurry rider that was supposed to be him was in fact much clearer than it actually was—that "he portrays me with a decorum of attitude which was foreign to my actual conduct at the time." All the same, he acknowledged, "it is a good picture."[33]

But there were at least two problems with Remington's firsthand depiction of the "Charge of the Rough Riders at San Juan Hill." First, Remington hadn't seen the charge himself. He had been sick, lost his sketchbook. And second, the Rough Riders hadn't charged San Juan Hill at all. It had been Kettle Hill.

Remington's old friend Poultney Bigelow thought the painting was hilarious. America's "Cowboy Napoleon spurring a fiery steed," he cracked. Besides, Bigelow continued, "Remington knew that Roosevelt was never on San Juan Hill—he told me so when I joked him about his picture."[34] At least a few people saw the painting for what it was: a dime novel illustration masquerading as history, a little like Cody's cowboy reenactors firing real bullets.

Like much of the Rough Riders legend—from their name, borrowed from Cody's show; to Roosevelt's salvaged six-gun; to the very notion of a cowboy warrior—Remington's painting was deliberately tinged with romance. Roosevelt knew that Remington hadn't actually witnessed the charge. Roosevelt was counting on the public's trust that Remington was painting the "real" war, just as he painted the "real" west. And he was correct. One critic singled out the painting as "the best of the scores of illustrations" of the war, writing that it clearly "show[ed] the colonel mounted on his pony several paces ahead of his men."[35] But the blurry faces did no such thing. When it came to the war and to the west, people saw what they wanted to see.

As he always did when he needed to get away, Remington lit out for the west. In the summer of 1899, he traveled to Wyoming and Montana. He attended a ball at Cody's house and had a great time.[36] He also started thinking about his next project. Earlier that year, Harper and Brothers had published *Sundown Leflare*, a collection of Remington's previously published short stories, but had made it available only by mail and not in the shops, much to Remington's irritation.[37] Now he began thinking about another collection of previously published articles, titled after a bit of self-created slang that Remington liked to use to describe naturally tough men: "men with the bark on."[38]

But as summer turned into fall, he couldn't stop thinking about the war. Perhaps he was bothered by the dishonesty of passing off as journalism an act of military heroism he actually never witnessed. Whatever it was, spending time out west helped him realize something. As he wrote to Wister in September, "'that was my War'—that old cleanup of the West."[39] Cuba hadn't been his war at all, he seemed to decide. His war had been the ongoing conquest of the west by white Americans. It was a lot easier to romanticize cowboy conquest when it was closer to home.

When he returned home, Remington started working on the illustrations for Wister's short story "The Game and the Nation," another one featuring his popular "Virginian" cowboy hero. The story, which would run in *Harper's* magazine the following year, was premised on the irreconcilable opposition between aristocratic superiority, what Wister called "quality," and democratic parity, which he called "equality." "All America," Wister wrote in the story, "is divided into two classes—the Quality and the Equality. The latter will always recognize the former when mistaken for it."[40] In other words, equality was little more than a pretense, one that always fell away before a superior man.

When Wister later reworked this story into one of the centerpieces of his novel *The Virginian*, he made the antidemocratic theme even clearer, adding that in America, the Declaration of Independence "acknowledged the *eternal inequality* of man" which "gave freedom to true aristocracy," or Jefferson's fabled natural aristocracy.[41] This fundamental conflict between inferior and superior men was often buried in the east, Wister suggested, but out west, it was readily apparent. Out west, the Darwinian battle for supremacy would allow for the emergence of America's true and naturally selected leaders.

Such naturally selected leaders would be men, perhaps, like Roosevelt. On a freezing cold morning in Albany on January 2, 1899, Roosevelt was inaugurated as governor of the state of New York.

He wasn't the only Rough Rider to try to leverage his newfound fame for political gain. A number of the men ran for elective office. Less than a year after the war, the Speaker of the House and president of the Senate in New Mexico were both former Rough Riders. The Rough Riders' fame was fast approaching that of their namesake, Cody's "Congress of Rough Riders of the World." That name, which originally referred to circus-like performances of western conquest, now referred to an actual military regiment of actual cowboys. The line between soldier and actor became blurry. Sixteen former Rough Riders joined Cody's show as performers.[42]

In a nod to Cody's famous love of realism, many of those former Rough Riders were cast in roles as Rough Riders. In March 1899, Cody brought the show to Madison Square Garden in New York. He had added a new segment titled "The Battle of San Juan Hill" that included the Ninth and Tenth regiments. (One writer noted that the "colored troops were received with great applause—even greater than that accorded to the Rough Riders themselves."[43])

Six years earlier at the World's Fair, electric lights had still been a startling novelty. Now, Cody used electric lights to dramatic effect. The house lights dimmed as if at dawn. Close to 500 performers marched in. There were pack mules, tents, sentries. There was a "stocky man on horseback" playing Theodore Roosevelt.[44] Then the sun rose with a sudden electric glare, the bugles sounded, and the cavalry marched on San Juan Hill—not Kettle Hill—which had been built near Fourth Avenue. There was a roar of gunfire, a mad rush up the hill, and at last the American flag was planted on the hilltop. The audience cheered wildly.[45]

There had long been a number of connections between Roosevelt and Cody. Both had made their names as representatives of a quick-receding past. In 1874, Alexander Moore (the uncle of Edith Carow, who would become Roosevelt's second wife) had tracked and killed a bear with Cody near the Freezeout Mountains in Wyoming. Roosevelt recalled with pride that Cody had kept the bearskin for years afterward.[46] At a private dinner at Delmonico's in New York in 1887, Cody had confided that he felt "Theodore Roosevelt is the only New-York dude that has got the making of a man in him."[47] Roosevelt later repaid the compliment, calling Cody "an American of Americans," a man who "embodied those traits of courage, strength, and self-reliant hardihood which are vital to the well-being of the nation."[48]

Roosevelt attended Cody's show during its two-week run at the Garden. Afterward, he shook the hands of the former Rough Riders and pronounced the show "accurate."[49] The circle of cowboy playacting had been closed. Roosevelt was a onetime easterner who had gone west to try his hand at an older mode of life, then tried to make use of those acquired traits in the new frontier of Cuba. Now he was an easterner again, watching an actor pretending to be Theodore Roosevelt leading hundreds of men. Some were actors pretending to be cowboy soldiers, others actually were cowboy soldiers pretending to be themselves.

The charge up Kettle Hill had transmuted into Cody-produced "Battle of San Juan Hill," which the real Roosevelt had never even fought in. It was no matter. The romance had become reality. And the rancher had become the governor.

NOTES

1. Roosevelt *Rough*, 223.
2. Qtd. in Samet, 226.
3. TR letter to John Hay, 1 September 1898.
4. TR letter to Francis Ellington Leupp, 3 September 1898.
5. "Roosevelt to Colored," 2.
6. "Roosevelt to Colored," 2.
7. Philips, 59.
8. "Roosevelt to Colored," 2.
9. "Roosevelt to Colored," 2.
10. Lovelace, 5.
11. Wallace "Rough," 10.
12. Roosevelt "Rough," 435, 436.
13. Qtd. in Washington et al. *New*, 57–58. See also Gatewood Jr., 92–97.
14. Qtd. in Washington et al. *New*, 60.
15. Washington et al. *New*, 37.
16. "Roosevelt to Colored," 2.
17. Washington *Up*, 40–41.
18. TR letter to T. Thomas Fortune, 30 March 1899; TR letter to William Henry Lewis, 26 July 1900.
19. TR letter to Owen Wister, 27 April 1906, in Wister *Roosevelt*, 255.
20. *Third*, 11.
21. "Wit," 6.
22. Washington "Progress," 299.
23. For a full analysis of Black soldiers' responses to Roosevelt, see Bold "Where," 273–297.
24. Bold "Where," 280.
25. "Richard," 4.
26. Roosevelt *Rough*, 219–220.
27. "Men's," 3.
28. TR letter to Frederic Remington, 19 September 1898, in Splete, 231.
29. FR letter to Theodore Roosevelt [September 1898].
30. Qtd. in Roosevelt *Rough*, 2.
31. Roosevelt *Rough*, 8.
32. Roosevelt "Rough," 421.
33. TR letter to Bradley Tyler Johnson, 31 July 1899.
34. Bigelow *Seventy*, 283. The fact that Roosevelt had never charged San Juan Hill was not a secret. As one writer noted in 1916, people could simply "refer to the

records of the War Department, which will show that Roosevelt had nothing to do with the taking of San Juan hill" (Pettigrew, 978).

35. "Book," 762.
36. Samuels *Frederic*, 292.
37. FR letter to J. Henry Harper, 6 February [1899].
38. Remington *Men*, FR letter to Poultney Bigelow, 29 January [1893].
39. FR letter to Owen Wister, 1 September 1899.
40. Wister "Game," 884.
41. Wister *Virginian*, 95.
42. Roosevelt *Rough*, 101, 318.
43. "Wild West at the Garden," 4.
44. Reddin, 125.
45. "Wild West Show," 4.
46. Roosevelt *Wilderness*, 319–320.
47. "Dinner," 5.
48. Qtd. in Russell, 469.
49. Qtd. in Reddin, 133.

Chapter 30

The Virginian and the White House

In 1902, Wister finally published the novel he had been working on for over a decade. He had been drafting parts of *The Virginian* in earnest since 1896, but its titular cowboy hero had been born even earlier, in an episode he recorded in his journal in 1891 and fictionalized into the short story "Balaam and Pedro."[1]

The book was the culmination of years' worth of thinking and writing. It was the product of Wister's travels in the west, his conversations with Remington and Roosevelt, and his legal training, shaped by his conversations with his friend and jurist Oliver Wendell Holmes Jr. He had even rewritten a portion of it based on a note from Roosevelt, who felt that the violence in one scene had gone too far. Wister dutifully toned it down.[2]

By the early twentieth century, Wister had established himself as the nation's leading teller of stories about the American west. A few years earlier, a writer for *Harper's Weekly* had painted him as the heir to Bret Harte. The lessons to be found in Wister's depictions of the west, the critic added, could be broadly applied: "A man who can see men in the West can see them everywhere."[3] As the writer seemed to acknowledge, Wister had arrived at the same insight as Roosevelt: that stories about western men were somehow not only about men in the west. They were also stories about men in the world.

To thank his old friend for all he had done to shape the book, Wister dedicated *The Virginian* to Theodore Roosevelt, writing in the book's front matter, "some of these pages you have seen, some you have praised, one stands new-written because you blamed it; and all, my dear critic, beg leave to remind you of their author's changeless admiration."[4]

Just below that, Wister added a few lines from one of Horace's Odes to complete the dedication: "*mihi parva rura et / Spiritum Graiae tenuem Camenae / Parca non mendax dedict, et malignum / Spernere vulgus,*" meaning, "for myself I have only a poor little country property and the gentle breath of the Greek Muse; these are the gifts of honest Fate which at the same time teaches me to disdain the spiteful crowd."[5] Given the novel that followed, Wister's epigraph was appropriate. It told the story of someone a little like Roosevelt, a young man who sought a world far from the clatter and crush of the east, someone who used the west to distinguish himself from the *"vulgus."* *Vulgus*, which can be translated as *crowd*, is perhaps better rendered as *commoners*. Western lands were where a man went to become a natural aristocrat, to set himself apart from the common man.

The novel was published on May 30, 1902. It was an instant success. The first printing sold out in three days, and it was soon on its way to becoming the best-selling novel of the year.[6]

A week after the publication of *The Virginian*, Roosevelt wrote to Wister to tell him that "it is a remarkable novel."[7] He added that if he could be quoted on the matter, he would have liked nothing better than to write a review of it. But unfortunately, he couldn't. He was the president.

By then, all the members of Roosevelt's circle of westerners were comfortably positioned on the national stage. Frederic Remington was widely recognized as a figure of deep and prodigious talents: a skilled illustrator, painter, sculptor, and writer. In 1900, Yale awarded its star dropout an honorary degree. The director of the Yale Art School told Remington that he was now the school's "most distinguished pupil."[8] In December 1901, Remington had his first fine art exhibition at Clausen's Gallery in New York.[9] He also kept in touch with Roosevelt, who continued to congratulate him on his art, invited him to Washington, and even discussed the occasional presidential appointment with him.

Inspired by Wister, Remington wrote his own western novel. *John Ermine of the Yellowstone* was published on November 12, 1902, six months after Wister's *Virginian*.[10] The novel told the story of John Ermine, a white man raised by a tribe of Crow Indians who becomes a scout for the United States Army. Ermine was something like James Fenimore Cooper's hero Natty Bumppo, updated for a new age of American expansion.[11] Critics were amazed that Remington's talents extended to novel writing, and saw the book as an extension of the western themes he explored in his drawings and sculpture. One reviewer said that the book "might worthily rank with those lifelike and virile drawings in which he has recorded that passing period on the Western frontiers."[12] By 1902, Remington had become one of the leading depicters of how America saw its frontier past.

"Buffalo Bill" Cody had just tilted to the downslope of his career. In the years after Cuba, the Rough Riders who joined the show gave it a new infusion of energy. But on October 28, 1901, a show train full of Cody's performers and animals collided with another train, killing over a hundred animals and seriously injuring a number of performers, including Annie Oakley.[13] Cody's current business partner, James A. Bailey, decided to bring Barnum and Bailey's Circus back from Europe and send out Cody's Wild West in its place for one last tour. Cody, like the show, was showing his age. He had worn a wig for years; now he needed his eyeglasses to do his shooting act.[14] Though attendance was sometime sparse, Cody's ambition had not left him. "I am going to organize a ten million dollar Company and make the boldest dash I ever dreamed of attempting," he declared to his sister.[15]

But the rise of Wister and Remington meant that Cody was no longer America's chief proprietor of the cowboy myth. Cody had once pointed out that until his show "introduced the cow-boy to the world at large, the great majority of people had altogether wrong notions about him."[16] But now Wister's new cowboy hero, the Virginian, was taking wry digs at Cody in Wister's novel, saying that *he* was the real thing, and "no wild-west show, after all."[17] Yet even if Cody's popularity was diminished, it was not gone entirely. The show would continue touring as an independent production until 1908, and in 1913, Cody would mount an ambitious new production: a film titled *Indian War Pictures* that sought to update the wild west show for a new age of mass entertainment.[18]

A decade after his groundbreaking talk at the World Columbian Exposition in Chicago, Frederick Jackson Turner had reached the pinnacle of his field. He had risen to become a full professor at the University of Wisconsin. To prevent him from moving to the University of Chicago, Wisconsin expanded his department into an entire School of History and named him its director. Under his leadership, student interest in history at Wisconsin boomed, leaping from 603 students enrolled in 1900 to 822 in 1902. Though he perhaps never fulfilled the soaring promise suggested by that summer night at the World's Fair, Turner's ideas nonetheless transformed the way generations of historians thought about the American west. Well into the late twentieth century, many historians were still working within the paradigm Turner established back in 1893.[19]

In 1902, Turner gave a talk at Northwestern University in which he praised the "old democratic admiration for the self-made man," yet worried that the rise of modern corporations would make it difficult to sustain that ideal. Even though the "individualism of the frontier" had been preserved in principle, he explained, Darwinian competition continued apace, which drove ever-greater corporate consolidation. The tremendous success of the Gilded Age barons who had disproportionately benefited from the nation's individual striving, he continued, raised the question "as to whether democracy under such conditions can survive" at all. The issue worried him. But he thought the solution lay in a rebirth of conservative western individualism. He concluded that we must "look for Western influence upon democracy in our own days," to ensure that "the ideals of the pioneer in his log cabin" persist, so as to harness those ideals for the common good.[20] Western individualism had contributed to a new set of modern problems, he acknowledged. But perhaps it could also solve them.

Roosevelt, of course, had risen highest and fastest of all. After Cuba, he served for a little over a year and a half as governor of New York and then was put on the Republican ticket as President McKinley's running mate in November 1900. McKinley was inaugurated for his second term in March 1901, but had scarcely been in office for six months before an anarchist shot him twice in the abdomen at point-blank range. He died in the early morning of September 14, 1901. Roosevelt was inaugurated that day.

Roosevelt steeled himself to the occasion at once. Wister recalled Roosevelt telling him that "I can't know that I have the ability, but I do know that I have the will, to carry out the task that has fallen to me."[21] He told Henry Cabot Lodge something similar: "here is the task, and I have got to do it to the best of my ability; and that is all there is about it."[22]

Newspapers made a point of recounting the new president's colorful story. One headline proclaimed him an "Author, Soldier, Historian, Cowboy, Statesman" who "Believes in the Strenuous Life."[23] It would not take long before Roosevelt, who newspapers wasted little time in dubbing the "cowboy president," became one of the nation's most popular figures.[24]

Roosevelt never completely outgrew the western conservatism he had nurtured as a younger man. As he later said, he saw his job as turning the Republican Party into "a party of progressive conservatism, or conservative radicalism, for of course wise radicalism and wise conservatism go hand in hand."[25] In 1904, he was reelected in a landslide victory, winning over 2.5 million more popular votes than his Democratic opponent Alton B. Parker. At the time, it was the largest margin of victory in American history.

When it was published a little over eight months after Roosevelt's first inauguration, Wister's *The Virginian* heralded a new type of novel. It would later be recognized as having invented the western genre—the primogenitor of later works like Zane Grey's *Riders of the Purple Sage* (1912), Walter Van Tillburg Clark's *The Ox-Bow Incident* (1940), or Jack Schaefer's *Shane* (1949). *The Virginian* dramatized the story that Roosevelt and his circle had been telling for years: that retrogressions into the "primitive" west would try an easterner, potentially revealing him as fit enough to be a ruler of men.

The Virginian's central conflict concerned its titular hero and his onetime friend Steve, a cowboy-turned-rustler who is caught by the Virginian and hanged for his crimes. Though the book seemed to be mostly about cowboys and cattle, it was also about the law. Wister based the book on the Johnson

County War, the labor conflict in which powerful ranchers sought to lynch men they labeled rustlers.

The hero of *The Virginian*, Wister decided, would be one of the men lynching to defend the interests of the powerful. His training as a lawyer and his deep philosophical interest in the law convinced him that the Johnson County War represented something significant about legal power, natural law, and inequality. Wister was following in the footsteps of de Tocqueville, who had written that "in a society in which lawyers occupy without dispute the elevated position that naturally belongs to them, their spirit will be eminently conservative and will show itself as antidemocratic."[26]

Wister's friend and mentor Oliver Wendell Holmes Jr. would be recess-appointed to the Supreme Court by Roosevelt three months after the publication of *The Virginian*. It was clear that Holmes, along with the many conversations he and Wister had about the law and the American west, was on Wister's mind as he was finishing the book.

A few weeks before the novel was published, Wister penned a letter to Holmes—"My dear Judge," he wrote affectionately—letting him know his copy of the novel was on its way. The book, Wister promised Holmes, told the story of a man of "American genius," and the reader would become aware of such genius through "*action*, sir, action and manifestation."[27] Wister felt that the book was, in its own way, a novel of ideas. Many of Holmes's conservative ideas about law, natural selection, and the principle of competition provided the intellectual heft for Wister's tale of "American genius."

The Virginian was a novel obsessed with aristocracy. Using language he had first used two years earlier, in his short story "The Game and the Nation," Wister's unnamed narrator mused about the role of aristocracy in America. For him, the Declaration of Independence "abolished a cut-and-dried aristocracy," and in doing so, "acknowledged the *eternal inequality* of man." This development, in turn, "gave freedom to true aristocracy," because it enacted an organizing principle of Darwinian competition: letting "the best man win." That devotion to competition, he feels, is "true democracy. And true democracy and true aristocracy are one and the same thing."[28]

The point was simple. Darwinian competition was a straightforward way of establishing America's natural aristocracy. And America, Wister suggested, was *designed* to be a place of inequality, one in which a true aristocracy emerges through a perpetual battle for power and resources.[29]

Seemingly inspired by Herbert Spencer, Wister suggested that society was really an extension of nature, which meant it had to be governed by natural laws such as "survival of the fittest," as one character puts it.[30] In the novel, demonstrating merit through competition—being smarter or faster or stronger—means being, in a Darwinian sense, *more fit*.

The Virginian's central conflict involved the execution of two men stealing calves from wealthy ranchers. The men are lynched by the Virginian and other representatives of the natural aristocracy. In the aftermath of the lynching, the Virginian chokes up, sobbing. He has, after all, just killed a man he once counted as a friend. Yet he doesn't regret his actions in the slightest. The narrator agrees "that only [by lynching] could justice be dealt in this country."[31]

But Molly Wood, the Virginian's fiancée, is less certain. Her skepticism of the lynching sparks the novel's elaborate legal and philosophical defense of the hangings, voiced by a character who is a former federal judge, wealthy rancher, and the Virginian's employer, a man named Judge Henry. Though the character of the judge was not based on Oliver Wendell Holmes Jr., Wister nevertheless hoped the character would, in some way, speak to him. In a speech articulating a conservative view of law and civil society alike, the judge not only defends the Virginian's actions, he offers a vision of the American west as an opportunity to bring the social compact more fully in line with the laws of nature: to discard any dreams of equality and establish, once and for all, a natural aristocracy among men.

The novel gives no reason to doubt that cattle rustlers' committed the crime. They must be lynched, readers are told, because it is unlikely they would be convicted in democratic courts of law. Jury nullification refers to the legal right of juries to acquit defendants who would otherwise be guilty, typically in response to an unjust law or an unjust application of a law. And whether out of corruption or a principled nullification, juries in the novel refuse to convict the rustlers. The Virginian then feels obliged to bring them to justice, which means, paradoxically, disregarding the procedures of the justice system.

To put it another way, the character of Judge Henry has to convince Molly Wood not of the moral guilt of the rustlers, nor of the moral correctness of their punishment, but rather that their punishment is valid in a civic or legal sense given that their guilt has not been established by any civic or legal institution.

Wister had created a problem for himself. He needed his characters not just to defend extrajudicial killing but to do so on intellectual and legal grounds. Recognizing that lynching was difficult to disentangle from America's larger history of racial oppression, Wister had his judge first draw a distinction between lynching in the west and lynching in the south. The judge does say he opposes southern lynching, but not for reasons having anything to do with legal or racial justice. Because southern lynching involves torture and spectacle, he argues, it represents "proof that the South is semi-barbarous," whereas western lynching is "proof that Wyoming is determined to become civilized."[32] In his view, extrajudicial punishment is not axiomatically wrong. Applied correctly, it can be a tool of a civilized and law-abiding society.

This paradox—that by disregarding due process of law, people can produce a law-abiding society—is not lost on the character of Molly. She points out that both southern and western lynching defy law and order, because the moment citizens decide to act as judge, jury, and executioner, they "take the law in their own hands."[33]

The judge shoots back that those citizens are where the law comes from in the first place, as they "chose the delegates who made the Constitution." As a result, "when they lynch they only take back what they once gave." This leads him to his conclusion. "The courts, or rather the juries, into whose hands we have put the law, are not dealing the law." As a result, the "ordinary citizen" must "take justice back into his own hands where it was at the beginning of all things. Call this primitive, if you will. But so far from being a *defiance* of the law, it is an *assertion* of it—the fundamental assertion of self-governing men, upon whom our whole social fabric is based."[34]

In a number of ways, Wister risked his whole novel on this single speech. It was what justified the Virginian's role in the lynching and part of what established him as the book's hero. Perhaps most important, it was in that speech that Wister was most expansive in his conservative vision of America.

In the speech, the judge first offers a fairly democratic philosophy of the law. He suggests that laws originate in "ordinary citizens": not in gods or natural law, but simply in the will of the public. But then he turns and offers a second, thoroughly contradictory, view. The lynching is justified, he concludes, because the courts are simply "not dealing the law."

Yet for it to be possible for legal institutions to not deal the law, the law would have to be something external to the judiciary, rather than something that emerges through its normal procedures. In explaining law in this way, Wister seemed to be channeling Holmes's *The Common Law*, which described the law as if it were somehow a living thing, existing in a symbiotic relationship to humans.

It is clearly this second argument that the judge—and Wister—thinks will justify the lynching. But its plausibility is undercut by the first argument. As the judge initially suggests, legal judgments aren't transcendent moral judgments. They are simply the result of the civil institutions and procedures established by ordinary citizens.

But if were otherwise—if laws did claim to enact transcendental or moral justice—then the law would have to reside outside of the wishes and institutions of the citizens. And if civil law did exist apart from ordinary citizens, as the judge clearly wants it to, at least two consequences would follow. First, it would be possible for the usual legal institutions to apply that law incorrectly. And second, it would be possible for certain elite individuals outside the usual legal institutions—what Wister called the "true aristocracy"—to apply that law correctly.

This was the real intellectual potency of *The Virginian*. The judge had found a way to justify the existence of a natural aristocracy superior to the democratic institutions of ordinary citizens. His west is one in which extrajudicial executions are legitimized by a group of natural aristocrats whose merit has been proofed by the testing grounds of the American west.

This is a vision of society that Wister, in the novel, viewed not just as authentic but as natural. The novel expressed a deep, almost spiritual longing to return to "the beginning of all things," as the judge says, in an atavistic return of some fundamental law of nature. The west thus represents a second chance, an opportunity to begin America anew. To this way of thinking, the west isn't a place of equality at all. Instead, it's a place where Darwinian principles can help sort out a new American ruling class, creating a true and natural aristocracy.

For Wister, the American west allowed conservatism to be *about* something. It offered a mythic space for selecting an American elite. Its spare, sweeping vistas allowed him to imagine a hard and Spartan freedom, one in which transcendental natural laws would, aided by a natural aristocracy, resolve social conflicts through brutal means.

There's no quality inherent to the act of lynching that would seem to require it to twist itself around the trunk of American conservatism. Yet for Wister and Roosevelt alike, lynching was not a repudiation of civil law; lynching preceded civil law. The idea that stepping westward meant stepping backward—returning to a primitive age without the protections of modern civil law—had long been a lodestar guiding the travels and politics of Roosevelt and his circle.

That's not to say that Wister's conservatism in particular, which was shaped by his friendship with Holmes, meant that Holmes supported lynching. Yet there was an interesting commonality between the legal philosophy espoused by Wister's fictional Judge Henry and the philosophy espoused by Holmes. Many years after *The Virginian*, Holmes would write the dissent for a Supreme Court case in which he argued that under certain circumstances, courts of law could sometimes, as Wister's Judge would have said, "not deal the law" correctly. "Mob law," Holmes wrote, "does not become due process of law by securing the assent of a terrorized jury." The court ought to "declare lynch law as little valid when practised by a regularly drawn jury as when administered by one elected by a mob intent on death."[35] In other words, even though the jury had reached its verdict through normal legal procedures, Holmes somehow felt that they had still not dealt the law correctly. In his view, the trial had been tantamount to lynching.

To put it differently, Wister and Holmes both suggested that true authority was always just beyond the grasp of ordinary citizens. Even though they arrived at different conclusions—Wister's judge defended the legitimacy of lynching; Holmes denied it—the reasoning they used to reach those conclusions was identical. They both suggested that law is procedural and democratic, save when those procedures produce a judgment contrary to a law known only by the elite. To put it another way: American law is equitable and democratic at all times, except for when the ruling classes say it isn't.

In *Popular Tribunals*, his 1887 book about lynching in the west, historian Hubert Howe Bancroft had made a number of points that would be echoed by Wister in *The Virginian* five years later. Bancroft thought that lynching provided an important restorative function for the republic, especially in the western regions. "Compare the laws of evolution as applied to government with the behavior of the mixed population of California when left without government," he wrote, and "we find the two in perfect accord."[36] A government enacting the Darwinian principle of natural selection and westerners carrying vigilante justice were, in Bancroft's view, essentially the same.

Common to Wister, Holmes, and Bancroft alike was a basic wariness of what Bancroft called the "despotism of democracy."[37] Their conservatism was premised on a sense that democratic law should be essentially subordinate to the will of America's natural aristocracy. Because that aristocracy would, as Bancroft wrote, be selected by the "laws of evolution," its decisions, whether made in courts of law or under a hanging tree, would be more legitimate—would be more natural—than those reached through the whims of democratic law.

Wister once wrote to Richard Harding Davis that the character of the Virginian was "meant by me to be just my whole American creed in flesh and blood."[38] But the character was more than a creed. He also represented the story of Roosevelt and his circle. *The Virginian* told the story of a man who came west, to a place where letting "the best man win" was the law of the land. That man proved himself shrewd and strong, able to stand beyond the laws of ordinary citizens and bring them to justice as he saw fit. The west was where he was recognized as a member of America's natural aristocracy. And that recognition did not just make him great. It also made him rich.

At the end of the novel, the Virginian accompanies his wife Molly to her family home in Bennington, Vermont. Her great aunt sizes up the Virginian, who is wearing a perfectly tailored suit. She asks if all the men seeking their fortunes in the west become wealthy. "All the good ones do," he replies coolly. The Virginian, a killer of men, is supposed to be one of those good ones. By the end of the novel, he has become rich and powerful. He is no longer merely a westerner, but a man for all corners of America. After herding hundreds of head of cattle, buying acres of land, and executing two rustlers, the outcome is clear: the "cow-boy could be invited anywhere and hold his own."[39]

Wister might as well have been describing Roosevelt. Or Cody or Remington or even himself, for that matter. As Remington said of Roosevelt, shortly after he took the oath of office to become president, "he is more than a man now; he is an idea, and he doesn't exactly belong to himself."[40] Roosevelt, like the Virginian, had become a kind of American character. And he was well as on his way to becoming an icon of the Republican Party.

NOTES

1. Scharnhorst *Owen*, 34.
2. Wister *Roosevelt*, 34.
3. Martin, 754.
4. Wister *Virginian*, xxx.
5. Wister *Virginian*, xxx; trans. Coleman *Gallo-Roman*, 49.
6. Scharnhorst *Owen*, 154.
7. Wister *Roosevelt*, 105–106.
8. Splete, 312.
9. FR letter to Owen Wister 4 October [1901].
10. Samuels *Frederic*, 334.
11. Alter, 42–46.
12. Ballantrae, 2.
13. Bridger, 420.
14. Reddin, 145, 147; Kasson 144.
15. Qtd. in Reddin, 147.
16. Qtd. in Reddin, 145.
17. Wister *Virginian*, 320.
18. Kasson, 255.
19. Bogue, 158–186; Handley, 43–46.
20. Turner "Contributions," 90, 91, 92, 96.
21. Wister *Roosevelt*, 86.
22. TR letter to Henry Cabot Lodge, 23 September 1901.
23. "President Roosevelt," 12.
24. "Cowboy," 16; "Roosevelt as a Factor," 2.
25. TR letter to Sydney Brooks, 20 November 1908.
26. De Tocqueville, 253.
27. Qtd. in Wister *Owen*, 16.
28. Wister *Virginian*, 95.
29. Literary historians have often studied *The Virginian*'s conservatism. For an overview, in addition to Scharnhorst *Owen* see Graulich, xvii; Hutson, 129; Kuenz, 101; Kollin, 238; Mitchell "When," 67; Robinson "Roosevelt-Wister," 114; Slotkin, 178; and White *"It's,"* 622.
30. Wister *Virginian*, 147.

31. Wister *Virginian*, 246.
32. Wister *Virginian*, 280. For an analysis of southern and western lynching in film, see Jackson, 102–120.
33. Wister *Virginian*, 281.
34. Wister *Virginian*, 281–282.
35. *Frank v. Mangum*, 347, 350.
36. Bancroft *Popular*, 430. For a current study of the history of western lynching, see Gonzalez-Day.
37. Bancroft *Popular*, 432.
38. Qtd. in Scharnhorst *Owen*, 45.
39. Wister *Virginian*, 322, 320.
40. Qtd. in "Guarding," 6.

Epilogue
The Cowboy President

The connection between the fictional Virginian and the real-life Roosevelt, the "cowboy president," would only grow.[1] In time, it would expand to include the entire Republican Party. Roosevelt had long said that he would want cowboys with him if it ever became necessary to go to war, a desire he was eventually able to bring to fruition. The warrior-cowboys he had sought out as Rough Riders were, he later wrote, men exactly like Wister's Virginian.[2]

Over time, fact and fiction became slowly fused in Roosevelt and Wister's conservative vision of America. Decades after the novel's publication, *The Virginian* was made into a television show. In one episode, the character of the Virginian actually enlists in Roosevelt's Rough Riders, traveling to Cuba to teach the regiment how to use the skills of the American frontier west to ensure military victory.[3]

The conservative individualism of Roosevelt and his circle, with its dream of using the west to select America's natural aristocracy, was a dream that attracted a later generation of conservatives. In 1914, *The Virginian* was made into a feature-length film, directed by Cecil B. DeMille and starring Dustin Farnum as the Virginian.[4] Farnum was returning to the role he had pioneered on Broadway ten years earlier, when he had first starred as the Virginian in the Wister-penned adaption of the novel.[5] DeMille was a prominent Republican whose conservatism was unusual not just in Hollywood, but even within his family. (By coincidence, his sister-in-law was the daughter of the liberal economist and onetime Roosevelt political opponent Henry George.[6])

The Virginian was filmed again in 1923 and then again in 1929. The 1929 adaptation starred Gary Cooper as the Virginian, in his first western film role. Cooper, too, would become well known as a conservative. DeMille would later direct Cooper as "Wild Bill" Hickok in *The Plainsman* (1936), a fictional account of the adventures of George Custer and "Buffalo Bill" Cody.[7] Yet DeMille and Cooper were not just linked by their films. They were also linked by their politics.

In 1944, with the Allied forces continuing to push back the Axis alliance, Franklin Delano Roosevelt was running for an unprecedented fourth term as president. His Republican opponent was New York governor Thomas E. Dewey. By then, the word "conservative" had come to refer to nearly any set of ideas that opposed the New Deal program.[8] Many in the Hollywood establishment supported Roosevelt.

In September, a small group of Hollywood Republicans, led by DeMille, organized a rally for Dewey at the Los Angeles Coliseum.[9] Nearly 93,000 spectators came to applaud Hollywood luminaries, including Cooper, and watch Dewey try to harness western individualism to the modern age. The evening began with actor Leo Carillo leading a Buffalo Bill-style team of cowboys and cowgirls in a riding exhibition around the artificial turf of the Coliseum.[10] In his speech, Dewey emphasized the need for an "American system," rather than the collectivism offered by the New Deal.[11] As the *Los Angeles Times* reported, Dewey promised an "end to the Roosevelt New Deal," stressing the need for "freedom for the individual."[12]

It was a spectacular night. The rally for the Republican nominee featured a cowboy show of expert riders, a stirring commitment to American individualism, and the Virginian himself, Gary Cooper. It was like the dawning of a new conservative era, one yet tethered to the old symbols of the west.

Seven months earlier, Cooper had joined the conservative Motion Picture Alliance for the Preservation of American Ideals. The group, which would eventually include DeMille, Walt Disney, John Ford, Ayn Rand, John Wayne, and many others, would soon urge the House Un-American Activities Committee to investigate Communist influences in Hollywood. Three years later, Cooper would testify as a friendly witness before the House Un-American Activities Committee.[13] He was there with the new president of the Screen Actors Guild, a charismatic actor named Ronald Reagan.

As it had with Cooper, the public would grow accustomed to seeing Reagan as a westerner, both on-screen and off. Among other roles, he starred as George Custer in *Santa Fe Trail* (1940); played a gunslinger in *Cattle Queen of Montana* (1954); and starred as Cowpoke in *Tennessee's Partner* (1955), a film loosely based on a short story by Bret Harte, whose words had inspired Wister and graced the front matter of Roosevelt's *The Rough Riders*.

As Reagan completed his long slow climb from entertainer to California governor to eventually president of the United States, he began to think of himself as a spokesman for modern American conservatism.[14] He wore a cowboy hat and well-scuffed cowboy boots on his California ranch.[15] After he was elected president in 1980, it would not take long before some writers, connecting Reagan's western persona to his new brand of conservatism, began using a phrase to describe Reagan that an earlier generation of journalists had first applied to Theodore Roosevelt: the "cowboy president."[16]

Reagan's western persona promised a regeneration of what he called "the robust individualism of the American experience."[17] Whether he realized it or not, he was walking on the path that had been cut by Roosevelt, Cody, Remington, Turner, and Wister nearly a century before. In their minds, the west was a place of Darwinian self-distinction, a place where extraordinary individualism could mark one as a member of America's fittest. Like those men, Reagan seemed to promise a future blurred by nostalgia, a romantic belief America should be led by its own natural aristocrats: perhaps individuals who, like him, had been fitted by the far west.

Seen one way, the association of western iconography with the Republican Party was simply a by-product of America's changing political geography. With changes in regional population density and racial politics, the second half of the twentieth century saw the conservative base of the Republican Party shift from the northeast to the south and west. When the conservative Arizona senator and onetime Republican presidential nominee Barry Goldwater spoke at the 1980 Republican convention, a number of observers were already viewing Reagan's nomination that year as the long-delayed fulfillment of Goldwater's own promise from sixteen years earlier. As one *Washington Post* column put it that year, "Goldwater had been the prophet of the western movement for the Republicans—the conservatives."[18] For some journalists at the time, Goldwater's conservatism was simply the most obvious antecedent of Reagan's own. For them, the triumph of Reagan was in large part a triumph of political demography.

But seen another way, the late-century westernization of conservativism had been shaped by a much longer legacy of western symbols and stories. Goldwater was occasionally photographed in a cowboy hat and western shirt, and during his failed 1964 run for president, the press made much of the connection between his conservative politics and his family's deep western roots.[19]

Those roots reportedly included two different western executions. One 1964 *Los Angeles Times* article about Goldwater reported that in 1898, Goldwater's uncle Morris Goldwater, then serving in various elected positions in Prescott, Arizona, had been associated with the hanging of a man who had escaped from the Prescott jail. Fifteen years before that, an alleged member of a gang who robbed his great-uncle Joe Goldwater's store in Bisbee had been lynched.[20]

Such stories of western violence could still tap into something deep within the American psyche. They seemed designed to endow Goldwater with an air of destiny, suggesting he was a westerner in the mode of Roosevelt, Cody, and others. The journalist went on to observe that much of Goldwater's appeal was "based on his constant reiteration of the Western values of enterprise, individualism and industry," as well as on westerners' "natural hankering for the man of action rather than the man of intellect."[21] And although Goldwater lost the 1964 election spectacularly, carrying only six states, in his efforts to speak to America's future in part by pantomiming its past, he was using the signs of the west to gesture at a much larger conservative aesthetic. That aesthetic was, as the *Times* put it, a "tradition of rugged individualism," but also a Darwinian tradition of social order in which the fittest would be selected for leadership and enforce the law as they saw fit.[22] After Goldwater, when national politicians such as Reagan or George W. Bush donned western clothing or told stories to establish their connections to the west, it sent unmistakable signals about their conservatism. It seemed to say, *Here is a man with a gimlet-eyed sense of the dialectic of freedom and punishment, the indifference and inequality of nature, the power of the individual. Here is a conservative man of action.*

By the second decade of the twenty-first century, conservatism had become something quite different from what it had been a hundred years earlier. No longer could conservatism be associated only with universal-sounding appeals to individualism, meritocracy, and natural law. For many, American conservatism had become about authoritarianism, nationalism, and racial grievance.[23] That sense was thrown into sharp relief with the 2016 election of the forty-fifth president, Donald Trump.

How conservatism turned into Trumpism, or whether it had in fact been some clandestine proto-Trumpism all along, is a question journalists and scholars will continue to ponder.

No one, of course, could confuse Trump, the son of a wealthy New York real estate developer who had spent decades cultivating the image of a flashy new-money plutocrat, with a self-reliant westerner. Unlike conservative Republican forebears like Reagan and Bush, who promoted their western bona fides and were occasionally photographed wearing cowboy boots and Stetson hats, Trump seldom spent time west of the Mississippi River and was rarely seen in anything other than a suit and tie.

Yet, despite the seeming incongruity of Trump tapping into a well of western-influenced conservative aesthetics, his language did, at times, seem pitched to draw on that same groundwater.

On August 27, 2020, Trump accepted the Republican nomination to run for a second term as president. In his acceptance speech, he made a point of proclaiming his adherence to the rule of law. That summer, cities and towns throughout the country had seen widespread protests against police brutality toward African Americans, protests that arose in the aftermath of the killing of George Floyd, an African American man, by a white Minneapolis police officer. Generally speaking, the protests were associated with the political left; the counter-protesters were associated with Trump and the political right.

In his speech, Trump claimed that the protests over racism and policing, which were generally peaceful, were in fact widely beset by "left-wing anarchy and mayhem." The remedy, he insisted, was allegiance to what he called "law and order."[24] Adhering to such a principle would seem to be straightforward: the first amendment rights of peaceful protesters should be observed, and any violent or criminal elements could be arrested and charged by law enforcement professionals.

Except that wasn't what Trump meant at all. Two days before Trump's speech, a white seventeen-year-old Illinois resident named Kyle Rittenhouse had attended one of those protests in Kenosha, Wisconsin, armed with a military-style rifle. That particular protest concerned the recent shooting of Jacob Blake, an African American man, by a white police officer.

Rittenhouse was a vocal supporter of Trump and a strong supporter of the police, even though he also seemed to think that trained and certified law officers somehow needed the assistance of armed civilians who were neither trained nor certified.[25] Before the night was over, Rittenhouse had allegedly killed two protesters and injured a third.

His vigilantism—his apparent willingness to commit violence ostensibly in the name of the law, despite not being a law officer—reminded some of the sort of extrajudicial western killings that were romanticized by Roosevelt and his circle. In an article about Rittenhouse, one Chicago journalist found it shocking that he and others were "allowed to carry guns in the streets as if they live in the Wild West."[26]

The day before Trump's convention acceptance speech, Rittenhouse was arrested at his home in Illinois, facing charges of first-degree intentional homicide. In Trump's efforts to depict himself as a candidate devoted to the rule of law, Rittenhouse's alleged crimes would seem to be obvious targets for censure, the type of thing he could easily weave into his speech.

But Trump did not mention Rittenhouse in his speech at all. Instead, he romanticized the myth of American meritocracy, the belief that "in America, anyone can rise with hard work." Like Roosevelt before him, he proclaimed that Emersonian self-reliance had built the nation. He didn't say anything about Rittenhouse's alleged cowboy-style vigilantism, yet he still made a point of bringing up America's legacy of frontier gunslingers. "Our American ancestors," he said in his speech, always "set out West for the next adventure. Ranchers and miners, cowboys and sheriffs, farmers and settlers. They pressed on past the Mississippi to stake a claim in the wild frontier. Legends were born. Wyatt Earp, Annie Oakley, Davy Crockett, and Buffalo Bill."[27]

He was not just calling up a nostalgic myth of the American west. He was trying to pull off a bit of legerdemain, suggesting that the extrajudicial lawlessness that Americans loved to associate with the romance of the wild west had culminated in his self-proclaimed identity as a "law and order" candidate.

A law-and-order candidate who was, it seemed, not particularly interested in condemning the alleged street killing of two left-wing protesters, at least when that killing had been done by a young supporter of his.

In Wister's *Virginian*, the judge had felt that when juries reached a verdict he didn't like, it was because they were "not dealing the law" correctly.[28] Now, Trump was implying something very similar. *Upholding law and order*, he seemed to be suggesting, *means upholding only the parts of it that I agree with.*

Over a hundred years earlier, the blinkered romance of western vigilantism had helped launch the careers of Roosevelt and his circle. Audiences were electrified by their stories and exploits. But in Trump's telling, one signifier of western conservatism—a thrillingly pitiless Darwinism—looked less like rugged self-reliance and more like simple brutality.

Days after Trump's convention acceptance speech, he had still not condemned Rittenhouse, and in fact had begun to defend his actions.[29] Shortly after his speech, more political violence erupted. A left-wing activist named Michael Reinoehl was suspected of killing Aaron Danielson, a supporter of a far-right group, during another protest in Portland, Oregon. Danielson had been participating in a rally for Trump when Reinhoehl allegedly shot and killed him.[30]

Even though Reinhoehl had not been arrested nor charged with the crime, Trump seemed to endorse an old west-style execution as recompense. He wanted, as he put it, "retribution" for the killing of the supporter of the far-right group. "I put out, 'when are you going to go get him,'" Trump recalled in an interview. "And the U.S. marshals went in to get him. There was a shootout. This guy was a violent criminal, and the U.S. marshals killed him. And I'll tell you something—that's the way it has to be. There has to be retribution."[31] Five days after Danielson's death, Reinhoehl was shot and killed by federal agents.[32]

In short, within a week of giving a speech promoting himself as a candidate of law and order, Trump had defended the actions of an underage right-wing supporter who had allegedly killed two individuals associated with the political left. And he had also seemed to demand the government kill a different individual, one who had been neither arrested nor charged with a crime, in retribution for allegedly killing someone associated with the political right.

Both of these actions, while shocking, would also seem to be not even remotely conservative, at least in the common sense of the word. In defending vigilante violence or encouraging federal agents to take retribution against a citizen, the president was weakening, rather than conserving, democratically accountable institutions like the justice system. Despite proclamations that he was an unwavering supporter of the rule of law, his words suggested he was nothing of the sort.

Yet viewed another way, Trump's rhetoric was also a strange descendant of the Darwinian, western-influenced conservatism imagined by Roosevelt and his circle. Like Roosevelt with the boat thieves, or the Virginian with the rustlers, Trump seemed to arrogate for himself the authority to determine innocence, guilt, or punishment. This was a strongman sort of individualism, marked by the circular belief that power should flow to exceptional individuals, whose exceptionalism can be recognized by the power they already wield.

It would be foolish to push the comparison too far, of course. In a number of ways both large and small, Trumpism was little like the conservative aesthetics of Roosevelt and his circle. Yet the persistent allure of grand myths of extrajudicial frontier violence—the way stories of heroic lone gunslingers taking the law into their hands have persisted over centuries, like a smothering vine that is never fully rooted out—also makes it possible to identify much darker descendants of their conservatism.

Roosevelt and his circle tried to uphold a respect for natural science, a commitment to environmental conservation, and a sense, however misguided, that contests of merit could build a fair society. But over time, those values could too easily mutate into malignancy. One darker inheritance of those same conservative impulses can be seen in a veneration of physical and racial supremacy, a ruthless indifference to natural resource management, and a cruel abrogation of the rule of law.

Roosevelt and his circle often seemed to be hunting for the great men of history, men they believed could be selected in the natural arena of the American west. In their minds, such competitions ensured the course of American history would evolve imperfectly toward progress.

Yet their optimism about evolution, the west, and American destiny could easily be recast into another shape entirely. A century after their deaths, romantic stories about the nature of freedom and the American west—Darwinian stories glorifying a natural aristocracy—had become a rulebook for a kind of tournament society: an all-destroying competition to determine the legatees of American individualism, the victors of history, the last men.

NOTES

1. "Cowboy," 16.
2. Roosevelt *Autobiography*, 120.

3. Green, 232. The Virginian joins the Rough Riders in the episode titled "Riff-Raff" (1962).
4. Birchard, 14–18.
5. Scharnhorst *Owen*, 170–180.
6. Higashi, 28.
7. Birchard, 293.
8. Rosen, 58, 79.
9. Critchlow, 67.
10. Jordan, 231.
11. Moscow, 9.
12. Palmer, 1, 2.
13. Meyers, 206–208; Kaminsky, 146–147.
14. Edwards, 466.
15. Barletta, 96. For more on western myths and American politics, see Goldberg 13–50 and Corkin, 1–18.
16. Smith "Reagan," A1. See also Lindsey, B7; Safire, A23; and Yemma.
17. Reagan, 96.
18. Quinn "The 1980," D1.
19. Perlstein, 16–20.
20. Mulligan "Goldwater," C2. Although a number of writers suggest Morris Goldwater directly participated in the 1898 hanging of Fleming Parker, no contemporary accounts support that assertion. See Anderson *Story*, 476.
21. Mulligan "Goldwater," C2.
22. Mulligan "Goldwater," C2.
23. Stevens *It*, 1–36; Kobes Du Mez, 1–32.
24. Thrush "Full."
25. MacFarquhar "Suspect"; Allam "Vigilante."
26. Mitchell "Don't."
27. Thrush "Full."
28. Wister *Virginian*, 281.
29. Carvajal et al. "Trump."
30. Wilson "Suspect."
31. Qtd. in Bouie "Trump's."
32. Hill et al. "Straight."

Works Cited

Abbott, Lawrence Fraser. *Impressions of Theodore Roosevelt*. New York: Doubleday, Page & Co., 1920.
Adams, Henry Carter. "Democracy." *The New Englander* 4.163 (Nov. 1881): 752–772.
Adams, Herbert B. *Methods of Historical Study, Second Series, I-II*. Baltimore: Johns Hopkins U, 1884.
Alitt, Patrick. *The Conservatives: Ideas and Personalities Throughout American History*. New Haven: Yale University Press, 2009.
Allam, Hannah. "Vigilante? Militia? Confusion and Politics Shape How Shooting Suspect is Labeled." *NPR*. Washington, DC (28 Aug. 2020): < https://www.npr.org/2020/08/28/907130558/vigilante-militia-confusion-and-politics-shape-how-shooting-suspect-is-labeled>.
Alschuler, Albert W. *Law Without Values: The Life, Work, and Legacy of Justice Holmes*. Chicago: University of Chicago Press, 2000.
Alter, Judith. "Frederic Remington's Major Novel: *John Ermine*." *Southwestern American Literature* 2 (1972): 42–46.
"Amusements." *Daily Inter Ocean* 22.32. Chicago, IL (25 Apr. 1893): 6.
Anderson, Parker. *Story of a Hanged Man*. Prescott, AZ: Kubera, 2016.
Andersson, Rani-Henrik. *The Lakota Ghost Dance of 1890*. Lincoln: University of Nebraska Press, 2008.
Ankersmit, F. R. *Aesthetic Politics: Political Philosophy Beyond Fact and Value*. Stanford: Stanford University Press, 1996.
Arnold, C. D. "World's Columbian Exposition, Boone and Crockett Club." [Photograph.] 1893. Historical Architecture and Landscape Image Collection, c. 1865–1973; Ryerson & Burnham Archives, the Art Institute of Chicago Libraries. n.p.
Arthur, Chester A. "First Annual Message." 6 Dec. 1881. *A Compilation of the Messages and Papers of the Presidents, 1789–1897, Volume VIII*. James D. Richardson, ed. Washington: Authority of Congress, 1898. 37–65.

"Bad Lands." *Stoddart's Encyclopedia Americana, Volume I*. New York: J. M. Stoddart, 1883. 389–390.
Ballantrae. "Out on the Western Border." *Kansas City Star*. Kansas City, MO (30 Nov. 1902): 2.
Bancroft, Hubert Howe. *History of Nevada, Colorado, and Wyoming, 1540–1888 [The Works of Hubert Howe Bancroft, Volume XXV]*. San Francisco: History Company, 1890.
_____. *Popular Tribunals*. San Francisco: History Company, 1887.
Bannister, Robert C. *Social Darwinism: Science and Myth in Anglo-American Social Thought*. Philadelphia: Temple University Press, 1979.
Barletta, John R. *Riding with Reagan: From the White House to the Ranch*. New York: Citadel, 2005.
Barlow, Aaron. *The Cult of Individualism: A History of an Enduring Myth*. Santa Barbara, CA: Praeger, 2013.
Baym, Nina. *Women Writers of the American West, 1833–1927*. Champaign: University of Illinois Press, 2011.
Beadle, John Hanson. *Western Wilds, and the Men Who Redeem Them*. Cincinnati: Jones Brothers & Company, 1880.
Beard, George M. *A Practical Treatise on Nervous Exhaustion (Neurasthenia): Its Symptoms, Nature, Sequences, Treatment*. New York: E.B. Treat, 1888.
Bederman, Gail. *Manliness and Civilization: A Cultural History of Gender and Race in the United States, 1880–1917*. Chicago: University of Chicago University Press, 1995.
Beecher, Henry Ward. *Evolution and Religion, Part I: Eight Sermons, Discussing the Bearings of the Evolutionary Philosophy on the Fundamental Doctrines of Evangelical Christianity*. London: James Clark & Co., 1885.
_____. *The Original Plymouth Pulpit: Sermons of Henry Ward Beecher, Volume X: March to September, 1873*. Boston: Pilgrim, 1873.
Beecher, Jonathan. *Charles Fourier: The Visionary and His World*. Berkeley: University of California Press, 1986.
Bell, Jr., Malcolm. *Major Butler's Legacy: Five Generations of a Slaveholding Family*. Athens: University of Georgia Press, 1987.
Berg, Manfred. *Popular Justice: A History of Lynching in America*. Chicago: Ivan R. Dee, 2011.
Bigelow, Poultney. *Seventy Summers* [Vol. I]. New York: Longmans, Green & Co., 1925.
Billings, Frank S. "Conservatisms". *The Conservative* 2.3 (27 Jul. 1899): 12–13.
_____. "Conservatisms." *The Conservative* 2.6 (17 Aug. 1899): 13.
_____. "Conservatisms." *The Conservative* 2.12 (28 Sep. 1899): 11.
_____. "The Spanish-American Imbroglio." *The Conservative* 2.3 (27 Jul. 1899): 7–12.
Billington, Ray Allen. *The Genesis of the Frontier Thesis: A Study in Historical Creativity*. San Marino: Huntington Library, 1971.
Birchard, Robert S. *Cecil B. DeMille's Hollywood*. Lexington: University Press of Kentucky, 2004.
Blight, David. *Race and Reunion: The Civil War in American Memory*. Cambridge: Belknap, 2001.

Bloom, Jack M. *Class, Race, and the Civil Rights Movement.* Bloomington: Indiana University Press, 1987.

Bogue, Allan G. *Frederick Jackson Turner: Strange Roads Going Down.* Norman: University of Oklahoma Press, 1998.

Bold, Christine. *The Frontier Club: Popular Westerns and Cultural Power, 1880–1924.* New York: Oxford University Press, 2013.

_____. "Where Did the Black Rough Riders Go?" *Canadian Review of American Studies* 39.3 (2009): 273–297.

Bonner, Robert E. *William F. Cody's Wyoming Empire: The Buffalo Bill Nobody Knows.* Norman: University of Oklahoma Press, 2007.

"Book Reviews: *The Rough Riders.*" *Public Opinion* 26.24 (15 Jun. 1899): 761–762.

Booth, Arthur John. *Saint-Simon and Saint-Simonism: A Chapter in the History of Socialism in France.* London: Longmans, Green, Reader, and Dyer, 1871.

Boston *Herald*, The, ed. *Commercial and Financial New England, Illustrated.* Boston: Boston Herald, 1906.

Bouie, Jamelle. "Trump's Perverse Campaign Strategy." *New York Times.* New York, NY (15 Sept. 2020): <https://www.nytimes.com/2020/09/15/opinion/caputo-trump-2020.html?action=click&module=Opinion&pgtype=Homepage>.

Bourke, John G. *On the Border with Crook.* 2nd ed. New York: Scribner's, 1896.

Bowler, Peter J. *The Eclipse of Darwinism: Anti-Darwinian Evolution Theories in the Decades around 1900.* Baltimore: The Johns Hopkins University Press, 1983.

Brander Matthews Letters, Rare Book and Manuscript Library, Columbia University Library.

Bremer, Fredrika. *The Homes of the New World: Impressions of America, Volume I.* New York: Harper & Brothers, 1853.

Brennan, Mary C. *Turning Right in the Sixties: The Conservative Capture of the GOP.* Chapel Hill: University of North Carolina Press, 1995.

Bridger, Bobby. *Buffalo Bill and Sitting Bull: Inventing the Wild West.* Austin: University of Texas Press, 2002.

Bright, William. *Native American Placenames of the United States.* Norman: University of Oklahoma Press, 2004.

Brinkley, Douglas. *The Wilderness Warrior: Theodore Roosevelt and the Crusade for America.* New York: HarperCollins, 2009.

"The British Cue for Uncle Sam in Foreign and Colonial Policy." *The Review of Reviews* 13 (Dec. 1898): 562–563.

Brooks, Van Wyck. "On Creating a Usable Past." *The Dial* 64 (11 Apr. 1918): 337–341.

"Buffalo Bill's" Wild West Company. *Buffalo Bill's Wild West: America's National Entertainment, Led By the Famed Scout and Guide Buffalo Bill* [1884 Program]. Hartford: Calhoun, 1884.

_____. *Buffalo Bill's Wild West: America's National Entertainment, An Illustrated Treatise of Historical Facts and Sketches* [1887 Program]. London: Allen, Scott & Co., 1887.

_____. *Buffalo Bill's Wild West and Congress of Rough Riders of the World* [1893 Program]. Chicago: Blakely, 1893.

Burg, David F. *Chicago's White City of 1893*. Lexington: University Press of Kentucky, 1976.

Burke, Edmund. *Reflections on the Revolution in* France. 1790. Ed. Frank M. Turner. New Haven: Yale University Press, 2003.

Burns, Jennifer. *Goddess of the Market: Ayn Rand and the American Right*. New York: Oxford University Press, 2009.

Cameron, Sharon. "The Way of Life by Abandonment: Emerson's Impersonal." *Critical Inquiry* 25.1 (1998): 1–31.

Cappon, Lester J., ed. *The Adams-Jefferson Letters: Volume II, 1812–1826*. Chapel Hill: University of North Carolina Press, 1959.

Carter, Robert A. *Buffalo Bill Cody: The Man Behind the Legend*. New York: John Wiley, 2000.

Carvajal, Nikki, et al. "Trump Refuses to Denounce Violent Actions by Right-Wing Agitators." *CNN*. Atlanta, GA (31 Aug. 2020): < https://www.cnn.com/2020/08/31/politics/trump-supporters-violence/index.html>.

Catlin, George. *Illustrations of the Manners, Customs, and Condition of the North American Indians, Volume I*. 1841. 5th ed. London: Henry G. Bohn, 1845.

Cavell, Stanley. *Emerson's Transcendental Etudes*. Stanford: Stanford University Press, 2003.

———. *Conditions Handsome and Unhandsome: The Conditions of Emersonian Perfectionism*. Chicago: University of Chicago Press, 1990.

Cherny, Robert W. *A Righteous Cause: The Life of Williams Jennings Bryan*. 1985. Second ed. Norman: University of Oklahoma Press, 1994.

Chicago of Today, The Metropolis of the West: The Nation's Choice for the World's Columbian Exposition. Chicago: Acme, 1891.

Chinard, Gilbert, ed. *The Letters of Lafayette and Jefferson*. 1929. New York: Arno Press, 1979.

"Chronicle and Comment [Geographical Map of American Literature]." *Bookman* 7.6 (Aug. 1898): 468–469.

Claghorn, Kate Holladay. "Burke: A Centenary Perspective." *Atlantic Monthly* 80.477 (Jul. 1897): 84–95.

Clark, Champ. "American Policy of Expansion." *The Conservative Review* 1.1 (Feb. 1899): 78–112.

Clark, James Hyde. *Cuba and the Fight for Freedom*. Philadelphia: Globe Bible, 1896.

Clift, George D. "The Kansas Settler" *The Kansas Magazine* 3.2 (Feb. 1873): 152–156.

Cody, William F. *An Autobiography of Buffalo Bill*. New York: Farrar & Rinehart, 1920.

———. *The Life of Hon. William F. Cody, Known as Buffalo Bill, the Famous Hunter, Scout and Guide*. Hartford, CT: Frank E. Bliss, 1879.

———. *Story of the Wild West and Camp-Fire Chats* [etc.]. Chicago: R.S. Peale & Co., 1888.

Coffin, William A. "American Illustration of To-Day: Third Paper." *Scribner's Magazine* 11.3 (Mar. 1892): 333–350.

_____. "Remington's 'Bronco Buster.'" *The Century* 52.2 (Jun. 1896): 318–319.
Cohen, Nancy. *The Reconstruction of American Liberalism, 1865–1914*. Chapel Hill: University of North Carolina Press, 2002.
"A Cold Snap: A Western Sketch." *All the Year Round* No. 200. Third Series. (29 Oct. 1892): 418–422.
Coleman, Dorothy Gabe. *The Gallo-Roman Muse: Aspects of Roman Literary Tradition in Sixteenth-Century France*. Cambridge: Cambridge University Press, 1979.
Connelly, Owen. *The French Revolution and Napoleonic Era*. Fort Worth: Harcourt, 1999.
Cook, David J. *Hands Up; Or, Thirty-Five Years of Detective Life in the Mountains and on the Plains*. Denver: W. F. Robinson, 1897.
Cook, Nancy. "The Romance of Ranching; or, Selling Place-Based Fantasies in and of the West." *Postwestern Cultures: Literary, Theory, Space*. Susan Kollin, ed. Lincoln: University of Nebraska Press, 2007, 223–243.
Cooke, George Willis. *Ralph Waldo Emerson: His Life, Writings, and Philosophy*. 1881. Honolulu: University Press of the Pacific, 2003.
Cooke, Jacob E., ed. *The Federalist*. Middletown: Wesleyan University Press, 1961.
Cooper, James Fenimore. *The Last of the Mohicans*. 1826. Ontario: Broadview, 2009.
Cooper, Laurence D. *Rousseau, Nature, and the Problem of the Good Life*. Pennsylvania: The Pennsylvania State University Press, 1999.
Coquillette, Daniel R. and Bruce A. Kimball. *On the Battlefield of Merit: Harvard Law School, the First Century*. Cambridge: Harvard University Press, 2015.
Corkin, Stanley. *Cowboys as Cold Warriors: The Western and U.S. History*. Philadelphia: Temple University Press, 2004.
"The Cowboy." *Morning News*. Dallas, TX (3 Aug. 1902): 16.
"The Cowboy Regiments: Theodore Roosevelt's Command to be Picked from the Best Fighters and Riders of the West." *New York Times*. New York, NY (28 Apr. 1898): 1.
Crafts, W. A. *The Southern Rebellion: Being a History of the United States from the Commencement of President Buchanan's Administration Through The War for the Suppression of the Rebellion*. Boston: Samuel Walker, 1862.
Critchlow, Donald T. *When Hollywood Was Right: How Movie Stars, Studio Moguls, and Big Business Remade American Politics*. New York: Cambridge University Press, 2013.
Cronon, William. "Turner's First Stand: The Significance of Significance in American History." *Writing Western History: Essays on Major Western Historians*. Richard W. Etulain, ed. Albuquerque: University of New Mexico Press, 1991. 73–101.
Cunningham, Raymond J. "The German Historical World of Herbert Baxter Adams: 1874–1876. *The Journal of American History* 68.2 (1981): 261–275.
Cushing, Charles Phelps. "What Can a Thin Man Do?" *The World's Work* 32.4 (Aug. 1916): 385–396.
"Custer's Last Charge: Ghastly Details of the Fight in Which the Brave General Perished." *The Inter Ocean*. Chicago, IL (7 Jul. 1876): 1, 4.

Cutright, Paul Russell. *Theodore Roosevelt: The Making of a Conservationist.* Urbana: University of Illinois Press, 1985.

Darwin, Charles. *The Descent of Man, and Selection in Relation to Sex: The Concise Edition.* Ed. Carl Zimmer. 1871. New York: Plume, 2007.

———. *The Origin of Species and The Voyage of the Beagle.* New York: Knopf, 2003.

Darwin, Erasmus. *Zoonomia; or the Laws of Organic Life, Volume I.* 1794. Boston: Thomas & Andrews, 1809.

Davies, Peter. *The Extreme Right in France, 1789 to the Present: From de Maistre to Le Pen.* London: Routledge, 2002.

Davis, Richard Harding. *The Cuban and Porto Rican Campaigns.* New York: Charles Scribner's Sons, 1898.

Demolins, Edmond. *Anglo-Saxon Superiority: To What it is Due.* Trans. Louis Bertram Lavigne. New York: R. F. Fenno & Company, 1899.

De Tocqueville, Alexis. *Democracy in America.* 1835, 1840. Harvey C. Mansfield and Delba Winthrop, trans. Chicago: University of Chicago Press, 2000.

———. *Democracy in America.* Henry Reeve, trans. New York: Colonial, 1889.

Di Silvestro, Roger L. *Theodore Roosevelt in the Badlands: A Young Politician's Quest for Recovery in the American West.* New York: Walker & Co., 2011.

"Dinner to Mr. Roosevelt: The Federal Club Entertains Him." *New York Tribune.* New York, NY (12 May 1887): 5.

Dyer, Thomas G. *Theodore Roosevelt and the Idea of Race.* Baton Rouge: Louisiana State University Press, 1980.

"Editorial Notes." *New York Observer* 76.40. New York, NY (6 Oct. 1898): 438–440.

Editorial Staff of the Mentor Association. "Frederic Remington." *The Mentor* 3.9, Serial No. 85, 1915: n.p.

Edwards, Anne. *Early Reagan.* New York: William Morrow, 1987.

Eisler, Benita. *The Red Man's Bones: George Catlin, Artist and Showman.* New York: W. W. Norton, 2013.

Ellingson, Ter. *The Myth of the Noble Savage.* Berkeley, University of California Press, 2001.

"The Emerson Mania [review of Emerson's *Essays*]." *The English Review* 12.23 (Sep. 1849): 139–152.

Emerson, Ralph Waldo. *The Early Lectures of Ralph Waldo Emerson, Volume I: 1833–1836.* Stephen E. Whicher and Robert E. Spiller, eds. Cambridge: Belknap, 1966.

———. "Lectures on the Times: Introductory Lecture read at the Masonic Temple in Boston, Thursday Evening, December 2, 1841." *The Dial* 3.1 (Jul. 1842): 1–18.

———. "Lectures on the Times: Lecture II. The Conservative: Read at the Masonic Temple in Boston, 9 Dec. 1841." *The Dial* 3.2 (Oct. 1842): 181–197.

———. "Remarks at a Meeting for the Relief of the Family of John Brown." *The Tribunal: Responses to John Brown and the Harpers Ferry Raid.* John Stauffer and Zoe Trodd, eds. Cambridge: Belknap, 2012. 114–116.

———. "Self-Reliance." 1841. *Ralph Waldo Emerson: Selected Essays, Lectures, and Poems.* Robert D. Richardson, Jr., ed. New York: Bantam, 1990.

_____. *Nature.* 1836. *Ralph Waldo Emerson: Selected Essays, Lectures, and Poems.* Robert D. Richardson, Jr., ed. New York: Bantam, 1990.

Faragher, John Mack. *Daniel Boone: The Life and Legend of an American Pioneer.* New York: Henry Holt, 1992.

_____. *Rereading Frederick Jackson Turner: "The Significance of the Frontier in American History" and Other Essays.* New Haven: Yale University Press, 1998.

Farber, David. *The Rise and Fall of Modern American Conservatism: A Short History.* Princeton: Princeton University Press, 2010.

Federici, Michael P. *The Political Philosophy of Alexander Hamilton.* Baltimore: The Johns Hopkins University Press, 2012.

Fletcher, Jefferson B. "The Visual Image in Literature." *Sewanee Review* 6.4 (Oct. 1898): 385–401.

Flint, Timothy. *The First White Man of the West, or the Life and Exploits of Colonel Daniel Boone.* 1833. Cincinnati: E. Morgan & Co., 1850.

Foner, Eric. *Freedom's Lawmakers: A Directory of Black Officeholders During Reconstruction.* New York: Oxford University Press, 1993.

Foord, John. "Agricultural and Other Resources of Cuba." *The Louisiana Planter and Sugar Manufacturer* 20.23 (4 Jun. 1898): 360–361.

Forty-Second Congress, Session II. "An Act to set apart a certain Tract of Land lying near the Head-waters of the Yellowstone River as a public Park." *U.S. Statutes at Large, Vol. 17.* (1 Mar. 1872): 32–33.

Frank v. Mangum. 237 US 309. Supreme Court of the United States. 1915. <http://supreme.justia.com/cases/federal/us/237/309/case.html>. 29 Jun. 2012.

Franklin, Benjamin. "Information to Those Who Would Remove to America." 1782. *The Writings of Benjamin Franklin, Volume VIII.* Albert Henry Smyth, ed. New York: MacMillan, 1906. 603–614.

Fresonke, Kris. *West of Emerson: The Design of Manifest Destiny.* Berkeley: University of California Press, 2003.

Gatewood, Jr., Willard B. *"Smoked Yankees" and the Struggle for Empire: Letters from Negro Soldiers, 1898-1902.* 1971. Fayetteville: University of Arkansas Press, 1987.

Geffert, Hannah. "They Heard His Call: The Local Black Community's Involvement in the Raid on Harpers Ferry." *Terrible Swift Sword: The Legacy of John Brown.* Peggy A. Russo and Paul Finkelman, eds. Athens: Ohio University Press, 2005. 23–45.

"Gen. Custer's Last Fight: Gen. Terry's Official Report." *New York Times.* New York, NY (9 Jul. 1876): 1.

George, Jr., Henry. *The Life of Henry George.* London: William Reeves, 1900.

Geronimo. *Geronimo's Story of His Life.* S. M. Barrett, ed. 1906. Williamstown: Corner House, 1973.

Goldberg, Robert A. "The Western Hero in Politics: Barry Goldwater, Ronald Reagan, and the Rise of the American Conservative Movement." *The Political Culture of the New West.* Jeff Roche, ed. Lawrence: University Press of Kansas, 2008. 13–50.

Gonzalez-Day, Ken. *Lynching in the West: 1850–1935.* Durham: Duke University Press, 2006.

Gosling, F. G. *Before Freud: Neurasthenia and the American Medical Community, 1870–1910*. Urbana: University of Illinois Press, 1987.
"Grand Thing: Our Victorious War with Spain." *Evening Journal* 65.21427 (22 Nov. 1898): 1.
Graulich, Melody. "Introduction." *Reading* The Virginian *in the New* West. Melody Graulich and Stephen Tatum, eds. Lincoln: University of Nebraska Press, 2003. xi–xix.
Graves, Robert. "The 'White City': Robert Graves Visits the World's Fair Grounds at Chicago." *Daily Spy*. Worcester, MA (22 Feb. 1893): 6.
Greeley, Horace. "The Preëmption System." *The New-Yorker* 5.23 (Saturday, 25 Aug. 1838): 361.
Green, Paul. *A History of Television's* The Virginian, *1962–1971*. Jefferson: McFarland, 2006.
Gressley, Gene M. "Teschemacher and deBillier Cattle Company: A Study of Eastern Capital on the Frontier." *Business History Review* 33.2 (1959): 121–137.
Grinnell, George Bird. "Big-Game Refuges." *American Big Game in Its Haunts: The Book of the Boone and Crockett Club*. George Bird Grinnell, ed. New York: Harper & Brothers, 1914. 442–454.
———. "The Boone and Crockett Club." *Forest and Stream* 31.26 (17 Jan. 1889): 513.
———. "The Boone and Crockett Club." *Forest and Stream* 40.3 (19 Jan. 1893): 49.
———. "Brief History of the Boone and Crockett Club." *Hunting at High Altitudes: The Book of the Boone and Crockett Club*. Ed. George Bird Grinnell. New York: Harper & Brothers, 1913. 433–491.
———. "In Buffalo Days." *American Big-Game Hunting: The Book of the Boone and Crockett Club*. Theodore Roosevelt and George Bird Grinnell, eds. New York: Forest and Stream, 1893. 155–211.
———. "Hunting Trips of a Ranchman [Book Review]." *Forest and Stream* 24.231 (2 Jul. 1885): 451.
———. "Introduction." *Hunting Trips of a Ranchman* [and] *Ranch Life and the Hunting Trail: The Works of Theodore Roosevelt*. National Edition. New York: Charles Scribner's Sons, 1926. xiii–xxv.
———. "Theodore Roosevelt." *American Big Game in Its Haunts: The Book of the Boone and Crockett Club*. George Bird Grinnell, ed. New York: Harper & Brothers, 1914. 13–24.
"Guarding the President." *Springfield Republican*. Springfield, MA (25 Sep. 1901): 6.
Gunn, Robert Lawrence. *Ethnology and Empire: Languages, Literature, and the Making of the North American Borderlands*. New York: New York University Press, 2015.
Hagedorn, Hermann. *Roosevelt in the Bad Lands*. Boston: Houghton Mifflin, 1930.
Halverson, Cathryn. *Playing House in the American West: Western Women's Life Narratives, 1839–1987*. Tuscaloosa: University of Alabama Press, 2013.
Handford, Thomas W. *Roosevelt: The Pride of the Rough Riders, an Ideal American*. Chicago: Donohue, Henneberry & Co., 1899.

Handley, William R. *Marriage, Violence, and the Nation in the American Literary West*. New York: Cambridge University Press, 2002.

Hanson, Paul. *Historical Dictionary of the French Revolution*. 2nd Ed. London: Roman & Littlefield, 2015.

Harper, J. Henry. *The House of Harper: A Century of Publishing in Franklin Square*. New York: Harper & Brothers, 1912.

Hartz, Louis. *The Liberal Tradition in America*. 1955. San Diego: Harcourt Brace, 1991.

Hawley, Joshua David. *Theodore Roosevelt: Preacher of Righteousness*. New Haven: Yale University Press, 2008.

Hay, John. *Addresses of John Hay*. 1890. New York: Century, 1906.

Helo, Ari. *Thomas Jefferson's Ethics and the Politics of Human Progress: The Morality of a Slaveholder*. Cambridge: Cambridge University Press, 2014.

Higinbotham, Harlow Niles. *Report of the President to the Board of Directors of the World's Columbian Exposition, Chicago, 1892–1893*. Chicago: Rand, McNally, 1898.

Higashi, Sumiko. *Cecil B. DeMille and American Culture: The Silent Era*. Berkeley: University of California Press, 1994.

Hill, Evan, et al. "'Straight to Gunshots': How a U.S. Task Force Killed an Antifa Activist." *New York Times*. New York, NY (13 Oct. 2020): <https://www.nytimes.com/2020/10/13/us/michael-reinoehl-antifa-portland-shooting.html>.

Himmelstein, Jerome L. *To the Right: The Transformation of American Conservatism*. Berkeley: University of California Press, 1990.

Hobbes, Thomas. *Leviathan*. 1651. A. R. Waller, ed. Cambridge: Cambridge University Press, 1904.

Hofstadter, Richard. *The American Political Tradition and the Men Who Made It*. 1948. New York: Vintage, 1973.

_____. *Social Darwinism in American Thought*. 1944. Boston: Beacon, 1992.

Holmes Jr., Oliver Wendell. "Buck v. Bell: 274 U.S. 200." 1927. *The Essential Holmes*. Richard A. Posner, ed. Chicago: University of Chicago Press, 1992. 103–105.

_____. "Codes, and the Arrangement of the Law." 1870. *The Collected Works of Justice Holmes, Volume 1*. Sheldon M. Novick, ed. Chicago: University of Chicago Press, 1995. 212–221.

_____. *The Common Law*. 1881. *The Collected Works of Justice Holmes, Volume 3*. Sheldon M. Novick, ed. Chicago: University of Chicago Press, 1995. 109–324.

_____. "The Soldier's Faith." 1895. *The Essential Holmes*. Richard A. Posner, ed. Chicago: University of Chicago Press, 1992. 87–93.

Hunter, Robert, ed. *The American Encyclopaedic Dictionary*. Chicago: R. S. Peale and J. A. Hill, 1897.

Hutson, Richard. "Early Film Versions of *The Virginian*." *Reading* The Virginian *in the New* West. Melody Graulich and Stephen Tatum, eds. Lincoln: University of Nebraska Press, 2003. 126–147.

"Indian Troubles." *Daily Courant*. Harford, CT (24 Apr. 1876): 3.

"Internal Policy." *The Quarterly Review* 42.83 (Jan. 1830): 228–277.

Jackson, Robert. "A Southern Sublimation: Lynching Film and the Reconstruction of American Memory." *The Southern Literary Journal* 40.2 (Spring 2008): 102–120.

Jacobs, Wilbur R. *The Historical World of Frederick Jackson Turner: With Selections From his Correspondence.* New Haven: Yale University Press, 1968.

James, William. "Herbert Spencer." *Atlantic Monthly* 94.561 (Jul. 1904): 99–107.

Jenson, Joan M. and Darlis A. Miller. "The Gentle Tamers Revisited: New Approaches to the History of Women in the American West." *Women and Gender in the American West.* Eds. Mary Ann Irwin and James F. Brooks. Albuquerque: University of New Mexico Press, 2004. 9–35.

Johannsen, Robert W. *Stephen A. Douglas.* 1973. Champaign: University of Illinois Press, 1997.

Jones, W. "Frederic Remington's Pictures of Frontier Life." *Harvard Monthly* 27.5 (Feb. 1899): 186–190.

Jordan, David M. *FDR, Dewey, and the Election of 1944.* Bloomington: Indiana University Press, 2011.

Kaminsky, Stuart M. *Coop: The Life and Legend of Gary Cooper.* New York: St. Martin's, 1980.

Kammen, Michael G. *People of Paradox: An Inquiry Concerning the Origins of American Civilization.* 1972. Ithaca: Cornell University Press, 1990.

Kaplan, Amy. "Nation, Region, and Empire." *The Columbia History of the American Novel.* Eds. Emory Elliott et al. New York: Columbia University Press, 1991. 240–266.

Kasson, Joy S. *Buffalo Bill's Wild West: Celebrity, Memory, and Popular History.* New York: Hill and Wang, 2000.

Kateb, George. *Emerson and Self-Reliance.* 1995. Lanham: Rowman & Littlefield, 2002.

Kazin, Michael. *A Godly Hero: The Life of William Jennings Bryan.* New York: Anchor, 2007.

Kegel, W. Percy. "Throngs Heard Roosevelt Speak: The Vice President Given a Continuous Ovation During the Exercises of the Morning." *Colorado Springs Gazette.* Colorado Springs, CO (3 Aug. 1901): 6, 9.

Kidd, Benjamin. *Social Evolution.* New York: Macmillan, 1894.

King, Charles. *Campaigning with Crooks and Stories of Army Life.* New York: Harper and Brothers, 1890.

Kipling, Rudyard. *The Second Jungle Book.* 1895. Leipzig: Bernhard Tauchnitz, 1897.

Kirk, Russell. *The Conservative Mind.* 1953. Miami: BN, 2008.

Kley, Dale Van, ed. *The French Idea of Freedom: The Old Regime and the Declaration of Rights of 1789.* Stanford: Stanford University Press, 1994.

Kobes Du Mez, Kristin. *Jesus and John Wayne: How White Evangelicals Corrupted a Faith and Fractured a Nation.* New York: W. W. Norton, 2020.

Kolko, Gabriel. *The Triumph of Conservatism: A Reinterpretation of American History, 1900–1916.* New York: Free Press, 1977.

Kollin, Susan. "Wister and the 'New West.'" *Reading* The Virginian *in the New* West. Melody Graulich and Stephen Tatum, eds. Lincoln: University of Nebraska Press, 2003. 233–254.

Kuenz, Jane. "The Cowboy Businessman and 'The Course of Empire': Owen Wister's *The Virginian.*" *Cultural Critique* 48 (Spring 2001): 98–128.
Ladino, Jennifer K. *Reclaiming Nostalgia: Longing for Nature in American Literature.* Charlottesville: University of Virginia Press, 2012.
Lakoff, George. *The Political Mind: Why You Can't Understand 21st-Century Politics with an 18th-Century Brain.* New York: Viking, 2008.
Lamarck, J. B. *Zoological Philosophy: An Exposition with Regard to the Natural History of Animals.* Trans. Hugh Elliott. 1809. London: Macmillan, 1914.
Lamont, Victoria. *Westerns: A Women's History.* Lincoln: University of Nebraska Press, 2016.
Larson, Kerry. "Illiberal Emerson." *Nineteenth-Century Prose* 33.1 (2006): 28–72.
Lawson, Joseph A. "Legal By-Ways." *Proceedings of the New York State Bar Association Twenty-Fifth Annual Meeting.* Albany: Argus, 1902. 422–428.
Lears, T. J. Jackson. *No Place of Grace: Antimodernism and the Transformation of American Culture, 1880–1920.* New York: Pantheon, 1981.
Leckie, William H., with Shirley A. Leckie. *The Buffalo Soldiers: A Narrative of the Black Calvary in the West.* Rev. ed. Norman: University of Oklahoma Press, 2003.
Leeson, Michael A., ed. *History of Montana, 1739–1885.* Chicago: Warner, Beers & Co., 1885.
LeMenager, Stephanie. *Manifest and Other Destinies: Territorial Fictions of the Nineteenth-Century United States.* Lincoln: University of Nebraska Press, 2004.
Lemons, William E. "History by Unreliable Narrators: Sitting Bull's Circus Horse." *Montana: The Magazine of Western History* 45.4 (Autumn/Winter 1995): 64–74.
Lichtman, Allan J. *White Protestant Nation: The Rise of the American Conservative Movement.* New York: Grove, 2008.
The Life, Trial and Execution of Captain John Brown, Known as 'Old Brown of Ossawatomie,' With a Full Account of the Attempted Insurrection at Harper's Ferry. New York: Robert M. De Witt, 1859.
Limerick, Patricia Nelson. *The Legacy of Conquest: The Unbroken Past of the American West.* 1987. New York: W. W. Norton, 2006.
Lincoln, Abraham. "Address at Cooper Institute, New York City." *Lincoln: Speeches and Writings, 1859–1865.* New York: Library of America, 1989. 111–129.
Lindsey, Robert. "A Cowboy Hero, Myth and Reality." *New York Times.* New York, NY (21 Jan. 1981): B7.
"Literature: A Social Economist's Land Tax Cure for Poverty." *New York Herald.* New York, NY (15 Dec. 1879): 6.
Locke, John. [Selections from] *The First Treatise of Government.* 1689. *The Selected Political Writings of John Locke.* Paul E. Sigmund, ed. New York: W. W. Norton, 2005. 5–16.
———. *The Second Treatise of Government.* 1689. *The Selected Political Writings of John Locke.* Paul E. Sigmund, ed. New York: W. W. Norton, 2005. 17–125.
Lockhart, John Gibson. *The History of Napoleon Buonaparte.* London: J. M. Dent, 1906.
Lora, Ronald. "*Conservative*: 1898-1902." *The Conservative Press in Twentieth-Century America.* Ronald Lora and William Henry Longton, eds. Westport: Greenwood, 1999. 23–36.

Lough, Alex Wagner. "Henry George, Frederick Jackson Turner, and the 'Closing' of the American Frontier." *California History* 89.2 (2012): 4–23.

Lovelace, Carl. "Beautiful Letter, Waco Rough Rider: Carl Lovelace Writes a Graphic Description of Hot Times Around Santiago. [Letter dated 26 Jul. 1898.] *Times-Herald*. Waco, TX (15 August 1898): 5.

Lowenberg, Bert James. *Darwinism Comes to America: 1859–1900*. Philadelphia: Fortress, 1969.

Lowenthal, David. "Nostalgia Tells It Like It Wasn't." *The Imagined Past: History and Nostalgia*. Malcolm Chase and Christopher Shaw, eds. New York: Manchester University Press, 1989. 18–32.

Lowndes, Joseph E. *From the New Deal to the New Right: Race and the Southern Origins of Modern Conservatism*. New Haven: Yale University Press, 2008.

Lynch, John R. *The Facts of Reconstruction*. New York: Neale, 1913.

MacFarquhar, Neil. "Suspect in Kenosha Killings Lionized the Police." *New York Times*. New York, NY (27 Aug. 2020): < https://www.nytimes.com/2020/08/27/us/kyle-rittenhouse-kenosha.html>.

Mackie, J. L. "The Law of the Jungle: Moral Alternatives and Principles of Evolution." *Philosophy* 53.206 (1978): 455–464.

Marshall, Arthur F. "Socialism: Its Harm and Its Apology." *The American Catholic Quarterly Review* 18.69 (Jan. 1893): 151–165.

Martin, E.S. "This Busy World." *Harper's Weekly* 38.1944 (11 Aug. 1894): 754.

_____. "This Busy World." *Harper's Weekly* 38.1979 (24 Nov. 1894): 1114.

Marx, Karl, and Friedrich Engels. *The Communist Manifesto*. 1848. Jeffrey C. Isaac, ed. New Haven: Yale University Press, 2012.

McCloskey, Robert Green. *American Conservatism in the Age of Enterprise, 1865–1910*. Cambridge: Harvard University Press, 1951.

McCullough, David. *Mornings on Horseback: The Story of an Extraordinary Family, a Vanished Way of Life, and the Unique Child Who Became Theodore Roosevelt*. 1981. New York, Simon and Schuster, 2001.

McDermott, John D. "Writers in Judgment: Historiography of the Johnson County War." *Wyoming Annals* (Winter 1993–1994): 20–35.

McGirr, Lisa. *Suburban Warriors: The Origins of the New Right*. Princeton: Princeton University Press, 2001.

McLaughlin, James. *My Friend the Indian*. Boston: Houghton Mifflin, 1910.

"Men's Gift to Roosevelt: The Rough Riders Present Their Colonel with a Replica of 'The Broncho Buster.'" *New York Times*. New York, NY (14 Sep. 1898): 3.

Mexal, Stephen J. *Reading for Liberalism: The* Overland Monthly *and the Writing of the Modern American West*. Lincoln: University of Nebraska Press, 2013.

Meyers, Jeffrey. *Gary Cooper: American Hero*. New York: Morrow, 1998.

Middleton, Stephen. *Black Congressmen During Reconstruction: A Documentary Sourcebook*. Westport: Greenwood, 2002.

Miles, Nelson A. *Personal Recollections and Observations of General Nelson A. Miles*. Chicago: Werner, 1897.

Mill, John Stuart. "On Liberty." *J.S. Mill: On Liberty and Other Writings*. 1859. Stefan Collini, ed. Cambridge: Cambridge University Press, 1989. 1–116.

Mitchell, Lee Clark. "'When You Call Me That . . . ': Tall Talk and Male Hegemony in *The Virginian*." *PMLA* 102.1 (1987): 66–77.
Mitchell, Mary. "Don't Make 17-Year-Old Kenosha Shooter a Hero." *Chicago Sun-Times*. Chicago, IL (28 Aug. 2020): <https://chicago.suntimes.com/opinion/2020/8/28/21406302/kenosha-kyle-rittenhouse-no-hero-jacob-blake>.
Mitchell, S. Weir. "Rest in the Treatment of Nervous Disease." *A Series of American Clinical Lectures Volume I, Number IV*. E. C. Seguin, ed. New York: G. P. Putnam's Sons, 1875. 83–102.
_____. *Wear and Tear: Or, Hints for the Overworked*. 1871. Philadelphia: J. B. Lippincott, 1897.
Mokler, Alfred James. *History of Natrona County, Wyoming: 1888–1922*. Chicago: Lakeside, 1923.
Morison, Elting E., ed. *The Letters of Theodore Roosevelt, Volume I: The Years of Preparation, 1868–1898*. Cambridge: Harvard University Press, 1951.
_____. *The Letters of Theodore Roosevelt, Volume II: The Years of Preparation, 1898–1900*. Cambridge: Harvard University Press, 1951.
_____. *The Letters of Theodore Roosevelt, Volume III: The Square Deal, 1901–1903*. Cambridge: Harvard University Press, 1951.
_____. *The Letters of Theodore Roosevelt, Volume IV: Panama: From Acquisition to Commission, continued, January 1904–March 1904*. Cambridge: Harvard University Press, 1951.
_____. *The Letters of Theodore Roosevelt, Volume VI: The Big Stick, 1907–1909*. Cambridge: Harvard University Press, 1952.
Morris, Edmund. *The Rise of Theodore Roosevelt*. New York: Coward, McCann & Geoghean, 1979.
Morton, J. Sterling. "The Conservative." *The Conservative* 1.1 (Jul. 14, 1898): 1.
Moscow, Warren. "Dewey Demands Old-Age Pensions for All Classes." *New York Times*. New York, NY (23 Sep. 1944): 1, 9.
"Mr. Bryan's Radical New Party." *The Review of Reviews* 14.4 (Oct. 1896): 391–392.
Mulligan, Hugh A. "Goldwater Character Owes Much to Arizona." *Los Angeles Times*. Los Angeles, CA (30 Aug. 1964): C2, C3.
Nash, George H. *The Conservative Intellectual Movement in America Since 1945*. 1976. Wilmington: Intercollegiate Studies Institute, 1996.
"Nebraska at the Fair: Twenty-Five Thousand Visitors See the State Headquarters Dedicated." *Daily Inter Ocean* 22.77. Chicago, IL (9 Jun. 1893): 7.
Nelson, John S. *Cowboy Politics: Myths and Discourses in Popular Westerns from* The Virginian *to* Unforgiven *and* Deadwood. Lanham: Lexington, 2017.
Newfield, Christopher. *The Emerson Effect: Individualism and Submission in America*. Chicago: University of Chicago Press, 1996.
Novick, Sheldon M., ed. *The Collected Work of Justine Holmes, Volume 1*. Chicago: University of Chicago Press, 1995.
_____. *Honorable Justice: The Life of Oliver Wendell Holmes*. Boston: Little, Brown, 1989.
"Nubs of News." *Daily Herald* 12.164. Grand Forks, ND (10 May 1893): 8.

Oakeshott, Michael. "On Being Conservative." 1956. *How Conservatives Think.* Philip W. Buck, ed. Middlesex: Penguin, 1975. 153–162.

Olmsted, Kathryn S. *Right Out of California: The 1930s and the Big Business Roots of Modern Conservatism.* New York: The New Press, 2015.

Olson, James C. *J. Sterling Morton.* Lincoln: University of Nebraska Press, 1942.

Ostrander, Gilman M. "Turner and the Germ Theory." *Agricultural History* 32.4 (1958): 258–261.

Page, Thomas Nelson. *The Old Dominion: Her Making and Her Manners.* 1908. New York: Charles Scribner's Sons, 1910.

———. *The Old South: Essays Social and Political.* New York: Charles Scribner's Sons, 1892.

Paine, Thomas. "*The American Crisis*: Number I, December 19, 1776." *Thomas Paine: Collected Writings.* New York: Library of America, 1955. 91–99.

Palmer, Kyle. "Dewey Coliseum Address Cheered." *Los Angeles Times.* Los Angeles, CA (23 Sep. 1944): 1, 2.

Palmquist, Peter E. and Thomas R. Kailbourn. *Pioneer Photographers of the Far West: A Biographical Dictionary, 1840–1865.* Stanford: Stanford University Press, 2000.

Parker, Edith H. "William Graham Sumner and the Frontier." *Southwest Review* 41 (Autumn 1956): 357–365.

Payne, Darwin. *Owen Wister: Chronicle of the West, Gentleman of the East.* Dallas: Southern Methodist University Press, 1985.

Penry, Tara. "The Chinese in Bret Harte's *Overland*: A Context for Truthful James." *American Literary Realism* 43.1 (2010): 74–82.

Perlstein, Rick. *Before the Storm: Barry Goldwater and the Unmaking of the American Consensus.* New York: Hill and Wang, 2001.

Perry, Bliss, ed. *The Heart of Emerson's Journals.* 1926. New York: Dover, 1995.

"Personal Tributes [to J. Sterling Morton]." *The Conservative* 4.47 (May 29, 1902): 4–10.

Pettigrew, R. F. "The Real Roosevelt." *The Public* 19.967 (13 Oct. 1916): 978–979.

Philips, James R. "The Little-Known Negro Rough Riders." *Negro History Bulletin* 27.3 (1963): 59.

"The Pitt Clubs Defended." *The Antijacobin Review* 217.50 (Jun. 1816): 550–567.

Pierce, Jason E. *Making the White Man's West: Whiteness and the Creation of the American West.* Boulder: University Press of Colorado, 2016.

Poirier, Suzanne. "The Weir Mitchell Rest Cure: Doctors and Patients." *Women's Studies* 10.1 (1983): 15–40.

Porter, Robert P. "Distribution of Population According to Density: 1890." Extra Census Bulletin 2 (20 Apr. 1891). Washington: Department of the Interior, U.S. Census Office. 1–4.

———. "The Future of Cuba." *The North American Review* 168.509 (Apr. 1899): 418–424.

Postell, Joseph W., and Johnathan O'Neill. *Toward an American Conservatism: Constitutional Conservatism During the Progressive Era.* New York: Palgrave MacMillan, 2013.

"President at Cannon's Home." *Daily Republican.* Springfield, MA (5 Jun. 1903): 7.

"President Roosevelt: New Chief Executive." *The Columbus Enquirer-Sun.* Columbus, GA (15 Sept. 1901): 12.

Pringle, Henry F. *Theodore Roosevelt: A Biography.* New York: Harcourt, Brace, 1931.

Prodger, Phillip. *Time Stands Still: Muybridge and the Instantaneous Photography Movement.* New York: Oxford University Press, 2003.

Punke, Michael. *Last Stand: George Bird Grinnell, the Battle to Save the Buffalo, and the Birth of the New West.* New York: Smithsonian, 2007.

Putnam, Carleton. *Theodore Roosevelt, Volume I: The Formative Years, 1858–1886.* New York: Charles Scribner's Sons, 1958.

Quinn, Sally. "The 1980 Way: Go West, Old Party." *The Washington Post.* Washington, DC (17 July 1980): D1, D3.

Rabiee, Robert Yusef. "Feudalism, Individualism, and Authority in Later Emerson." *ESQ* 62.1 (2016): 77–114.

Randolph, Thomas Jefferson, ed. *Memoirs, Correspondence, and Private Papers of Thomas Jefferson, Vol. I.* London: Henry Colburn and Richard Bentley, 1829.

Reagan, Ronald. *Speaking My Mind: Selected Speeches.* New York: Simon and Schuster, 1989.

Reddin, Paul. *Wild West Shows.* Urbana: University of Illinois Press, 1999.

Reid, Captain Mayne. *The Scalp Hunters.* London: Charles J. Skeet, 1851.

Reid, Elizabeth. *Mayne Reid: A Memoir of His Life.* London: Ward and Downey, 1890.

Reif, Rita. "Silent Witnesses to War and Fellowship." *New York Times.* New York, NY (23 Dec. 2001): AR38.

Reiger, John F. *American Sportsmen and the Origins of Conservation.* 1975. 3rd ed. Corvallis: Oregon State University Press, 2001.

Remington, Frederic. "An Appeal for Justice." 1892. *The Collected Writings of Frederic Remington.* Peggy and Harold Samuels, eds. New York: Doubleday, 1979. 94–95.

———. "Buffalo Bill in London." *Harper's Weekly* (3 Sep. 1892): 847.

———. "Chasing a Major-General." 1890. *The Collected Writings of Frederic Remington.* Peggy and Harold Samuels, eds. New York: Doubleday, 1979. 50–56.

———. "The Colonel of the First Cycle Infantry." *Harper's Weekly* 39.2004 (18 May 1895): 468–469.

———. "A Few Words From Mr. Remington." *Collier's* 34.25 (18 Mar.1905): 16.

———. "A Gallop Through the Midway." 1893. *The Collected Writings of Frederic Remington.* Peggy and Harold Samuels, eds. New York: Doubleday, 1979. 110–113.

———. *Men with the Bark On.* New York: Harper & Brothers, 1900.

———. "A Scout with the Buffalo-Soldiers." 1889. *The Collected Writings of Frederic Remington.* Peggy and Harold Samuels, eds. New York: Doubleday, 1979. 22–30.

———. "The Sioux Outbreak in South Dakota." 1891. *The Collected Writings of Frederic Remington.* Peggy and Harold Samuels, eds. New York: Doubleday, 1979. 67–69.

_____. "With the Fifth Corps." *Harper's New Monthly Magazine* 97.582 (Nov. 1898): 962–975.
Report: Reports of Senate Committees, 36th Congress, 1st Session, No. 278; Testimony: Testimony of Lewis W. Washington, January 5, 1860, 29–40.
"Representative Men [review of Emerson's *Representative Men*]" *The Eclectic Magazine* 26.3 (Jul. 1852): 360–368.
"Republicans for Roosevelt: A Strong Partisan Muster at Cooper Institute." *New York Herald*. New York, NY (28 Oct. 1886): 4.
"[Review of] *French and German Socialism in Modern Time*s [by Richard T. Ely]." *The Popular Science Monthly* 24 (Nov. 1883): 122–123.
"Richard Harding Davis." *Daily Independent*. Harrisburg, PA (27 Dec. 1898): 4.
Richardson, Heather Cox. *How the South Won the Civil War: Oligarchy, Democracy, and the Continuing Fight for the Soul of America*. New York: Oxford University Press, 2020.
_____. *To Make Men Free: A History of the Republican Party*. New York: Basic Books, 2014.
Richardson, Jr. Robert D. *Emerson: The Mind on Fire*. Berkeley: University of California Press, 1995.
"*Richmond Whig*, 'Editorial,' November 18, 1859." *The Tribunal: Responses to John Brown and the Harpers Ferry Raid*. Ed. John Stauffer and Zoe Trodd. Cambridge: Belknap, 2012. 257–258.
Rico, Monica. *Nature's Noblemen: Transatlantic Masculinities and the Nineteenth-Century American West*. New Haven: Yale University Press, 2013.
Robin, Corey. *The Reactionary Mind: Conservatism from Edmund Burke to Sarah Palin*. New York: Oxford University Press, 2011.
Robinson, Corinne Roosevelt. *My Brother Theodore Roosevelt*. New York: Charles Scribner's Sons, 1921.
Robinson, Forrest G. "The Roosevelt-Wister Connection: Some Notes on the West and the Uses of History." *Western American Literature* 14.2 (1979): 95–114.
Rogers, W.A. *A World Worth While: A Record of "Auld Acquaintance."* New York: Harper & Brothers, 1922.
"Roosevelt Accepts a Command." *The Sun*. New York, NY (26 Apr. 1898): 5.
"Roosevelt as a Factor." *Idaho Falls Times*. Idaho Falls, ID (13 Nov. 1902): 2.
"Roosevelt to Colored Men." *New York Times*. New York, NY (15 Oct. 1898): 2.
Roosevelt, Theodore. *An Autobiography*. 1913. New York: Charles Scribner's Sons, 1920.
_____. "The Boone and Crockett Club." *Harper's Weekly* 37 (18 Mar. 1893): 267.
_____. "Citizenship in a Republic." *History as Literature and Other Essays*. New York: Charles Scribner's Sons, 1913. 135–174.
_____. "A Colonial Survival." *The Cosmopolitan* 14.2 (Dec. 1892): 229–236.
_____. "Coursing the Prongbuck." *American Big-Game Hunting: The Book of the Boone and Crockett Club*. Theodore Roosevelt and George Bird Grinnell, eds. New York: Forest and Stream Publishing Co., 1893. 129–139.
_____. "Degeneration and Evolution II: Kidd's 'Social Evolution.'" *The North American Review* 161.464 (Jul. 1895): 94–109.

———. *Diary of Theodore Roosevelt from 1-31 August 1871.* Theodore Roosevelt Collection. MS Am 1454.55 (7). Harvard College Library. Theodore Roosevelt Digital Library. Dickinson State University.

———. "History as Literature." *History as Literature and Other Essays.* New York: Charles Scribner's Sons, 1913. 1–36.

———. *Hunting Trips of a Ranchman.* New York: G.P. Putnam's Sons, 1885.

———. "Message Communicated to the Two Houses of Congress at the Beginning of the First Session of the Fifty-Ninth Congress, December 5, 1905." *Presidential Address and State Papers of Theodore Roosevelt, Part Four.* New York: P.F. Collier & Son, 1906. 560–658.

———. "Personal Diary 1880, Jan. 1-Dec. 31." Reel 429, Theodore Roosevelt Papers, Manuscript Division, Library of Congress, Washington, DC.

———. "Personal Diary 1884, Feb. 14-Dec. 17" Reel 430, Theodore Roosevelt Papers, Manuscript Division, Library of Congress, Washington, DC.

———. "The Pioneer Spirit and American Problems." *The Outlook* 96.2 (10 Sep. 1910): 56–60.

———. *Ranch Life and the Hunting-Trail.* 1888. New York: The Century Co., 1902.

———. *The Rough Riders.* New York: P.F. Collier & Son, 1899.

———. "The Rough Riders: The Cavalry at Santiago." *Scribner's Magazine* 25.4 (Apr. 1899): 420–440.

———. "Sheriff's Work on a Ranch." *The Century Magazine* 36.6 (May 1888): 39–52.

———. "The Strenuous Life." 1899. *The Strenuous Life: Essays and Addresses.* New York: The Century Co., 1905. 1–21.

———. "The Trusts, the People, and the Square Deal." *The Outlook* (18 Nov. 1911): 649–656.

———. "Washington's Forgotten Maxim." 1897. *American Ideals.* New York: G.P. Putnam's Sons, 1920. 240–262.

———. *The Wilderness Hunter.* New York: G. P. Putnam's Sons, 1893.

———. "Wilderness Reserves." *American Big Game in Its Haunts: The Book of the Boone and Crockett Club.* George Bird Grinnell, ed. New York: Harper & Brothers, 1914. 23–51.

———. *The Winning of the West Volume I: From the Alleghanies to the Mississippi, 1769–1776.* New York: G.P. Putnam's Sons, 1889.

———. *The Winning of the West Volume II: From the Alleghanies to the Mississippi, 1777–1783.* New York: G.P. Putnam's Sons, 1897.

———. *The Winning of the West, Volume III: The Founding of the Trans-Alleghany Commonwealths, 1784–1790.* New York: G. P. Putnam's Sons, 1894.

Roosevelt, Theodore, and George Bird Grinnell, eds. *American Big-Game Hunting: The Book of the Boone and Crockett Club.* New York: Forest and Stream, 1893.

———. "The Boone and Crockett Club." *American Big-Game Hunting: The Book of the Boone and Crockett Club.* Theodore Roosevelt and George Bird Grinnell, eds. New York: Forest and Stream, 1893. 9–15.

Rosen, Eliot A. *The Republican Party in the Age of Roosevelt: Sources of Anti-Government Conservatism in the United States.* Charlottesville: University of Virginia Press, 2014.

"The Rough Riders." *Evening Star.* Washington, DC (19 May 1898): 11.
Rusk, Ralph L., ed. *The Letters of Ralph Waldo Emerson, Volume One.* New York: Columbia University Press, 1939.
Russell, Don. *The Lives and Legends of Buffalo Bill.* Norman: University of Oklahoma Press, 1960.
Russett, Cynthia Eagle. *Darwin in America: The Intellectual Response: 1865–1912.* San Francisco: W. H. Freeman, 1976.
Rydell, Robert W., and Rob Kroes. *Buffalo Bill in Bologna: The Americanization of the World, 1869–1922.* Chicago: University of Chicago Press, 2005.
Safire, William. "Ronnie Le Cowboy." *New York Times.* New York, NY (16 Jun. 1980): A23.
Samet, Elizabeth D. *Willing Obedience: Citizens, Soldiers, and the Progress of Consent in America, 1776–1898.* Stanford: Stanford University Press, 2004.
Samuels, Peggy and Harold Samuels. *Frederic Remington: A Biography.* New York: Doubleday, 1982.
_____. *Teddy Roosevelt at San Juan: The Making of a President.* College Station: Texas A&M University Press, 1997.
Sanial, Lucien. *The Socialist Almanac and Treasury of Facts: Volume I, Number 1.* New York: Socialist Labor Party of the United States, 1898.
Scharnhorst, Gary. *Bret Harte: Opening the American Literary West.* Norman: University of Oklahoma Press, 2000.
_____. *Owen Wister and the West.* Norman: University of Oklahoma Press, 2015.
Schneider, Gregory L. *The Conservative Century: From Reaction to Revolution.* Lanham: Rowman and Littlefield, 2009.
Schoenwald, Jonathan. *A Time for Choosing: The Rise of Modern American Conservatism.* New York: Oxford University Press, 2001.
Shaler, N.S. "An Ex-Southerner in South Carolina." *Atlantic Monthly* 26.153 (Jul. 1870): 53–62.
"In Short Meter." *News Tribune.* Duluth, MN (14 Apr. 1893): 1.
"Sketch of William Graham Sumner." *Popular Science Monthly* 35 (Jun. 1889): 261–268.
Slotkin, Richard. *Gunfighter Nation: The Myth of the Frontier in Twentieth-Century America.* Norman: University of Oklahoma Press, 1992.
Smith, Franklin. "Signs of Decadence in the United States." *The Conservative Review* 5.2 (Sep. 1901): 193–211.
Smith, Hedrick. "Reagan Goal: Dispel Doubt." *New York Times.* New York, NY (11 Nov. 1981): A1.
Smith, Helena Huntington. *The War on Powder River.* New York: McGraw-Hill, 1966.
Smith, Henry Nash. *Virgin Land: The American West as Symbol and Myth.* Cambridge: Harvard University Press, 1950.
Smith, Joseph. "The Spanish-American War: Land Battles in Cuba, 1895–1898." *Military Power: Land Warfare in Theory and Practice.* 1997. Brian Holden Reid, ed. London: Routledge, 2013. 37–58.

Smith, Rogers M. *Stories of Peoplehood: The Politics and Morals of Political Membership.* Cambridge: Cambridge University Press, 2003.

Snyder, Carl. "Engineer Ferris and His Wheel." *The Review of Reviews* 8.3 (Sep. 1893): 269–276.

Sobel, Robert. *The Money Manias: The Eras of Great Speculation in America, 1770–1970.* 1973. Washington: Beard Books, 2000.

Spencer, Herbert. *An Autobiography: Volume I.* New York: D. Appleton, 1904.

———. "The Evanescence of Evil." *On Social Evolution: Selected Writings.* J. D. Y. Peel, ed. Chicago: University of Chicago Press, 1972. 8–13.

———. "The Social Organism." *On Social Evolution: Selected Writings.* J. D. Y. Peel, ed. Chicago: University of Chicago Press, 1972. 53–70.

———. "Social Statics and Social Dynamics." *On Social Evolution: Selected Writings.* J. D. Y. Peel, ed. Chicago: University of Chicago Press, 1972. 17–29.

Splete, Allen P. and Marilyn D. Splete. *Frederic Remington: Selected Letters.* New York: Abbeville Press, 1988.

Stanlis, Peter James. *Edmund Burke and the Natural Law.* Ann Arbor: University of Michigan Press, 1958.

Steiner, Michael C. "Frederick Jackson Turner and Western Regionalism." *Writing Western History: Essays on Major Western Historians.* Richard W. Etulain, ed. Albuquerque: University of New Mexico Press, 1991. 103–135.

Stevens, Robert. *Law School: Legal Education in America from the 1850s to the 1980s.* Chapel Hill: University of North Carolina Press, 1983.

Stevens, Stuart. *It Was All a Lie: How the Republican Party Became Donald Trump.* New York: Knopf, 2020.

Stoner, Jr., James R. *Common Law and Liberal Theory: Coke, Hobbes, and the Origins of American Constitutionalism.* Kansas: University Press of Kansas, 1992.

"Subscribers for 1880." *The Harvard Register* 2.6 (Dec. 1880): 247–250.

Sullivan, D.J. "[Letter to the] Editor Courier." *Prescott Mourning Courier.* Prescott, AZ (10 Aug. 1901): 2.

Sumner, William Graham. *Folkways: A Study of the Sociological Importance of Usages, Manners, Customs, Mores, and Morals.* Boston: Ginn and Company, 1906.

Tanenhaus, Sam. *The Death of Conservatism.* New York: Random House, 2009.

Tatum, Stephen. *In the Remington Moment.* Lincoln: University of Nebraska Press, 2010.

Theodore Roosevelt National Park. Theodore Roosevelt Digital Library. Dickinson State University. <theodorerooseveltcenter.org>.

Thomas, Addison C. *Roosevelt Among the People.* Chicago: L.W. Walter Company, 1910.

Thomas, Augustus. "Recollections of Frederic Remington." *The Century* 86.3 (Jul. 1913): 354–361.

Thoreau, Henry David. *Walden.* 1854. Princeton, NJ: Princeton University Press, 1989.

Thornton, Russell. "The Demography of the Trail of Tears Period: A New Estimate of Cherokee Population Losses." *Cherokee Removal: Before and After.* William L. Anderson, ed. Athens: University of Georgia Press, 1991. 75–95.

Thrush, Glenn. "Full Transcript: President Trump's Republican National Convention Speech." *New York Times*. New York, NY (28 Aug. 2020): <https://www.nytimes.com/2020/08/28/us/politics/trump-rnc-speech-transcript.html>.

Tolstoï, Lyof N [Leo Tolstoy]. *Anna Karénina* [Vols. I-III]. Nathan Haskell Dole, trans. New York: Thomas Y. Crowell & Co., 1899.

Trilling, Lionel. *The Liberal Imagination*. 1950. New York: New York Review Books, 2008.

Turner, Frederick Jackson. "Contributions of the West to American Democracy." *Atlantic Monthly* 91.543 (Jan. 1903): 83–95.

———. "Dominant Forces in Western Life" *Atlantic Monthly* 79.474 (Apr. 1897): 433–443.

———. "The Problem of the West." *Atlantic Monthly* 78.67 (Sep. 1896): 289–297.

———. "Roosevelt's Winning of the West." *The Nation* 60.1552 (28 Mar. 1895): 240–242.

———. "The Significance of the Frontier in American History." 1893. *Annual Report of the American Historical Association for the Year 1893*. Washington: Government Printing Office, 1894. 199–227.

———. "Social Forces in American History." *The American Historical Review* 16.2 (1911): 217–233.

Ulman, Lloyd. *The Rise of the National Trade Union*. Cambridge: Harvard University Press, 1955.

Utley, Robert M. *The Indian Frontier of the American West, 1846–1890*. Albuquerque: University of New Mexico Press, 1984.

———. *The Last Days of the Sioux Nation*. 2nd ed. New Haven: Yale University Press, 2004.

Van Dulken, Stephen. *American Inventions: A History of Curious, Extraordinary, and Just Plain Useful Patents*. New York: New York University Press, 2004.

Van Zanden, Jan L. "Wages and the Standard of Living in Europe, 1500-1800." *European Review of Economics History* 3.2 (1999): 175–197.

Vollweiler, Albert Tangeman. "Roosevelt's Ranch Life in North Dakota." *Quarterly Journal of the University of North Dakota* 9.1 (Oct. 1918): 31–49.

Vorpahl, Ben Merchant. *Frederic Remington and the West: With the Eye of the Mind*. Austin: University of Texas Press, 1978.

———. *My Dear Wister: The Frederic Remington-Owen Wister Letters*. Palo Alto: American West, 1972.

Waldrep, Christopher. *The Many Faces of Judge Lynch: Extralegal Violence and Punishment in America*. New York: Palgrave Macmillan, 2002.

Wallace, Alexander H. "A Rough Rider's Story: Alexander H. Wallace's Interesting Letters to His Sister, Mrs. S. F. Johnson." *Daily Eagle*. Brooklyn, NY (29 Jul. 1898): 10.

Wallace, Alfred Russel. *Darwinism: An Exposition of the Theory of Natural Selection with Some of its Applications*. London: Macmillan, 1891.

Ward, Lester F. *Neo-Darwinism and Neo-Lamarckism: Annual Address of the President of the Biological Society of Washington, Delivered January 24, 1891*. Washington: Gedney & Roberts, 1891.

Waring, Jr., George E. "The Horse in Motion." *The Century* 24.3 (Jul. 1882): 381–388.
Warren, Louis S. *Buffalo Bill's America: William Cody and the Wild West Show*. New York: Knopf, 2005.
Washington, Booker T. "Progress of the American Negro." 1904. *The Negro in Business*. Atlanta: Hertel, Jenkins & Co., 1907. 293–302.
_____. *Up from Slavery: An Autobiography*. New York: A.L. Burt Co., 1901.
Washington, Booker T., N. B. Wood, and Fannie Barrier Williams. *A New Negro for a New Century*. 1900. New York: Arno, 1969.
Watts, Sarah. *Rough Rider in the White House: Theodore Roosevelt and the Politics of Desire*. Chicago: University of Chicago Press, 2003.
Webster, Noah. *An American Dictionary of the English Language*. New York: Harper and Brothers, 1830.
_____. *An American Dictionary of the English Language*. New York: Harper and Brothers, 1844.
_____. *An American Dictionary of the English Language*. New York: Harper & Brothers, 1848.
_____. *An American Dictionary of the English Language*. Philadelphia: J. B. Lippincott & Co., 1857.
_____, Chauncey A. Goodrich. et. al. *An American Dictionary of the English Language*. Springfield: G&C Merriam, 1865.
Wenzer, Kenneth C., ed. *Henry George: Collected Journalistic Writings Volume I: The Early Years 1860–1879*. New York: M.E. Sharpe, 2003.
West, Cornel. *The American Evasion of Philosophy: A Genealogy of Pragmatism*. Madison: University of Wisconsin Press, 1989.
Wetmore, Helen Cody. *Buffalo Bill: Last of the Great Scouts: The Life Story of Colonel William F. Cody, "Buffalo Bill."* 1899. Lincoln: University of Nebraska Press, 1965.
White, G. Edward, ed. *The Common Law*. 1881. Oliver Wendell Holmes, Jr. Cambridge: Belknap, 2009.
_____. *The Eastern Establishment and the Western Experience: The West of Frederic Remington, Theodore Roosevelt, and Owen Wister*. New Haven: Yale University Press, 1968.
White, Richard. "Frederick Jackson Turner and Buffalo Bill." *The Frontier in American Culture*. James R. Grossman, ed. Berkeley: University of California Press, 1994. 7–66.
_____. *"It's Your Misfortune and None of My Own": A New History of the American West*. Norman: University of Oklahoma Press, 1991.
White, Trumbull. *Pictorial History of Our War with Spain for Cuba's Freedom*. N.P.: Freedom, 1898.
_____, and William Igleheart. *The World's Columbian Exposition, Chicago, 1893*. Philadelphia: International, 1893.
Whitman, Walt. "Song of Myself." 1855. *Song of Myself and Other Poems*. Robert Hass, ed. Berkeley: Counterpoint, 2010. 7–70.
"Wild West at the Garden: Opening of the Season of Buffalo Bill's Exhibition." *New York Tribune*. New York, NY (30 Mar. 1899): 4.

"Wild West Show Opens: Madison Square Garden Crowded with an Enthusiastic Audience." *New York Times*. New York, NY (30 Mar. 1899): 4.

Wilson, Conrad. "Suspect in Fatal Shooting of Portland Right-Wing Protester Killed by Law Enforcement." *NPR*. Washington, DC (4 Sept. 2020): <https://www.npr.org/2020/09/04/909515885/protester-suspected-in-portland-shooting-death-killed-by-law-enforcement>.

Wister, Fanny Kemble, ed. *Owen Wister Out West: His Journals and Letters*. Chicago: University of Chicago Press, 1958.

Wister, Owen. "Among the Cow-Boys—Random Notes of a Tenderfoot and Sportsman in Wyoming." 1892. *Journal of the West* 37.2 (1998): 64–69.

_____. "The Evolution of the Cow-Puncher." *Harper's New Monthly Magazine* 91.544 (Sep. 1895): 602–617.

_____. "The Game and the Nation." *Harper's New Monthly Magazine* 100.600 (May 1900): 884–905.

_____. *Lin McLean*. 1897. New York: Harper & Brothers, 1905.

_____. "Remington—An Appreciation." *Collier's* 34.25 (18 Mar. 18 1905): 15.

_____. *Roosevelt: The Story of a Friendship, 1880–1919*. New York: Macmillan Company, 1930.

_____. *The Virginian*. 1902. New York: Penguin, 1988.

_____. "The White Goat and His Country." *American Big-Game Hunting: The Book of the Boone and Crockett Club*. Theodore Roosevelt and George Bird Grinnell, eds. New York: Forest and Stream, 1893. 26–60.

"Wit and Humor." *Enquirer-Sun*. Columbus, GA (12 Jul. 1898): 6.

Witschi, Nicolas S. *Traces of Gold: California's Natural Resources and the Claim to Realism in Western American Literature*. Tuscaloosa: University of Alabama Press, 2002.

Woodworth-Ney, Laura E. *Women in the American West*. Santa Barbara: ABC-CLIO, 2008.

Worden, Daniel. *Masculine Style: The American West and Literary Modernism*. London: Palgrave Macmillan, 2011.

Wrobel, David M. *Global West, American Frontier: Travel, Empire, and Exceptionalism from Manifest Destiny to the Great Depression*. Albuquerque: University of New Mexico Press, 2013.

Yemma, John. "As Reagan Gallops Out of West, Mideast Jockeys for Position." *The Christian Science Monitor*. Boston, MA (20 Nov. 1980): <https://search.proquest.com/docview/1039012674?accountid=9840>. 29 Jan. 2018.

Young, Arthur Nichols. *The Single Tax Movement in the United States*. Princeton: Princeton University Press, 1916.

Zunac, Mark, ed. *Literature and the Conservative Ideal*. Lanham: Lexington, 2016.

Index

acquired traits: Lamarck and, 10, 55–57, 118, 120–21, 123, 139–40, 228, 287; Turner and, 230
Acton, Thomas C., 165n2
Adams, Henry Carter: democracy and, 132; socialism and, 33, 131–32, 175
Adams, Herbert Baxter, 219–22, 228
Adams, John (president), 100
African American Calvary Regiments: as buffalo soldiers, 274–75; on Kettle Hill, 14, 274–76, 290; Ninth and Tenth Calvary as, 14, 274–76, 282–84, 288, 290; Roosevelt, T., on, 7, 14, 275, 282–86. *See also* Blacks
Alcott, Bronson, 32, 109
Alden, Henry Mills, 192, 234–35
America: American west creating, 220, 223–25; artists changing, 68–69; Badlands freedom and, 62; characteristics of, 2–3; Chicago World's Fair on, 195–99, 201–2, 295; cowboys as, 237, 306; Darwin and, 120–22; European liberalism for conservatism and, 96–97, 109; frontier virtues and, 2–3, 221–25, 227–32, 236; on Indians, Mexicans and British, 62; individualism as, 102, 108, 307–8; Lamarck and, 120–21; merit and history of, 13; natural aristocracy and, 99–100, 133, 294, 305, 307; primitive west on, 1; as racist and antiracist, 81; Roosevelt, T., on, 178–79; socialism and, 130–32; "survival of the fittest" and, 120–22; as white identity, 7–8, 141–42, 182, 224; whites on Indians, 50–51, 141–42

American Big-Game Hunting, 201, 214–15
American conservatism, 16n36; aesthetics of, 5, 8; after Civil War, 127, 129–30; after World War II, 8, 10–11; aristocracy and, 135, 210, 301, 311; of art, literature, ideas, 11; from banking and western development, 5; from Darwinism, 3, 134–35; European liberalism for, 96–97, 109; for historical status quo, 7–8; principles of, 7; as self-reliance, 3; white males on, 6, 135–36
American west: America by, 220, 223–25; Badlands and, 62; Buffalo Bill's Wild West on, 79, 88–90, 156; census report on, 221–22, 231, 271; Chicago World's Fair and, 195–99, 201–2, 295; Cody, W., and, 4, 13, 81–84, 196, 294–95, 305–6, 309; conservative politics and, 28, 156,

335

306–8; Cuba as, 270–71; Darwinian fitness and, 1–3, 5, 307; democracy and, 211–12; as economic solution, 134; equality and, 20; freedom and, 60, 90, 142; free land and, 223, 227, 230–31; frontier virtues from, 2–3, 221–25, 227–32, 236; for future, 220; Harte stories on, 170, 234, 237, 287, 293, 306; as homogenizing, 53; for individual freedom, 24, 26, 28; law and, 75; laws of nature and, 21; Locke on, 97, 179; Louisiana Purchase for, 81, 101, 134, 229; lynching in, 298–99; for male neurasthenia, 4, 34–35; for manhood, 19, 62–63; nostalgia on, 161–62, 164–65; Paine and, 90; as passing away, 160–64, 235, 261, 290; for personal regeneration, 3–4; Porter on settlement and, 221, 271; race and, 5; railroads on, 23; Remington, F., capturing, 42–43, 47–50, 167–69; Republican Party as cowboys and, 305, 307; as retrogressions, 9–10, 145, 191, 215, 224–25, 281, 296; rich white males on, 135, 140; Roosevelt, T., on, 4–5, 58, 62, 139–41, 178–79; Roosevelt circle on aesthetics and, 14; self-reliance and, 9–10, 161, 163; stories on precarious, 11–12; with superior males, 62–63; as temporal shift, 37; U.S. government on, 24; values of primitive, 1; violence and romance in, 2; Wister and, 35–37, 75, 243–44, 300; Wister stories on, 13, 37, 192–93, 243–45, 247, 259, 261, 263–64, 293; writers on, 5–6, 15n21

Apache tribe, 49–51, 159, 170

Arapaho tribe, 85

aristocracy: American conservatism and, 135, 210, 301, 311; Bancroft and, 301; Burke and, 107, 127, 129; conservatism from, 99, 106, 109, 112, 127; cowboys as, 215, 263; Darwinian fitness and, 270; democracy and, 212; Emerson and, 107, 113n6, 127; of Europe, 110, 112, 196, 214, 243; as hierarchical society, 101; Holmes and, 4, 301; as inherited, 100; law and, 301; Morton, J., on, 213–14; Page on southern, 127–29; property-owning men as, 145–46; de Tocqueville on, 101; *The Virginian* on, 289, 293, 296–301, 302n29, 305; white southerners as, 129; Wister on Anglo-American, 4, 75, 80, 239, 243, 289, 297–301. *See also* natural aristocracy

Aristotle, 95, 118

Arthur, Chester A. (president), 80

assimilation, 48, 53–54

Atlantis, 164, 165n24

authoritarianism, 3, 308

Badlands: for American freedom and history, 62; competition in, 174; as primeval, 178; Roosevelt, T., in, 23–25, 28, 53, 57, 59, 62, 139–40, 164–65; Roosevelt, T., leaving, 173; vigilantes and, 145, 261–62

Bancroft, Hubert Howe, 301

Barnum, P. T., 79, 295

Bartholdi, Frédéric Auguste, 196

Beard, George M., 34

Beecher, Henry Ward, 82, 123–24

Benton, Thomas Hart, 28, 159

Bigelow, John, 25

Bigelow, Poultney, 1; *Outing* magazine of, 65, 167; Remington, F., and, 44–46, 65, 233–35, 240, 246, 251, 259, 288; on Roosevelt, T., 263, 288

de Billier, Frederic O., 25, 29n28, 36, 46, 189, 191

Billings, Frank S., 213–14

bison. *See* buffalo

Blacks, 106; Cody, W., and soldiers as, 290; as "The Colored Rough Riders", 282–83; democracy and, 128–30; Roosevelt, T., on soldiers

and, 7, 14, 275, 282–86; self-reliance of, 274–75; Shaler on, 129; southerners on democracy and, 128–30. *See also* African American Calvary Regiments; race
Blake, Jacob, 309
Boone, Daniel: Bumppo from, 60–62, 83, 140, 167; "fire-hunting" by, 205
Boone and Crockett Club: *American Big-Game Hunting* and, 201, 214–15; Chicago World's Fair cabin of, 201–2; on conservation, 13, 201, 204–6, 208, 311; on democracy, 210–11; on "fire-hunting," 205; *Forest and Stream* magazine and, 202–3, 207, 214; Grinnell co-founding, 202–17; on individual freedom, 210; Roosevelt co-founding, 201–3; Wister and, 201–2, 205; on Yellowstone, 42, 206–7, 216, 234–35
bootstraps, 285
Bothwell, Albert J., 189–90
Brandeis, Louis, 75
Bremer, Fredrika, 109–11, 130, 173
"The Bronco Buster" (Remington, F.), 4, 246–47, 253, 286–87
Brown, John, 82, 117
Bryan, William Jennings, 249–50
Buckley, William F., 10
buffalo: Cody, W., and, 84, 155; as disappearing, 155, 203, 210, 215–16; as hunted, 23–25, 84, 210, 215; nostalgia and, 215–16
Buffalo Bill. *See* Cody, William F.
Buffalo Bill's Wild West. *See* "The Wild West, Rocky Mountain, and Prairie Exhibition"
"Buffalo Bill's Wild West and Congress of Rough Riders of the World" (Congress of Rough Riders), 195–96, 199, 290
buffalo soldiers, 274–75
Bumppo, Nathaniel (Natty), 58–59, 156, 294; from Boone, 60–62, 83, 140, 167

Buntline, Ned. *See* Judson, Edward Z. C.
Burke, Edmund, 11–12, 108, 113, 128, 134–35, 163; aristocracy and, 107, 127, 129; on conservation, 98–99; Emerson and, 105–7; on French Revolution, 98–99, 101; on individual freedom, 98–102
Bush, George W. (president), 308
Butler, Pierce Mease, 31–32

Calvin, John, 107
capitalism: American west and, 134; conservatism of, 190; cowboys and, 189–90; ethical economists and, 132–33, 135; Gilded Age of, 34, 130, 132, 295; as laissez-faire, 5, 20, 113n6, 123, 130–33, 135, 233; lynching for, 189–90; nostalgia after, 162; Panic of 1873 and, 130, 133–34; *Progress and Poverty* on, 130–33, 135; Sumner and competition in, 122–23
Carow, Edith Kermit (Roosevelt wife), 160, 173
Caten, Eva, 45, 47
Catlin, George, 79, 206–7; Remington, F., on, 41–42
cattle rustlers: cowboys and, 13, 25, 143–46, 189–91, 296–98, 301–2, 311; Johnson County War on, 6, 25, 144, 189–90, 192, 195, 296–97; lynching of, 6, 25, 143–44, 189–90, 192, 195, 257–58, 296–97; Roosevelt, T., on, 13, 143–47, 300, 311; *The Rustlers* on, 6; stockgrowers on, 25, 143–44, 190, 257–58; *The Virginian* on, 298, 301–2, 311
census report, 221–22, 231, 271
Central Labor Union party, 132, 160
Chambers, Whittaker, 10
Cherokee tribe, 268; Trail of Tears and, 59, 63n30
Cheyenne Club, 36

Cheyenne tribe: on "buffalo soldiers," 275; Cody, W., and, 4, 79, 85–87
Chicago World's Fair. *See* World's Columbian Exposition
Chimney Butte ranch, 24, 26, 139
Civil War: American conservatism after, 127, 129–30; Confederacy starting, 118; conservative and, 12, 112–13; Reconstruction after, 113, 124, 127–30, 197, 237, 282; Remington, F., on, 251–52; white identity after, 12; on Wister, 32
Clark, Champ, 270
Clark, James Hyde, 261
Clark, John Bates, 132
Clark, William, 41, 62
Cleveland, Grover (president), 213, 258
Cody, Isaac, 81–83, 91n15
Cody, William F. (Buffalo Bill): as American west showman, 4, 13, 81–84, 196, 294–95, 305–6, 309; with Black regiments, 290; on buffalo, 84, 155; Buffalo Bill's Wild West by, 79, 88–90, 156; Chicago World's Fair and, 198–99; on cowboys, 79–80, 295; Custer and, 84, 86–88, 154, 186, 305–6; description of, 153; Europe tour by, 181–82, 185, 196, 295; Ghost Dance and, 169–71, 181–86; Grinnell and, 203; in *Harper's Weekly*, 195, 233; *A Horse's Tale* on, 87; on Indians, 86–88, 154, 183, 195, 197–98; *Indian War Pictures* by, 295; individualism of, 153; Judson writing, 84; manhood and, 153; Miles and, 49–50, 170–71, 181–82, 251–52; name of, 84; natural aristocracy and, 153; with nostalgia, 4, 89; *The Red Right Hand* by, 87–88; Remington, F., and, 167, 233–34, 289; retrogressions into "past" and, 88, 90, 182, 248; Roosevelt, T., and, 290–91; rough riders and, 248, 262, 288, 290, 294; as scalping, 79, 84, 86–88, 154, 156; self-reliance and, 153; Sitting Bull and, 154–55, 170–71, 181–83, 185–86, 186n13; *Story of the Wild West* by, 167; "survival of the fittest" and, 90; Twain on, 87, 130–31, 156; Victoria performance by, 87, 156; Virginian as, 302; western expansion and, 81–82; Wetmore as sister and, 90, 195; Wister and, 80; World's Columbian Exposition and, 195–97, 201, 295; on Yellow Hair, 86–88, 154
"The Colored Rough Riders," 282–83
common law: as conservative, 73–74; Holmes on, 72–75, 77, 244–45; natural selection in, 76–77
The Common Law (Holmes), 72–74, 299
Communist Manifesto (Marx and Engels), 110
competition: as conservative, 76; Darwinism and, 5, 13, 76, 113, 118–19, 121–22, 134–35, 141, 170–71, 174, 211, 244, 295, 297; hierarchical society from, 142–44; Holmes and, 74, 76, 257, 297; Indian land and, 141; Lamarck and, 10; for progress, 118–19; Remington, F., and, 245–46, 252–53; retrogressions into "past" and, 141–42, 175, 178–79, 271; Roosevelt, T., on, 5, 142, 174–78, 211, 257, 268, 311; Rough Riders testing, 268; Sumner on economic, 122–23; as warfare, 178–79
Confederacy. *See* southerners
Congress of Rough Riders. *See* "Buffalo Bill's Wild West and Congress of Rough Riders of the World"
conservation: actions for, 215–16; Boone and Crockett Club on, 13, 201, 204–6, 208, 311; Burke on, 98–99; conservatism and, 209–10, 215–17; democracy and, 210–11, 214; from future and past, 204; hierarchical society for, 210; individual freedom *vs.*, 206, 209–17;

Morton, J., on, 213–14; politics and, 209–17; Roosevelt circle on, 305, 311; term of, 204
conservatism. *See specific subjects*
conservative: term of, 111–13, 115n37; theatricality of, 202. *See also specific subjects*
"The Conservative" (Emerson), 108–9
The Conservative Mind (Kirk), 10–11
Constitution (U.S.), 31, 100, 123, 176, 239, 299
contests of merit, 1, 13, 261–63, 297, 300; as Darwinian, 135, 140, 177, 214; Roosevelt, T., on, 142, 311
Cook, David J., 89–90
Cooper, Gary, 305–6
Cooper, James Fenimore, 5–6, 15n21, 54, 237, 247; Bumppo character by, 58–61, 83, 156, 294; life of, 59–60
"Cowboy Napoleon," 1, 288
"cowboy of Dakota," 133, 159–60, 165n2
"cowboy philosophy," 12, 48, 50, 196
cowboy president, 307
cowboys: as American, 237, 306; as aristocrat, 215, 263; attire of, 60–61; cattle rustlers and, 13, 25, 143–46, 189–91, 296–98, 301–2, 311; Cody, W., on, 79–80, 295; individualism and, 80; Johnson County War and, 6, 25, 189–90, 192, 195, 296–97; as Mexican, 7, 238; pay and wealth of, 189–90; Remington, F., on, 12, 50, 237–38, 246; Republican Party as western, 305, 307; Rough Riders as, 1, 262, 267, 286–87; sailors as, 259–60; as white southerners, 238–39; Wister on, 7, 237–39, 243–45
Crockett, David, 61–62, 167, 309
Cuba, 2, 13; conservatism of, 270–71; frontier past conquering, 262–63; imperialism on, 270–71, 273; Kettle Hill and, 14, 274–77, 288, 290–91; *Maine* battleship and, 262, 276; Morton, J., on, 270; as new state of nature, 261; Remington, F., and, 258–59, 269–70, 272, 276–77; as retrogressions into "past," 270–71; Roosevelt, T., in, 1, 11, 258, 262–64, 269–70, 272–77; Rough Riders in, 262–63, 272–76; San Juan Hill and, 14, 273–74, 276, 288, 291n34; U.S. armada to, 269–70; U.S. trading partner as, 258
Curtis, Emma Ghent, 6
Curtis, George William, 46
Custer, George: Cody, W., and, 84, 86–88, 154, 186, 305–6; Grinnell and, 203; Indian battle by, 85–86, 171, 203, 274

Darwin, Charles: America and, 120–22; *The Descent of Man* by, 121–22; on development and evolution, 12, 54–55, 62, 73, 118, 121–24, 129, 139–40, 271; hierarchical society and, 124; on Lamarck, 118; *On the Origin of Species* by, 54–55, 113, 118–21, 173; Roosevelt, T., on, 5, 124, 140; transmutation theory of, 118
Darwin, Erasmus, 55, 118
Darwinism: American conservatism from, 3, 134–35; American west and, 1–3, 5, 307; aristocracy and, 270; competition and, 5, 13, 76, 113, 118–19, 121–22, 134–35, 141, 170–71, 174, 211, 244, 295, 297; contests of merit as, 135, 140, 177, 214; individualism in, 10, 21, 268–69; natural selection of, 12, 54, 56, 118–19, 121, 124, 135, 174, 214, 301; Remington, F., and, 50; Roosevelt, T., civilization as, 178–79; Rough Riders and, 272; Spencer and, 21, 55, 119, 297; Sumner on, 12, 122–23, 131–35, 173–74; Wounded Knee as, 184. *See also* "survival of the fittest"
Davis, Richard Harding, 259, 269–71, 273, 286, 301
Debs, Eugene V., 244

Declaration of Independence (U.S.), 96–98, 176, 261, 289, 297
DeMille, Cecil B., 305–6
democracy, 162; Adams, Henry, and, 132; American west and, 211–12; aristocracy and, 212; Bancroft on despotism of, 301; Beecher on, 123–24; Black suffrage *vs.*, 128–30; Boone and Crockett Club on, 210–11; conservation and, 210–11, 214; despotism of, 301; Emerson on, 113n6; equality and, 100–101; as "flannel-shirted," 243–44; Google on, 125n29; individual freedom and, 101, 211–12; Kansas Territory on, 81–83; as "negro domination," 128–30; as physical, 20; Sumner on, 122; de Tocqueville and, 101, 105, 132, 134, 297; trees and, 214; Turner on, 295–96; Whitman on, 123–25; Wister on, 245, 249, 297
Democratic Party: Bryan and, 249–50; Clark, C., and, 270; Douglas and, 81; Emerson and, 113n6; Hewitt in, 132–33, 160; Jackson and, 59; Parker and, 296; Roosevelt, F., and, 306; Van Wyck and, 282
Demolins, Edmond, 268–69
Depew, Chauncey M., 268
The Descent of Man (Darwin, C.), 121–22
"The Development Hypothesis" (Spencer), 119, 121
Dewey, Thomas E., 306
Douglas, Stephen A., 81
Dow, Wilmot, 139, 146–48

Eiffel, Gustave, 196, 198
Elkhorn Ranch, 53, 57, 59, 146, 148; as retreat, 27, 139–41; Roosevelt shutting, 160, 173
Emerson, Ralph Waldo: aristocracy and, 107, 113n6, 127; Burke and, 105–7; on conservatism, 12; "The Conservative" by, 108–9; on democracy, 113n6; Democratic Party and, 113n6; on government, 106–7; history and, 9, 12, 105–15; individualism and, 12, 107–8, 113n6; individual merit and, 140; on manhood, 106; on past and future, 107; Republican Party and, 113n6; Roosevelt, T., influenced by, 56–57; self-reliance and, 6, 12, 107–8, 113–14, 149, 210, 212, 250, 309; "Self-Reliance" by, 106, 113n6; Spencer on, 119
Endicott, William, 159
Engels, Friedrich, 110
England: Buffalo Bill's Wild West in, 87, 156; conservative in, 111; Victoria of, 87, 156
equality: American west and, 20; democracy and, 100–101; fairness not in, 142–43; individual superiority over, 3, 7; inequality and, 113, 124–25; Kidd on, 173–75, 178; meaning of, 150; "might makes right" *vs.*, 76, 150; Roosevelt, T., on, 20
ethical economists, 132–33, 135
eugenics, 76–77
Europe: American conservatism from liberalism and, 96–97, 109; aristocracy of, 110, 112, 196, 214, 243; Cody, W., touring, 181–82, 185, 196, 295
evolution: common law in, 73–74; Darwin, C., on development and, 12, 54–55, 62, 73, 118, 121–24, 129, 139–40, 271; lynching and, 301; Roosevelt, T., on, 140, 284
"Evolution of the Cow-Puncher" (Wister), 237–39, 243–45

Ferris, George Washington Gale, 198, 219–20
Ferris, Joe, 24–25
Ferris, Sylvane, 26, 262
"fire-hunting," 205
Floyd, George, 308–9

Index

Forest and Stream magazine, 202–3, 207, 214
Forsyth, James W., 183
Fourier, Charles, 110
Franklin, Benjamin, 142
freedom: American west and, 60, 90, 142; Badlands and, 62; Roosevelt, T. on fitness and, 54
free land, 223, 227, 230–31
French Revolution, 11–12, 97, 109, 190; Burke on, 98–99, 101; conservatism after, 111; Eiffel and, 196, 198
frontier: American west and, 2–3, 221–25, 227–32, 236; Cuba as, 262–63; of India, 234; manhood by, 9–10; term of, 222
future: American west looking, 220; conservation from past and, 204; conservatism toward, 3, 8–10, 14, 37–38, 163, 225; Emerson on past and, 107; manhood superiority on, 9–10; present capturing for, 42–43. *See also* retrogressions into "past"

George, Henry: in Central Labor Union party, 132, 160; *Progress and Poverty* by, 130–33, 135; Republican Party and, 160; on Roosevelt, T., 133, 160; as socialist, 130–33, 135, 160, 249, 258
Geronimo, 49–51, 159, 170
Ghost Dance: Cody, W., and, 169–71, 181–86; retrogressions into "past" and, 181–82; Wounded Knee and, 13, 183–85, 198
Gilded Age, 34, 130, 132, 295
The Gilded Age (Warner and Twain), 130
Goldwater, Barry, 10, 307–8
Goldwater, Morris, 312n20
Google, 125n29
Gorringe, Henry Honychurch, 22–23, 79
Gould, Benjamin Apthorp, 121
government: Emerson on, 106–7; House Un-American Activities Committee and, 306; on hunting, 205–6; individual consent and, 95–96, 98; Locke for liberalism, 11, 96–97, 109; meritocracy and, 177, 308–9; Roosevelt, T., on, 175–77; Spencer on, 120
Grant, Ulysses S. (president), 23, 207
great man of history, 9, 105–15
Greeley, Horace, 82, 134
Grinnell, George Bird, 202–17

Harper, J. Henry, 48–49, 289
Harper's Weekly: Remington, F., and, 13, 42–43, 46–49, 65, 169–71, 251–52, 260; Remington, F., and Cody, W., in, 195, 233; Remington, F., and Wister at, 234–36, 243, 289; Remington, F., on Cuba and, 272, 274, 277; Wister and, 192, 234, 261, 293
Harte, Bret, 170, 234, 237, 287, 293, 306
Hawthorne, Nathaniel, 110
Hay, John, 163, 239
Hayes, Rutherford B. (president), 128–29
Hearst, William Randolph, 259, 269
Hewitt, Abram, 132–33, 160
hierarchical society: aristocracy as, 101; competition producing, 142–44; conservation needing, 210; conservatism and, 7, 170–71; conservative merit in, 8, 113n6, 177, 213, 308–9; contests of merit, 1, 13, 135, 140, 142, 214, 261–63, 297, 300, 311; Darwin and, 124; race and merit in, 267–68, 282–83, 285; Roosevelt circle on natural, 8
history: American conservatism and, 7–8; Badlands freedom and, 62; Buffalo Bill's Wild West on, 155; conservatism and, 7–8, 75–76, 108–9, 170–71, 224–25, 227, 232; Emerson and, 12, 105–15; linear-progressive model of, 73, 165, 178,

223–24, 227; Turner on American, 13, 244, 249, 295–96. *See also* retrogressions into "past"
Hobbes, Thomas, 95, 175
Hofstadter, Richard, 15n14
Holliday, Presley, 284
Holmes, Oliver Wendell, Jr.: aristocracy and, 4, 301; on "average man," 73–74; on common law, 72–75, 77, 244–45; *The Common Law* by, 72–74, 299; competition and, 74, 76, 257, 297; on eugenics, 76–77; fascist ideology of, 76; law and, 32–34, 71–75, 244, 297, 299–301; on natural selection, 76–77, 297; Roosevelt, T., on, 257; as Supreme Court judge, 74–76, 293, 297–98, 300; on war, 257. *See also* Wister, Owen
horses, 42, 49, 66–69; Remington, F., on galloping, 67–68; of Sitting Bull, 186, 186n13
A Horse's Tale (Twain), 87
House Un-American Activities Committee (U.S.), 306
Houston, Samuel, 62
Howells, William Dean, 32, 34–35, 71, 246
hunting: *American Big-Game Hunting* on, 201, 214–15; buffalo, 23–25, 84, 210, 215; "fire-hunting" in, 205; government on, 205–6; *Hunting Trips of a Ranchman* on, 27, 60–61, 139, 163, 203; *Ranch Life and the Hunting Trail* on, 27, 61, 139, 163–64, 167; as retrogressions into "past," 215–16; *The Scalp-Hunters* and, 57–58, 60, 203; *The Wilderness Hunter* on, 28
Hunting Trips of a Ranchman (Roosevelt, T.), 27, 60–61, 139, 163, 203

imperialism: on Cuba, 270–71, 273; Remington, F., on, 170, 234, 236–37, 274; of U.S., 178, 239–40, 287

India, 170, 234
Indians: America on, 50–51, 62, 141–42; Apache tribe, 49–50; Arapaho tribe, 85; Catlin painting, 41, 79, 206–7; Cherokee, 59, 63n30, 268; Cheyenne tribe, 4, 79, 85–87, 275; Cody, W., and, 86–88, 154, 183, 195, 197–98; competition on land and, 141; Custer battle with, 85–86, 171, 203, 274; free land and, 223, 227, 230–31; Geronimo as, 49–51, 159, 170; Ghost Dance of, 13, 169–71, 181–86, 198; Jackson on, 59, 62, 101; Lakota tribe, 13, 85, 154, 171, 183, 185, 197; McLaughlin on, 155, 170, 181–82; No-Name as, 198–99; Red Cloud, 197–98; Remington, F., on, 171, 184–85, 237; Roosevelt, T., on land and, 141, 143; Roosevelt circle on, 7; Sitting Bull as, 154–55, 170–71, 181–83, 185–86, 186n13; Trail of Tears, 59, 63n30; Turner on, 227–28; wars with, 13, 49, 85, 88, 154–55, 171, 183–86, 198; whites on, 60, 85, 141–42; Wounded Knee and, 13, 183–85, 198; Yellow Hair as, 86–88, 154
Indian War Pictures (Cody, W.), 295
individual freedom: American west for, 24, 26, 28; Boone and Crockett Club on, 210; Brown and, 82, 117; Burke on, 98–102; conservation *vs.*, 206, 209–17; democracy and, 101, 211–12; Dewey on, 306; evolution on assimilation and, 54; government and, 95–96, 98; as laissez-faire capitalism, 5, 20, 113n6, 123, 130–33, 135, 233; laws of nature and, 12, 95, 97, 99–100; Locke on, 9, 12, 95–101, 106, 176; Roosevelt, T., self-promoting, 263–64, 276, 280; vigilantes for, 146
individualism: as American, 102, 108, 307–8; bootstraps and, 285; Bremer

on, 109–10, 130, 173; Clark, J. B., on socialism and, 132; of Cody, W., 153; cowboys and, 80; Darwinism on, 10, 21, 268–69; democracy fostering, 101, 211–12; Demolins on, 268–69; Emerson and, 107–8, 113n6; Holmes on "average man," 73–74; over equality, 3, 7; Panic of 1873 and, 130, 133–34; politics and, 10; Remington, F., and, 48; Roosevelt, T., civilization as, 178–79; Roosevelt, T., on, 20–21, 28, 142; Saint-Simon on, 109–10; science of, 134–35; "Self-Reliance" and, 106; self-reliance as, 10; socialism contested by, 10, 109–11, 130; as strongman, 311; Sumner and, 131–35; by de Tocqueville, 102, 108; for white males, 105

individual merit: Emerson and, 140; Roosevelt, T., cult of, 13, 140, 142, 266–68, 282–83, 285

Irving, Washington, 41–42

Jackson, Andrew (president): on Indians, 59, 62, 101; de Tocqueville on, 101

James, Henry, 32–33

James, William, 71, 119

Jefferson, Thomas (president): Declaration of Independence by, 96–98, 176, 261, 289, 297; as democrat, 100, 107; Lafayette and, 97–98, 110, 117; on Locke, 96–97; on natural aristocracy, 3, 8, 100, 107, 136, 178, 289; natural selection and, 214; slavery and, 100; state of nature and, 12

John Ermine of the Yellowstone (Remington, F.), 294

Johnson County War, 6, 25, 144, 189–90, 192, 195, 296–97

Judson, Edward Z. C. (Ned Buntline), 84

Kansas Territory, 81–83

Kemble, Fanny, 31–33

Kettle Hill: Black Calvary on, 14, 274–76, 290; Roosevelt, T., on, 275–77, 288, 291n34; Rough Riders and, 275–77, 288, 290–91; San Juan Hill and, 14, 273–74, 276, 288, 291n34

Kidd, Benjamin, 173–75, 178

Kipling, Rudyard, 165n24, 242n35; Remington, F., on, 170, 239–40; Wister and, 234, 236–37

Kirk, Russell, 10–11

Kirkland, Caroline, 6

Lacey, John F., 207–8

Lafayette, Marquis de (Gilbert du Motier), 97–98, 110, 117

Lakota tribe, 13, 85, 154, 183, 185; Red Cloud of, 197–98; Sitting Bull in, 170–71

Lamarck, Jean Baptiste: on acquired traits, 10, 55–57, 118, 120–21, 123, 139–40, 228, 287; competition and, 10; Darwin, C., on, 118; Roosevelt, T., on, 139–40; self-reinvention and, 5; Spencer on, 120–21; on transmutation theory, 118

Langdell, Christopher Columbus, 71

law: American west and, 75; aristocracy and, 301; common law in, 72–77, 244–45, 299; Holmes and, 32–34, 71–75, 244, 297, 299–301; stockgrowers manipulation of, 25, 148, 189–90; Supreme Court and, 74–76, 293, 297–98, 300; Wister on, 71–72, 75, 244–45, 296–302

laws of nature, 7; American west and, 21; equality and, 113, 142–43; individual freedom and, 12, 95, 97, 99–100; individualism science in, 134–35; Page on, 128; on slavery, 127; social power in, 76; society in, 119–20; state of nature and, 9, 12, 95, 97, 131, 175, 179, 261; Turner on, 221

Lee, Alice Hathaway (Roosevelt wife), 19, 23, 26
Lee, George Cabot, 21
Lee, Robert E., 117
Lewis, Meriwether, 41, 62
liberalism, 11, 96–97, 109
Lincoln, Abraham (president), 112, 118
linear-progressive history model, 73, 165, 178, 223–24, 227
Lin McLean (Wister), 192–93, 234, 259, 261
Liszt, Franz, 33
Locke, John: on American west, 97, 179; Emerson on, 106; on individual liberty, 9, 12, 95–101, 106, 176; Jefferson and, 96–97; liberalism government by, 11, 96–97, 109; on rule of property, 96; as self reliant, 107; on state of nature, 9, 97, 131, 179, 261; on wilderness, 24
Lodge, Henry Cabot, 159, 161, 276, 296
London, Jack, 5
Louisiana Purchase, 81, 101, 134, 229
Lovelace, Carl, 283
Lynch, John R., 129
lynching: Bancroft on, 301; Bothwell and, 189–90; for capitalism, 189–90; of cattle rustlers, 6, 25, 143–44, 189–90, 192, 195, 257–58, 296–97; evolution and, 301; example of, 307; Johnson County War on, 6, 25, 189–90, 192, 195, 296–97; Roosevelt, T., and, 13, 143–47, 300; in southern states *vs.* west, 298–99; Spencer on, 120; stockgrowers and, 25, 143–44, 190, 257–58; vigilantism and, 190–92; *The Virginian* and, 298–300; Wister on, 4, 25, 191–92, 296–97, 300–301

Madison, James (president), 123
Magie, Elizabeth, 131
Malthus, Thomas, 118–19, 134, 176

manhood: American west for, 19, 62–63; Cody, W., and, 153; Emerson on, 106; on "fire-hunting," 205; frontier conquest for, 9–10; on future, 9–10; individualism and, 311; opera and, 32; Remington, F., and, 44, 169; Roosevelt circle on, 9–10; as self-reliant, 27; Wister on, 31
Martí, José, 258
Marx, Karl, 110, 173–74
mass media, 68
Matthews, James Brander, 245
McElrath, Frances, 6
McKinley, William (president), 2, 249, 258, 296
McLaughlin, John, 155, 170, 181–82
merit: conservatism and, 8, 113n6, 177, 213, 308–9; contests of, 1, 13, 135, 140, 142, 214, 261–63, 297, 300, 311; in hierarchical society, 267–68, 282–83, 285; hierarchy and conservative, 8, 113n6, 177, 213, 308–9; race and, 267–68, 282–83, 285. *See also* individual merit
meritocracy, 177, 308–9
Merrifield, William J., 24, 26, 160
Mexican: America on, 62; cowboys, 7, 238
"might makes right," 76, 150
Miles, Nelson A.: Cody, W., and, 49–50, 170–71, 181–82, 251–52; McLaughlin on, 155, 170, 181–82
Mill, John Stuart, 96–97
Mitchell, Silas Weir, 34–35, 38n19, 192
Morès, Marquis de, 23
Morton, Julius Sterling: on conservation, 213–14; on Cuba, 270; on self-reliance, 214
Morton, Paul, 213
Moses, Phoebe Ann (Annie Oakley), 89, 309
Motier, Gilbert du. *See* Lafayette, Marquis de
Muybridge, Eadweard James, 66–69, 169
mythic depictions, 15n21

natural aristocracy: America and, 99–100, 133, 294, 305, 307; Cody, W., and, 153; cowboys and natural, 80, 215, 243; Jefferson on, 3, 8, 100, 107, 136, 178, 289; Roosevelt, T., on natural, 25, 62–63, 140, 145–47, 177, 305, 311

natural selection: in common law, 76–77; of Darwinism, 12, 54, 56, 118–19, 121, 124, 135, 174, 214, 301; Holmes on, 76–77, 297; Jefferson and, 214; Roosevelt, T., on, 62, 141, 174–76, 178; U.S. and, 120–24, 301

The Naval War of 1812 (Roosevelt, T.), 22–23, 27, 258

"negro domination," 128–29

neurasthenia, 4, 34–35

New York: Roosevelt, T., as governor and, 2, 280–82, 289–91; Roosevelt, T., for mayor and, 159–60, 165n2, 173

Ninth and Tenth Calvary, 14, 274–76, 282–84, 288, 290

No-Name, Johnny Burke, 198–99

Norris, Frank, 5, 269

nostalgia: bison and, 215–16; Cody, W., show with, 4, 89; Reagan on, 307; Roosevelt, T., on, 161–62, 164–65; term of, 162

Oakley, Annie. *See* Moses, Phoebe Ann

Olmsted, Frederick Law, 197

On the Origin of Species (Darwin, C.), 54–55, 113, 118–21, 173

Outing magazine, 65, 167

Page, Thomas Nelson, 127–29

Paine, Thomas, 90

Panic of 1873, 130, 133–34

Parker, Alton B., 296

Parsons, Charles, 42

passing away of American west, 160–64, 235, 261, 290

photography: Muybridge and, 66–69, 169; Remington, F., using, 65–66; Stanford using, 66; Zoöpraxiscope and, 66–67, 169

Pierce, Franklin (president), 81

politics: American west and, 28, 156, 306–8; Central Labor Union party and, 132, 160; conservation and, 209–17; "cowboy of Dakota," 133, 159–60, 165n2; individualism and, 10; "left" and republicanism in, 100; Populist Party and, 233, 236, 249–50; on race and grievance, 308; Rough Riders in, 289–90; Turner on, 249–50. *See also* Democratic Party; Republican Party

Pollard, Edward A., 127

popular sovereignty, 81

Populist Party, 233, 249–50; populism and, 236

Porcellian Club, 4, 32–33, 192, 275

Porter, Robert P., 221, 271

Presbyterian Irish, 62

Proctor, Alexander Phimister, 197–99, 200n15

progress: competition driving, 118–19; retrogressions into "past" for, 60, 217

Progress and Poverty (George), 130–33, 135

race, 5; Adams, Herbert, on, 219–22, 228; Blake and violence on, 309; Floyd and violence on, 308–9; in hierarchical society, 267–68, 282–83, 285; merit and, 267–68, 282–83, 285; politics and grievance on, 308; Presbyterian Irish and, 62; racist and antiracist America on, 81; Remington, F., on, 47, 50, 259; Roosevelt, T., on, 7, 14, 275, 282–86; Rough Riders and, 268, 282; Turner on, 221; whites on Indians and, 60; Wister on, 238–39, 285–86. *See also* Blacks

Ranch Life and the Hunting Trail (Roosevelt, T.), 27, 61, 139, 163–64; Remington, F., and, 68, 167–68

Reagan, Ronald (president), 306–8
Reconstruction, 113, 124, 127–30, 197, 237, 282
Red Cloud, 197–98
The Red Right Hand; or, Buffalo Bill's First Scalp for Custer (Cody, W.), 87–88
Reid, Mayne, 54, 57–58, 60, 203
Reinoehl, Michael, 310
Remington, Frederic: art of, 44–45, 51n16, 294; Bigelow, P., and, 44–46, 65, 233–35, 240, 246, 251, 259, 288; "The Bronco Buster" by, 4, 246–47, 253, 286–87; camera work of, 65–66; on Catlin, 41–42; on Civil War, 251–52; Cody, W., and, 167, 233–34, 289; on competition, 245–46, 252–53; on Congress of Rough Riders, 195–96; on conservatism, 170–71; "cowboy philosophy" and, 12, 48, 50, 196; on cowboys, 12, 50, 237–38, 246; Cuba and, 258–59, 269–70, 272, 276–77; Darwinian judgments by, 50; on "Evolution of the Cow-Puncher," 237–39, 243–45; family loss of, 45–46; on galloping horses, 67–68; in *Harper's Weekly*, 13, 42–43, 46–49, 65, 169–71, 251–52, 260; *Harper's Weekly* and Cuba by, 195, 233; *Harper's Weekly* with Cody, W., and, 272, 274, 277; *Harper's Weekly* with Wister and, 234–36, 243, 289; on imperialism, 170, 234, 236–37, 274; on Indians, 171, 184–85, 237; individualism and, 48; *John Ermine of the Yellowstone* by, 294; on Kipling, 170, 239–40; life of, 43; on manhood, 44, 169; on Mexican cowboys, 7, 238; Miles and, 49–50, 170–71, 181–82, 251–52; on military, 43–45, 184–85; on Muybridge photography, 66–69, 169; in *Outing* magazine, 65, 167; on race, 47, 50, 259; *Ranch Life and the Hunting Trail* and, 68, 167–68; Republican Party and, 44, 251; Roosevelt, T., and, 68, 167–68, 239–40, 247, 259–61, 288, 294, 302; on sculpture, 241, 245; self-reliance and, 47, 170, 196, 274–75; talents of, 4, 13; Thomas on west and, 48; Virginian as, 302; war and, 13, 250–53, 258–59, 261, 269, 276–77, 289; west captured by, 42–43, 47–50, 167–69; *The Winning of the West* and, 260; Wister and, 168, 234–36, 258–59, 269, 289
Remington, Seth, 43, 251–52
Republican Party: Acton in, 165n2; Bush, G. W., and, 308; Cooper, G., in, 305–6; DeMille in, 305–6; Dewey and, 306; Emerson and, 113n6; George and, 160; Goldwater, B., and, 307; Lacey and, 207–8; Lincoln to, 112, 118; McKinley and, 249, 296; Reagan and, 306–8; Remington, F., and, 44, 251; republicanism, 100, 123; Roosevelt, T., and, 22, 133, 159–60, 165n2, 249, 281–82, 296, 302, 305; socialism and, 132; to south and west, 307; Stanford, L., and, 66; Trump and, 308; as western cowboys, 305, 307
retrogressions into "past": American west as, 9–10, 145, 191, 215, 224–25, 281, 296; Cody, W., and, 88, 90, 182, 248; competition and, 141–42, 175, 178–79, 271; Cuba as, 270–71; Ghost Dance and, 181–82; hunting as, 215–16; practical conservatism and, 2; progress through, 60, 217; for self-reliance, 9–10, 13, 107; Turner on, 4, 224–25, 228, 230–32, 250, 270; vigilantism and, 145
Ripley, George, 110
Rittenhouse, Kyle, 309–10
Rocky Mountain Detective Agency, 89–90
Rogers, William A., 42–43
Roosevelt, Alice Lee (daughter), 26

Roosevelt, Anna (sister), 19, 27, 54, 161, 249, 262
Roosevelt, Corinne (sister), 54, 56, 139, 150, 163, 179, 262
Roosevelt, Elliott (brother), 19–20, 54
Roosevelt, Franklin Delano (president), 306
Roosevelt, Martha Bulloch (mother), 5, 19, 26
Roosevelt, Theodore (president): on acquired traits, 139–40, 287; on American civilization, 178–79; on American west, 4–5, 58, 62, 139–41, 178–79; on assimilation and vigor, 53–54; Badlands and, 23–25, 28, 53, 57, 59, 62, 139–40, 164–65, 173; on Benton, 28, 159; Bigelow, P., on, 263, 288; on Black Calvary, 7, 14, 275, 282–86; Boone and Crockett Club by, 201–3; "Bronco Buster" to, 286–87; Bumppo character inspiring, 58–61, 83, 156, 294; Carow as wife and, 160, 173; cattle rustlers lynching and, 13, 143–47, 300, 311; at Chimney Butte ranch, 24, 26, 139; Cody, W., and, 290–91; in Colorado Springs, 1–2; on competition, 5, 142, 174–78, 211, 257, 268, 311; conservatism and, 112, 163, 177–78, 296; on contests of merit, 142, 311; as "Cowboy Napoleon," 1, 288; as "cowboy of Dakota," 133, 159–60, 165n2; as cowboy president, 307; Cuba and, 1, 11, 258, 262–64, 269–70, 272–77; cult of individual merit and, 13, 140, 142, 266–68, 282–83, 285; on Darwin, 5, 124, 140; Elkhorn Ranch of, 27, 53, 57, 59, 139–41, 146, 148, 160, 173; Emerson influencing, 56–57; on equality, 20; on evolution and white identity, 140, 284; on freedom and fitness, 54; on George, 133, 160; on government, 175–77; on his body, 57–58, 275–76; Hofstadter on, 15n14; on Holmes, 257; on homogenizing west, 53; on Indian land, 141, 143; on individualism, 20–21, 28, 142; Kettle Hill and, 275–77, 288, 291n34; on Lamarck, 139–40; Lee, A. H., as wife, 19, 23, 26; mayoral race by, 159–60, 165n2, 173; McKinley preceding, 2, 249, 258, 296; meritocracy and, 177, 308–9; on natural aristocracy, 25, 62–63, 140, 145–47, 177, 305, 311; on natural selection, 62, 141, 174–76, 178; *The Naval War of 1812* by, 22, 27, 258; as New York governor, 2, 280–82, 289–91; on nostalgia, 161–62, 164–65; on "old iron days," 2–3; Porcellian Club and, 4, 32–33, 192, 275; presidency of, 294, 296; Proctor and, 197–99, 200n15; Remington, F., and, 68, 167–68, 239–40, 247, 259–61, 288, 294, 302; Republican Party and, 22, 133, 159–60, 165n2, 249, 281–82, 296, 302, 305; *The Rough Riders* by, 281–84, 287, 306; Rough Riders of, 1–2, 4, 11, 13–14, 159, 248, 262–63, 267–68, 272–76, 281–84, 286–88, 290, 294, 305–6; as ruler of men, 1, 287–88; on sailor cowboys, 259–60; San Juan Hill and, 14, 288, 291n34; self promotion by, 263–64, 276, 280; on self-reliance, 3, 5, 20, 141, 149, 161, 163, 175, 211–12, 215, 282, 285; on socialism, 20, 175, 249–50; vigilante justification by, 148–50, 191; vigilantism and, 143–48, 159, 257–58, 310; Virginian as, 302, 305; on warfare, 13, 141–42, 159, 257–58, 261–62, 269; on western costumes, 60–62; on west passing away, 160–64, 261, 290; *The Winning of the West* by, 27–28, 53, 59, 139, 220–21; Wister and, 31,

240, 261, 293, 296; young health of, 54–56, 58
Roosevelt, Theodore, Sr. (father), 55–56
Roosevelt circle: on American west aesthetics, 14; on conservation, 305, 311; on hierarchical society, 8; on Indians, 7; malignant mutations from, 311; on manhood superiority, 9–10; Virginian as, 301; as white males, 3–4, 6–7
rough riders, 159, 195–96; Blacks as, 282–83; Cody, W., and, 13, 248, 262, 288, 290, 294
Rough Riders: "The Bronco Buster" from, 286–87; on competition, 268; as cowboy regiment, 1, 262, 267, 286–87; in Cuba, 262–63, 272–76; as Darwinian supremacy, 272; on Kettle Hill, 275–77, 288, 290–91; in politics, 289–90; races in, 268, 282; Roosevelt, T., and, 1–2, 4, 11, 13–14, 159, 248, 262–63, 267–68, 272–76, 281–84, 286–88, 290, 294, 305–6; San Juan Hill and, 14, 273–74, 276; Virginian and, 305, 312n3; Wister on, 262
The Rough Riders (Roosevelt, T.), 281–84, 287, 306
Rousseau, Jean-Jacques, 9
Rouvroy, Claude Henri de. *See* Saint-Simon
The Rustlers (McElrath), 6

Saint-Simon (Claude Henri de Rouvroy), 109–10
Salsbury, Nathan, 79–80, 89, 156
Saltonstall, Richard, 21
San Juan Hill: Kettle Hill and, 14, 274–77, 288, 290–91; Roosevelt, T., and, 14, 288, 291n34; Rough Riders and, 14, 273–74, 276
The Scalp-Hunters (Reid), 57–58, 60, 203
scalping, 228; Cody, W., as, 79, 84, 86–88, 154, 156; violence of, 87–88, 120

Schell, Fred B., 171
self-reliance: American conservatism as, 3; American west and, 9–10, 161, 163; of Blacks, 274–75; Cody, W., and, 153; Emerson and, 6, 12, 107–8, 113–14, 149, 210, 212, 250, 309; as individualism, 10; Locke and, 107; manhood and, 27; Morton, J., on, 214; Remington, F., and, 47, 170, 196, 274–75; retrogressions into "past" for, 9–10, 13, 107; Roosevelt, T., on, 3, 5, 20, 141, 149, 161, 163, 175, 211–12, 215, 282, 285; Sumner on, 123; Trump on, 309–10
"Self-Reliance" (Emerson), 106, 113n6
Sewall, Bill, 139, 144–48, 161, 173
Shakespeare, William, 31, 80, 107
Shaler, Nathan S., 129
"The Significance of the Frontier in American History" (Turner), 220–24, 227, 231
Sitting Bull: arrest and death of, 171, 182–83, 185; Cody, W., and, 154–55, 181–82, 185–86, 186n13; independence of, 170–71
slavery, 106; Brown on, 82, 117; Jefferson and, 100; Kansas Territory and, 81–83; laws of nature on, 127; "negro domination" after, 128–29; Pierce on, 81; popular sovereignty on, 81; Roosevelt mother and, 19; U.S. compromises on, 81–82; Wister and, 31–32, 239
Smedley, William Thomas, 192–93
Smith, Lillian, 89
Social Evolution (Kidd), 173–75, 178
socialism: Adams, H. C., for, 33, 131–32, 175; America and, 130–32; Bremer on, 109–10, 130, 173; Clark, J. B., on individualism and, 132; Demolins on, 268–69; ethical economists on, 132–33, 135; by Fourier, 110; George and, 130–33, 135, 160, 249, 258; individualism contesting, 10, 109–11, 130;

Progress and Poverty and, 130–33, 135; Republican Party and, 132; Roosevelt, T., on, 20, 175, 249–50; by Saint-Simon, 109–10; trade unions and, 132–33, 244; *The Wages Question* and, 131–32, 231
society as organism, 219–21
southerners: on Brown, 82, 117; Civil War by, 118; conservatism of, 133; cowboys and, 238–39; on democracy and Blacks, 128–30; Lee, R., leading, 117; Lincoln to, 112, 118; lynching by, 298–99; Page on genteel, 127–29; on racist simplicity, 128; Reconstruction and, 113, 124, 127–30, 197, 237, 282; Republican Party to, 307
Spencer, Herbert: Darwinism and, 21, 55, 119, 297; "The Development Hypothesis" by, 119, 121; on Emerson, 119; on government, 120; on Lamarck, 120–21; on lynching, 120; on "survival of the fittest," 119–20
Stanford, Leland, 66
Stanford University, 66
state of nature: Cuba as new, 261; freedom and, 97, 261; Hobbes on, 95, 175; Jefferson and, 12; Locke on, 9, 131, 179, 261. *See also* laws of nature
stockgrowers: on cattle rustling, 25, 143–44, 190, 257–58; Cheyenne Club for, 36; Chimney Butte ranch and, 24, 26, 139; laws manipulated by, 25, 148, 189–90; Locke and property of, 96; vigilantism by, 145–46
Story of the Wild West (Cody, W.), 167
stranglers, 143, 145–46, 148
Stuart, Granville, 143
Sumner, William Graham, 12, 173–74; conservatism of, 133–34; on economic competition, 122–23; for individualism, 131–35; on self-reliance, 123; on Walker, 131
"survival of the fittest," 55, 134–35, 175, 248, 297, 308; America and, 120–22; Cody, W., and, 90; Cuba and, 270–71; Spencer on, 119–20; Sumner on, 123; warfare for, 141–42
Sweetwater incident, 190–91

Teschemacher, Hubert E., 25, 36, 46, 189, 191
Thomas, Augustus, 48, 245
Thoreau, Henry David, 177, 207
de Tocqueville, Alexis: democracy and, 101, 105, 132, 134, 297; individualism by, 102, 108; on Jackson, 101
Trail of Tears, 59, 63n30
transmutation theory, 118
Trilling, Lionel, 10–11
Trimble, Richard, 25
Trump, Donald J. (president), 308–11
Turner, Frederick Jackson: on acquired traits, 228; on American history, 13, 244, 249, 295–96; on democracy, 295–96; on Indians, 227–28; on politics, 249–50; on race, 221; on retrogressions into "past," 4, 224–25, 228, 230–32, 250, 270; "The Significance of the Frontier" by, 220–24, 227, 231; on vigilantism, 222; on *The Winning of the West*, 4, 229, 231, 240, 244
Twain, Mark, 247; on Cody, W., 87, 130–31, 156; *The Gilded Age* by, 130; *A Horse's Tale* by, 87

unions, 132–33, 244
United States (U.S.): on American west, 24; Chicago World's Fair and, 195–99, 201–2, 295; Constitution of, 31, 100, 123, 176, 239, 299; to Cuba, 269–70; Cuba trading partner as, 258; Declaration of Independence

of, 96–98, 176, 261, 289, 297; Endicott and, 159; on Ghost Dance, 13, 169–71, 181–86, 198; House Un-American Activities Committee and, 306; imperialism of, 178, 239–40, 287; imperialism on Cuba, 270–71, 273; Indian wars by, 13, 49, 85, 88, 154–55, 171, 183–86, 198; natural selection and, 120–24, 301; on slavery compromises, 81–82; Wounded Knee and, 13, 183–85, 198

Van Wyck, Augustus, 282
Victoria (queen), 87, 156
vigilantism: Badlands and, 145, 261–62; Bancroft on, 301; for individual freedom, 146; lynching and, 190–92; by property-owning men, 145–46; retrogression of, 145; Rittenhouse and, 309–10; Roosevelt, T., and, 143–48, 159, 257–58, 310; Roosevelt, T., justifying, 148–50, 191; as stranglers, 143, 145–46, 148; Sweetwater incident in, 190–91; Trump and, 308–11; Turner on, 222; Wister and, 13, 190–92
Villard, Henry, 23
The Virginian (Wister), 289, 293, 296–97, 302n29, 305; on cattle rustlers, 298, 301–2, 311; lynching in, 298–300
Virginian character, 245–47, 289, 301; Rough Riders and, 305, 312n3

The Wages Question (Walker), 131–32, 231
Wagner, Richard, 33
Walker, Francis Amasa, 131–32, 231
Wallace, Alexander H., 283
warfare: competition as, 178–79; Ghost Dance and Indian, 13, 169–71, 181–86, 198; Holmes on, 257; Remington, F., desiring, 13, 250–53, 258–59, 261, 269, 276–77, 289; Remington, F., on military

and, 43–45, 184–85; Roosevelt, T., desiring, 13, 141–42, 159, 257–58, 261–62, 269; for "survival of the fittest," 141–42; World War II and, 8, 10–11; Wounded Knee ending Indian, 13, 183–85, 198. *See also* Civil War
Waring, George E., Jr., 67–69
Waring, Guy, 192
Warner, Charles Dudley, 130
Washington, Booker T., 284–86
Washington, George (president), 97–98, 110, 117
Wear and Tear: Or, Hints for the Overworked (Mitchell), 34–35, 38n19, 192
Wetmore, Helen Cody, 90, 195
white identity: after Civil War, 12; America from, 7–8, 141–42, 182, 224; conservatism with, 127; cowboys and, 238–39; democracy vs., 128–30; on Indians, 60, 85, 141–42; on "negro domination," 128–29; popular sovereignty and, 81; Roosevelt, T., for, 140, 284; as southern aristocracy, 129
white males: American west for, 62–63; American west for rich, 135, 140; aristocracy as property-owning, 145–46; around Roosevelt, T., 3–4, 6–7; on conservatism, 6, 135–36; individualism for, 105; vigilantism by, 145–46; Wister on "fit," 75–76
Whitman, Walt, 123–25
The Wilderness Hunter (Roosevelt, T.), 28
"The Wild West, Rocky Mountain, and Prairie Exhibition" (Buffalo Bill's Wild West), 237; on American west, 79, 88–90, 156; as Buffalo Bill's Wild West, 80, 88–90, 195, 231, 233; by Cody, W., 79, 88–90, 156; in England, 87, 156; in Europe, 181–82, 185, 196, 295; on history, 155
The Winning of the West (Roosevelt, T.), 27–28, 53, 59, 139, 220–21;

Remington, F., and, 260; Turner on, 4, 229, 231, 240, 244

Wister, Owen, 44; American west and, 35–37, 75, 243–44, 300; on Anglo-American aristocracy, 4, 75, 80, 239, 243, 289, 297–300; Boone and Crockett Club and, 201–2, 205; Civil War on, 32; Cody, W., and, 80; on cowboys, 7, 237–39, 243–45; on democracy, 245, 249, 297; on eugenics, 75–76; "Evolution of the Cow-Puncher" by, 237–39, 243–45; *Harper's Weekly* and, 192, 234, 261, 293; *Harper's Weekly* with Remington, F., and, 234–36, 243, 289; Harte heir as, 170, 234, 237, 287, 293, 306; on Holmes and law, 32–34, 71–75, 244, 297, 299–301; Kipling and, 234, 236–37; on law, 71–72, 75, 244–45, 296–302; Lee, G., and, 21; *Lin McLean* by, 192–93, 234, 259, 261; on lynching, 4, 25, 191–92, 296–97, 300–301; on manhood, 31; with neurasthenia, 4, 34–35; on race, 238–39, 285–86; Remington, F., and, 168, 234–36, 258–59, 269, 289; Roosevelt, T., and, 31, 240, 261, 293, 296; on Rough Riders, 262; slavery and, 31–32, 239; on strikers, 244; on vigilantes, 13, 190–92; Virginian as, 302; western stories by, 13, 37, 192–93, 243–45, 247, 259, 261, 263–64, 293; on whites as "fit," 75–76

Wolcott, Frank, 36, 189–91

women, 106; as overlooked, 6

World's Columbian Exposition (Chicago World's Fair): Boone and Crockett Club cabin at, 201–2; Cody, W., and, 198–99; Ferris, G., with wheel and, 198, 219–20; U.S. and, 195–99, 201–2, 295

World War II, 8, 10–11

Wounded Knee, 13, 183–85, 198

Yellow Hair, 86–88, 154

Yellowstone national park, 42, 206–7, 216, 234–35

Zola, Emile, 33–34

Zoonomia (Darwin, E.), 55

Zoöpraxiscope, 66–67, 169

About the Author

Stephen J. Mexal is a professor of English at California State University, Fullerton. His writing has appeared in a number of scholarly and popular venues, including *The Chronicle of Higher Education*, *Pacific Standard*, and *Smithsonian*. He is the author of *Reading for Liberalism: The Overland Monthly and the Writing of the Modern American West*.

www.ingramcontent.com/pod-product-compliance
Lightning Source LLC
Chambersburg PA
CBHW021340300426
44114CB00012B/1015